Bridging Knowledge Cultures

Bridging Knowledge Cultures

Rebalancing Power in the
Co-Construction of Knowledge

Edited by

Walter Lepore, Budd L. Hall and Rajesh Tandon

BRILL

LEIDEN | BOSTON

Cover illustration: iStock.com/Kedar Diwakar Mandakhalikar

All chapters in this book have undergone peer review.

The Library of Congress Cataloging-in-Publication Data is available online at https://catalog.loc.gov

Typeface for the Latin, Greek, and Cyrillic scripts: "Brill". See and download: brill.com/brill-typeface.

ISBN 978-90-04-68774-5 (paperback)
ISBN 978-90-04-68775-2 (hardback)
ISBN 978-90-04-68776-9 (e-book)
DOI 10.1163/9789004687769

This book is printed on acid-free paper and produced in a sustainable manner.

Contents

PART 3
Learning to Bridge Knowledge Cultures

Foreword

A slow-motion standoff is being witnessed in the relationship between communities and researchers from formal institutions. Linda T. Smith captures the most poignant expression of this face-off:

> The term 'research' itself stirs up in local communities a silence, conjures up bad memories that still offends the deepest sense of our humanity.... It galls non-Western societies that western researchers, intellectuals and scientists trained in that tradition can claim to know ALL that there is to know about other societies, on the basis of brief and superficial encounters with those societies. It often appalls indigenous societies that Western science [and researchers trained in that tradition] can desire, extract, and claim ownership of people's way of knowing, and then simultaneously reject those people who created those ideas, and deny them the opportunities to be the creators of their culture and own notions. (Smith, 1999, p. 1)

Coming from Africa, I assume an African perspective in my analysis of the broader implications of recognising community knowledges worldwide. On entry to the system that associates the non-Western, the non-'developed' with 'bad', it quickly becomes known to indigenous and African children that what is relevant for the West, its insights, its values, its tastes and eccentricities alike, becomes the model for the world. From then on, everything one does and thinks, is defined and compared using Western norms, leaving all else bundled together as the 'rural other', the 'non-urban', often equated with 'community'. This 'other' is the cosmologies of Africa, the Native American, Saami from Scandinavia, Asia and Latin America – otherwise collectively known as the 'Third World'. In fact, it took less than 20 years since President Truman launched the concept of 'underdevelopment' in his inaugural speech in 1949 (Sachs, 1992), to make two billion people define themselves as such (Illich, 1981). With the launching of this concept, all social totalities were collapsed into one single model; all systems of science into one mega science; all development to growth, to GNP. The attitude to what is referred to as 'rural', or 'community', in development jargon, still bears, like father, like son, the hallmarks of subjugative paternalism.

Critiquing the Western, scientific research model without offering an alternative will not be helpful for universities to play a different role and give voice to those who don't have voice. *Bridging Knowledge Cultures* addresses this need for transformation and equity in the political economy of knowledge production. In examining the allocation, use and utilisation of human, financial and infrastructural resources available to the academy, the policy domain and community-based organisations, it faces the question: In establishing trusting and respectful community-university research partnerships, how can diverse knowledge cultures be bridged so that extant power inequalities between collaborating partners are taken into consideration to make these connections sustainable and secure over time?

In urging the fostering of community knowledge cultures and co-construction of knowledge, leading to transformation and healing between the academy and the communities, knowledge power inequalities between the two have been taken into account in this book. These power differentials at individual and institutional level not only influence the role of partnership members in the entire research process, but also create hierarchies of knowledge(s) based on existing institutional or socio-cultural norms and assumptions. What we need to do is deepen our analysis at the diagnostic level so that action can proceed. This book is a step in that direction.

The intractable problems of modernity cannot be solved within the paradigms of modernity (Odora Hoppers & Richards, 2011). The universities must see to it that its roles include the verification, validation and legitimation of community knowledge, locally and internationally, through sustained dialogue. Equitable relations between the academy and the indigenous knowledge holders must create within its strategic objectives a process in which the marginalised have a 'presence' and 'voice'. It is through affirmation of the multiplicity of worlds, and the recognition that forms of knowledge other than that sanctioned by science *exist*, that it becomes possible to redefine the relationship between objectivity and representation, between subject and object (CODESRIA, 1998), between university and community – a *healing moment* (Nouwen, 1972) in this long chain of *vicarious disenfranchisement*.

Catherine A. Odora Hoppers

References

CODESRIA. (1998, September 14–18). *Introduction to the international symposium on social sciences and the challenges of globalization in Africa* (pp. 1–2). Johannesburg.
Illich, I. (1981). *Shadow work: Vernacular values examined*. Marion Boyars Inc.
Nouwen, H. (1972). *The wounded healers*. Doubleday.

Odora Hoppers, C. A., & Richards, H. (2011). *Rethinking thinking. modernity's "other" and the transformation of the university.* UNISA.

Sachs, W. (Ed.). (1992). *The development dictionary: A guide to knowledge as power.* Zed Books.

Smith, L. T. (1999). *Decolonizing methodologies: Research and indigenous peoples.* Zed Books.

Acknowledgements

This book would not have been possible without the support, contributions and participation of numerous individuals and organisations who have generously given their time, knowledge and expertise. First and foremost, we would like to express our deep appreciation to the community members and university partners who have collaborated with us through this three-year research project titled *Bridging Knowledge Cultures: The Knowledge for Change Global Consortium on Training of Community-Based Participatory Research*, also known as the BKC project. Our partners' valuable insights, perspectives and experiences have enriched this book and made it a true reflection of the power and potential of community-university research partnerships, and of the diversity and complexity of knowledge cultures in a variety of settings and geographic regions.

To Gloria Aber, Maura Adshead, Andrés Astaiza, Minali Banerjee, René Walter Botha, Beatrix (Bibi) Bouwman, Anuradha Chakraborty, Tanya Clarmont, Hendri Coetzee, Suriani Dzulkifli, Irma Flores, Luisa Fernanda González, Carol Hal, Siraz Hirani, Muhamad Hanapi bin Jamaluddin, Jufitri Joha, Norhyisyamudin Bin Kami, Niharika Kaul, Ahmad Kipacha, Alice Veronica Lamwaka, Daniel Lopera, Darren Lortan, Savathrie Margie Maistry, Haikael D. Martin, Aminuddin Mohamed, David Monk, Alfi Moolman, Misbakhul Munir, Mahazan Abdul Mutalib, Nabiela Naily, Khairunneezam Mohd Noor, Martin Odoch, George Openjuru, Mohd. Dzulkhairi Mohd. Rani, Mwemezi Johaiven Rwiza, Manish Sharma, Priyamvada Shrivastava, Sebastian Silva, Crystal Tremblay, Helmi Umam, Andrea Vargiu, Aniksha Varoda, Karen Venter, Reeta Venugopal, Noor Wahyudi, Clive Allens William-Hunt, Lesley Wood, Izawati Wook, Madhura Yadav – your contributions have made this book stronger. The BKC project and our efforts to advance equal, transparent, accountable and trust-based community-university research partnerships would not have been possible without your dedication, commitment and enthusiasm. Thank you.

We would also like to thank the Social Sciences and Humanities Research Council (SSHRC) of Canada, the University of Victoria and Participatory Research in Asia (PRIA), which have provided us with the resources and support necessary to carry out this project. Their financial support, research facilities and other resources have been essential to the success of the BKC project.

We would also like to thank our colleagues (academics and practitioners) who provided us with invaluable feedback and support throughout the research and writing process. Their encouragement, critical insights and constructive comments have been instrumental in shaping this book. We are particularly grateful to Barbara Jenni and Sumitra Srinivasan who have provided us with valuable feedback and guidance on this book. Their input, suggestions and editorial work have helped to refine and strengthen the content and structure of our work. We would like to express our gratitude to our family and friends who have provided us with unwavering support, love and inspiration throughout this journey. Their patience, understanding, and encouragement have been essential to our success.

Special thanks to Lorna Wanosts'a7 Williams, for agreeing to write an endorsement of this book, and Catherine Odora Hoppers, for the Foreword.

Figures and Tables

Figures

Tables

Notes on Contributors

Gloria Aber
is a part-time lecturer in medical ethics at PHARMBIOTRAC-Gulu, a project
manager, a researcher and a lawyer. She has a graduate degree in law from
Makerere University, a Post Graduate Diploma in Legal Practice from the Law
Development Centre, a Post Graduate Diploma in Hospital and Health Care
Management, a Master's degree in Management specialising in Hospital and
Health Care from Uganda Management Institute, and an Executive Master's in
Business Administration from NIBM, India. Her research interests are related
to health management, governance and community engagement.

Andrés Astaiza
is a professor-researcher with experience in the field of higher education in
the areas of psychology, social sciences and systemic thinking. She also has
experience in planning and coordinating educational projects and providing
individual and group psychopedagogical support to students. Since 2018, she
has been working at the University of Ibagué, Colombia, conducting research
on the teacher-researcher training processes in the university context, citizen
training and systemic thinking. She is a member of the fourth cohort of the
Mentor Training Program of the UNESCO Chair in Community Based Research
and Social Responsibility in Higher Education.

Minali Banerjee
is a certified mentor of Community Based Participatory Research (CBPR) and a
growing economist and academician. She is Assistant Professor in Department
of Economics, School of Humanities & Social Sciences, Manipal University
Jaipur. An avid participatory researcher, her current areas of interest lie in
engaged teaching-learning pedagogy, engaged research, community engagement and its institutionalization among Indian higher education institutions.

René Walter Botha
is the Coordinator for Community Based Education and Rural Health, Faculty
of Health Sciences, University of the Free State, South Africa. He has a Master's
degree in Diagnostic Radiography, and doctorate in Health Professions
Education from the same university. His areas of research include Community
Based Education, Service-learning, Interprofessional Education and Radiation
Science. He is responsible for the planning, implementation and monitoring of
the Faculty of Health Sciences Rural Community Initiative based in three rural
towns (see https://www.ufs.ac.za/health/faculty-of-health-sciences-home/

faculty/community-based-education). As a former member of the Health Professions Council of South Africa, he is still involved with governance and accreditation of decentralised training facilities.

Beatrix (Bibi) Bouwman

is the current Director for Sustainability and Community Impact at North-West University (NWU), South Africa. She has experience as a development practitioner, academic and researcher in the field of microbiology, agriculture, business, sustainable development, in technology transfer, as well as community engagement management for more than 15 years. She has an MSc degree from the University of Johannesburg and an MBA from NWU. As a member of the SA Global Reporting Initiative Focal point, she is driving impact measurement in community engagement. As longest serving executive member of the South African Higher Education Community Engagement Forum (SAHECEF) and previous chairperson, she is well-informed on the latest community engagement developments in South Africa and keen to facilitate the practice of service-learning as a pedagogy in African universities by working with all external stakeholders.

Anuradha Chakraborty

is a faculty in Centre for Women's Studies, Pt. Ravishankar Shukla University, Raipur, Chhattisgarh, India. She has a Master's in Physical Anthropology and Indian classical music and is a recipient of gold medals for the same. She completed her PhD in Life Sciences. Her areas of interest include epidemiological studies, community health, tribal and rural developmental issues, gender disparities, and education.

Tanya Clarmont

is Teme-Augama Anishnabai on her father's side and French Canadian on her mother's side, and has committed her life to improving relations among all Canadians. She works as the Director of Management Services with Victoria Native Friendship Centre, which includes managing the Victoria Urban Reconciliation Dialogue. She has worked with Friendship Centres for 18 years and held positions at the national, provincial and local levels. Along with her certification under the UNESCO Chair's Mentor Training Program, Tanya holds BA's in Native Studies, Law & Justice, and Creative Writing.

Hendri Coetzee

is an extraordinary associate-professor at the North-West University's COMPRES research unit and the director of the Nature's Valley Trust. As an engaged scholar, his main research focus encompasses community, conservation and social-environmental topics such as human-environment interactions, community engagement, community well-being, community impact, community-based conservation, human-wildlife conflict and the conservation of the ground-hornbill, to mention but a few. He also has a passion for botany and ornithology.

Suriani Dzulkifli

is the programme manager and co-instructor/facilitator of the UNESCO Chair's Knowledge for Change Global Consortium training programme in community based participatory research. She is also a certified CBPR mentor of the Salish Sea K4C hub. Suriani is a PhD Candidate in Leadership Studies-Adult Education and Community Engagement at the University of Victoria. She is from Malaysia but currently based in Canada.

Irma Flores

is an Associate Professor in the Faculty of Education of the University of los Andes, Colombia. Her interest, both in research and teaching, focuses on teacher training in qualitative and participatory research, ethnoeducation, diversity and curricular transformation. She has a PhD in Social Sciences, Childhood and Youth; a Master's degree in Educational and Social Development, a specialization degree in Community Development and a graduation degree in Psychology. She is a certified CBPR mentor of the Mentor Training Program of the UNESCO Chair in Community Based Research and Social Responsibility in Higher Education. She is the coordinator of the Colombia K4C hub.

Luisa Fernanda González

is a researcher at University of los Andes, Colombia. Her research agenda focuses on issues of inclusive education, teacher training and support, teacher evaluation, curriculum, practices, public policies and social responsibility in higher education. Luisa has a Bachelor's in Biology and Chemistry from the University of Caldas, a Master's in Education and is a PhD candidate in Education at the University of the Andes.

Budd L. Hall

is Professor Emeritus with the School of Public Administration, University of Victoria, Canada, and Co-Chair of the UNESCO Chair in Community Based Research and Social Responsibility in Higher Education. He was Former Dean of the Faculty of Education at the University of Victoria, Chair of the Adult Education Department of the University of Toronto, and Secretary-General of the International Council for Adult Education. He is a member of the

International Adult Education Hall of the Fame and was selected for the 2005 Canadian Bureau of International Education Innovation in Education Award.

Carol Hall

is Director of Strategic Initiatives with the Victoria Foundation, which is a partner in the Salish Sea K4C hub. She has worked in community development in Victoria, British Columbia and globally to mobilise knowledge and tools to strengthen community wellbeing in an era of rapid change. Prior to moving to Victoria, she was executive director of a foundation in New England that conserved farms and natural areas, and worked on community economic development in southern Africa. She holds a BA from the University of Pennsylvania, and Master's degrees from Georgetown University and University College London, UK.

Siraz Hirani

is a senior professional with 20 years of strategic and operational experience with international development organisations, including 10 years at leadership positions at global and national levels. He holds an MSc in Disaster Mitigation, MSc in Life Sciences and an MBA with specialisation in finance. He is an alumni of the Harvard Kennedy School with work experience in multi-cultural & challenging countries like India, Bangladesh, Afghanistan, Tajikistan and Myanmar. His sectoral experience includes habitat development, climate change and disaster risk management. He is a certified CBPR mentor of the Mentor Training Program of the UNESCO Chair in Community Based Research and Social Responsibility in Higher Education. He presently works as Senior Programme Management Specialist at Mahila Housing Sewa Trust (MHT).

Muhamad Hanapi bin Jamaludin

has a Bachelor's degree in Social Science and Humanity (Malay Studies) and a Master of Arts (Theory of Knowledge and Epistemology) from National University of Malaysia (UKM). He is currently part of the Secretariat Executive of Youth Advisors to Malaysia's Prime Minister, a Committee Member of OIC Youth Forum, Research Fellow of Malaysia Youth Council President, Head of Information for 4B Youth Club, President of WAMY Club Malaysia, and President of Kerapatan Graduan Muda Youth Organisation (KAGUM). He is also an active Malay author of books. Some of his most recent books are *Barat dari Cerminan Watan* (2021) and *Gelintaran Fikiran Al-Attas dan Pendita Za'ba* (2021). He acts as Research Fellow for Jejak Tarbiah, Deputy Secretary of Federasi Kebangsaan Pekerja Belia (FKPB), Manager of Sekolah Pembangunan Pekerja Belia dan Komuniti (SPKB), Co-founder of District Intellectual Discourse Secretariat, and Secretary of Minang Intellectuals Organisation Malaysia. He is now an invited speaker and part of the Mizan K4C Hub as a social activist.

Barbara Jenni

is of Swiss, French and German ancestry and now lives in W̱SÁNEĆ and lək̓ʷəŋən territories in Victoria (Canada). She has a Master's degree in Linguistics and has worked for over a decade in various capacities supporting community-led/based research projects. Barbara is a PhD Candidate in the Faculty of Education at the University of Victoria, where she investigates the circumstances, experiences and practices of those doing the labour of knowledge sharing at/from universities. As a Research Assistant, UNESCO Chair in Community-Based Research and Social Responsibility in Higher Education, she has played a coordinating role in the Bridging Knowledge Cultures project.

Jufitri Joha

is former President of Malaysian Youth Council (MBM). He is Vice President, Muslim Youth Movement of Malaysia (ABIM) in charge of youth and intellectual development. He obtained an LLB from International Islamic University of Malaysia (IIUM) and a Master's degree in Community and Youth Work from Durham University, United Kingdom. Currently, he is pursuing his PhD in Youth Studies at Institute for Social Science Studies (IPSAS) of University Putra Malaysia (UPM).

Norhyisyamudin Bin Kamil

(AAP) was born in Kuala Pilah, N. Sembilan, Malaysia. He studied TESL education at the University College of St. Mark & St. John, Plymouth, United Kingdom. After teaching for eight years in a school, he joined the Institute of Teacher Education, Sultan Mizan Campus, Besut. He currently works at the Institute of Teacher Education, Tengku Ampuan Afzan Campus, Kuala Lipis, Pahang. His serious involvement in the development of indigenous education lead to his appointment as Deputy Head at The National Centre of Excellent for Indigenous Pedagogy (PKPPK). He continues to contribute in various fields, especially in indigenous pedagogy, teacher training and professional support, module writing and motivational programmes for indigenous education.

Niharika Kaul

has been a Research Associate at PRIA, New Delhi, working with Drs. Tandon and Hall. She completed her undergraduate degree in Sociology from Delhi University and her Bachelor of Laws from University of Durham. She has worked extensively with the UNESCO Chair in Community Based Research towards making higher education institutions community-driven and inclusive. Niharika has been engaged in research and advocacy with relevant stakeholders on building knowledge democracy and bridging knowledge cultures between academia and communities. She recently co-authored the chapter 'Towards Societally Embedded Higher Education: A Panoramic Overview of Asia & Oceania' in GUNi Higher Education in the World Report 8 Special Issue (2022), and authored the book *The Knowledge for Change Global Consortium* (2021). She is currently pursuing a post-graduate degree in Gender, Policy and Inequalities at the London School of Economics and Political Science, United Kingdom.

Ahmad Kipacha

works as Senior Lecturer in the School of Business Studies and Humanities of the Nelson Mandela African Institution of Science and Technology (NM-AIST) in Arusha, Tanzania. He has a PhD from the University of London (SOAS) and a Master's degree in Applied Linguistics from the University of Dar es Salaam, Tanzania. He has been associated with interdisciplinary projects and research, and lecturing in areas of research writing in sciences, languages (Swahili and English), ethics in sciences, culture and social entrepreneurship. His current research is about forensic analysis of Swahili texts, academic writing styles, data visualisation, ethics in sciences and community-based research, and the complexity in modern Tanzanian cultural issues in literary and media outlets. Dr. Kipacha has been engaged in PACE Research Network: Project on Post-proverbial in African Cultural Expressions sponsored by Alexander von Humboldt Alumni Awards for Networking Initiatives Post-proverbial in African Studies, in collaboration with Ibadan University. He is a certified CBPR mentor of the Mentor Training Program of the UNESCO Chair in Community Based Research and Social Responsibility in Higher Education with the Nyerere K4C hub.

Alice Veronica Lamwaka

holds a PhD in Clinical Pharmaceutical Sciences and Pharmacogenomics. She is Senior Lecturer, Head, Pharmacy Programs and Principal Investigator of Covilyce Natural Products used in the management of Covid-19 cases. Her interest in teaching, research and community engagement focuses principally on indigenous knowledge, indigenous cultures and indigenous knowledge systems, on how these can be translated into science that can be well understood by the community. While her work is aligned towards discovery of medicines for managing both communicable and non-communicable diseases including epidemics, she has carried out extensive research on biodiversity,

traditional medicine, and alternative medicines principally towards addressing Sustainable Development Goals for improving socioeconomic development of the local peoples of Northern Uganda. She is the Centre Leader for the
Pharmaceutical Biotechnology and Traditional Medicine Centre of Excellence
at Gulu University, Uganda.

Walter Lepore

is Assistant Professor in the School of Public Administration at the University
of Victoria, and co-founder of the Salish Sea K4C hub that provides training in community-based research and indigenous research methodologies.
He is also the Research Director for the UNESCO Chair in Community-Based
Research and Social Responsibility in Higher Education and former coor-
dinator of the Knowledge for Change (K4C) Consortium. Before joining the
University of Victoria, Dr. Lepore was an Associate Professor at the Division
of Public Administration of Centro de Investigación y Docencia Económicas
(Mexico), and Associate Faculty at the Schools of Leadership Studies, and of
Environment and Sustainability at Royal Roads University (Canada).

Daniel Lopera

is Industrial Designer from the Universidad Javeriana, Colombia, with a
Master's in Design Futures from Griffith University in Australia and a Master's
in Education from Universidad de los Andes, Colombia. He teaches in the
areas of design futures, ontological design and research. He has carried out
action-research projects in which peasant, indigenous and ex-combatant communities have participated. He led the creation of the current Design academic
program at the University of Ibagué, Colombia, of which he was its director for
five years. Currently, he serves as Dean of the Faculty of Humanities, Arts and
Social Sciences of the University of Ibagué.

Darren Lortan

is Associate Professor of Mathematics at the Durban University of Technology
(DUT), is a teacher and an activist interested in sustaining an interest in
education at the grass roots level. Previously, he has held several leadership
positions in DUT, including Executive Dean, Acting Deputy Vice-Chancellor:
Academic, and Acting Senior Director: Engagement. His interest in community engagement began through a project which marketed STEM professions
to high school students. Over the years, the focus of his community engagement interests included early childhood development, youth development
and educational support, adult basic education, post-school training and local

community skills development, and social entrepreneurship. He serves on the boards of the South African Higher Education Community Engagement Forum (SAHECEF), and the International Association for Research on Service Learning and Community Engagement (IARSLCE). DUT joined the global K4C Consortium under his leadership.

Savathrie Margie Maistry
is currently a Research Associate at Rhodes University and the Durban University of Technology. She has held numerous positions at a number of institutions, including director of *community engagement* at Rhodes University; lecturer and head of department (*social work and social development*) at University of Fort Hare; lecturer in the Centre for Continuing Education, University of Waikato, New Zealand; and served as the Africa Region Programme Manager of Volunteer Services Abroad, New Zealand. As a Research Associate with the Durban University of Technology, she was responsible for curriculum development at the Master's and Bachelor's level in Community Development. In addition, she supervised Master's and doctoral postgraduate students in *community engagement* and in an *articulation research* project within the South African Post School Education and Training sector. She has extensive experience in social work and community development practice, management, education and research. She is a member of the national task team established by the Department of Social Development, Community Development Directorate for the professionalization of community development. She has researched and published in the areas of social work, community development, higher education, community engagement, integral education, community based participatory research and women's studies.

Haikael D. Martin
is a human nutritionist with experience working in Tanzania, particularly in nutrition and health. She is working for The Nelson Mandela African Institution of Science and Technology as a senior Lecturer in Human Nutrition and Dietetics. She strives to implement nutrition and nutritional-related programs and interventions that are responsive to societal issues. She is a certified CBPR mentor of the Mentor Training Program of the UNESCO Chair in Community Based Research and Social Responsibility in Higher Education under the Nyerere Hub in Tanzania. She experiences and competencies in human nutrition and health include maternal and child nutrition, adolescent nutrition, nutritional management of disease/conditions (diabetes, hypertension and cancers), advocating for nutrition in different sectors, mentorship of

District Nutrition Officers, nutrition surveys, nutrition stakeholders mapping and assessment, agriculture, and nutrition linkages.

Aminuddin Mohamed

earned his PhD from the National University of Malaysia in 2017 after completing his thesis entitled *Kelestarian KEDAP dalam Pembangunan Modal Insan Masyarakat Orang Asli*. He is now working as a lecturer and also heads the Indigenous Pedagogy Centre of Excellence, Kampus Tengku Ampuan Afzan Teacher's College, Pahang, Malaysia. He is actively involved in various research in the field of indigenous pedagogy and socio-cultural study at both national and international levels.

David Monk

is Lecturer in the Faculty of Education and Humanities at Gulu University, Uganda and an honorary Associate Professor in the Faculty of Education at the University of Nottingham, United Kingdom. He is also special advisor to the UNESCO Chair in Lifelong Learning Youth and Work and coordinator of the Gulu K4C Hub. His research and community work revolve around inclusive lifelong learning, developing healthy community university relationships, environmental sustainability and innovation, participatory community economics and social entrepreneurship, and understanding the vibrant social skills learning ecosystem in northern Uganda.

Alfi Moolman

is coordinating the University of the Free States's engaged- and e-engaged scholarship activities. She has more than 20 years' experience in community development and project management. She has worked in various industries including government, local and international funding, and corporate, private and tertiary education sectors. Alfi studied psychology and is an SAQA accredited facilitator and assessor. She is a certified CBPR mentor of the Mentor Training Program of the UNESCO Chair in Community Based Research and Social Responsibility in Higher Education, and affiliated with the Global University of Lifelong Learning, in support of community development.

Misbakhul Munir

is an activist and social worker for the Indonesian Traditional Fishermen Association (KNTI) in East Java Province. Munir is active in the advocacy, liberation and empowerment of local fishermen on social inequality, economy and climate change issues.

Mahazan Abdul Mutalib
is Associate Professor at the Faculty of Leadership and Management, Universiti Sains Islam Malaysia (USIM). He obtained his PhD from College of Business, Universiti Utara Malaysia (UUM) in 2013, a Master's degree in Organisational Leadership from Monash University in 2008, and a Bachelor's degree in Da'wah and Islamic Management from Universiti Sains Islam Malaysia (USIM) in 2005. He has published various books and articles in the field of Islamic leadership, management and community studies. He was the Director for Research Management and Innovation Centre (RIMC), USIM, and Deputy Dean (Academic and Research), Faculty of Leadership and Management, USIM. He is currently Director, Islamic Science Institute (ISI), USIM. He is also the coordinator for Mizan Research Centre (MRC), USIM and a mentor for the Mizan K4C hub. His interest of research is in Islamic leadership and management, community studies and Islamic sociology.

Khairunneezam Mohd Noor
is Associate Professor and Head of Management with Tourism Program in Faculty of Leadership and Management, Universiti Sains Islam Malaysia (USIM). Holds a Bachelor of Science (Human Resource Development), Master of Science (Human Resource Development) from Universiti Teknologi Malaysia, and a PhD in Management from La Trobe University, Melbourne. His writings and research revolve around leadership issues, job satisfaction, work-life balance and higher education sector issues.

Nabiela Naily
is a lecturer at faculty of Sharia and law in UIN Sunan Ampel Surabaya, Indonesia. Her focus of expertise is family law, Islamic law, gender and women-children protection, and university-community engagement.

Martin Odoch
tragically passed away prior to the publication of this book. Prior to joining the Faculty of Agriculture and Environment at Gulu University as a senior lecturer, Dr. Odoch spent 20 years working as a scientist in the private sector. He was trained to teach CBPR and was a leader at Gulu University. He was best known for his integrity as a lecturer and researcher and for his advocacy and action for human rights and community development. He is missed terribly.

George Openjuru
is Vice Chancellor of Gulu University, and the chair of the board of Vice Chancellors in Uganda. He is also the coordinator for the UNESCO Chair in

Lifelong Learning Youth and Work, a founding director of the Youth Education and Work network, and the founding director of the Gulu K4C hub. His academic background is oriented in adult and lifelong learning and Participatory Action Research. Professor Openjuru is a champion of knowledge democracy and community engaged scholarship in Uganda.

Mohd. Dzulkhairi Mohd. Rani
is a medical doctor and an Associate Professor in Public Health Medicine at Universiti Sains Islam Malaysia (USIM). His research interests include community based intervention, rural medicine and population health. He is also a certified CBPR mentor at the Mizan K4c hub since 2022.

Mwemezi Johaiven Rwiza
is Senior Lecturer in the School of Materials, Energy, Water, and Environmental Sciences (MEWES) at the Nelson Mandela African Institution of Science and Technology (NM-AIST), Tanzania. Dr. Rwiza is a certified CBPR mentor of the Mentor Training Program of the UNESCO Chair in Community Based Research and Social Responsibility in Higher Education. He is an Editorial Advisory Board member of the *African Journal of Engineering and Environmental Research* (AJEER). Dr. Rwiza also serves as an African Host University (AHU) coordinator in the Partnership for Skills in Applied Sciences, Engineering and Technology–Regional Scholarship Innovation Fund (PASET-RSIF), an African governments-led initiative to strengthen science, technology, and engineering capability in sub-Saharan Africa. He was a Co-Principal Investigator and Programme Coordinator in the just-ended Queen Elizabeth Scholarship-Advanced Scholars Program (QES) that was implemented by Carleton University (Ottawa, Canada) in partnership with Mzuzu University (Mzuzu, Malawi), Nelson Mandela African Institute for Science and Technology (Arusha, Tanzania), and the University of Ghana (Accra, Ghana).

Manish Sharma
is Assistant Professor at School of Architecture and Design, Manipal University Jaipur. His primary research interest focuses on community-university engagement, community knowledge cultures, the concept of an empowered community-university network, urban resilience, urban utilities and urban water, specific to developing nations. He is a certified CBPR mentor of the Mentor Training Program of the UNESCO Chair in Community Based Research and Social Responsibility in Higher Education. He, along with his students, collaborates frequently with various organisations, institutes and local authorities

on community-based research projects. He has authored and co-authored several book chapters and research articles. He is a recipient of two international scholarships during his post-graduation and doctoral studies.

Priyamvada Shrivastava

is Professor and Dean of Psychology, Associate Director at the Centre for Women's Studies, and coordinator at the Sangwari K4C hub at Pt. Ravishankar Shukla University, Raipur, Chhattisgarh, India. She has taught undergraduate and postgraduate classes in teacher's training in psychology for thirty years. Her area of specialization is health psychology, with research interests women and health, gender issues, guidance and counseling, psychopathology and educational psychology and personality.

Sebastian Silva

is a management consultant and owner of Roundtable Consulting Inc. He has a Master's degree in international law and is a member of the Salish Sea K4C Hub. He supports projects with Indigenous communities in British Columbia, as well as reconciliation initiatives that bring together all levels of government and community groups to address racism and create more equitable systems. As a community-based researcher, he is keen to explore how mainstream institutions can learn from Indigenous protocols that guide community engagement and the transfer of knowledge.

Rajesh Tandon

is an internationally acclaimed leader and practitioner of participatory research and development. He founded Participatory Research in Asia (PRIA) in 1982 and continues to be its chief Functionary. He is Co-Chair of the UNESCO Chair in Community based Research and Social Responsibility in Higher Education along with Professor Budd L. Hall. Dr. Tandon has authored more than 100 articles, a dozen books and numerous training manuals. He was inducted to the International Adult and Continuing Education (IACE) Hall of Fame (class of 2011).

Crystal Tremblay

is a faculty member and Co-chair of the Map Shop in the Department of Geography and Director of CIFAL Victoria at the University of Victoria, Canada. Since 2018, Dr. Tremblay has been the academic lead of the Salish Sea K4C Hub, working to build capacity in CBPR in higher education and communities to advance the United Nations Sustainable Development Goals.

M. Helmi Umam

is a lecturer at Faculty of Ushuluddin and Philosophy. His focus of expertise, which also is his current research, is the integration of community engagement in social work in higher education in Indonesia.

Andrea Vargiu

is Associate Professor of Sociology in the Department of Humanities and Social Sciences of the University of Sassari, Italy. He directs the FOIST Laboratory for Social Policies and Training Processes, which runs CBPR programs since its foundation in 1977. Andrea is Rector's delegate for Third Mission (H&SS) and serves as President of the MA Course in Social Work and Social Policies. He has a solid record in action research and CBPR. He studies civic engagement of universities, social policies, and organised solidarity. He presently co-ordinates impact evaluation of national and regional projects to contrast educational poverty.

Aniksha Varoda

is Research Assistant at the Centre for Women's Studies, and a PhD Research Scholar, School of Studies in Anthropology, Pt. Ravishankar Shukla University, Raipur, Chhattisgarh, India. Her research interests include women and children, health and social problems, gender, education, rural development, tribal community issues and Sustainable Development Goals.

Karen Venter

heads the Service-Learning Division within the Directorate of Community Engagement at the University of the Free State, South Africa. Having a PhD in Higher Education Studies, she is responsible for advancing the institutionalisation and glocal networking of engaged scholarship. Her research focuses on the use of appreciative inquiry for flourishing of engaged scholarship in community university research partnerships.

Reeta Venugopal

is Professor and Head of Physical Education, Director at the Centre for Women's Studies, and coordinator and mentor in the Sangwari K4C hub at Pt. Ravishankar Shukla University, Raipur, Chhattisgarh, India. She has taught undergraduate and postgraduate classes in teacher's training in physical education for 29 years. Her research interests include women and health, gender issues, tribal women, and children, specialising in exercise physiology.

Noor Wahyudi

is a lecturer in the Faculty of Economics and Business at UINSA, Indonesia. His focus of expertise is accounting information systems, governance, and university-community engagement.

Lesley Wood

(DEd, MA, BASS, BA, PGCHE) is an experienced action researcher of international repute. She has developed and conducted action research training for professional development, organisational development and community development in different contexts. She is founding Director of the research entity, Community-Based Educational Research, at North-West University, South Africa, and has been awarded several national and international grants. She is a National Research Foundation rated researcher and has published over 100 articles, book chapters and books. Her latest books include *Participatory Action Learning and Action Research: Theory, Process and Practice* (Routledge, 2020), and *Community-based Research with Vulnerable Populations* (Palgrave McMillan, 2022)

Izawati Wook

is teaching law at the Faculty of Syariah and Law, Universiti Sains Islam Malaysia (USIM). She graduated with an LLB (Hons) and a Master of Comparative Laws from the International Islamic University Malaysia. She obtained a PhD from the College of Law and Justice, Victoria University, Melbourne Australia. She was also admitted and enrolled as an Advocate and Solicitor of the High Court in Malaya. Her research interests are indigenous peoples and law, and legal education. She is a mentor at the Mizan K4C hub since 2018.

Madhura Yadav

is an architect-planner with over two-and-a-half-decade experience in academics, administration and research. She is a recipient of the AICTE scholarship for her doctoral research, along with several awards like Asia Pacific Global Award 2017, Education Leadership Award 2019, and Indo Pacific Architecture Excellence Award 2021, in recognition of her sustained commitment to architecture education. She is on several committees/expert groups set up by the Government of India, serves as a jury member of various architectural and design competitions, and a member of editorial boards of architecture, urban design and urban planning journals in India. Her current research interests are sustainable architecture and cities with inclusive approaches and community-based participatory research. She is currently the Dean of the Faculty of Design at Manipal University Jaipur.

PART 1

Theoretical Perspectives

∴

CHAPTER 1

Introduction

Walter Lepore, Budd L. Hall and Rajesh Tandon

We are delighted to share the latest book in our series of explorations over the past years of knowledge democracy, community-university research partnerships (CURP), social responsibility in higher education, and the creation of locally contextualised knowledge for social justice and sustainability. This chapter provides the background to our interest in the concept of knowledge cultures, a literature review that has helped us understand knowledge cultures in a variety of settings and a brief overview of the Bridging Knowledge Cultures (BKC) project, conducted between 2020 and 2022, that forms the basis of the case studies and reflections presented in this book.

We start by recognising that knowledge is created everywhere. It is created by everyone in negotiating the life in which they are immersed. We create our own knowledge individually as we grow and experience life. We usually refer to this as 'learning' when it happens on an individual level. The social construction of knowledge happens everywhere as well. Families, neighbourhoods, communities, workplaces create knowledge through shared experience to enable them to survive or flourish depending on their contexts. Indigenous peoples around the world have accumulated knowledge over the millennia through interaction with rest of nature, including the spirit world. Civil society organisations create knowledge with a focus on finding solutions to community or global challenges, and/or to back up requests for financial or political support for their work (Leadbeater et al., 2011; Lutz & Neis, 2008). Trade unions work with knowledge creating capacities of working individuals to fight for better pay and healthier workplaces. Social movements create knowledge through their conversations internally and through their interactions with the authority and the broader public outside their movements. In higher education institutions, which are often seen as the only place where 'real' knowledge is created, knowledge is constructed, used, shared and acted upon in quite different ways. In the broadest terms, knowledge within the academy serves several purposes, such as deepening theoretical understandings of disciplinary fields, contributing to career advancement, and sometimes to support community or policy partners (Britten & Maguire, 2016; Newman et al., 2016).

While the English language word 'knowledge' is used in all the above settings, we cannot assume that people in diverse organisational, institutional, political, or jurisdictional contexts understand, create and use knowledge in the same way. In each of these sites of knowledge creation and sharing, a *knowledge culture* exists. Briefly, we understand knowledge culture as the set of formal and informal roles, structures, norms and practices, shared meanings, and cultural forms (e.g., language, symbols, rituals), which influence how knowledge is understood, valued, assembled, shared, and acted upon in specific settings, such as the academic world, civil society organisations, social movements, Indigenous communities, and more.

In the face of global crises and the challenges posed by socio-ecological systems and economic and political uncertainties, a variety of knowledge workers, such as academic researchers, practitioners, policymakers, governments and community members – each with a particular knowledge culture and different interests invested into knowledge processes – are called to work together in the long term to co-develop practical solutions to pressing societal issues. In this context, CURP have been presented as inter-organisational/institutional arrangements able to involve university and community partners in a mutually beneficial, iterative process of learning, reflection and action, whereby the results of such a process are useful to create positive social and institutional change (Hall et al., 2015). To achieve such goals, CURP deploys various strategies: capacity-building, knowledge translation, participatory research, citizen-centric development, and policy advocacy, to name a few.

Community-university research partnerships are often based on the assumption (or the ideal) that both the community organisation and the university are – or should be – equal partners and co-owners of the research process as well as the research outputs (Hall et al., 2018; Tandon, 2005). CURP can be also seen as autonomous 'entities', 'mechanisms' or even 'machines' that can be designed and adjusted in a relatively simple way to deliver its promises (Fransman et al., 2021). However, tensions commonly arise in most types of research partnerships based on real or perceived power differences between the academy and the community, for instance, in terms of: decision-making and control of funding; governance and direction of the partnership; ownership of the research process and knowledge outcomes; different understandings of what research and knowledge mean; dynamics of time; analysis and sharing of research results. Structurally, universities often lead community organisations that typically have insufficient institutional and financial capacity to support research activities and collaborations (Hall et al., 2011; Tremblay, 2015), thus putting communities at an unfair disadvantage. Sullivan and Skelcher (2002) refer to such practices as 'pessimist collaboration', a term that indicates one party's "attempts to control or influence the other's activities", thus emphasising that power "resides implicitly in the other's dependency" (p. 40).

Almost all of the key activities carried out in CURP can be seen as deeply rooted in power relations – from setting a research agenda and administering funds to communicating research findings – with individuals from partner organisations also occupying diverse positions of power, and bringing with them a wide range of personal and professional understandings, agendas, practices and identities (Fransman et al., 2021). These power differentials at individual and institutional level not only influence the role of partnership members in the entire research process, but also create hierarchies of knowledge(s) based on existing institutional or socio-cultural norms and assumptions. Failure to fully recognise that power dynamics and tensions between partners are real and inevitable can lead to reaffirming and amplifying certain voices and knowledge while excluding others, particularly those already marginalised and experiencing structural disadvantage, thus undermining the real benefits that CURP can bring (Cornish et al., 2017).

One of the biggest challenges faced by those in the academia working in the field of CURP is indeed the establishment of truly respectful, mutually beneficial and equitable knowledge creation partnerships with diverse communities, social movements and organisations. Not unusually, conflicts between knowledge cultures are based on divergent views of ownership of the research process and control over its knowledge creation, validation and dissemination. Conflicts between the worldviews and traditions of different knowledge cultures in research partnerships remain, rather than being the exception, reifying power differences that inhibit consensus building among partners, and leading to the privileging of one knowledge system over others. These considerations lead us to ask the following question: *in establishing trusting and respectful CURP, how can diverse knowledge cultures be bridged so that perceived or actual power inequalities between collaborating CURP partners are taken into consideration in a way that makes these connections sustainable, secure over time, and able to contribute to better lives, social justice, climate solutions or healthier communities?*

To answer this general question, we decided to lead a global research project titled "Bridging Knowledge Cultures" (BKC) that looked at 10 CURP experiences working on different research areas, such as prenatal health, water management, education, etc. Broadly speaking, in this context we use the term *bridging* to refer to transformative changes at policy, institutional and individual level, which reconfigure system dynamics and power relationships within CURP and lead to the development of inclusive partnership governance arrangements that ensure co-responsibility between academic researchers and a range of research stakeholders (including community and voluntary groups, civil society organisations, state agencies, industry, and professionals).

Our understanding of 'bridging' is informed by Sherry Arnstein's (1969) ladder on citizen involvement in planning processes, and by the work of others on community-engaged research (see Lepore & King, 2023). Thus, activities related to bridging knowledge cultures can be classified as different levels of community participation, empowerment and decision-making capacity on a continuum that indicates increasing control, involvement and active participation by the community in participatory research projects.

We used the Knowledge for Change (K4C) Consortium as a 'laboratory' that allowed us to analyse the interaction between diverse (even conflicting) knowledge cultures involved in CURP, and how collaborating partners within and outside academia address extant power inequalities. The K4C Consortium is an international partnered training and research initiative of the UNESCO Chair in Community-Based Research and Social Responsibility in Higher Education. Launched in 2017, the K4C Consortium aims to develop research capacities for the co-creation of knowledge through collective action by community groups and academics working together in training hubs around the world on issues related to the UN Sustainable Development Goals, such as Indigenous wellbeing, water governance, poverty and inequality, climate action, gender equality and violence against women. Each local K4C hub is a formal CURP made up of at least one Higher Education Institution (HEI) and a Civil Society Organisation (CSO) working together on strengthening individual research capacities and professional skills using a variety of training methods, such as classroom-based instruction, professional development workshops, open online courses, field research projects and individual mentorship. These training hubs support trans-disciplinary research partnerships that provide practical experience to students, and co-create and mobilise knowledge to university and community members and to local, national and international policy makers. There are currently 22 K4C hubs in 10 countries around the globe (Indonesia, India, Malaysia, Ireland, Italy, Canada, South Africa, Colombia, Cuba, Uganda and Tanzania).

The reason for focusing on the K4C Consortium for conducting this research on power inequalities among knowledge cultures is that, while the Consortium was launched with strong support in its various sites, we cannot yet know the extent to which the hubs have been able to overcome the challenges inherent in developing trusting and egalitarian relations between the distinct knowledge cultures of their partners. In some of the K4C hubs (e.g., Victoria, Canada; Gulu, Uganda; and Arusha, Tanzania) work on bridging different knowledge cultures and power relations is well underway. However, in other locations, it is now clear that it will take more research to uncover how far bridging has proceeded, and how and to what extent those hubs have overcome knowledge cultures challenges. Studying the K4C Consortium thus let us gain deeper understanding of the specific practices, norms and values of intellectuals and their partners, which are in play in academic and community settings as they work together to co-create knowledge.

The BKC project allowed us to create a process of collective knowledge exchange and self-reflection about the nature of the academic and non-academic partnerships in the distinct cultural, institutional and political environments where the K4C hubs are located. In the process, we tried to identify and build more robust forms of networking and co-construct reciprocal understandings about knowledge, power, trust and equality to strengthen the K4C Consortium in particular, and contribute to an in-depth understanding of structural barriers and power dynamics that prevent mainstream research institutions from collaborating effectively with community groups, in more general terms.

1 The Bridging Knowledge Cultures Project

To conduct the BKC project, in September 2019 a research team led by Hall and Tandon submitted a partnership development grant proposal to the Canadian Social Sciences and Humanities Research Council (SSHRC). The partnership development funding stream provides funds for formal partnerships between postsecondary institutions and/or organisations of various types to develop research-related activities that can result in best practices or models. In preparing the grant application, the lead team was supported by a diverse set of K4C partners from various regions, with experience in different local, cultural and institutional settings. In order to achieve the project goals, we envisaged a decentralised governance structure able to reflect the diversity of knowledge cultures of our partners. The K4C hubs participating in the BKC project were divided into four regions – Latin America, Africa, Southern Asia, Global North (Canada and Europe) – and a research team was conformed in each region to develop, plan and conduct studies with their regional K4C partners, which would contribute to answering the BKC research question. The teams were led by a member of a K4C hub, who would be responsible for collecting and analyzing primary data from other hubs in their region through field work and community engagement, and for preparing a synthesis of secondary data illustrating the existing knowledge cultures in their regions.

The grant application was positively evaluated and approved by SSHRC, and funds were provided in March 2020. The onset of the Covid-19 global pandemic, however, disrupted the original research plans severely. The Covid-19 restrictions declared in countries where the BKC case studies were to be conducted made it impossible for the regional leaders and their teams to travel internationally to conduct field research. To avoid delays in initiating the project while waiting for local and global health restrictions to be lifted, the lead team together with the participating K4C partners decided that, instead of regional teams being responsible for pulling together all the experiences from the hubs in their region, funding was to be provided to each hub to conduct its own case study on their local knowledge cultures. Participating hubs received research funds upon submission a Plan of Action approved by the editorial team, describing how each team would conduct the study locally, including methodology, timeline and deliverables.

Each case study is informed by an analytical framework on knowledge cultures (see Chapter 2 for more details) designed from inputs from the regional syntheses prepared by the four research teams. The authors of the case studies, which are presented in different chapters of this book, were asked to reflect on the socio-political context where the hub is embedded and the nature of their partnership, to describe the case study methodology, to present a 'map' of knowledge cultures in the hub, to conduct a comparative analysis of academic and community knowledge cultures found in the hub, and to make suggestions for bridging knowledge cultures that could be applied locally in their hubs and transferred to other similar research partnerships.

The empirical part of the project (case studies) started in March 2021. Taking into consideration that local Covid-19 sanitary restrictions might have delayed different stages of the research process (especially for those teams that planned to collect data through art-based methods and community engagement), the teams were given one year to complete their research and submit a final version of their case study. After three rounds of reviews by the editorial team, the outcomes of this global study are presented in this book. Later in the year, this book will be accompanied by a practical guide with recommendations for bridging knowledge cultures within CURP in diverse contexts.

The use of the K4C hubs as individual case studies has allowed for a better understanding of: (a) how university and their community partners understand knowledge, its creation and use; (b) what challenges the hubs have faced in working across both trans-disciplinary and community-university boundaries; (c) what the hubs have done to date to help bridge different knowledge cultures; and (d) what positive stories do they have of co-creation and development of trust and respect between hub members. Thus, we hope that the BKC project will not only contribute to strengthening and developing the K4C Consortium by engaging the hubs in a research and reflection process on the processes of partnership development that they have undertaken, but it will also contribute to a more equal approach to CURP to be used by others.

2   The Road to the Bridging Knowledge Cultures Project

This research is a continuation of an extensive story about knowledge, community action and learning that for two of the editors began in the mid-1970s. Budd L. Hall, working in Tanzania at the time, and Rajesh Tandon, working in southern Rajasthan in India, both found themselves confronted by a challenge to their work as researchers. Trained in the mainstream research orthodoxies of the 1960s and 1970s, both found that their training did not prepare them for making the practical contributions to adult education and community development that they had hoped for. This story on the formulation of the discourse on participatory research and subsequent creation of the International Participatory Research Network has been written about in many places over the years (e.g., Hall et al., 1982; Hall, 2005; Hall & Tandon, 2017; Tandon, 1981). Budd L. Hall and Rajesh Tandon are co-holders of the UNESCO Chair in Community-Based Research and Social Responsibility in Higher Education, created in 2012. In 2014, Walter Lepore, originally from Argentina with six years of experience working in higher education in Mexico, joined Tandon and Hall as Research Coordinator of the Next Gen research project. At the time, Lepore was a PhD candidate in Public Administration interested in researching how to address highly complex, dynamic and uncertain social issues (also known as wicked problems), which require a new generation of decision and policy makers to play an important role as network facilitators to create the conditions that enable interactions between diverse (and often conflicting) stakeholders, and/ or as knowledge brokers to promote the use of various forms of knowledge co-created by different partners (see Lepore, 2018).

The first study conducted by the UNESCO Chair in 2013 study explored three questions: What are the roles of knowledge in society? What are the roles of higher education in society? And how can CURP be mainstreamed and contribute to knowledge democracy? (see Hall et al., 2015). It was in this study that we first articulated our understanding of knowledge democracy. We noted that the terms knowledge economy and knowledge society, while making specific suggestions on how to understand some roles of knowledge and society, did not bring into question the near monopoly of Eurocentric knowledge systems or the exclusion of experiential or Indigenous knowledges. Knowledge democracy, we suggested, combined an openness to a multiplicity of knowledges, and a much broader set of participatory and arts-based tools for creating, validating, and using knowledge (Hall et al., 2013; see also Gaventa, 2005; In 't Veld 2010; Visvanathan 2009). We have found knowledge democracy is the discourse that best encompasses the various approaches, values and practices of participatory research, as it places collective knowledge at the heart of processes of social transformation and social justice (Lepore et al., 2021).

The main findings of this first project were published in the book *Strengthening Community University Research Partnerships: Global Perspectives* (Hall et al., 2015). The evidence presented in the book shows the prevalence and diversity of CURP around the world. Further, it indicates the strong desire of post-secondary institutions for CURP to co-create knowledge with the community, and to enact positive change in the society through collaboration, but also the need for a range of policies, infrastructure and funding for bringing such partnerships into practice. Our findings also showed that democratic knowledge partnerships, where community action is united with academic knowledge, have the potential for social transformation in ways that the narrow application of university scientific knowledge solutions cannot achieve. Another major finding of the study was that there were few places for university students or practitioners to formally learn about community-based approaches to research.

This led to the next study published in *Knowledge and Engagement: Building Capacity for the Next Generation of Community Based Researchers* (Tandon et al., 2016), in which we explored three further questions: Where and how have people been learning about community-based research (CBR)? What pedagogical principles have emerged from the teaching and learning practices? What kinds of partnerships have facilitated effective learning of CBR? Overall, the study makes evident that there is a high interest in CBR training around the world, demanding diversified training and teaching modalities in a variety of settings. The results also show that a variety of skills are needed for the new generation of community-based researchers to contribute to engaged research processes and knowledge democracy; for instance, group facilitation skills, continuous reflection on ethics issues, and the creation of community-based advisory communities for long-term projects. However, we also learned that most people never received formal training in CBR or simply learn to do it through trial and error, and that the predominant ways of acquiring participatory research capabilities are autodidactic, self-directed learning and on-the-job training. Perhaps the most significant finding was that the training supply itself is skewed. That is, the training taking place in university settings typically focuses on theoretical or procedural approaches to participatory research, while training by community organisations puts emphasis on practical work in the field.

Based on our previous studies and after consultations with our partners in various parts of the world, we decided to design a pedagogical model that offers formal, structured opportunities for the next generation of young people to learn both the theories and practices of community-based participatory research. We named this the Knowledge for Change (K4C) Global Consortium for the Training of Community-Based Participatory Research. The K4C hubs are placed at the heart of the Consortium. As explained earlier, a K4C hub is a formal partnership between a CSO and a HEI, whereby the partners agree to work together to provide learning opportunities to both community workers and university students. The goal of the K4C Consortium is to equip community-based researchers with historical, cultural and scientific understanding of participatory approaches to knowledge creation, and to cultivate in them the expertise, competencies and skills required to collaborate with others to contribute productively to economic, social and technological change at local/regional level. The hubs were established with the explicit goal of institutionalising egalitarian knowledge partnerships. Within the K4C Consortium reciprocal knowledge relations are not just an aspiration, but a requirement. However, to what extent have these goals been achieved to date? How can we share what seems to be working to bridge knowledge cultures and illuminate pitfalls going forward? As we investigated the K4C hubs through the BKC project, we identified their practical challenges, learning from their experiences, and exchanging new knowledge within and beyond the K4C.

3   The BKC Project in Context: A Transformative Moment in Higher Education and Knowledge Production

Traditionally, representations of knowledge in academic settings have often been defined as what Nowotny et al. (2006) call Mode 1 research that is characterised by "the hegemony of disciplinary science, with its strong sense of an internal hierarchy between the disciplines and driven by the autonomy of scientists and their host institutions, the universities" (p. 39). Mode 1, which includes natural and social sciences, linguistics, and literature (Gibbons, 2013), represents a discipline-based research structure, where knowledge validation and quality is controlled primarily by disciplinary peers within a system with powerful hierarchies built into the higher education institutions (Carayannis & Campbell, 2019). In the last few decades, we have been witnessing an expansion of scientific knowledge production towards 'Mode 2' and 'Mode 3' research paradigms. Mode 2 knowledge is "socially distributed, application-oriented, trans-disciplinary and subject to multiple accountabilities" (Nowotny et al.,

2006, p. 39). Mode 3 is based on the acceptance and fostering of a pluralism of different knowledge and research paradigms, mutual cross-learning of diverse knowledge modes, and "interdisciplinary thinking and transdisciplinary application of interdisciplinary knowledge" (Carayannis & Campbell, 2019, p. 21).

This changing approach to knowledge production is reflected in the concept of *engaged research* that can be seen in the intersection of various strands of scholarship and practice that have one overlapping characteristic: a democratisation of knowledge and its production. This ambition has led to a renewed interest in how researchers and research institutions interact with non-academic knowledge workers. Engaged researchers, often in collaboration with community groups and/or non-governmental organisations, are at the vanguard of this approach. Such a collective approach to responsibility requires support by public debate and democratic involvement in governance, paralleled by wider and more active participation of citizens in the research and innovation processes. From this perspective, the production of knowledge is conceived as a two-way learning process that redefines how conventional academia investigates and relates to other forms of knowledge production that are developed in the daily life of communities.

Yet, while the idea and practices of engaged research are not new, a generalised growing interest in engaged research is observed within the academic community during the past decades all over the world (Hall et al., 2014; Stoker, 2019; Tapia, 2018). A great variety of studies and initiatives on the ground have indeed flourished in various disciplinary fields in relation to diverse societal issues (Fransman, 2018). In consequence, the list of methods and approaches that identify themselves as a form of engaged research can seem bewildering. Etmanski et al. (2014) identified 27 different types of knowledge production configurations that fall under the umbrella of the community-based research approach. A national survey of Irish researchers carried out in 2017 discovered 47 different terms that were used by different kinds of researchers to describe their collaboration with communities (Campus Engage, 2017). The difference between prevalent engaged research methodologies is, however, often artificial, reflecting distinctive disciplinary concerns and scopes. For instance, what health researchers refer to as 'public patient involvement', other scientists may call 'citizen science'. What some social scientists call 'participatory action research', is called 'action research' in business studies. This varied group of approaches to research are all characterised by an intention to include as many people as possible in deliberative fora designed to provide advice, tacit knowledge and insights for political action and/or policy interventions. Some of the methods employed in engaged research deliberately seek out relevant expertise (e.g., Delphi) or specialised knowledge (e.g., Indigenous ways of knowing), while others – such as discussion circles, autoethnographies, narratives, intergenerational dialogues and the systematisation of experiences – are more inclusive and open in nature. However, they all are characterised by deliberation and consensus building in relation to proposed activities, actions and/or processes. Notwithstanding the new-found enthusiasm for engaged research, it must be acknowledged that this flourishing of alternative participatory methodologies means that we also risk creating a variety of new knowledge cultures, each incapable of speaking to the other.

Community-university research partnerships are a central component of the engaged research approach in the training hubs that make up the K4C Consortium, as they provide a medium/platform/network arrangement that brings university scholars into involvement with those in the community who are often the most disempowered (e.g., newly arrived immigrants, homeless individuals, people with disabilities, etc.) (Silka et al., 2008). To date, research partnerships have expanded remarkably in Canada and internationally as an effective approach to community-university engagement and the co-creation of knowledge. We have reached a stage of maturity in understanding: (a) benefits of collaboration between diverse knowledge actors; (b) changes in research from a focus on individual and institutionally grounded partnerships to broader knowledge systems with their own cultures and incentive structures (Fransman et al., 2021); and (c) a wealth of descriptive and prescriptive literature and toolkits instructing different groups on how to do partnerships (Aniekwe et al., 2012; Cornish et al., 2017; KFPE, 2014; Stevens et al., 2013; Winterford, 2017). We have also found evidence that expressions of power inequalities persist in knowledge creation collaborations, especially in issues related to structures and processes, roles and relationships, artefacts and discourses, partnership configurations and transformations over time, and partners' identities and status. These challenges are further complicated by issues of gender, race, abilities, urban-rural differences, language and social class, which impact the way people engage with research and knowledge, hindering the transformative potential of CURP (Chouinard & Cram, 2020; Cornish et al., 2017; Muhammad, & Wallerstein, 2015; Wallerstein, 1999; Zurba et al., 2022). What seems to continue to be overlooked are the more analytical and practical questions around how to address power inequalities between a wide range of stakeholders (some with divergent interests and values) in research partnerships. The BKC project aimed to fill this knowledge gap and provide practical recommendations to help remove a range of structural barriers and address power dynamics, which prevent mainstream research institutions from collaborating effectively with community groups.

4   The Structure of This Book

Following this Introduction, in Chapter 2 we develop an in-depth review of previous literature on the concept of knowledge cultures, including mainstream references, grey literature and global sources produced and/or identified by our K4C hub research teams during the pre-investigation phase of the BKC project. Based on findings coming from this literature review, we make the case for a refined and expanded understanding of the concept of knowledge cultures, and an original analytical framework for the purposes of addressing the goals of the BKC project. Chapter 3 focuses on understanding what is community knowledge and the ways in which it is produced, stored, shared and used for action.

Chapters 4 to 13 present the 10 case studies written by our K4C hub research teams. Chapter 14 synthesises the learnings from the case studies, reflecting on possibilities and ways in which the gap between academic and community knowledge cultures can be bridged. Chapter 15 provides final thoughts on the importance of the concept of knowledge cultures, and the need for community voice in our discussions about knowledge and epistemology, raising questions about how best to implement the findings from this and related studies into our community-university research partnerships.

References

Aniekwe, C. C., Hayman, R., Mdee, A., Akuni, J., Lall, P., & Stevens, D. (2012). *Academic-NGO collaboration in international development research: A reflection on the issues* [Working paper]. https://www.ssrn.com/abstract=2995689

Britten, N., & Maguire, K. (2016). Lay knowledge, social movements and the use of medicines: Personal reflections. *Health*, 20(2), 77–93.

Campus Engage. (2017). *Engaged research – Society & higher education working together to address grand societal challenges.* Irish Universities Association. https://www.iua.ie/wp-content/uploads/2019/09/Campus-Engage-Irish-Research-Council-Engaged-Research-Report-Jan-2017-revised1.pdf

Carayannis, E. G., & Campbell, D. F. J. (2019). Mode 1, mode 2, and mode 3: Triple helix and quadruple helix. In E. G. Carayannis & D. F. J. Campbell (Eds.), *Smart quintuple helix innovation systems: How social ecology and environmental protection are driving innovation, sustainable development and economic growth* (pp. 17–30). Springer International Publishing AG.

Chouinard, J. A., & Cram, F. (2020). *Culturally responsive approaches to evaluation: Empirical implications for theory and practice.* Sage.

Cornish, H., Fransman, J., & Newman, K. (2017). *Rethinking research partnerships: Discussion guide and toolkit.* Christian Aid Centre of Excellence for Research, Evidence and Learning. https://www.christianaid.org.uk/sites/default/files/2022-08/discussion-guide-ngo-academic-research-oct2017.pdf

Etmanski, C., Hall, B. L., & Dawson, T. (2014). *Learning and teaching community-based research: Linking pedagogy to practice.* University of Toronto Press.

Fransman, J. (2018). Charting a course to an emerging field of 'research engagement studies': A conceptual meta-synthesis. *Research for All, 2*(2), 185–229.

Fransman, J., Hall, B., Hayman, R., Narayanan, P., Newman, K., & Tandon, R. (2021). Beyond partnerships: Embracing complexity to understand and improve research collaboration for global development. *Canadian Journal of Development Studies, 42*(3), 326–346. https://doi.org/10.1080/02255189.2021.1872507

Gaventa, J. (2005). Towards participatory governance: Assessing the transformative possibilities. In S. Hickey & G. Mohan (Eds.), *Participation – from tyranny to transformation? Exploring new approaches to participation in development* (pp. 25–41). Zed Books.

Gibbons, M. (2013). Mode 1, mode 2, and innovation. In E. G. Carayannis (Ed.), *Encyclopedia of creativity, invention, innovation and entrepreneurship.* Springer. https://doi.org/10.1007/978-1-4614-3858-8_451

GUNi. (2014). *Higher education in the world 5. Knowledge, engagement and higher education: Contributing to social change.* Palgrave-Macmillan.

Hall, B. (2005). In from the cold? Reflections on participatory research 1970–2005. *Convergence, 38*(1), 5–24.

Hall, B., Lepore, W., & Bhatt, N. (2018). The community-based university. In C. D. Wang, M. Sirat, & D. A. Razak (Eds.), *Higher education in Malaysia. A critical review of the past and present for the future* (pp. 164–177). Penerbit University Sains Malaysia.

Hall, B., Gillette, A., & Tandon, R. (Eds.). (1982). *Creating knowledge: A monopoly?* Participatory Research in Asia.

Hall, B., Jackson, E., Tandon, R., Lall, N., & Fontan, J. M. (Eds.). (2013). *Knowledge, democracy and action: Community-university research partnerships in global perspectives.* Manchester University Press.

Hall, B., & Tandon, R. (2017). Participatory research: Where have we been, where are we going? A dialogue. *Research for All, 1*(2), 365–374.

Hall, B., & Tandon, R. (Eds.). (2021). *Socially responsible higher education: International perspectives on knowledge democracy.* Brill.

Hall, B., Tandon, R., & Escrigas, C. (Eds.). (2014). *Higher education in the world 5. Knowledge, engagement and higher education: Contributing to social change.* GUNI and Palgrave-MacMillan.

Hall, B., Tandon, R., & Tremblay, C. (Eds.). (2015). *Strengthening community university research partnerships: Global perspectives.* University of Victoria Press and PRIA.

Hall, P., Smith, J., Kay, A., Downing, R., MacPherson, I., & McKitrick, A. (2011). Introduction: Learning from the social economy community-university research partnerships. In P. Hall & I. MacPherson (Eds.), *Community-university research partnerships: Reflections on the Canadian Social Economy Experience*. University of Victoria.

In 't Veld, R. J. (2010). Towards knowledge democracy. In R. J. In 't Veld (Ed.), *Knowledge democracy: Consequences for science, politics and media* (pp. 1–11). Springer-Verlag.

KFPE. (2014). *A guide to transboundary research partnerships*. https://naturalsciences.ch/uuid/564b67b9-c39d-5184-9a94-e0b129244761?r= 20170706115333_1499301166_3898d31d-7a25-55d7-8208-d9cbeada1d05

Leadbeater, B., Bannister, E., & Marshall, E. A. (2011). *Knowledge translation in context: Indigenous, policy and community settings*. University of Toronto Press.

Lepore, W. (2018). *Government attention on wicked problems* [Doctoral dissertation, University of Victoria]. https://dspace.library.uvic.ca/handle/1828/10447

Lepore, W., & King. L. (2023). Weaving knowledge systems: Challenges and possible solutions through community-engaged research in Canada and Nordic countries. In M. Singh, P. Bhatt, W. Singh, & K. S. Pareek (Eds.), *Community engagement in higher education: From theory to practice*. Routledge India.

Lepore, W., Hall, B., & Tandon, R. (2021). Knowledge for change consortium: A decolonising approach to international collaboration in capacity-building in community-based participatory research. *Canadian Journal of Development Studies*. (Special issue: *Next-Generation Models for Improved Collaboration in International Development*), 42(3), 347–370. https://doi.org/10.1080/02255189.2020.1838887

Lutz, J., & Neis, B. (2008). *Making and moving knowledge: Interdisciplinary and community-based research in a world on the edge*. McGill-Queen's University Press.

Muhammad, M., & Wallerstein, N. (2015). Reflections on researcher identity and power: The impact of positionality on Community Based Participatory Research (CBPR) processes and outcomes. *Critical Sociology*, 41(7–8), 1045–1063.

Munck, R., McIllrath, L., Hall, B., & Tandon, R. (Eds.). (2014). *Higher education and community based research: Creating a global vision*. Palgrave MacMillan.

Newman, J., Cherney, A., & Head, B. W. (2016). Do policy makers use academic research? Reexamining the two communities. *Public Administration Review*, 76(1), 24–32.

Nowotny, H., Scott, P., & Gibbons, M. (2006). Re-thinking science: Mode 2 in societal context. In E. G. Carayannis & D. F. J. Campbell (Eds.), *Knowledge creation, diffusion, and use in innovation networks and knowledge clusters: A comparative systems approach across the United States, Europe, and Asia* (pp. 39–51). Praeger Publishers.

Silka, L., Toof, R., Turcotte, D., Villareal, J., Buxbaum, L., & Renault-Caragianes, P. (2008). Community-university partnerships: Achieving the promise in the face of changing goals, changing funding patterns, and competing priorities. *New Solutions*, 18(2), 161–175. https://doi.org/10.2190/NS.18.2.g

Stevens, D., Hayman, R., & Mdee, A. (2013). 'Cracking collaboration' between NGOs and academics in development research. *Development in Practice, 23*(8), 1071–1077. https://doi.org/10.1080/09614524.2013.840266

Stoker, N. (2019). *Increasing awareness of public engagement.* National Co-ordinating Centre for Public Engagement. https://www.publicengagement.ac.uk/whats-new/blog/finding-common-ground-defining-our-differences-useful-map-public-engagement

Sullivan, H., & Skelcher, C. (2002). *Working across boundaries: Collaboration in public services.* Palgrave MacMillan.

Tandon, R. (1981). Participatory research in the empowerment of people. *Convergence, 14*(3), 20.

Tandon, R. (2005). *Participatory research: Revisiting the roots* (Rev ed.). Mosaic Books.

Tandon, R., Hall, B., Lepore, W., & Singh, W. (Eds.). (2016). *Knowledge and engagement: Building capacity for the next generation of community based researchers.* University of Victoria and PRIA. http://bit.ly/KnowledgeandEngagement

Tapia, M. N. (2018). *El compromiso social en al curriculo de la Educación Superior.* CLAYSS.

Tremblay, C. (2015). Global trends in community-university research partnerships. In B. Hall, R. Tandon, & C. Tremblay (Eds.), *Strengthening community university research partnerships: Global perspectives.* University of Victoria Press and PRIA.

Visvanathan, S. (2009). *The search for cognitive justice. Knowledge in question.* A Symposium on Interrogating Knowledge and Questioning Science. http://bit.ly/3ZwMD2

Wakeford, T., & Rodriguez, J. S. (2018). *Participatory action research: Towards a more fruitful knowledge.* University of Bristol and the AHRC Connected Communities Programme.

Wallerstein, N. (1999). Power between evaluator and community: Research relationships within New Mexico's healthier communities. *Social Science & Medicine, 49*(1), 39–53.

Winterford, K. (2017). *How to partner for development research.* Research for Development Impact Network.

Zurba, M., Petriello, M. A., Madge, C., McCarney, P., Bishop, B., McBeth, S., Denniston, M., Bodwitch, H., & Bailey, M. (2022). Learning from knowledge co-production research and practice in the twenty-first century: Global lessons and what they mean for collaborative research in Nunatsiavut. *Sustainability Science, 17*(2), 449–467. https://doi.org/10.1007/s11625-021-00996-x

CHAPTER 2

A Theoretical Framework to Bridge Knowledge Cultures

Walter Lepore and Barbara Jenni

Abstract

In this chapter we explore the notion of knowledge cultures (KC) in the context of community university research partnerships (CURP), a particular institutional arrangement not previously considered in the literature on KC. Starting with a review of how KC have been conceptualized in various contexts, we develop an analytical framework that accounts for the tensions and conflicts that may emerge between CURP partners stemming from uneven power dynamics. In this chapter, we pay particular attention to and rely on the knowledge processes existing in diverse settings and geographical regions, beyond Western academia.

Keywords

knowledge culture – community-university research partnership – community knowledges – general knowledge environment – institutional/organizational knowledge environment – knowledge setting/practice

1 Introduction

Despite its ubiquitous presence in the Western academic literature, the concept of knowledge cultures (KC) has not yet been used in studying community university research partnerships (CURP). As explained in the first chapter, our work across the K4C Consortium makes us particularly interested in understanding KC in the context of CURP. In the mainstream literature, KC is often defined in relation to a unified or single organisational arrangement to indicate, for instance, how organisational culture affects the way knowledge is valued and shared (Mas Machuca & Martínez-Costa, 2012), a set of organising practices (Knorr Cetina, 2007), or the internal sense-making processes and structures of meaning (Tsouvalis et al., 2000). However, CURP, as understood in the context of the Bridging Knowledge Cultures (BKC) project, represents a particular institutional arrangement made up of at least two organisations with typically distinctive structures, norms, processes, interests and goals, which are called upon to co-create alternative knowledge drawing on local, community-based and multiple epistemological resolutions.

In the Introduction, we briefly defined KC as the set of formal and informal roles, structures, norms and practices, shared meanings and cultural forms (e.g., language, symbols, rituals), which influence how knowledge is understood, valued, assembled, shared and acted upon in a specific setting. In this chapter, we aim to further elaborate this definition in a manner adequate to capture the intrinsic complexity of KC, and to develop an analytical framework which considers both the role of the CURP context, as well as the different settings in which the BKC project takes place. The overarching goal of the BKC project is to contribute to a transformative change that reconfigures system dynamics and CURP power relationships. Our conceptualisation of KC therefore needs to account for tensions and conflicts that may emerge between partner organisations operating with unequal power while determining how voices, expertise and knowledge are valued and amplified (or lost) in the research process, as well as how decisions are made regarding how, when and to whom research is communicated.

To develop a framework for the analysis of KC in diverse settings and geographical regions, we began with an examination of existing definitions of KC, which is available primarily in the Western academic literature in the organisational context and in cultural and social studies, where the term KC is used productively. We also relied on studies about occupational culture that offer an alternative perspective to the study of KC. In recognising the limitations of looking solely to the Western academic literature, we then review insights from four regional syntheses produced by K4C members involved in the BKC project, which describe knowledge processes based on their respective local literatures and community contexts. Methodologically, this ensures value alignment with the proposed framework being able to address how the diverse ways of knowing in communities, social movements and community organisations are validated, and not seeing higher education institutions (HEI) as the only places where 'real' knowledge is created. We conclude this chapter by offering a definition of KC and describing our proposed analytical framework.

2   Knowledge Culture in Western Academic Literature

Western literature provides several theoretical groundings of KC primarily from an organisational perspective and, as such, deals with considerations of KC within a closed or limited system (Dickinson, 2013; Dilmaghani et al., 2015). For example, Oliver and Reddy Kandadi (2006) developed a framework to account for ten factors affecting the KC of an organisation, including organisational structure, leadership, reward systems and time allocation. Their key argument is that effective KC must be nurtured through careful consideration of each of these factors. The authors show that the physical configuration of the work environment can facilitate how knowledge is shared within an organisation. Developing a KC requires sufficient allocation of time for learning, collaboration and sharing, including supporting communication infrastructures. The creation of hybrid positions combining functional role and task-based job responsibilities related to knowledge processes allows for everybody to be involved in the spread of the KC throughout an organisation. The findings of this study are useful to our conceptualisation of KC in that they acknowledge some of the logistical and day-to-day contexts that either support or hinder successful collaboration between research partners in the context of CURP.

Continuing from this argument, Svetlana & Jucevičius (2011) put forth that KC is a multi-level structure, combining "cultural features (culture), typical to organisations (organisational culture) that stress the importance of knowledge and its effective management (organisational knowledge culture)" (p. 533). The authors argue that KC entails attributes at each of these three levels, including *artifacts*, i.e., the physical environment, creations, rituals, etc.; *espoused values*, i.e., the settled ways of accepted norms, attitudes and beliefs; and *basic assumptions*, i.e., the basic values accepted without proof. Svetlana & Jucevičius (ibid.) make a useful contribution to our own conceptualisation of KC, as the co-construction of knowledge in the context of CURP typically involves different structural/institutional levels, and these different spheres are not limited to either ideas and beliefs, or a physical infrastructure.

Mas Machuca and Martínez-Costa (2012) suggest that KC consists of "trust, transparency, flexibility, collaboration, commitment, honesty and professionalism" (p. 30). Specifically, they find that trust is the most relevant value in a KC, followed by transparency and flexibility. The authors observe that groups of values (called 'cultural factors') support people to share what they know. The study shows that KC is made up of values that exist not in isolation but those that interact with each other, creating (or not) a trustworthy atmosphere. This is relevant to the study of CURP, where stakeholders – each with their own values, biases and interests – engage with each other in a typically power-imbalanced setting. With perceptions of trust, professionalism, flexibility and transparency varying within an organisation, differences in these value-driven aspects are even more pronounced where universities and community partners must open and share their respective knowledges to collaborate and co-create effectively and safely. Another relevant take-away from this work is the observation that the term *culture* encompasses values, norms and actions of the environment in which knowledge co-creation takes place. We will return to this point in our discussion of organisational and occupational dimensions of KC.

Among the key global developments of the 21st century is the shift towards knowledge-based economies whose continuous growth depends on generating new knowledge from existing knowledge (Chorev & Ball, 2022). It is no surprise that in this context, knowledge management emerges as a prevalent academic discipline to "explain how it enables organisational learning and innovation" (Syed et al., 2018, p. 2). Over time, KC has become adopted as a key principle of knowledge management by most companies, as well as within the knowledge management literature (Miklosik et al., 2019). KC is equated with business culture in general, where existing KC is deployed as mediator in the implementation of knowledge management systems and routines (Ahmad & Hossain, 2018).

Travica (2013) provides a definition of KC and framework that serves as a useful heuristic to identify requirements for *knowledge management* processes in organisations. The author proposes the following basic definition: "Knowledge culture is a form of organisational culture that combines elements of individualistic, group and macro-organisational cultures to facilitate a heedful management of the entire knowledge management process" (p. 95). This definition puts emphasis on a combination of micro-, meso-, and macro-cultural aspects that facilitate and represent knowledge production activities (e.g., knowledge generation, validation, diffusion, utilisation and evaluation) and forms of knowledge that correspond to different types of organisation (i.e., bureaucracy, decentralised companies, small business and universities, and project-driven firms). Travica's work aligns particularly well with our understanding that KC entails values, beliefs and assumptions, while also depending on structural supporting factors. Travica's approach to KC is, however, less suitable to capture, identify or address the power dynamics inherent in CURP, where at least two partner organisations meet.

Related to knowledge management, the novel notion of *knowledge governance* proposes that "understanding rules around knowledge-based processes can help navigate complex relationships between science and practice" (van Kerkhoff & Pilbeam, 2017, p. 32). This concept explores how knowledge-based processes are shaped by formal and informal rules and conventions and, importantly, reaches beyond the limitations of the singular organisation. The linking of knowledge creation practices to politics, history and institutions aligns with CURP dynamics, through its consideration of the complexities inherent within governance arrangements aimed at "engaging actors in innovative ways of solving societal issues" (van Kerkhoff, 2013, p. 84). However, spaces where knowledge production takes place inherently contain power dynamics in which universities often assume control and ownership of research-related processes and activities (Hall et al., 2011; Wakeford & Rodriguez, 2018). Knowledge governance models thus recognise that certain knowledge-to-action processes and outcomes are allowed or restricted under a given governance arrangement. The potentials for power imbalances among partners are even more pronounced where governance is – or aims to be – shared between community-based and academic entities.

Tsouvalis et al. (2000) address the inherent rules of what counts as 'legitimate knowledge', which is a contentious aspect within CURP as research partners often have dissimilar epistemological and ontological assumptions. Central to their conceptualisation of KC is the notion that it is not a theoretical or technical *form* of knowledge, but rather that it "provides a means for the interactions with others that instructs them about the cultural significance [an object, practice, or idea] has for the community of which they are a part" (p. 912). The observation that what counts as knowledge is constantly negotiated is relevant to our own understanding of KC in the context of CURP. We agree with Tsouvalis and her colleagues in that the boundaries between diverse forms of knowledge(s) are fluid or porous, and that the processes of knowledge production are either constrained or enabled by the rules, norms and values in which knowledge is created. At the same time, as those authors also suggest, the extant power relations between Western 'expert' knowledge and 'other' forms of knowledges are not in balance. It is these power imbalances that to date have remained largely unresolved in CURP, and which we argue require a careful exploration of how a KC is conceived of and understood across and between partners. Relatedly, Somers (1999) argues that "claims to knowledge and truth are [...] culturally embedded – that is, mediated through symbolic systems and practices" (p. 125). Cultural structures always interact empirically with the political, social or economic structures, which allow some KC to achieve a degree of imprint onto these structures and the subsequent exclusion of other knowledges or KC.

Finally, Peters and Besley (2006) introduce the term KC in their work on higher education, knowledge and economy. The authors specifically focus on social learning and development in the context of the knowledge economy/society. They define KC as "the cultural preconditions that must be established before economies or societies based on knowledge can operate successfully as genuine democratic cultures" (p. 29). These preconditions include trust, reciprocal rights as well as responsibilities between different knowledge partners, institutional routines, regimes and strategies. We agree with their understanding that KC s "embody culturally preferred ways of doing things, i.e., learning styles, processes, economies, and systems often developed over many generations" (ibid., p. 29). The authors consider knowledge primarily as being fundamentally different from other commodities. This perspective is somewhat limiting for our context as it is less inclusive of understandings of knowledge – and by extension of KC – which diverge from the dominant Western academic perspectives. In the context of the BKC project, a conceptualisation of KC must account for knowledge(s) as understood beyond Western academia and encompass community or experiential knowledges that fundamentally differ from the view of knowledge as a commodity.

3   Knowledge Culture as a Community of Practice

Over the years, we have come to value CURP as groups of people bonded together by shared expertise and passion for the same type of work, involving values, norms, identities and common meanings – a perspective also reflected in the notion of *occupational communities* or *communities of practice* (Wenger & Snyder, 2000; Kalliola & Nakari, 2007). Relevant to the BKC project, such a community generates, maintains and reproduces a distinctive stock of knowledge – its primary 'output' – which provides involved individuals with identities and significant reference groups within and outside their respective 'home' organisation, i.e., a CSO or HEI (Gregory, 1983; Wenger & Snyder, 2000). It is reasonable to assume that people doing similar work, such as co-producing knowledge within a CURP, have a common jargon, similar approaches to tasks, and a unique repertoire of routines and procedures, symbols, gestures and stories, which define similar attitudes and expectations related to the work to be performed and the context in which it is carried out (Kwantes & Boglarsky, 2007). A community of practice, such as a CURP, certainly contributes to the development of collective identities and sense-making processes. However, as indicated in the preceding sections, it might also hold the potential for conflict and power struggles between the different contributing groups or individuals of the CURP, given that status and control are negotiated between communities within an organisation and involved partners (Bechky, 2006). One potential source of conflict and power inequalities lies, for example, in the way some research partnerships are set up, assigning university researchers the so-called expert status and limiting community partners' decision-making authority and control over equitable resource distribution (Fransman et al., 2021).

The lens of occupational cultures helps here to shed light on the existence of sub-cultures within and across organisational boundaries, each of them with their own structures of meanings and different ways of developing and maintaining group identity among its members (Gregory, 1983; Kwantes & Blogarsky, 2007). The inherent values and ideologies, i.e., feelings that are often unconscious and manifested trough practices or cultural forms such as symbols, heroes and rituals, are at the core of any culture (Hofstede et al., 1990; Trice, 1993). In our case, we will refer to these as occupational and organisational (sub)-dimensions of KCs, as they are practiced within the context of a CURP, such as the different K4C hubs contributing in the BKC project.

Practices are of course carried out by individuals or groups of people, and KC may be seen as "a constitutive force that operates in the interface between political-economic efforts and individuals' agency" (Nerland, 2012, p. 27). KC thus exists through the structures and processes used to organise knowledge and express themselves through shared practices. This observation can be extended to the context of the BKC project, with the organisational member of each K4C hub representing a site of practice where individuals learn as well as replicate and express their respective KC. We believe that fundamental to building trust-based and equitable knowledge partnerships is the recognition by all parties involved in the co-construction of knowledge of the differences in their respective KC. Failure to understand that the ways knowledge is validated and used differ in academic and non-academic settings contributes to a perpetuation of the power imbalances noted above, and places a roadblock on the bridges to working together. The development of an analytical framework for the study of KC in the context of CURP, especially if they involve organised communities (e.g., non-for-profit organisations) with a particular professional/practical expertise and body of knowledge, must thus provide the possibility to also study conflicts, tensions and power inequalities, as they exist in CURP. We argue that the analysis of KC can contribute to a better understanding of the power relations at play in CURP, and eventually lead to transforming and redressing the extant hierarchies imposed on different knowledges. In turn, this will aid organisations operating from different (even conflicting) worldviews to work together more productively and equitably.

4 Community-Based Understandings of Knowledge Cultures

Our review of the concept of KC thus far has been sourced from Western academic literatures and an overly Eurocentric knowledge base, which provide useful – but limited – perspectives and elements for the development of an analytical framework for the BKC project. To better reflect the reality and environment of the local K4C hubs and to build a more inclusive understanding of what may constitute a KC beyond the preceding literature review, we felt the need to also draw from the vast wisdom of the diverse academic and non-academic communities that work in the BKC project and the global K4C Consortium. To deepen the notion of what we are calling 'knowledge cultures', four regional research teams composed of members of the K4C Consortium were created (Latin America, Africa, South Asia, Global North).[1] Using academic and so-called grey literature published in local languages, each team produced a regional synthesis on the typical knowledge production processes (creation, validation, dissemination and use) in local academic and community settings, and extant power inequalities in CURP found in their regions.

In our own work, we use the term *community knowledges* as a shorthand to differentiate from otherwise Western academic knowledge. One of the dangers in talking about community knowledges of course is to assume that they are very much alike across the world, without sufficient consideration of the linguistic, cultural, experiential and regional diversity of peoples and communities. We intentionally use the plural term *knowledges* to recognise the significant role the millions of Indigenous peoples and local communities hold in sustaining the diversity of the world's cultural and biological landscape (UNESCO, n.d.).

Based on the information provided by our K4C partners in their regional syntheses, a variety of ways in which knowledge is created, passed on and shared falls under the big umbrella term *community knowledges*, such as traditional knowledge, Indigenous knowledge, tacit knowledge, and others. What follows are brief outlines without any claim to being able to do justice to their diversity and richness. The different types of community knowledges introduced here will contribute to our understanding of KC and further inform our conceptual framework.

4.1 *Traditional Knowledge*

Traditional knowledge (TK) has many definitions, but the central theme consists of cultural beliefs and traditions transmitted orally from generation to generation (Hiebert & Van Rees, 1998). TK can be acquired through firsthand experience, has a spiritual component, is mainly of a practical nature – particularly in fields as agriculture, fisheries, health, horticulture, and forestry – and it is also dynamic, evolving and adapted to the local culture and environment (Stevenson, 1998; Secretariat of the Convention on Biological Diversity, 2007). What makes certain knowledges 'traditional' is not its antiquity – much of this knowledge can be contemporary or new – but the way it is acquired and used, its social meaning and legal character, and the social process of learning and sharing such knowledge that is unique to each culture (Four Directions Council, 1996). The essence of TK is found in the language of the people, which is the vehicle by which taxonomic systems, metaphysical perceptions and codified knowledge are passed from generation to generation. TK is based upon customary law and involves the practices of the Elders, who are essential to the relaying of oral traditions (Opheim, 2018).

4.2   *Indigenous Knowledges*

Indigenous knowledge is a holistic and inclusive form of knowledge, i.e., cultural traditions, values, beliefs, skills, philosophies, and worldviews, that is the product of Indigenous peoples' direct experience and their long histories of interaction with their natural surroundings (Dei, 1993; Battiste, 2002; Nakashima et al., 2017; Ndlovu-Gatsheni, 2013; Odora Hoppers, 2021; Kambon, 2020). Indigenous knowledges contain linguistic categories, rules and relationships unique to each knowledge system, have localised content and meaning and established customs with respect to acquiring and sharing of knowledge (Battiste, 2002). As indicated by L. Little Bear (2000), an esteemed Blackfoot researcher, educator and First Nations advocate, common generalisations comparing Eurocentric and Indigenous epistemologies include binary classifications such as linear versus cyclical, objective versus subjective, secular versus spiritual, industrial versus nature- and context-based, and fragmentary versus integrated and holistic.

4.3   *Latin American Ancestral Knowledge*

As proposed by Chamorro and Sicard (2021), Latin American ancestral wisdom is re-created and adapted to different contexts through the transmission from one generation to another. Associated with the Spanish word *saberes,* ancestral wisdom is traditional knowledge that materialises in social interactions and with the environment in which the transmission occurs. People are understood to be actors in complex networks of interactions that involve social relations, relations with nature and relations with the planet, including the social and natural phenomena that surround the experience (ibid, 2020; Mendiwelso et al., 2020).

Latin American native communities maintain a relationship to the land and care for the common home through sensitive affection and care for the other, which allows people to recognise, cooperate, build, project, act, and transmit ancestral knowledge. Native peoples transfer their affection by teaching the production of their material culture in a manner that will guarantee, under their autonomy and cosmogony, the process is sustained and cared for over time (Chamorro & Sicard, 2021).

4.4 African Indigenous Knowledge Systems

A starting point to define African Indigenous knowledge systems (AIKS) is to conceive of it through cultural heritage (Wyk, 2012). AIKS is a systematic body of knowledge produced and acquired by local people strictly based on their lived experiences and through accumulation of experience, informal experiment and understanding of their environment (Tella, 2007; Zhu & Ringler, 2010). AIKS affect several aspects of the African society and the major influence is experienced within the culture domain, including poems (p'Bitek, 1969; Genis, 2019), proverbs (Mvanyashe, 2019), stories and folktales (Iseke, 2013), as well as dance (Nzewi, 2006). The practices appear supported by experiences between the communities to the physical and the metaphysical domains. Within African communities, practice usually creates norms and themes which in turn result in the generation of a new body of understanding, or knowledge. Importantly, once people's ways of being are based on learned practices, it is impossible to claim that they lack knowledge (Nyerere, 1967). Odora Hoppers (2021) points out that the value of AIKS resides in the understanding that culture is knowledge.

4.5 Tribal Knowledge Systems in South Asia

The diversity of ethnicities, religions, languages and cultures across South Asia has contributed to unique expressions of tribal community knowledges in this region (Gangadharan, 2021). Indigenous knowledge of tribal communities is both tangible and intangible, and concerns a wide range of topics relevant for local people's survival, well-being, as well as the equitable management of resources (Reddy, 2011). Appointed individuals often hold vast knowledges relevant to their communities, but this knowledge is also shared within a community through, for example, festivals and ceremonies, so as to sustain the connection between culture, daily practices and knowledge (NIRMAN, 2017; Kardooni et al., 2014). Transferring the knowledge systems from 'people to people' reflects the principle of a decentralised knowledge system (Gangadharan, 2021). While all natural resources belong to the Creator, community knowledge lives on through the human experience (Kardooni et al., 2014; Saini, 2016).

4.6   Tacit Knowledge/Experiential Knowledge

Tacit knowledge – as opposed to formal, codified, or explicit knowledge – is difficult to express or extract, and even more difficult to transfer to others by traditional means of writing it down or verbalising it (Polanyi, 1983). This can include personal wisdom, experience, insight and intuition. In the context of the BKC project, tacit knowledge is used to refer, for instance, to the important and valid knowledge possessed by immigrants, obtained in their home countries either formally or informally, which may be lost or not easily transposed through the process of integration and contribution to their recipient countries and their standards of what knowledge should look, feel or sound like. Experiential knowledge captures an individual's understanding through direct engagement with the physical, social or intellectual world (Borkman, 1976). Also described as lived experience, experiential knowledge can offer a source of practical and usable techniques to others with similar experiences in supporting their quality of life (Pols, 2014).

4.7   Community Knowledges in Perspective

As evident from the above contributions, *community knowledges* are local knowledges – i.e., knowledges unique to a given culture, group, or society – that form the basis for local-level decision-making in agriculture, health care, food preparation, education, natural resources management, as well as social, economic and political organisation. Their value stems in part from this localness, not only for the culture and context in, and from, which they evolve, but also for scientists and planners striving to improve conditions in local communities (Warren, 1991). The validity of *community knowledges* is demonstrated by the survival techniques that have been successfully used by countless generations over time within the local space. It does not, therefore, need to be further authenticated by using the criteria of modern occidental science (e.g., academic peer review process).

Another key takeaway relevant to our conceptualisation of KC is that *community knowledges* are transmitted through a diversity of conduits: poems, proverbs, documents on land ownership and access, music and dance, practices (harvesting, hunting, housing, planting), religion, ceremonies, arts and crafts, governance, sacred sites, local languages, and more. These different channels and media are essential to form a particular KC. They contribute to building collective memory (Genis, 2019), instilling a sense of pride, and helping to establish an identity (Mvanyashe, 2019). They also foster the nurturing of relationships and the sharing of knowledge in ways consistent with traditional worldviews and cosmologies (Iseke, 2013), ensuring minimal livelihoods for local people (Akullo et al., 2007), and supporting the resolution and management of conflicts (Jendia, 2019; Tshimba, 2015).

In the context of CURP, *community knowledges* may be represented in an organised format (e.g., through an Indigenous organisation partnering with a university), or more informally/unstructured (e.g., through the participation of community-based individuals and families in a research project). Either way, their presence introduces a rich diversity and breaks open the notion of CURP as a self-contained, singular organisation or one-dimensional community of practice, rooted in a single KC. While communities around the world have begun to assert "a kind of cultural and intellectual sovereignty" (Marker, 2019, p. 1), *community knowledges* remain at risk of being appropriated, suppressed, or marginalised by Western academic KC. Addressing this reality is of utmost importance as we develop our analytical framework for KC.

5   A Conceptual Framework for CURP: Knowledge Culture as a Local Practice

5.1   *Defining Knowledge Culture*

Using the words of Kollmar-Paulenz (2016), one core value of our project is to ensure that non-European knowledge cultures "do not emerge out of their obscurity and come into existence only in their relation and response to the encounter with Europe" (p. 233). Our conceptualisation of KC is thus grounded in the global diversity of understandings of knowledges. We began our work with a broad notion of KC as the ways in which knowledge is understood, valued, assembled, shared and acted upon in diverse settings, within and outside academia. The foregrounding of the environment that facilitates knowledge production allows knowledge and its production to be understood as a set of practices that comprises aspects of the environment, and with it its social, political, and philosophical categories (Knorr Cetina, 2007). This perspective further reveals the existence of diverging epistemic cultures, or practices, connected with creating and verifying knowledge (Knorr Cetina & Reichmann, 2015). Our review of K4C insights on community knowledges in their wide diversity and range powerfully illustrates this.

Our contribution to the understanding of KC in CURP contexts builds on the groundwork of Knorr Cetina, who defines KC as "the set of practices, arrangements and mechanisms bound together by necessity, affinity and[/or] historical coincidence" (2007, p. 363). This view of KC is echoed in Connell's (2022) notion of a *knowledge formation*; that is

a set of concepts, information and intellectual procedures that provides the framework for many specific knowledges and applications and
knowledge [that is also] a socially realised episteme [that] involves the
set of social practices, organisations and institutions through which the
episteme is brought into being, sustained, and developed. (p. 3)

Similarly, Somers (1999) identifies different varieties of KC, that could describe
certain practices: KC as the narrative structures that arrange relational elements in temporal and location patterns; KC as patterns of distinction or oppo-
sition, such as what criteria determine what is natural versus not-natural; and
KC as metanarratives, i.e., naturalised cultural forms, no longer accountable to
otherwise applied standards of rigor, and thus becoming "more foundational"
knowledge than other knowledge(s) (p. 132).

As shown in Chapter 1, one objective of the BKC project has been to identify
how to bridge different KCs. Our theoretical framework thus needs to differentiate the key components of a KC and the processes taking place at each
level in a KC. The act of bridging assumes distinct enough entities exist, even
if the boundary of each entity remains flexible. In the discussion of KC as a
concept used in cultural studies, Liebert (2016) identifies that a KC must have
inclusion and exclusion criteria, governing not only the belonging of people
to a KC, but also technologies, behaviours and objects. This means that, while
the boundaries of a KC may transform through interactions, a KC also is clearly
demarcated, even temporarily. The author explains that every KC contains axi-
oms and assumptions that are not questioned, and it entails traditions that
structure the recognised forms of storing, passing on, teaching and learning,
as well as evaluating KC-specific knowledge. A KC thus is both negotiated and
self-referential, able to contemplate inwardly and outwardly. Applied to our
exploration of extant power structures in the context of CURP, we expect that
community partners and universities both bring preconceived understandings
of their respective and the others' KC to the table, but through the process of
knowledge co-creation, one or multiple KC may change. Recognising whose
KC is valued, and exploring which side's traditions of legitimising prevail, will
make implicit power inequities salient.

Based on the factors and aspects of the various understandings of KC that
emerged from the literature review as relevant to the context of CURP, we thus
conceptualise *knowledge culture* as a set of local value-based practices, rules
and beliefs, which, in a given organisation, community, area of professional
expertise and/or discipline, create and reinforce shared meanings, expectations, identities and generalised rationales about knowledge production processes (creation, validation, dissemination and use). A *knowledge culture as it*

relates to CURP is embedded in the traditions and history of both, its participating members and its partnership configuration, and thus includes its own intra- and inter-organisational structures, alongside roles, division of labour, norms, formal and informal arrangements and mechanisms, collective beliefs, (im)personal interactions/relations and cultural forms – e.g., images, symbols, heroes, rituals and vocabulary/language. These cultural elements shape the way knowledge production is performed within and across organisations and/ or communities in any given CURP setting.

5.2   *Analytical Framework*

With our definition of KC in hand, we now shift our attention to formulating an analytical framework suitable to explore the concept in the context of the BKC project. We recap from the preceding pages that a wide variety of sub-cultures – with their own values, ideologies and cultural forms – exists within a CURP. In addition, CURP are not necessarily structured by a singular organisational or occupational culture, nor are they constrained by organisational boundaries. Likewise, CURP members may have an organisational culture in common alongside another unique occupational identity. From this starting point, we thus initiate a shift in emphasis from a holistic view of the organisational culture of CURP to one entailing changing, dynamic and conflicting interrelationships among varied sub-cultures and across different (micro, meso and macro) levels.

We believe our contribution here is suitable to recognise aspects and practicalities entailed in bridging power inequalities and differences in the co-creation of knowledge in the context of CURP. This framework also informed the BKC case studies as well as our subsequent global analyses presented in this book. We conceptualise our *knowledge cultures framework* according to three basic components that operate at different levels of analysis, as shown in Figure 2.1:

1.   General Knowledge Environment;
2.   Institutional/Organisational Knowledge Environment;
3.   Knowledge Setting/Practice

The three components are nested, reflecting the directionality of influence from the outer and middle to the center sphere. The framework further distinguishes between structural and procedural aspects at each level of analysis. The different levels facilitate and represent both knowledge activities and forms of knowledge (Travica, 2013). This highlights that KCs are both temporally and locally stable and bounded, but are also negotiated, evaluated, and exist through relations and traditions. Each sphere contains both ideas

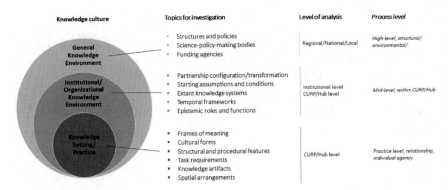

FIGURE 2.1   Knowledge culture framework

and beliefs as well as structural and physical dimensions. Further, the power dynamics present in each of these spaces is expressed in the varied aspects of the KC, i.e., the means through which significance of an idea or activity is attributed (Tsouvalis et al., 2000). We discuss each of the three components in more detail below.

5.3   Outer Sphere: General Knowledge Environment

The General Knowledge Environment exists at the regional, national, global, as well as local level, given that CURP cannot not be decontextualised from the broader historical and geopolitical places in which they are situated. KCs have real political, economic and social effects that are not neutral with respect to social structures and interests or with respect to economic growth (Knorr Cetina, 2007). The General Knowledge Environment shapes how cultural and political differences are reflected in the way research is set up and conducted (i.e., how one cultural order translates into or influences another) and how expert knowledge is embedded in legal frameworks, schemes of citizen participation, policymaking, and the like. In our framework, this sphere entails two aspects:

- Structures and policies that sustain or discourage certain epistemic outcomes, which includes for example, national education, science and innovation policies, professional standards, education systems and/or university models (e.g., French, British, German higher education models). These structures and polices determine what counts as legitimate knowledge or meets the social, political, or economic criteria to be prioritised over other forms of knowledge, and influence knowledge production processes.
- National/Regional science policy-making bodies and funding agencies, which have the political and financial capability to significantly influence the content and approach of knowledge production (i.e., research) at national and

regional levels (e.g., the supranational and national funding bodies of the European Union, like Horizon Europe, or the Tri-Council Agency of Canada).

General Knowledge Environments hold the highest degree of legitimisation power and resemble 'espoused values' – i.e., the settled ways of accepted norms, attitudes, and beliefs – and 'basic assumptions'– i.e., the basic values accepted without proof (Svetlana & Jucevičius, 2011) – about knowledge processes that are 'naturalised' and beyond accountability in many instances (Somers, 1999). This core component of KC effectively governs over most other KCs, or at least profoundly impacts the context and practice of CURP (van Kerkhoff & Pilbeam, 2017).

5.4 Middle Sphere: Institutional/Organisational Knowledge Environment

This sphere reflects the institutional arrangements and frameworks that direct co-producing, acquiring, exchanging and using knowledge in collaboration with community-based partners. We reference both, the HEI and the community organisation (formal and informal), to reflect that both 'sides' bring their own KC to the CURP.

This sphere is more contained in its format or structure than the General Knowledge Environment, but it is far more difficult to navigate, and a number of considerations are necessary at this level. For one, it often sets specific temporal and local boundaries to how academic and non-academic partners – and their KCs – interact with each other. The Institutional Knowledge Environment, although representative of a hegemonic model of knowledge production, is a site where more active negotiations take place. The 'artifacts', i.e., the physical environment and locals, creations, rituals, etc. (Svetlana & Jucevičius, 2011) of KC, and the 'logistics' of day-to-day interactions of CURP (Oliver & Reddy Kandadi, 2006) are worked out at this level. The social activities taking place here in and of themselves determine the meaning of those interactions and what significance the co-creation of knowledge has for both the institution and the community partners (Tsouvalis et al., 2000). The framework thus considers the following aspects:

– *Partnership configurations and transformations over time.* For example, the partners need to work out the assumptions and purposes of creating the CURP and which norms will be accepted for conducting research in a collaborative way. The role and status of each partner needs to be determined (e.g., who are the 'experts'), and how relationships will be maintained as the partnership changes in time and space.

- *Starting assumptions and conditions.* This element refers to the points of origin where the partnership was initiated by putting in motion a series of conditions and assumptions that will set the boundaries of the partnership itself. This may be influenced, for example, by previous research projects, participation in grant applications, events (e.g., networking and showcasing conferences), and discourses (e.g., around Sustainable Development Goals).
- *Extant knowledge systems.* This includes worldviews/epistemological and ontological frameworks that provide the orientation or the set of beliefs on the world or reality (i.e., what is the nature of reality? how can we know what is true and what is not true? how should we act in that reality?); related pedagogies (i.e., ways of knowing and learning); disciplinary approaches; social relationships that inform people's sense of themselves and their cultural values; and logical relationships that connect the content of knowledge to its value (utility).
- *Temporal frameworks.* With this we mean the pace of knowledge creation, which is usually different in community and university settings. For instance, community groups often have tight deadlines for action whereas academics may have years to develop a robust research project. CURP must therefore consider aspects such as temporal requirements to efficiently produce and reproduce knowledge; the temporalities of knowledge and expertise; or simply the conception of time (e.g., cyclical versus linear).
- *Subjects with epistemic roles and functions.* Here, we refer to, for example, internal and/or external actors with different roles in the various knowledge production processes (e.g., journal peer reviewers have a validating role that determines what academic knowledge is acceptable for dissemination; boundary-spanners mediate between academics and community and support knowledge translation; Elders act as knowledge holders in Indigenous communities).

5.5   *Inner Sphere: Knowledge Setting/Practice*

This sphere refers to the whole sets of arrangements, mechanisms, procedures and principles that serve knowledge co-creation and which unfold with its articulation (Knorr Cetina, 2007) within the CURP. Thus, we switch from an understanding of knowledge as the representational and technological product of research to an understanding of knowledge as practice. We therefore recognise the individuals (and groups of individuals) who carry out these practices. Their 'agency' enacts and re-creates the wide variety and diversity of KCs (Nerland, 2012). These actions require 'trust', 'transparency' and a willingness to be open and share with others (Mas Machuca & Martínez-Costa, 2012). At this level, the emphasis is put on the interiorised participatory processes of knowledge production in a K4C hub, and how they are framed, understood and executed. Thus, we would be able to 'observe' values and ideologies regarding knowledge 'practices' or cultural forms, as indicated by Hofstede et al. (1990) and Trice and Beyer (1993). Our framework considers the following aspects of this sphere:

- *Frameworks of meaning.* People enact their lives within frames of meaning via the specific constructions of the objects of knowledge, particular ontologies of instruments, and specific models of epistemic subjects. At this level, CURP members establish who or what are the epistemic subjects, – those we traditionally think of as the agents in scientific practice and the authors of scientific findings – and their ways of relating to the objects of knowledge in research. Frameworks of meaning include vocabulary/jargon, generalised rationales, cultural beliefs and shared passions (common meanings). Frameworks of meaning provide the underlying structure and context for sense-making, "a social activity [...] suffused by moral judgements and power relations" (Tsouvalis et al., 2000, p. 922).

- *Cultural forms.* This aspect contains the rituals, symbols, heroes, ceremonies and stories of success/failure of co-producing knowledge that each member brings to a CURP. In some KCs, knowledge may be primarily produced by experts or authorities following reproducible procedures, while in others, knowledge may be more decentralised and produced by a wider range of individuals and communities in a more informal way.

- *Structural and procedural features.* Within CURP, at least two sets of formal and informal hierarchical structure and rules meet, and along with them the (im)personal relations and ways in which knowledge processes are functionally organised and divided within and across partners. In other words, this aspect captures the allocation of tasks and responsibilities in terms of decision-making (e.g., research agenda setting and governance), funding (e.g., application, allocation and management), leadership (e.g., research design and implementation), validation (e.g., in terms of accuracy, usefulness for the partners and the relationship with existing knowledge), influence (e.g., research communication, uptake and adaptation), and impact (e.g., research use).

- *Task requirements.* Knowledge practices also require a unique body of knowledge or expertise (e.g., storytelling) to perform the particular sets of tasks and responsibilities related to knowledge production in CURP (e.g., knowledge sharing).

- *Knowledge artifacts.* The purpose of using a knowledge artifact is to share and transfer knowledge (Holsapple & Joshi, 2001). According to Newman and Conrad (2000), knowledge artifacts form the linkages between the activities and events that comprise knowledge flow. An artifact can be defined as a medium used to represent meaning and understanding. Knowledge

artifacts come in a variety of forms and shapes, ranging from tangible items such as documents, files and pictures to intangible entries such as nods and thoughts (Abuhimed et al., 2014).
- *Spatial arrangements.* CURP exist 'in the real world' and for members to collaborate they need some form of physical manifestation. This aspect refers to the places where knowledge creation, dissemination and application take place. This might include traditional benchwork laboratories, research centres (i.e., places where resources vital to a whole field come to be located), networks, but also locales within the community/territory or 'on the land' itself (Zurba et al., 2019), such as community circles.

6   Conclusion

The rise and development of CURP as a way to contribute to addressing and solving societal problems has neither been easy nor uncontroversial. One of the main challenges associated with this approach to research creation is the lack of strong evidence about how knowledge created in CURP might be translated into policy and actions. Even when the theoretical underpinnings of participatory, community-engaged research emphasise its action-orientation, what constitutes appropriate and sufficient 'action' is not always clear, with different partners holding diverse views on what types of outcomes could be described as social action and social change (MacFarlane & Roche, 2018). The claims for the effectiveness of CURP thus tend to be theoretical and/or conceptual, rather than empirical. As a consequence, there is considerable discrepancy between the acclamation and attention CURP receives in the literature, and the lack of empirical knowledge and understanding of the processes and dynamics of the partnerships' overall functioning (e.g., the process by which certain partnership conditions lead to various partnership-level outcomes). The literature also shows a strong bias that tends to conceive research partnerships as relatively static entities within a linear understanding of research-into-practice, without paying enough attention to the complex reality where such collaborative arrangements must be embedded (Tremblay et al., 2017).

To better explain the intricacies of power dynamics in collaborative research initiatives, in this chapter we have developed an analytical framework for the study of *knowledge cultures within CURP* that will help address the objectives of the BKC project. First, the offered framework helps explain CURP conflicts and power inequalities by the heterogeneity of co-existing KCs, each with its own system of meanings and identities. Not only do the various CURP members often compete for the same resources, but they also face the imposition of a guiding vision of how work should be organised, conducted and judged within and between partner organisations. Second, our framework suggests that the study of KCs benefits from considering occupational and organisational dimensions of CURP, to better understand and respond to power conflicts that emerge from diverging aspects of KCs.

In practical terms, our analytical framework offers a way to recognise and manage the diverse KCs inherent in CURP. When CURP members meet for the purposes of knowledge co-creation, considering and understanding the coexisting cultural elements and sub-cultures in the partnership will go a long way toward reducing or resolving conflicts, especially where similar values may still lead to conflicting priorities (Gregory, 1983). Helping CURP members work more effectively across epistemological differences requires sensitivity to the presence of diverging values, beliefs, ideologies and cultural forms at various levels, which may otherwise bring research partners into conflict.

Yet, we do not believe that the task of those leading and coordinating research partnerships is to avoid conflict, but rather to know how to manage conflicts in a productive way. Through the interaction and deliberation with other epistemological actors, 'productive conflicts' allow for a more open exploration and evaluation of competing ideas and knowledge claims in order to achieve new ideas, insights and practical solutions (Cuppen, 2012). This does not entail the homogenisation of diverse knowledge (sub-)cultures within the CURP by changing or creating a single dominating mono-culture – something which occurs too often by the imposition of Western academic KC, or the absorption of Indigenous knowledge systems into scientific systems. Rather, our framework suggests the way is to first recognise and embrace cultural differences within the partnership, and then find workable compromises that allow (sub-) cultures to maintain their own identity, while at the same time formulating a distinct KC that aims to achieve a balanced incorporation of diverse knowledges within the CURP. Paraphrasing the suggestions by Kalliola and Nakari (2004, p. 92), the critical task of partnership coordinators and leaders is to build and maintain a sustainable system of shared meanings in the CURP as a whole, without losing sight of the wide variety of KCs – with their own values, ideologies and cultural forms – that exist within the partnership. This is what we succinctly mean by *bridging knowledge cultures*, admittedly a goal easier stated than realised in daily practice. However, we believe that working on building bridges between KCs can provide more practical benefits than attempting to modify the core organisational culture or KC of each CURP partner, a task that in and of itself is difficult to achieve (Hofstede et al., 1990). We hope that our framework offers a starting point for moving beyond the limiting holistic view of CURP, and for recognising and embracing the changing, dynamic and even conflicting inter-relationships among sub-cultures of knowledge that make up CURP. Making salient the power dynamics inherent in CURP is the key to materialising and harnessing the potential of their epistemological diversity.

Note

1   Each research team was led by a K4C partner: Irma Flores Hinojos (U. Andes, Colombia), David Monk (Gulu U., Uganda), Nabiela Naily (UINSA, Indonesia), Maura Adshead (U. Limerick, Ireland). With the support of other members of the Consortium in their regions, the teams collected and analysed secondary data to help us establish a baseline of what we know now about the knowledge cultures of the diverse communities with which the K4C hubs work.

References

Abuhimed, D., Beheshti, J., Cole, C., Alghamdi, M., & Lamoureux, I. (2014). Knowledge artefacts: Lessons learned and stories as a means to transfer knowledge amongst cohorts of high school students working on an inquiry-based project. *Proceedings of the American Society for Information Science and Technology, 50*. https://doi.org/10.1002/meet.14505001146

Ahmad, A., & Hossain, M. A. (2018). Assimilation of business intelligence systems: The mediating role of organizational knowledge culture. In *Lecture notes in computer science (including subseries lecture notes in artificial intelligence and lecture notes in bioinformatics)* (Vol. 11195 LNCS). Springer International Publishing. https://doi.org/10.1007/978-3-030-02131-3_43

Akullo, D., Kanzikwera, R., Birungi, P., Alum, W., Aliguma, L., & Barwogeza, M. (2007). *Indigenous knowledge in agriculture: A case study of the challenges in sharing knowledge of past generations in a globalized context in Uganda*. World Library and Information Congress.

Battiste, M. (2002). *Indigenous knowledge and pedagogy in first nations education: A literature review with recommendations*. National Working Group on Education.

Bechky, B. A. (2006). *Gaffers, gofers, and grips: Role-based coordination in temporary organizations. Organization. Science, 17*(1), 3–21.

Borkman, T. (1976). Experiential knowledge. A new concept for the analysis of self-help groups. *Social Service Review, 50*(3), 445–456.

Chamorro, M., & Sicard, A. (2021). Las sabidurías ancestrales como tecnologías vivas en diálogos con el diseño. Caminos para vivir la inspiración y el cuidado. In C. Córdoba Cely and M. C. Ascuntar Rivera (Eds.), *Investigación + creación a través del territorio* (pp. 351–376). Editorial Universidad de Nariño.

Chorev, N., & Ball, A. C. (2022). The knowledge-based economy and the Global South. *Annual Review of Sociology, 48*(19), 1–21.

Connell, R. (2022). Putting Southern perspectives to work: Paths forward for our practice. In A. Bueno, M. Teixeira, & D. Strecker (Eds.), *De-centering global sociology: The peripheral turn in social theory and research* (pp. 1–19). Taylor & Francis.

Cuppen, E. (2012). Diversity and constructive conflict in stakeholder dialogue: Considerations for design and methods. *Policy Science, 45,* 23–46.

Dei, G. (1993). Sustainable development in the African context: Revisiting some theoretical and methodological issues. *African Development, 18*(2), 97–110.

Dickinson, H. D. (2013). Crossing boundaries: Creating, transferring & using knowledge. In J. Dzisah & H. Etzkowitz (Eds.), *The age of knowledge: The dynamics of universities, knowledge, and society* (pp. 143–165). Haymarket Books.

Dilmaghani, M., Fahimnia, F., Ardakan, M. A., & Naghshineh, N. (2015). Function of knowledge culture in the effectiveness of knowledge management procedures: A case study of a knowledge-based organization. *Webology, 12*(1), 1–21.

Four Directions Council. (1996). *Forests, Indigenous peoples and biodiversity: Contribution of the four directions council.* Submission to the Secretariat for the Convention on Biological Diversity. Four Directions Council.

Fransman, J., Hall, B., Hayman, R., Narayanan, P., Newman, K., & Tandon, R. (2021). Beyond partnerships: Embracing complexity to understand and improve research collaboration for global development. *Revue Canadienne D'études Du Développement, 42*(3), 326–346. https://doi.org/10.1080/02255189.2021.1872507

Gangadharan, V. G. G. (2021). *Local knowledge, social movements & participatory research: Indian perspectives* [Webinar]. Participatory Research in Asia.

Genis, G. (2019, January). Indigenous South African poetry as conduits of history. *Yesterday and Today,* pp. 60–87.

Gregory, K. L. (1983). Native-view paradigms: Multiple cultures and culture conflicts in organizations. *Administrative Science Quarterly, 28*(3), 359–376. https://doi.org/10.2307/2392247

Hall, B. L., Clover, D. E., Crowther, J., & Scandrett, E. (2011). Social movement learning: A contemporary re-examination. *Studies in the Education of Adults, 43*(2), 113–116. https://doi.org/10.1080/02660830.2011.11661607

Hiebert, D., & Van Rees, K. (1998). *Traditional knowledge on forestry issues within the Prince Albert Grand Council* [Unpublished manuscript]. Prince Albert Model Forest.

Hofstede, G., Neuijen, B., Ohayv, D. D., & Sanders, G. (1990). Measuring organizational cultures: A qualitative and quantitative study across twenty cases. *Administrative Science Quarterly, 35*(2), 286–316. https://doi.org/10.2307/2393392

Holsapple, C. W., & Joshi, K. D. (2001). Organizational knowledge resources. *Decision support systems, 31*(1), 39–54. https://doi.org/10.1016/S0167-9236(00)00118-4

Iseke, J. (2013). Indigenous storytelling as research. *International Review of Qualitative Research*, 6(4), 559–577.

Jendia, C. (2019). The cultural factor in conflict management/resolution: A case study of the Acholi of Northern Uganda. *African Journal of History and Culture*, 11(2), 15–25. https://doi.org/10.5897/AJHC2018.0425

Kalliola, S., & Nakari, R. (2007). Renewing occupational cultures—Bridging boundaries in learning spaces. *International Journal of Educational Research*, 46(3–4), 190–203. https://doi.org/10.1016/j.ijer.2007.09.010

Kambon, O. (2020). Editorial book critique: The origin of the word Amen: Ancient knowledge the Bible has never told. *Ghana Journal of Linguistics*, 9(1), 72–96.

Kardooni, R., Kari, F. B., Yahaya, S. R. B., & Yusup, S. H. (2014). Traditional knowledge of Orang Asli on forests in peninsular Malaysia. *Indian Journal of Traditional Knowledge*, 13(2), 283–291. https://nopr.niscpr.res.in/bitstream/123456789/27915/1/IJTK%2013%282%29%20283-291.pdf

Knorr Cetina, K. (2007). Culture in global knowledge societies: Knowledge cultures and epistemic cultures. *Interdisciplinary Science Reviews*, 32(4), 361–375. https://doi.org/10.1179/030801807X163571

Knorr Cetina, K., & Reichmann, W. (2015). Epistemic cultures. In *International encyclopedia of the social & behavioral sciences* (2nd ed., Vol. 7, pp. 873–880). Elsevier. https://doi.org/10.1016/B978-0-08-097086-8.10454-4

Kollmar-Paulenz, K. (2016). Of Yellow teaching and Black faith: Entangled knowledge cultures and the creation of religious traditions. In C. Bochinger & J. Rüpke (Eds.), *Dynamics of religion: Past and present proceedings of the XXI World Congress of the International Association for the History of Religions* (pp. 231–250). De Gruyter, Inc. https://doi.org/10.1515/9783110450934-013

Kwantes, C. T., & Boglarsky, C. A. (2007). Perceptions of organizational culture, leadership effectiveness and personal effectiveness across six countries. *Journal of International Management*, 13(2), 204–230.

Liebert, W.-A. (2016). Wissenskulturen. In L. Jäger, W. Holly, P. Krapp, S. Weber, & S. Heekeren (Eds.), *Sprache - Kultur - Kommunikation: Ein internationales Handbuch zu Linguistik als Kulturwissenschaft*. De Gruyter, Inc.

Little Bear, L. (2000). Jagged worldviews colliding. In M. Battiste (Ed.), *Reclaiming Indigenous voice and vision* (pp. 77–85). UBC Press.

MacFarlane, A., & Roche, B. (2018). Blurring the boundaries between researcher and researched, academic and activist. In S. Banks & Brydon-Miller (Eds.), *Ethics in participatory research for health and social well-being* (pp. 56–79). Routledge.

Marker, M. (2019). Indigenous knowledges, universities, and alluvial zones of paradigm change. *Discourse: Studies in the Cultural Politics of Education*, 40(4), 500–513. https://doi.org/10.1080/01596306.2017.1393398

Mas Machuca, M., & Martínez-Costa, C. (2012). A study of knowledge culture in the consulting industry. *Industrial Management and Data Systems, 112*(1), 24–41. https://doi.org/10.1108/02635571211193626

Mendiwelso-Bendek, Z., Reyes, A., & Plata, J. (2020). Construcción de Paz en Colombia, Alianza entre la Universidad y la Comunidad. *Co Lab Paz: Marco de referencia sobre la Investigación y la Acción con comunidades.* Editorial Universidad de los Andes.

Miklosik, A., Evans, N., Hasprova, M., & Lipianska, J. (2019). Reflection of embedded knowledge culture in communications of Australian companies. *Knowledge Management Research & Practice, 17*(2), 172–181.

Mvanyashe, A. (2019). IsiXhosa proverbs and idioms as a reflection of Indigenous knowledge systems and an education tool. *Southern African Journal for Folklore Studies, 29*(2), 1–14.

Nakashima, D., Rubis, J., Bates, P., & Ávila, B. (2017). *Local knowledge, global goals.* UNESCO. https://unesdoc.unesco.org/ark:/48223/pf0000259599

Ndlovu-Gatsheni, S. J. (2013). The entrapment of Africa within the global colonial matrices of power: Eurocentrism, coloniality, and deimperialization in the twenty-first century. *Journal of Developing Societies, 29*(4), 331–353. https://doi.org/10.1177/0169796X13503195

Nerland, M. (2012). Professions as knowledge cultures. *The Knowledge Economy and Lifelong Learning: A Critical Reader, 1994,* 207–228. https://doi.org/10.1007/978-94-6091-915-2

Newman, B., & Conrad, K. (2000, October 30–31). *A framework for characterizing knowledge management methods, practices, and technologies.* PAKM 2000, Third International Conference on Practical Aspects of Knowledge Management, Proceedings of the Third International Conference, Basel, Switzerland.

NIRMAN. (2017). Burlang Yatra: The annual indigenous seed festival. *Seed Freedom.* https://seedfreedom.info/events/burlang-yatra-the-annual-indigenous-seed-festival/

Nyerere, J. K. (1967). Education for self-reliance. *The Ecumenical Review, 19*(4), 382–403.

Nzewi, M. (2006). African music creativity and performance: The science of the sound. *Voices: A World Forum for Music Therapy, 6*(1). https://doi.org/10.15845/voices.v6i1.242

Odora Hoppers, C. (2021). Research on Indigenous knowledge systems: The search for cognitive justice. *International Journal of Lifelong Education, 40*(4), 310–327. https://doi.org/10.1080/02601370.2021.1966109

Oliver, S., & Reddy Kandadi, K. (2006). How to develop knowledge culture in organizations? A multiple case study of large distributed organizations. *Journal of Knowledge Management, 10*(4), 6–24. https://doi.org/10.1108/13673270610679336

Opheim, D. (2018, May 11). Governance (Indigenous Life in Canada: Past, Present, Future)/Oral Traditions and Storytelling (Indigenous Life in Canada: Past,

Present, Future)/Spirituality (Indigenous Life in Canada: Past, Present, Future)/
Stewardship (Indigenous Life in Canada: Past, Present, Future)/Treaties
(Indigenous Life in Canada: Past, Present, Future)/Truth and Reconciliation
(Indigenous Life in Canada: Past, Present, Future). *Canadian Review of Materials,
24*(1). http://myaccess.library.utoronto.ca/login?qurl=https%3A%2F%
2Fwww.proquest.com%2Fdocview%2F2045243287%3Faccountid%3D14771

p'Bitek, O. (1969). *Wer pa Lawino.* East African Publishing House.

Peters, M. A., & Besley, A. C. (2006). *Building knowledge cultures: Education and development in the age of knowledge capitalism.* Rowman & Littlefield.

Polanyi, M. (1983). *The tacit dimension.* Peter Smith.

Pols, J. (2014). Knowing patients: Turning patient knowledge into science. *Science,
Technology & Human Values, 39*(1), 73–97.

Reddy, S. T. S. (2011). Water management: The neeruganti way. *India Water Portal.*
https://www.indiawaterportal.org/sites/default/files/iwp2/Community_water_
management_in_Karnataka_The_Neeruganti_way_2011.pdf

Saini, A. (2016). Physicians of ancient India. *Journal of Family Medicine and Primary
Care, 5*(2), 254–258. https://doi.org/10.4103/2249-4863.192322

Secretariat of the Convention on Biological Diversity. (2007). *Year in review 2006.*
Montreal.

Somers, M. R. (1999). The privatization of citizenship. In V. E. Bonnell (Ed.), *Beyond
the cultural turn: New directions in the study of society and culture.* University of
California Press.

Stevenson, M. (1998). *Traditional knowledge in environmental management? From commodity to process.* Sustainable Forest Management Network.

Svetlana, Š., & Jucevičius, R. (2011). Investigation of critical attributes of the
organizational knowledge culture. In *Proceedings of the international conference
on intellectual capital, knowledge management & organizational learning* (pp. 529–
538). http://libaccess.mcmaster.ca/login?url=http://search.ebscohost.com/
login.aspx?direct=true&db=bth&AN=69713435&site=ehost-live&scope=site

Syed, J., Murray, P. A., Hislop, D., & Mouzughi, Y. (Eds.). (2018). *The Palgrave handbook
of knowledge management.* Palgrave Macmillan. https://doi.org/10.1007/978-3-319-
75620-2

Tella, R. D. (2007). Towards promotion and dissemination of indigenous knowledge.
A case of NIRD. *International Information & Library Review, 39*(3–4), 185–193.

Travica, B. (2013). Conceptualizing knowledge culture. *Online Journal of Applied
Knowledge Management, 1*(2), 85–104.

Tremblay, C., Singh, W., & Lepore, W. (2017). *Mutual learning and empowering support:
Networks and balance between local and global demands.* GUNi.

Trice, H. M., & Beyer, J. M. (1993). *The cultures of work organizations.* Prentice-Hall, Inc.

Tshimba, D.-N. (2015). Beyond the Mato Oput tradition: Embedded contestations in transitional justice for post-massacre Pajong, Northern Uganda, *Journal of African Conflicts and Peace Studies, 2*(2), 62–85. http://dx.doi.org/10.5038/2325-484X.2.2.3

Tsouvalis, J., Seymour, S., & Watkins, C. (2000). Exploring knowledge-cultures: Precision farming, yield mapping, and the expert-farmer interface. *Environment and Planning A, 32*(5), 909–924. https://doi.org/10.1068/a32138

UNESCO. (n.d.). *Indigenous peoples.* https://en.unesco.org/indigenous-peoples

van Kerkhoff, L. (2013). Knowledge governance for sustainable development: A review. *Challenges in Sustainability, 1*(2), 82–93. https://doi.org/10.12924/cis2013.01020082

van Kerkhoff, L., & Pilbeam, V. (2017). Understanding socio-cultural dimensions of environmental decision-making: A knowledge governance approach. *Environmental Science and Policy, 73,* 29–37. https://doi.org/10.1016/j.envsci.2017.03.011

Wakeford, T., & Rodriguez, J. (2018). *Participatory action research: Towards a more fruitful knowledge.* University of Bristol/AHRC Connected Communities Programme. http://hdl.handle.net/10871/36994

Warren, D. M. (1991, May 21–24). *The role of indigenous knowledge in facilitating the agricultural extension process.* [Paper presentation]. International Workshop on Agricultural Knowledge Systems and the Role of Extension, Bad Boll, Germany.

Wenger, E., & Snyder, W. M. (2000). Communities of practice: The organizational frontier. *Harvard Business Review, 78*(1), 139–145.

Wyk, M. M. (2012). [Re]claiming the Riel as Khoisan indigenous cultural knowledge. *Studies of Tribes and Tribals, 10*(1), 47–56.

Zhu, T., & Ringler, C. (2010). *Climate change implications for water resources in the Limpopo River Basin* (No. 961). International Food Policy Research Institute (IFPRI).

Zurba, M., Maclean, K., Woodward, E., & Islam, D. (2019). Amplifying Indigenous community participation in place-based research through boundary work. *Progress in Human Geography, 43*(6), 1020–1043. https://doi.org/10.1177/0309132518807758

CHAPTER 3

Understanding Community Knowledge Cultures

Walter Lepore and Niharika Kaul

Abstract

This chapter delves deeper into the concept of *community knowledge* introduced in Chapter 2, utilizing primary and secondary data from K4C hubs involved in the Bridging Knowledge Culture project. Our focus lies on the multifaceted nature of knowledge within community contexts. We pay particular attention to how knowledge is understood in community settings, the purposes of community knowledge, and how it is created, disseminated, and stored. We also discuss how power inequalities between research partners influence the utilization and validation of community knowledge vis-à-vis academic, scientific knowledge. The chapter concludes by summarizing seven essential attributes of community knowledge.

Keywords

community knowledge – knowledge creation, dissemination, validation and use – power – research partnerships – oral tradition – experiential learning

1 Introduction

Community knowledge remains an essential source of communities' survival across the globe, which helps them deal with health, environmental and other crises. Locations where K4C hubs are hosted have a rich base of community knowledge that has largely remained undervalued and undocumented. Community knowledge is often considered inaccurate compared to western formal sources of knowledge, since it does not adhere to the formal codes of academic knowledge production. While the introductory chapters of this book defined *knowledge cultures* (KC) in the context of CURP from a theoretical and conceptual perspective, the case studies will show the diverse influence of KC on knowledge production processes both in academic and community settings. This chapter contributes to the understanding of KC by further exploring community knowledge and related knowledge production practices – the inner circle of the BKC analytical framework presented in Chapter 2. Based on primary and secondary information provided in the case studies and regional syntheses, this chapter synthesizes the fundamental assumptions, patterns of meanings and power dynamics around knowledge production processes that characterise the diverse community knowledge cultures.

2   How Do Communities Describe Knowledge?

Knowledge is described in myriad ways by communities. Communities in the K4C regions illustrate the connection between diversity in cultures and ethnicities, and the number of local terms that can be translated into *knowledge* in the English language. For instance, within the national language of Indonesia, the term *pengetahuan* denotes knowledge as having the capacity to see, understand, and realise. In the Javanese tribe, a different ethnic group within the Indonesian nation, there exist the words *ngelmu* (deep understanding of certain disciplines), *kawruh* (physical and mental understanding), *pepadhang* (clarity of explanation), or *pitutur* (quotes). There are also many terms that have the same meaning in other tribes – *nyuprih pangaweruh* (exploring the depths of inner and outer knowledge) within the Sundanese community, *elmoh* (life knowledge beyond daily knowledge) among the Madurese, *isseng* (how things work) among the people at Makassar, *poting* (knowing how to control oneself) within the Batak peoples, *bakunya, bapadah, padah* and *tumbur* (to know and tell) among the Banjar ethnic community, and *nawang* (knowing) among Balinese people. In Malaysia, people also use the term *pengetahuan* when speaking of knowledge. It originates from the root word (verb) *tahu* meaning 'to be aware of'. It is defined in three ways in the context of: (a) *Ilmu* (which represents any form of knowledge, or a specific field pertaining to specific knowledge); (b) *Keadaan mengetahui* (which is the state of being); and (c) *Hal mengetahui* (which is the extent of how much knowledge one possesses; knowledgeable). There are other synonyms of *pengetahuan* including the words *faham, mengerti, mengetahui, sedar, mengakui,* and *enga*.

In Hindi, one of the official languages of India, the term *gyaan* means intellect or knowledge, while in Sanskrit *vidyā* means learning and originates from the word *vid* that means 'to know'. It refers to true knowledge of the self and entails a spiritual as well as philosophical dimension. In Urdu, the words *agaahi* or *shaoor* refer to 'awareness', while *marifat* means 'knowing'. Regional Indian languages also have different terms for knowledge, such as *jñāna* in Bengali.

The words used to translate knowledge into local or mother tongue languages not only indicate different aspects of reality that are known, but also different perceptual and cognitive processes involved in the act of knowing. For instance, in Spanish speaking countries, like Colombia where the University of Andes hub is located, knowledge is usually translated as *conocimiento*. This noun comes from the verb *conocer* that refers to a perceptual process that is direct and immediate, and indicates a conscious contact with the known object through experience and, in particular, perception. Accordingly, animals and human beings have the capacity of *conocer* (e.g., to know objects, persons, places). Another term in Spanish that can be translated into English as to know/knowing is *saber*. Contrary to *conocer*, the verb *saber* indicates an indirect, prolonged and inferential process supported by reason that also implies the ability to learn. In this case, only human beings have the capacity of *saber* (e.g., to know concepts, ideas, skills, etc.). The noun related to the verb *saber* is *sabiduria*, which is translated in English as 'wisdom'. *Sabiduria* not only involves knowledge, but also insight, judgement, attitudes and beliefs, age and experience. Another related word is *saberes*, which is associated with ancestral knowledge (Chamorro & Sicard, 2021; Mendiwelso-Bendek et al., 2020), referring to the traditional knowledge that arises from the daily relationship woven in the interactions between human beings, between human beings and nature, between human beings and the social and natural phenomena that surround the experience of encounter between academia and communities.

A clear difference between knowledge and wisdom is also stressed in the case study from the Durban University hub, which focuses on creating an integral education program underpinned by Indigenous knowledge values and the African philosophy of Ubuntu – a non-Western philosophy that rejects individuality and emphasises a relational form of personhood, in which one's sense of self is shaped by the relationships with other people (Ogudeet al., 2019). In the field of early child development, community partners agree that knowledge is what you know to teach a child, and that wisdom must come from within and must include love. "Information/knowledge is collected from an external source and wisdom comes from within the person. It is innate ... love comes from within to teach a child, so it is part of wisdom" (Research participant in Durban case study). Implicit in this observation is that knowledge is transmitted and/or acquired through instrumental understanding (thought-based), while wisdom does so through relational understanding (emotion-based). Knowledge can be learnt and taught, while wisdom is not always learnt as it comes from within and from experience, and depends on the exercise that is being accomplished, which illustrates the difference between the promotion of an instrumental versus a relational approach to knowledge creation and dissemination.

3 Purpose of Knowledge in Community Settings

Community knowledge is closely interwoven with people's everyday lives, and exists across a wide range of subject areas, depending on the needs of the specific community. It helps people complete their daily activities and provides useful means to cope with changes in their surroundings. For example, Ugandan Acholi sayings and stories for children about hygiene (e.g., not defecating in riverbanks, or sitting with an uncovered bottom on the grinding stone) can be seen as means to control human behaviour among the younger individuals of the community, and help them prevent diseases (African Manners, 2012; Banya, 2015).

Another example comes from the Maasai's knowledge that is used in traditional water management practices, which are highly effective in semiarid lands of Tanzania and considered by local people as "somehow better than what is usually taught in formal [engineering] classes" (Research participant in Tanzania hub case study). Application of community knowledge to water management practices is also found in Karnataka, South India, where a *neeruganti* (a highly appreciated member of the community and recognised for his high standards of justice) is appointed by the community to manage water in a just and equitable manner (Reddy, 2011). The neeruganti ensures equal water supply to all fields, decides on the water supply schedule for the community, informs about the schedule to the community, ensures proper maintenance of the outlets of tanks, and organises Ganga Pooja (worship ritual of the banks of the river) to invoke the blessings of the God for plentiful water in the tank. Despite often being illiterate, the neerugantis possess immense knowledge and skills in water management (ibid.).

In the Orang Asli community in Malaysia, the use of Indigenous knowledge is directed toward the preservation of society from any element, whether from supernatural powers or certain groups. Such knowledge is usually held by the Elders of the community, who are highly respected for their patience, enthusiasm, sense of justice and expertise in the mastery of knowledge, experience and skills. Such leaders normally have some specific set of skills, for example, traditional medicine, and are able to continue the legacy of Orang Asli customs and traditions, as well as act as mediators for any social issues surrounding the community. Similarly, the Baigas (a tribal group in Chhattisgarh, India) are well known for their knowledge of medicinal plants and healing practices, as well as for their traditionally minimalistic way of life. The Baigas create knowledge based on natural and traditional understanding of the world through the experience of living in continual movement with nature, especially forests. Local knowledge regarding traditional healing practices is not particular to Baigas, since almost every ethnic group in India has their own traditional healthcare system.

Traditional knowledge of Indigenous communities in Indonesia holds relevance regarding several subjects, including the early warnings for natural disasters. In several places in Papua island, such as Nabire and Manokwari, the local communities believe that the appearance of marine animals to the surface is a warning that a natural disaster will occur. Another example is the knowledge of farmers in Pliken village, Banyumas regency in Central Java. The farmers have the knowledge and the ability to protect the plantation ecosystem from pest attacks, by forming refugia around them to naturally inhibit pest attacks, using flowers such as *kenikir*, which are considered a highly effective in pest control. In a similar way, based on nature observation, Indigenous knowledge of tribal communities in India is used for weather forecasting. In Rajasthan, for instance, tribal communities have, over centuries, developed the ability to recognise patterns in weather changes and the appearance of certain species during specific seasons to draw conclusions about environmental and climatic conditions. The colour and location of clouds is the basis for assessing the probability of floods. Unusual sounds and behaviour of wildlife, changes in flow and colour of water, and change in wind direction helps in the assessment of climatic variations (Pareek, 2011).

4   How Do Communities Produce Knowledge?

Community knowledge is produced in several ways, but most often emerges from people's practical experience. As local knowledge is mostly gained through practice, the learning processes do not require formal education or training. For example, local health traditions in India are evidence-based and experiential, based on various streams of knowledge: oral folk stream (folk medicine); codified classical stream (Ayurveda, Siddha, and Unani medicine); allied systems (yoga and naturopathy); and systems of foreign origin (Homeopathy, western biomedicine). Folk stream knowledge systems have presence all over the country; they are diverse and varied, oral and undocumented. Such knowledge is dynamic, innovative, evolving and specific to the ethnic community. They are generated over centuries by sensitive and intelligent lay people – tribals, farmers, artisans, shepherds, barbers, housewives, wandering monks. They consist of home remedies, food and nutrition, obstetrics, bone setting, treatment of poison, chronic and common ailments, acupressure, pulse diagnosis, animal and mineral products, and medicinal plants, such as the use of the Alstonia scholaris tree to prevent malaria during monsoons (Gangadharan,

2021). Folk medicine in India is based on the use of over 8000 species of plants, several hundred species of animals and several minerals and metals, as well as around 50,000 herbal and natural product formulations. The folk stream has nutritional knowledge of thousands of ecosystem specific food resources that are not documented (ibid.).

In Gulu, Uganda much of the knowledge production and learning is done through ceremony, dreams, dance and food around the traditional learning space, for example, the campfire. Indigenous knowledge is created and shared based on a broader use of all the senses and on a relational ontology which interprets and creates knowledge in a multi-modal and collaborative way with the non-human world and non-linear temporal perspective.

In Maasai communities of Tanzania, knowledge is created and transferred in a dynamic and horizontal way. The Maasai knowledge system can indeed be considered a continuously evolving living classroom or laboratory, where there are no formal roles as 'teachers' and 'students', and everyone learns from each other:

> We have no teachers, we teach ourselves. And we are learning from each other. When a neighbour fails, you learn from their mistakes and do some-thing different. (Research participant in the Tanzania hub case study)

> We may not have received a formal education, but we know how life works here in the semiarid lands. We research, learn and acquire knowl-edge while working. You fail, you do it again, until you pass. (Research participant in the Tanzania hub case study)

Community knowledge is thus produced through oral and written practices, as well as through experiential learning. Most importantly, community knowl-edge is produced according to the needs of the particular community and, therefore, differs according to regional, cultural, linguistic and socio-economic specificities. The case study from Durban, South Africa, shows that knowledge creation depends on the context (space and time) within which the knowl-edge circle is located. If the location changes, it should be expected that the processes of co-construction may as well. Knowledge is understood by com-munity partners as coming from experiences and, out of these experiences, they choose what knowledge to use and how. Even in urban settings, like Victo-ria (Canada), community organisations use community knowledge to inform their programs, services and other projects, which are designed and built based on a needs-based approach. Thus, their services and programs are unique to their own site. In this regard, reflective practice is a helpful means to improve the effectiveness of their work and program when working with the community. The importance of reflection was also underscored by the Colombia hub to help think of knowledge production processes, incorporate and integrate the view of all the involved partners and stakeholders, and how knowledge products are generated.

5   How Do Communities Disseminate Knowledge?

Similar to knowledge creation, knowledge dissemination takes different forms in the community. In Indonesia, for instance, socialisation through informal gatherings, meetings and other forums are very common ways of knowledge sharing and transmission within the local community. Given that Indonesia is a country with communality as one of its integral features, it has many forms of informal gatherings. Religious ceremonies, ritual of the safety of pregnancy, rituals for sending prayers to those who have passed away, rituals for thanking God for the sea and land, and other traditional rituals are widespread. It is on such occasions that the local knowledge about life or community affairs is transmitted and shared.

Another form of knowledge sharing in communities is community festivals, such as the Indigenous community seed festival known locally as *Burlang Yatra* (Indigenous Biodiversity Festival) in Kandhamal, Odisha in India. This annual event collectivises millet farmers to share knowledge and practices, including exchange of Indigenous heirloom seeds. The festival rests on 'cultural sustainability', where food and nutrition interlock with seeds, and knowledge of an Indigenous food system. This can be linked to a sense of community defined as a process in which the members interact, draw identity, social support, and make their own contributions to the common good (NIRMAN, 2017). Similarly, among the Orang Asli in Malaysia, knowledge on the use and control of forest resources is shared in a ceremony titled *Cenagoh* that takes place where "permission is first sought from the friendly spirits before any land is opened for agriculture as a form of respect" (Kardooni et al., 2014).

Knowledge carriers of folk streams in India include, among others, birth attendants, bone setters, herbal healers and *visha vaidyas* who treat poisonous bites. The carriers of these knowledge systems transfer it from 'people to people', for instance from *gurus* (teachers) to their *shishyas* (students) guided by local cultural and ethical codes. It is a highly decentralised method of knowledge production. Looking across the social spectrum of knowledge creation and use, a particular ethnic community may specialise in certain local health practices. In India, for instance, the *navidhars* (the barber community of certain locations in Tamil Nadu) are experts in treating skin ailments; the *kurubas* in Karnataka and the *konars* of Tamil Nadu (the shepherd or cattle rearing communities) are experts in veterinary medicine; while the Irula tribe is known for their skills in treating poisonous bites. The prevalence of a particular category of knowledge in a locality is related to the local needs. For instance, *pashu vaidyas* (veterinary healers) can be found in North Karnataka where cattle rearing is a major occupation; and *visha vaidyas* exist in dry and drought prone areas where snakebites are common (Gangadharan, 2021).

In addition, knowledges related to practical skills in fields such as fishing and farming are usually passed on to the younger generations through direct teaching by the older generations at the site of work. These are experiential learning systems that have been practised and preserved through generations within local communities across the world. Information and awareness about environmental challenges is also communicated across generations in several communities. For example, in Ghata village in Haryana, India, access to clean drinking water is a pressing challenge. Local children are aware of this, learning about it from their parents and elders in their family, and they are now able to identify potable and unpotable water sources (PRIA, 2022).

In Gulu, Uganda, there is a strong focus on bringing Acholi Elders together to inform and lead gatherings, particularly in partnership with the herbal medicine community. This local knowledge is, however, difficult to transfer in written format as it is place-based, and requires telling, feeling and sensory experience. It goes beyond intertextual and inter-language experiences, and it cannot be easily understood through a Western lens.

In the predominantly patriarchal Maasai culture in Tanzania, knowledge dissemination can be considered an 'inheritance process', that is, a Maasai child stays close to his father while he performs his day-to-day duties, so the child sees his father working and acquires practical knowledge. Interestingly, this is not considered a one-way process; fathers and grandfathers also acquire knowledge from their children and grandchildren. Children, who can be creative and innovative, work alongside their fathers and relatives. The children do not passively watch their Elders to learn; it is a living classroom for both groups – demonstrating knowledge exchange between Elders and the younger generation.

In addition to cultural events hosted in the community, forms of traditional education and boarding schooling systems are also ways in which knowledge is shared and transmitted. In India, among the Muria tribe, young people stay and communicate with one another in institutions called *ghotul* (youth dormitories) where they share knowledge and life experiences. Similarly, among the Oraon tribal community in Jharkhand, there is the concept of the *dhum-kuria*, a youth dormitory, where youths participate actively in the process of knowledge sharing with each other. *Gurukul* is another traditional system of education where young scholars learn from Elders or *gurus* using experiential practices.

These, and several other examples explained in the case studies that follow, show how community knowledge production mechanisms cannot be separated from the knowledge dissemination process. Community knowledge is created in the process of sharing it in different, informal ways and through a variety of conduits. Oral traditions, rituals, customs and art forms of knowledge transmission and sharing have existed and sustained communities for millennia.

6   How Do Communities Store Knowledge?

Communities preserve their knowledge in ways very different from how academic scholars store knowledge. Academic knowledge is primarily stored in written texts and repositories like journals, newsletters, books and libraries. Very often such stored academic knowledge remains limited in its dissemination, locked behind pay walls and available to the privileged few. Community knowledge is stored in the oral traditions, folklore, art, music, dance, poetry, and even tattooing customs and practices. Community knowledge surpasses the barriers of language and written text, since it needs to be easily accessible in understandable forms for the benefit of the community.

In different geographical regions, Elders of the community become the knowledge holders and are responsible for passing on the knowledge to the next generation. Human memory is a repository of knowledge for a community. For example, among the Orang Asli in Malaysia, biodiversity is an integral part of their identity and land is the resource base of the community. Elders share traditional conservation and land management practices with the next generation (Kardooni et al., 2014). Medical practitioners in India emphasise learning verses of *Ashtangahrdayam* (a treatise of Ayurveda) while learning the practice of Ayurveda. In Kerala, the *ashta vaidyas* (a group of Ayurveda practitioners) begin their study of Ayurveda by memorising the 7120-odd verses of the Ashtangahrdayam (Menon & Spudich, 2010). Another way of storing community knowledge is through human experience. Sushruta (ancient Indian physician and considered 'Father of Surgery') in his teaching methods emphasised practical learning, where students watched and aided their teachers in the preparation of Ayurvedic medicines. Surgical training involved students practising surgical procedures on vegetables, fruits and body parts of animals. Careful observation of a dead body aided acquiring anatomical knowledge (Saini, 2016).

Indigenous communities store and transmit knowledge in myriad ways:

- Poems can be used to remember the past in the present, encapsulating the interplay of language and the socio-cultural and physical environments in memory construction (Genis, 2019). Poems are a form of production of Indigenous knowledge, but when diluted by modernisation, a part of it gets lost.

- Proverbs use figurative and literal meanings and carry lessons about ways of life that are most significant for the younger generation that has not experienced life in full and needs to learn about community customs and culture. Proverbs are a source of Indigenous knowledge that is useful in guiding, instilling a sense of pride and helping to establish an identity (Mvanyashe, 2019).

- Stories/folktales are a practice in Indigenous cultures that expresses their experiences, validates experiences, nurtures relationships and sustains communities. Indigenous peoples engage in oral traditions to examine current events and Indigenous understanding in ways consistent with traditional worldviews and cosmologies (Iseke, 2013). These stories/folktales have been passed down orally and there is scarce literature on them written by Indigenous peoples; most are documented by Westerners, therefore diluting and losing cultural integrity.

- Documents on land access and ownership, and communal/tribal lands is viewed as central to the identity and spirituality of Indigenous peoples. Indigenous peoples believe land is neither a commodity nor an individual possession, but a gift from the Creator. Land embraces the ecological, cultural, cosmological, social and the spiritual. The juridical considerations engrained in their social systems result in values, norms and observances, that is, Indigenous knowledge, that protects natural resources, the environment and wildlife (Tafira, 2015). However, when colonial modernity was ushered in, it brought a historical experience comprising murder, genocide, destruction of existing Indigenous knowledge and large-scale dispossession of lands.

- Music and dance are a frame of Indigenous African heritage and a conduit to rationalise and perform norms that aim to humanise the individual and bond humanity. The sound of music is a spiritual force that energises and enriches the mind. Dance, deriving from the conformation of musical structures, en-spirits the dancer, thereby imbuing benevolent spirituality and affording psychotherapeutic healing (Nzewi, 2006).

– Indigenous knowledge is also expressed in agricultural practices, equipment, materials, plant species and animal breeds. These knowledge systems represent mechanisms to ensure minimal livelihoods for local people.
Traditional knowledge systems are often elaborate and adapted to local
culture and environmental conditions, tuned to the needs of local people
and the quality and quantity of available resources (Akullo et al., 2007).
Indigenous knowledge pertaining to the use of wild plants is localised and
is generally unknown outside the immediate community where the species
are used. To broaden understanding and mainstreaming of such Indigenous
knowledge, there is a need for effective documentation and validation of
useful Indigenous technologies. Conservation and management of subsistence farming practices may be possible only if they are linked to the preservation of the cultural diversity and economic viability of the local farming
populations (Rankoana, 2017). Such Indigenous knowledge systems have
developed over generations through the process of man-environmental
interaction and its continuity depends on its transmission and the ability of
the younger generation to acquire and practice it.
– The relationships between the natural and supernatural world, the living
and the dead, and the normative continuity between an individual and
community is at the centre of how knowledge is transmitted through religion and spiritualism. With the introduction of Christianity and Islam, they
have become the most dominant religions in the African continent but,
through all adversity, the African traditional religion has endured as a vital
and prime Indigenous knowledge system that still holds the Indigenous
peoples together. The Acholi people of Northern Uganda maintain the cultural beliefs of the spirit world and social order with a wealth of knowledge inherent in the positive practices that are part of Acholi culture. Such
practices support the resolution and management of conflicts for peaceful
coexistence among those in the local communities through ritual purifica-
tion, cleansing and reintegration of individuals into community, and maintenance of peace and harmony in society (Jendia, 2019; Tshimba, 2015).

Owing to the fact that most Indigenous community knowledge is undocumented, it is all the more relevant to recognise, value and preserve such knowledge systems. Overall, we echo the words of Dr. Wanosts'a7 Lorna Williams,
one of Canada's leading experts on the promotion and restoration of Indigenous culture and language. The ways in which local communities, including Indigenous peoples, transmit and transfer their knowledge and wisdom
through varied and multiple practices and conduits have not been generally
accepted in the world of academia, and Euro-Western perspectives on local

knowledge tend to filter and place it in an abstract process in which knowledge creation, storage and transmission are disconnected rather than intertwined (Williams, 2019).

7 How Are Power Asymmetries Embedded in Knowledge Utilisation in Communities?

Validation of knowledge, that is, the process of ensuring that the knowledge being created, shared or used is trustworthy and can be relied upon to make informed decisions, is one of the knowledge production processes where power imbalances between research partners becomes more evident. In the academic world, knowledge is validated by pre-defined authoritative persons (i.e., 'the expert in the field', 'the peer reviewer'), who are 'qualified' to scrutinise the knowledge produced, according to specific rules and criteria (e.g., objectivity, reliability, generalisations) that define who can possess and share the knowledge (through journal articles or book chapters, for instance) in order to contribute to the advancement of that specific field or discipline. Community knowledge, on the other hand, is generally validated by its practical application, after its production and dissemination. When a certain knowledge, such as techniques for daily activities for fishing, farming or artwork, is practiced by the community, it is community-validated. In community settings, knowledge validation is crucial because information is often passed on through informal channels, and does not need to be fact-checked or peer-reviewed.

Such a validation process by communities may be seen as insufficient from a Western scientific perspective and the academic partner may not accept it as 'legitimate'. Community knowledge is then often not considered as authoritative or as accurate as knowledge that is produced and stored in the academic world. Traditional modes of knowledge sharing and transmission within communities (including direct sharing through generations, poems, storytelling, socialisation, through gatherings and so on) are not recognised as knowledge by academia. This reflects a clear power imbalance in favour of academia.

As a consequence, one can observe, in Eastern Africa for instance, a general displacement of the traditional African knowledge 'authors' from all forms of formal education. This has mainly resulted in the incompleteness and/or disruption of intergenerational knowledge transmission. There is indeed a vast amount of written academic literature on African knowledge cultures and community knowledge; however, it is almost always authored or funded by 'foreigners', or those outside the community that is being documented. The Indigenous-initiated literature available in written form is generally produced

for cultural preservation and activist healing of communities through a rec-
lamation of knowledge. A key observation coming from the African regional
synthesis is that much of the civil society and NGO literature is recycling
Euro-Western epistemology and demonising local knowledge. Civil society
organisations are using this recycled knowledge for a Western style of development and for reporting/attracting funders. At the same time, there are efforts
from university settings to produce and reclaim Indigenous knowledge. This is
reflected in academic writing and in community engaged programs such as the
Gulu University Indigenous medicine program that integrates practitioners
(students) with academics (teachers) in a certificate program. The Indigenous
interpretation of medicine is far broader than Western medicine, and so the
program encompasses holistic and integrated community learning.

The Gulu case study also highlights the importance of healthy relationships
(the hub itself is considered a network of very diverse partners) and, while participants generally agreed that most partnerships are community oriented, the
core problem that stakeholders observed was that community had little agency
when it comes to relationships. Often the Gulu hub and university programs
enter partnerships from a position of power, because they have resources and
understand the institutional systems. Decisions are also made by researchers
or the lead team, not the community. Starting a partnership with and within
the community is seen as an important strategy for sharing power and making sure that the research and results benefit those involved in it. Additional
challenges include accessing funding, navigating funders' demands, deficient
communication structures and challenging the deeply ingrained epistemic
injustice and narrow perspective of what is 'valid' research.

The NWU-SFU hub (South Africa) indicated that the community does not
really consider the knowledge it holds to be as important as that of the health
professionals from the university. However, they feel that their knowledge is
validated though generational successive use. They evaluate the knowledge
received by testing its usefulness in improving their health. A similar finding
was evident in the other South African hub at Durban, that is, community
knowledge is suppressed because community members do not have the necessary academic qualifications, even though "academics are lacking in practical
experience and have no love to share with the children" (Research participant
in Durban case study). Community members also mentioned fear as the main
obstacle to the co-creation of knowledge. "Fear is the major obstacle for communities: they hold back their knowledge because they are scared that they
do not know much. Fear of academics as experts" (Research participant in
Durban case study).

The Salish Sea hub case study also showcases a series of power imbalances, namely, a discrepancy in perception of what community knowledge is and the value it holds; challenges for local communities to navigate relationships with universities given the specific mandate and complex organisational structure of the institution; a lack of practice by academics in listening to communities; and an urgent need for reflection and cultural awareness when working with communities.

The regional syntheses and case studies developed for the BKC project suggest that globally traditional knowledges are often racialised or simply classified as inferior, evil or witchcraft. Scientific/academic knowledge receives higher appreciation and is considered 'more valid' and superior. It is in the construction of knowledge where dynamics of power and domination of the academic expert's vision are reproduced, which makes the de-anchoring of the expert a day-to-day ethical-political issue. Community members have a critical role in knowledge validation by questioning the accuracy of information, seeking out sources to confirm or refute such knowledge, and sharing their own worldviews and experiences to help validate or refine existing knowledge. Community organisations, such as those participating in the BKC project as hub partners, also play a role in knowledge validation by providing reliable information and resources to community members, facilitating conversations and information sharing, and promoting critical thinking and fact-checking skills. Knowledge validation in community settings can help overturn existing unequal power relations between HEIs and CSOs by bridging their diverse and sometimes conflicting knowledge cultures, in a way that helps prevent the spread of misinformation and build trust among community members, which is essential for effective communication, collaboration and decision-making.

8   Conclusion

The foregoing discussion in this chapter illustrates ways in which communities build their knowledge cultures, that is, produce, use, store and disseminate their knowledge. It shows community knowledge cultures are highly advanced that involve complex understandings of various subject areas. Since community knowledge is usually produced across long time periods, the insights drawn are thoroughly verified through several generations. Community knowledge cultures are inextricably linked with individual and collective values, as well as higher level philosophical and spiritual dimensions of human existence, which makes the learning process more meaningful.

Community knowledge can be said to have the following characteristics:

1. Knowledge built in communities is directly related to the needs of every-day life situations.
2. Community knowledge is both pragmatic and normative.
3. Traditional, culture-based forms of knowledge exist in primarily oral forms that are passed down from generation to generation.
4. The process of knowledge creation and transmission/dissemination are inherently intertwined and cannot be separated. Suffused with spiritu-ality and mediated through rituals of worship, community knowledge production and sharing are functional and need-based, rather than extractive and exhaustive (Gaudry, 2011).
5. Values of the community and surrounding eco-system shape internal validation of knowledge that is being produced, stored and shared. The validity of community knowledge is indeed demonstrated by the survival techniques that have been successfully used by countless generations, rather than by the criteria of modern occidental science.
6. Community protocols for knowledge validation are based on principles of cooperation (not competition), culturally resonant ethics (not pro-cedural and bureaucratic), and responding to changes in the 'business of life' (not pre-determined and permanent). 'Community certified' and respected Elders are designated and accepted as knowledge-keepers and behaviour 'regulators', which is not substantially different from elderly and tenured full professors and institutionally promoted officials as knowledgeable academics.
7. Community knowledge is disseminated through a variety of means. Language has a critical role in the transmission of community knowledge as it is the vehicle by which taxonomic systems, metaphysical percep-tions and codified knowledge are passed from generation to generation. The essence of community knowledge is indeed found in the language of the people. In order for community knowledge to survive and prove itself useful in the modern world, so must the language and oral tradi-tions to which it is intricately linked.

Cultural forms, such as everyday rituals, symbols, languages and practices, 'curate' community knowledge, so inner understanding of meanings, feelings and norms are essential to make sense of community knowledge. Such tra-ditional ways of knowing and being are however experiencing a significant decline, although in some countries like Canada efforts are underway to revi-talize Indigenous languages and appreciate traditional knowledge (see Boyd, 2015; Government of Canada, 2019). The oral nature of traditional knowledge makes it difficult to coexist with the current modern ways of knowledge production, resulting in traditional knowledge production being pushed aside since the introduction of modern ways of education and through other more aggressive colonial practices. In part, this is not surprising considering that traditional knowledge is created and shared based on a broader use of all of the senses and on a relational ontology that interprets and creates knowledge multi-modally and together with the non-human world in a non-linear temporal perspective. Putting such knowledge into text would be a difficult task because it requires telling, feeling, place, and sensory experience, which becomes limited as soon as it enters written format.

Modern/western education systems and pedagogies influence how people know community knowledge and their understandings of how such knowledge is understood, created and transmitted. It becomes a completely different story that gets told when knowledge production mechanisms are separated from knowledge dissemination. Community knowledge moves beyond inter-textual and inter-language experiences to a completely different realm and subset of knowledge. Embedded in communities' socio-economic, political, cultural and religious life, freely accessible and easily usable by all, this knowledge is from the community and for the community – which is what makes community knowledge so valuable.

References

African Manners. (2012). *Acholi proverbs (118 in total)*.
  https://africanmanners.wordpress.com/2012/07/07/acholi-proverbs-118-in-total/
Akullo, D., Kanzikwera, R., Birungi, P., Alum, W., Aliguma, L., & Barwogeza, M. (2007). *Indigenous knowledge in agriculture: A case study of the challenges in sharing knowledge of past generations in a globaized context in Uganda*. World Library and Information Congress.
Banya, A. A. (2015). *Traditions and sayings of the Acholi of Uganda*. Adoko Gwok Development Agency Ltd.
Boyd, G., (2015). *A closer look: Revitalizing Indigenous languages*. The Path Forward. Assembly of First Nations. Canada. https://policycommons.net/artifacts/2219928/a-closer-look/2976872/
Chamorro, M., & Sicard, A. (2021). Las sabidurías ancestrales como tecnologías vivas en diálogos con el diseño. Caminos para vivir la inspiración y el cuidado. In C. Córdoba Cely & M. C. Ascuntar Rivera (Eds.), *Investigación + creación a través del territorio* (pp. 351–376). Editorial Universidad de Nariño.

Gangadharan, V. G. G. (2021). *Local knowledge, social movements & participatory research: Indian perspectives* [Webinar]. Participatory Research in Asia. https://www.youtube.com/watch?v=09OdkX_g-Xw&ab_channel=PRIAIndia and https://www.pria.org/knowledge_resource/1639660371_WBR%2018_Local%20 Knowledge,%20Social%20Movt%20and%20PR.pdf

Gaudry, A. (2011). Insurgent research. *Wicazo Sa Review, 26*(1), 113–136.

Genis, G. (2019). Indigenous South African poetry as conduits of History: Epi-poetics – a pedagogy of memory. *Yesterday and Today, 22,* 60–87. https://doi.org/10.17159/ 2223-0386/2019/n22a4

Government of Canada. (2019). *Indigenous Languages Act,* S.C. 2019, c. 23. https://laws.justice.gc.ca/eng/acts/I-7.85/page-1.html

Iseke, J. (2013). Indigenous storytelling as research. *International Review of Qualitative Research, 6*(4), 559–577. https://doi.org/10.1525/irqr.2013.6.4.559

Jendia, C. (2019). The cultural factor in conflict management/resolution: A case study of the Acholi of Northern Uganda. *African Journal of History and Culture, 11*(2), 15–25.

Kardooni, R., Kari, F. B., Yahaya, S. R. B., & Yusup, S. H. (2014). Traditional knowledge of Orang Asli on forests in peninsular Malaysia. *Indian Journal of Traditional Knowledge, 13*(2), 283–291.

Mendiwelso-Bendek, Z., Reyes, A., & Plata, J. (2020). Construcción de Paz en Colombia, Alianza entre la Universidad y la Comunidad. In Z. Mendiwelso-Bendek, A. Reyes Alvarado & J. J. Plata Caviedes (Eds.), *Co-Lab Paz: Marco de referencia sobre la Investigación y la Acción con comunidades.* Editorial Universidad de los Andes.

Menon, I., & Spudich, A. (2010). *Ashtavaidya TRADITION.* Science and Society. https://www.ncbs.res.in/HistoryScienceSociety/content/ashtavaidya-tradition

Mvanyashe, A. (2019). IsiXhosa proverbs and idioms as a reflection of Indigenous knowledge systems and an education tool. *Southern African Journal for Folklore Studies,* 14.

NIRMAN. (2017). Burlang Yatra: The annual indigenous seed festival. *Seed Freedom.* https://seedfreedom.info/events/burlang-yatra-the-annual-indigenous-seed-festival/

Nzewi, M. (2006). African music creativity and performance: The science of the sound. *Voices: A World Forum for Music Therapy, 6*(1). https://doi.org/10.15845/ voices.v6i1.242

Ogude, J., Paulson, S., Strainchamps, A. (2019). *I am because you are: An interview with James Ogude.* Consortium of Humanities Centers and Institutes (CHCI). https://chcinetwork.org/ideas/i-am-because-you-are-an-interview-with-james-ogude

Pareek, A. (2011). *Cultural values and indigenous knowledge of climate change.* National Institute of Science Communication and Information Resources (NISCIR).

PRIA. (2022). *Breaking the vicious cycle: Planning water security in low-income urban neighbourhoods through co-creation. ARA Micro Grant Project (January–April 2022)*. https://www.pria.org/knowledge_resource/1651485365_ARA_Micro_Grant_Final_Report_(29%20April%202022).pdf

Rankoana, S. A. (2017). The use of indigenous knowledge in subsistence farming. In M. M. Bergman & H Jordaan (Eds.), *Toward a sustainable agriculture: Farming practices and water use. Frontiers in sustainability* (Vol. 1, pp. 63–72). MDPI AG. https://doi.org/10.3390/books978-3-03842-331-7-4

Reddy, S. T. S. (2011). Water management: The neeruganti way. *India Water Portal*. https://www.indiawaterportal.org/sites/default/files/iwp2/Community_water_management_in_Karnataka_The_Neeruganti_way_2011.pdf

Saini, A. (2016). Physicians of ancient India. *Journal of Family Medicine and Primary Care, 5*(2), 254–258. https://doi.org/10.4103/2249-4863.192322

Tafira, K. (2015). Why land evokes such deep emotions in Africa. *The Conversation*. https://theconversation.com/why-land-evokes-such-deep-emotions-in-africa-42125

Tshimba, D.-N. (2015). Beyond the Mato Oput tradition: Embedded contestations in transitional justice for post-massacre Pajong, Northern Uganda. *Journal of African Conflicts and Peace Studies, 2*(2), 62–85.

Williams, L. (2019). Ti wa7 szwatenem. What we know: Indigenous knowledge and learning. *BC Studies, 200*, 31–308.

PART 2

Case Studies

..

CHAPTER 4

What Academia Can Learn from the Kenjeran Community of Indonesia

Experiences of the UINSA K4C Hub, Surabaya, Indonesia

Nabiela Naily, M. Helmi Umam, Noor Wahyudi and Misbakhul Munir

Abstract

In Indonesia, University Community Engagement is strongly supported by policy, and UINSA has taken forward this policy with their Kuliah Kerja Nyata (KKN), or student community engagement program, with communities in East Java. The K4C Hub in UINSA shares learnings from documenting the knowledge generation processes among the Kenjeran coastal community, who are dependent on the sea for their lives and livelihoods. UINSA has a long history of collaborative works with the community, and the community is familiar with UINSA as many of their children study in the university.

Keywords

University Community Engagement – East Java – Kenjeran coastal community – Kulian Kerja Nyata (KKN) – knowledge traditions – fisherfolk

1 Introduction

The issue of knowledge democracy brings with it the exploration of what knowledge culture within a community looks like, and its role and importance in sustaining daily lives and livelihoods. The role of community knowledge got spotlighted during the recent Covid-19 pandemic when local traditions of health and healing gained momentum. Many people re-incorporated traditional herbs into their diets for both prevention and cure. In Indonesia, the *jamu* (traditional herb drink), ginger and curcuma have had their place within local health traditions for decades. In fact, at the beginning of the pandemic, the president of Indonesia, supported by the minister for health, promoted jamu as the local-wisdom-based immune booster (Farisa & Galih, 2020).

© NABIELA NAILY ET AL., 2024 | DOI: 10.1163/9789004687769_004

In Indonesia, awareness of the importance of linking education with community has been strong since independence, and University Community Engagement (UCE) is strongly supported by national policy. It has led to the emergence of what we in Indonesia call *Tridharma*.[1] Tridharma was formally integrated in the education system through Law Number 15 (1961) (Fahmi, 2007).

State support for UCE has been quite consistent, shown at national and local levels, both in form of laws and the more practical guidelines for lecturer's performance. The most recent law that is closely related to UCE is Law Number 12 (2012) on higher education. These laws obligate all universities in Indonesia to carry out education that involves teaching, research and community service. Furthermore, the state also obliges all lecturers to perform the three roles and hence makes community engagement mandatory for all (Law number 14, 2005). Within the Ministry of Religious Affairs (MORA), for example, there is a ministerial regulation regarding research and community work (Ministerial Regulation Number 55, 2014). In addition, there are also laws and regulations at the regional or local level.

In keeping with the state's policy, UINSA has developed an internal strategic policy on UCE which provides an institutional basis for managing and promoting UCE, including facilitating capacity building to undertake UCE (Coyle, 2016). UCE is mainstreamed within all activities of UINSA. Integration is premised on the concept of Tridharma, which means that the three roles – teaching, research and community service – should be seen, understood and practiced in an integrated manner (Naily & Mukaffa, 2013).

The UINSA K4C Hub based in Surabaya, Indonesia has been working through Kuliah Kerja Nyata (KKN), or student community engagement program, with communities in East Java. Several alumni of the Mentor Training Program (MTP) support the hub, mandated by MORA to facilitate UCE approaches including Asset-Based Community Development (ABCD), Community Based Participatory Research (CBPR), service learning, and so forth (Seftiawan, 2017). Among the hub's partners are Civil Society Organisations (CSOs), city offices, regional district governments, and community partners. The Hub promotes CBPR as one way to learn from and with communities through various collaborative projects.

When we were approached to be part of the BKC project, we were struck by how little we understood what is community (local) knowledge, and how it is produced, used, validated and transmitted. This chapter attempts to share our learnings from documenting the knowledge generation processes among the Kenjeran coastal community. We also asked: Have we been building truly equal partnerships with communities and respecting their knowledge culture? By analysing the similarities and differences between how knowledge is produced and used in the community and in academia, we attempted to understand what are the factors behind the seemingly unequal relationships that often characterise CBPR efforts. If we are to build true knowledge democracies, it is important to respect the community knowledge culture and build partnerships of equality between the community and university.

2   Context and Methodology

The Nambangan-Cumpat fishing community living on the Kenjeran coast is the locus of this research. The community are dependent on the sea for their lives and livelihoods. UINSA has a long history of collaborative works with the community, and the community is familiar with UINSA as many of their children study in the university.

Interestingly, despite the quite long association with the Kenjeran community, it still took us time to engage them for this case study. Understanding all aspects of their knowledge culture proved to be quite challenging. It took several meetings and discussions to finally come to a shared understanding of the goal of the research and the research questions. The key term, knowledge culture, was relatively new. Roughly, it translates into *budaya pengetahuan*. Munir, who has worked with us on earlier projects and was supporting us in this case study, was initially quite confused with regards to goals of this research, as he is more used to specific and explicit goals such as "What program are we going to evaluate?", or "What issues are we going to investigate in order to solve the problem?"

2.1   *Data collection*

We used interviews, Focus Group Discussions (FGDs) and observation as the tools to collect the data. These tools were selected because the community partners are more comfortable and familiar with informal discussions. In addition, observation was a key tool since we were aiming to map the culture within the community in relation their local practices and daily lives. We were keen to collect stories, anecdotes, poems, songs and other cultural expressions.

Interviews were conducted with several key figures in the Kenjeran community, among them Munir, Syukron, Hadi, Warsono, Atiyah, Nurul, Dewi Asiyah and Dewi Yulia. Munir is a leader of the Kenjeran community. In fact, he is now the chief of the fisher committee of the East Java region. Syukron is a fisher who also is active in the fisherman's cooperative. Hadi and Warsono are diving fishers. They are also active in several community associations. Atiyah and Nurul are women from the Kenjeran coastal community who are active in religious groups and women's associations within the community. Dewi Aisyah and Dewi Yulia are activists and stakeholders from Fatayat, the young women branch of NU, the largest Muslim organisation in Indonesia.

In addition to the primary data collected through interviews, observation and FGDs, we also undertook a literature survey to collect secondary data on state policies, academic modes of knowledge generation, and sociological or ethnological research of the northern coastal Java islands.

2.2   *Analysis*

The analysis of the observations and discussions focused on exploring the similarities and differences between community and academics in producing their knowledge cultures. A more active role, admittedly, was taken by the academics in the research team to analyse the perceptions and practices that were observed and mapped, and to systematise the discussions. Support for analysis was provided by Fatayat, a community partner the hub has worked with on several KKN programs. To make the data analysis more participatory, we formed a group on social media of all members of the research team, and shared emerging analysis and conclusions on this group, on a daily basis if required. In addition, the analysis also tries to employ critical thinking in assessing the level of power between the two parties: campus and community. It also explores how the differences between the two knowledge cultures might have led to the gap and inequality.

3   Knowledge Culture of the Kenjeran Community

Historically, the fisherman community of Nambangan-Cumpat in Kenjeran, Surabaya has existed since the 1700s. It is believed that the original settler of the community is Mbah Buyut Dirah, or Mbah Dirah, who came to the north coast of Surabaya from Gresik. He is believed to be a student of Mbah Sindu Joyo or Pangaskarto, a pious and powerful figure in Gresik. Mbah Sindu Joyo is believed to have lived in the 1600s.[2] Mbah Dirah is the *sesepuh* (the elder, the ancestor), symbolising *orang tua* (the parent) of the Nambangan-Cumpat fishing community. The term nambangan itself originates from the word *nambang*, which means 'going to the sea'. This commemorates the adventure of Mbah Dirah who went to the sea.

Mbah Dirah used to sail to Surabaya to trade and shop for necessities. For his stopovers in Surabaya, he built a place to rest on the beach, and began fishing. His fishing method, believed to be similar to that of his teacher Mbah Sindu Joyo, is known as the *sodoh* technique. This particular technique is performed using a net with small holes to catch the fish. The net is not tied at the front or back, so that the fish or shrimp that enter the net can easily find their way out and release themselves. This technique may surely be considered inefficient, ineffective, and even useless. But those who respect and believe in Mbah Dirah use the sodoh technique.

The uniqueness of Mbah Dirah's technique is its philosophical basis – that not all fish need to be caught. Mbah Dirah believed in the power of fate and nature – "What has been written (by fate/God/nature) as ours (our belonging) will be ours; what is not ours/not meant to be given to us by fate, will leave".

The Nambangan-Cumpat community formed organically and naturally over a long period of time. The fisherman of the community are traditional. In a more conceptual sense, traditional usually has stronger ties to ancestral beliefs and to the land, water and ecosystems. As fishermen, they can adopt more advanced fishing techniques and tools. Yet, they have chosen not to accommodate various advances in fishing into their traditional fishing methods. They have also affirmed their traditional character by joining the Indonesian Traditional Fishermen Association (KNTI).

3.1 Economic Roles in the Community

The composition and classification of the fisherman community of Nambangan-Cumpat is based on many working roles. There are those who play the main role of fishermen and are called *nelayan*. The term is used to refer to those who go out into the sea and catch fish. They are usually (if not all) males, between 20 and 60 years of age, own fishing equipment, and have the skill to carry out traditional fishing at sea. Then there are those called *ibu nelayan* (fisherman's wives), *buruh nelayan* (fishermen workers), and *pengepul* (fish marketers/brokers). Approximately, 60% of the community are fishermen and 40% are the others.

Syukron spoke of how his community has its own system of classification (beliefs) in regard to who can be called as nelayan, validated through generations. They classify fishers as those who earn less than two million rupiah (around 150 US dollars). This might be due to the fact that those who earn more than that are usually ship or boat owners.

It is worth noting that almost all roles within the Nambangan-Cumpat community are involved with sea-related activities, and the community is, in general, shaped by the culture and knowledge of fishing. Those who are not fishermen work in roles related to the fishing culture, such as making and repairing nets, or marketing the catch to earn money, which is the economic basis of the Kenjeran community.

3.2 Production and Validation of Knowledge among Nambangan-Cumpat Fishermen

One of the most interesting findings related to knowledge culture of the Nambangan-Cumpat community is the ways in which the community, particularly the *nelayan*, have developed their own mechanism and traditions in spotting, categorising and naming areas of the sea. When a fisherman goes to sea, his family and friends also know the name of the area towards which he is headed, and the direction. They argue this helps them if they need to go his rescue. Warsono spoke of how the naming also helps in terms of communality, as together they agree on which areas are in season (that is, offers large quantities of fish) or where to gather at certain times.

Location naming is validated by its continuous use in the daily lives of the fishermen. The validation process involves sharing the name locations of the sea among everyone in the community. They feel no need for a particular ceremony or even acknowledgement from the government to use these names.

Tradition is a hereditary process of transferring beliefs, knowledge and habits from one generation to the next. The story of Mbah Buyut Dirah as the ancestor of the Nambangan-Cumpat community that is told and transmitted over generations is an important part of the community's identity. More particularly, it is significant in the community's self-identification in terms of religion. He is profiled as the figure who opened and initiated the first village of Nambangan. He is a figure of a trader, a fisherman, and a devout Muslim. His adherence to religious teachings is attributed by the Nambangan community as someone with spiritual advantages and they consider him a *sunan/wali*, or guardian/saint. This sacredness is reinforced by the belief that Mbah Dirah is a student of Mbah Sindu Joyo who is also believed to be a sacred Gresik figure.

Based on the literature survey of sociological and ethnological research of the northern Java islands, we can see the coastal communities of Java have a unique relationship with Islam. Most researchers agree that Islam entered Indonesia first through contacts between preachers and coastal communities. The story of Mbah Dirah in Nambangan is identical to this narrative. The knowledge culture of the Nambangan-Cumpat fishermen is a holistic one, combining religious traditions with the tradition of trading and fishing. Knowledge is not broken into silos. As a community that grew with Islamic religious traditions, the fishermen accept and hold in high regard the values learned from

Mbah Dirah, which call for respect and preservation. Other figures respected by the community all have connections with Islamic religious leaders.

Another practice related to religious tradition is to echo and sing praises after the adhan, before the sholah, in the mandatory prayer. The lyrics of praise along with the melody are called *puji-pujian*, and the tradition is known as *rengeng, syiir* or *kidung*. Uniquely, these lyrics are heavily influenced by the life of a sea based community, containing specific advice for the fishermen, their families and the surrounding community. They praise the God that has blessed them with the wealth of the sea; it also contains the story of the daily life of fishermen.

The songs composed as part of the kidung are hummed while at sea looking for fish. The kidung songs narrate and illustrate life within the fishing community. It also describes the social system and the community's economic life. During the FGD, a fisherman hummed part of one song:

> the life of the traditional fishermen of Nambangan start in the morning and last until the afternoon-evening. When leaving, the men or husbands are provided with food and prayers by their wives and children. When they come home in the afternoon, the wife greets them with treats and a smile.

These songs are recited in certain repetitive rhythms that are easy to recall and spontaneously memorised by the community. They are stored in memory; no written documentation is necessary. Unfortunately, this tradition seems to be fading slowly now.

In our discussions, we explored the skills and techniques related to fishing that are daily practices of the fishermen. The fishing equipment used is, in general, similar to other fishermen – boats and nets. The have several types of boats – *sentik kicak*, which is 4 metres long, 0.5 metres wide with bamboo tubes on the right and left, *jukung*, which is 5–7 metres long and 1 metre wide, and *sro'ol*, which is 7 metres long and 2–3 metres wide – and nets, including trawl nets for middle strait fish, string nets for crabs, small trawl nets, and nets to be operated independently by individuals. The fishing technique (net fishing, petorosan fishing and diving) determines the net to be used.

Net and petorosan fishing do not need as much equipment as the diver fishermen. For diving, the equipment commonly carried is swimming goggles, compressed wetsuits, air compressor tubes, oxygen supply, and hose pipes. Fuel (diesel) for the boat and food for breakfast and lunch are brought for the trip to sea.

Knowledge of the fishing techniqes used by the Nambangan-Cumpat fishermen has been passed down from generation to generation. This means that fishermen understand and practice the techniques because they learn and practice them by observing senior fishermen. This transfer of knowledge of fishing techniques through learning by doing includes knowledge of climate, navigation, weather readings, character of water, currents and wind, at different times of the day, week and month. Technical knowledge of a physical nature, such as setting up and picking up nets for petorosan fishermen, diving and collecting marine products for diving fishermen, or how to cast nets for net fishermen, can be mastered relatively quickly by new, younger fishermen. Knowledge that is non-practical but needs experience, such as navigation and weather, usually takes longer. In fact, the ability to read weather and changing climate is still being honed by senior fishermen who discuss it among themselves and with retired fishermen who have stopped fishing due to age. This tradition of asking and receiving input and opinions from other fishermen reflects the ways in which knowledge is shared, used, and transmitted.

Petorosan fishermen carry out fishing activities by installing nets at special spots that have been historically determined. This spot is an area where piles have been built with coconut wood or palm wood. Petorosan nets are designed to be attached to poles and are intended to block the sea current so as to trap fish that swim with the current. Petorosan fishermen have deep knowledge of currents and sea flow paths. According to the fishermen, currents are formed by place, wind and time (date, week, month). The currents then determine water quality. The quality of sea water can change – from cloudy, to clear, cold, or warm. Each change in water quality has consequences on the number and type of fish that is availble of fishing.

Petorosan fishing has fundamental differences with other techniques. The ways in which net fishermen or dive fishermen can move between points according to their needs or predicted movement of fish cannot be applied by petorosan fishermen. Petorosan fishermen depend on the petorosan that is lodged in its place and location, and will continue to rely on the same location until it is no longer considered viable.

This type of fixed fishing technique has its own advantages and challenges, which the fishermen discussed during the FGD. The most visible advantage is the chance of higher yield because the nets are installed and removed after a specific time span. Another advantage is that the place or location where they put their petorosan is perceived to be their 'spot' and the right to fish at this spot belongs to them. This respect of fishing rights of petorosan fishermen at their locations is a non-written agreement within the community. As a consequence, the petorosan along with the potential to catch fish within this location is safe from intrusion from other fishermen. The risk of losing nets carried away by the current is relatively higher, in contrast to net fishermen who set up their nets and take them away everyday.

In general, knowledge related to changes in weather, currents, wind and water are not required much by petorosan fishermen. This is, again, an advantage of the technique since the location is fixed. Such knowledge is needed only at the beginning when building and setting up the petorosan pole. Site selection based on condition of the location, type of fish and flow of currents can be said to be the most important knowledge for the petorosan fishermen. It is learnt from the elders who are more experienced.

Moreover, installating a petorosan needs accuracy of position within the spot alongside several petorosans installed by other fishermen. There is a tradition in which a petorosan fisherman asks opinions from other petorosan fishermen when preparing and deciding the location for his petorosan. Although the more technical part of installing the petorosan is nowadays carried out by paid personnel (in the past it was carried out in *gotong royong*, people working together communally and voluntarily), the tradition of asking the community to determine the best location is still continued. The petorosan fishermen believe that determining the location of petorosan spots in conslutation with others is not only effective in producing sufficient catch, but is also an efficient way of avoiding conflicts between fishermen.

Another important skill that is primary and central for the fishermen is knowledge about nature. Nature here means the wind, the current, the seasons. Such knowledge is getting more crucial for those who use netting tecniques. In contrast to petorosan fishermen, net fishermen require detailed knowledge of nature, as they are highly dependent on the accuracy of their location for netting fish. This fishing technique involves high intensity and high interaction with high mobility that relies purely on instinct, or knowledge, of how to find the best spot at all times. The depth and width of knowledge in reading nature determines their success at sea. Net fishermen have their own traditional calendaring system including day/week/month.

Combined with direct observations at sea, this knowledge of time equips net fishermen to be able determine the status of wind, current and water. From this they are able to predict where and in which direction the fish are moving. Predicting the movement of fish plays a significant role in catching fish. It is based on instinct learned from everyday practice, combined with the knowledge shared and transmitted across generations.

The fishing profession of the Kenjaran is a combinaition of work experience and traditional values and beliefs, based in religious and other practices, ancestral stories, respect for ancestral graves sites, and ritual prayers, passed down from generation to generation. This complex knowledge culture encompasses both pragmatic and normative interests, and is important to understand in order to include community knowledge in CBPR.

3.3 Developments Affecting the Knowledge Culture of Nambangan-Cumpat Fishermen

The sea of Kenjeran is the strait between Madura and Java islands, and the Nambangan-Cumpat fishermen fall within the category of strait fishermen. Changes around the Madura strait directly affects and impacts these traditional fishermen. There are several changes that the fisherman spoke of in this context, such as the construction of the Perak international port, the Suramadu bridge, sand mining off the coast of Nambangan-Cumpat and the Covid-19 pandemic.

One of the biggest changes in the life of the Nambangan-Cumpat fisherman is the construction of Perak port and boxes that have been operating since 1925. Large scale ocean container ships and liners berth at the port. The development of this port was considered necessary for national development, representing the wider interest of the country rather than the interests of the Kenjeran fisherman, a smaller group. The other major change that has affected the fishing community's lives is the 5,438 metre long Suramadu bridge, constructed between 2003 and 2009, to connect Java and Madura islands.

These developments in the Kenjeran sea and Madura strait has undeniably changed the existing fishing practices of the traditional fishermen, especially the petorosan fishermen. Petorosan fishermen install fishing poles to trap fish in spots that are historically known to have a lot of fish. Such areas have been disturbed due to the traffic lanes of large ships. Petorosan fishing equipment has often been damaged, and the flow of fish has dramatically reduced. Unfortunately, the fishing community did not have the option to express their aspirations and opinions on the proposed development of the port and bridge, and were forced to adapt, to relocate the petorosan staking areas and use new tools in order to continue with fishing as their livelihood.

In addition, sand mining activities along the strait coast from 2006 to 2012 has destroyed the ecosystem. The fishermen community has shown resistance and several times have protested the award of mining rights to entrepreneurs. Some of the protests to the local government have been won by the fishermen.

Munir in his interview told us that the Covid-19 pandemic also had a major unavoidable economic impact on his community, as many restaurants were forced to close their businesses. These restaurants were major buyers of the local catch caught by the fisherman.

A more recent impact is that of climate change. There were moments during the discussions when fishermen told us they were confused and failed to understand the climate. "Things, sometimes, for the last several years, have been changing quite strangely", said Syukron. Despite the fact that they still share and consult the elders regarding the changes, the kenjeran fishermen like Syurkon and Warno also feel the need to adopt new ways of knowing about the changes they are observing. They realise that elders may not have all knowledge on climate. They have begun to realise that, several times, the causality and correlations they have learnt from the elders is not what they are observing in the sea. This is interesting and shows that new changes are happening in nature that the fishermen don't have knowledge of. For example, changes in the winds of the West and East monsoons causes changes in the strength of the currents in the southern and northern parts of the Java Sea. In the field of climate studies, sea currents are categorised as strong, moderate and weak. Uniquely, the strength and weakness of the sea currents are not always steady or routine because of the type of wind that blows. In certain years, the sea currents during the West monsoon are weaker while in other years they can be stronger. Many fishermen have also noticed that there is an erratic change in the character of the current compared to the change in the direction of the monsoon wind. This trend is recognised by the Kenjaran fishermen as a climate anomaly that sometimes cannot be understood quickly. This is why fishermen like Syukron admit it is more crucial now that they update their knowledge about changes in climate, and are open to learning from a variety of sources, while they continue their tradition of seeking knowledge and advice from elders.

The Nambangan-Cumpat fishing community has reacted to changes brought by external factors such as the building of Suramadu bridge, developing their own mechanisms for adaptation by relocating fishing areas, for example. They are also willing to learn new knowledge and skill sets by having a dialogue between scientific knowledge and their traditional knowledge for the survival of their community and way of life.

Communication, contact or interaction between the knowledge culture within the Kenjaran community and the scientific knowledge culture from academia is already there. There are a numerous modern products that the fisherman have begun to use, among them fish-finder devices, in order to detect fish movements, and GPS, for navigation. The dive fishermen have learnt new diving skills through technical guidance from the Frog Troop Command (Kopaska) of the Indonesian Navy. The fishermen have shown a high level of accommodation and acceptance of new technology and scientific knowledge, knowing that one way their community knowledge culture can survive is through interaction with other knowledge cultures.

The community mechanism through which they produce knowledge and learn from observing and viewing elders does not necessarily mean that space for reviewing, questioning and or even revising their knowledge is closed. There are indeed occasions when the younger generation finds that some of the knowledge they gain and learn from the seniors is no longer relevant. New issues such as climate change, ways in managing the fish produce more effectively, dealing with Covid-19 pandemic and waste management, are some of the interesting new knowledge lessons occurring within the Kenjeran community. The process of discussion, reviewing, rethinking and then revising is part of the knowledge production culture within the community to generate new knowledge that will later be communicated and transmitted to future generations. Arguably, knowledge transmission continues to be dominated by learning from the elders.

4   Differences in Academic and Community Knowledge Cultures

Understanding the differences in the knowledge cultures can be useful in bridging the gap with the community knowledge culture and support academic knowledge culture to adapt.

In Indonesia, academic knowledge is established through the scientific working mechanism. Knowledge generated in the academic world is shared and disseminated in several 'formal' ways: through scientific journals, academic reports/books, and through public media such as magazines, televisions or online magazines, as well as popular media. Secondary data gathered by the Indonesian hub shows that the academic world, in addition to its basic function of explaining things, also plays the role of predicting and controlling what is knowledge (in 't Veld, 2010). Publication in various media functions to approve the knowledge produced in academia, influencing what is known and is a test of its validity. Journals, conferences and scientific publications are acknowledged as proven ways to not only share but also validate academic knowledge (Dalkir, 2017).

Knowledge within the non-academic sphere, the community in this case, is usually established using three models: that which is common among people in society (common knowledge), what is special in the community related to a philosophy of life (philosophical knowledge), and that practised within the community adhering to a religion (religious knowledge) (Dewey, 2012).

In the process of knowledge creation, the academic and non-academic (community) realms have a relationship between each other, often exchanging and providing mutual inputs. Academia (science) receives its material from the non-academic realm, providing scientific explanations as well as validating science (Reijnders & Boersema, 2008).

An interesting exchange can be seen in relation to the naming of locations in the sea. The Suramadu bridge and sand mining activities have impacted, both directly and indirectly, the daily life of the community and the naming configuration for locations. There are locations that have become less active, or even almost inactive, due to the changes brought by these developments. Petorosan, especially in locations such as the one named mlirit, have been damaged, and fishermen now call these locations *mati* (dead). Dead does not necessarily mean that the locations no longer exist; it just means that locations no longer have relevance to the daily life of the Kenjeran community as there is no livelihood possible from that specific area of the sea. In addition, there are also impacts caused by the change in wind direction. Suramadu bridge is very tall and hence blocks some winds. This changes the condition of the sea which impacts the flow of fish within certain areas.

People on the mainland (*daratan*) have given names to places or locations in their neighbourhoods, districts and even at the regency level. Surabaya city has classifications and categorisations of areas from the level of the district. The naming is mostly produced locally by the community, and is formalised and validated at the mainland by the state through the local government (Vletter, 2009). Some names have myths associated with them. For example, Margorejo Tangsi is related to the fact that the area in the past functioned as a living centre for soldiers.

The Kenjeran community have also developed their own ways of giving names to locations, often aligning its reasons for naming a location with myth or a historical story. For example, the area called *carok*, which literally means fight, has a history of being the ground of a major battle. Naming can also be related to a particular feature. For example, one location named *ribath* is near a board-ing school for young Muslims, which is called *ribath*. What makes the Kenjeran naming system unique is the fact that once named, it gains validity through use by everyone in the community, with usually no rejection. Interestingly, validation and formalisation by the government is not sought by the Kenjaran community. The community is confident and comfortable using these names, transmitting them through generations with no formal written document.

Transmission of knowledge within the Kenjeran community does not involve writing and documentation. As a matter of fact, location names given by the Kenjeran cannot be found when searched on Google and other websites. Lack of willingness (or initiative) to write the names, let alone systematically document them, is starkly different from the ways in which names of regions and locations on the mainland are systematically and formally documented and validated. In discussions, some participants put forth the view that there is no relevance or need to register these location names formally with officials and get them put on a map. They perceive it as both unnecessary and complex. They live the experience of their own system – of spotting a location, creating the name, sharing it within the community and using it – which has proven effective for them through generations.

One finds a noticeable different style of communication between the government and community which, to some extent, indicates inequality in power relations. The government, according to some participants in the FGD, still operates under the belief that they are the only ones with authority to generate knowledge as well as policy. For example, there is a giant-size information screen installed by the government in the area. The screen is supposed to function as a guide for the Kenjeran community, particularly the fishermen, for getting weather forecasts, information on wind direction, and so. Unfortunately, it is remains ineffective as it is not user-friendly for the target community. The machine is not easy to use and the way in which it provides the information is highly technologically advanced. Furthermore, there seems to be lack of a socialisation strategy and other communication to help the community make use of the technology. They continue to use their traditional ways, while interestingly also incorporating modern technology as a source for information about the weather.

With regards to validation, there are several interesting differences. Within the academic community, knowledge is validated through rigid procedures and mechanisms. Validation has to come through an authoritative hierarchy, such as approval by experts in the respective field and/or publications in journals, books and other academic forms. In addition, presenting the findings in conferences is also a way to seek validation for the knowledge produced within the academic community. The conferences themselves have to have a stamp of approval from the academic world. In other words, if academic research findings are presented in conferences that are not approved by other academics in those respective fields, then the knowledge presented remains unvalidated.

It is difficult to find a model of community knowledge that rejects all previous or traditional knowledge that has been passed down from generation to generation. Existing knowledge is used to create new knowledge that has undergone a dialogic process of knowledge sharing and validation. Local

knowledge is validated through acceptance by the community. The acceptance is, most of the time, indicated by use of the knowledge or information
by the community in daily lives and activities, such as fishing, or managing
the sea produce. So, the use of spots or locations in the sea by the community
at large, and not just by the fishermen, is an indicator that the knowledge produced has been validated. Unfortunately, the power to validate what is knowledge is unequal, because community knowledge remains unvalidated until it
is proven by academia. We use the term 'community-validated' to counter the
commonly used term 'scientifically proven'.

There are differences in the transmission and sharing culture of knowledge
within communities and academics. Within the academic community, knowledge is shared through a formal system of curricula within a formal institution with authoritative persons such as teachers. Going to formal schools is
a prerequisite for gaining knowledge. There are rules with regards to who has
the authority to share and create knowledge. This authority is limited to those
who have been formally approved (lectures, teachers, researchers). Those who
likely hold indigenous knowledge and experiential-based knowledge with
regard to respective fields are not recognised. Learning about fisheries within
a formal educational institution and from skilled fishermen who have practised their skills through generations can enhance the knowledge a student
can learn about fishing.

Even though there are ways of sharing community knowledge within the
academy, such as conferences and jointly authored articles, these are still
designed and prescribed in certain ways by the academy. Traditional modes of
knowledge transmission such as inter-generational sharing, poems, storytelling, socialisation through community gatherings are not acknowledged ways
of knowledge sharing. Consequently, there is a reduction in the sources from
which we can procure knowledge and share it within the academy.

5   Challenges and Learnings

There are several lessons we learnt about defining knowledge, its production
and validation from documenting the case study of the Nambangan-Cumpat
fishing community.

The most challenging was translating the research questions in to practice and as activities to be undertaken with the community by the academic
partners. For traditional communities, such as the Nambangan-Cumpat fishing community, researching 'what is knowledge?', is an unfamiliar question.
Even for the academic researchers, questions like "How do you understand

and define knowledge?" were not automatically understood or translated. Researchers from the hub were well aware of this challenge before going to the community. The process of achieving a mutual understanding, optimal transparency and maximum disclosures about the research was time consuming. The process, especially at the beginning of the communication, required the campus and the community to engage in intensive discussion and dialogue to ensure that a common understanding of the purpose of the research was reached.

Second, explaining how we know something, or have knowledge, is usually not as easy as articulating the concept itself. For example, if we are asked what is participation, we can explain it through definitions and concepts. But it is more difficult to explain what is knowledge about participation. The notion of knowledge about something is often implied and contained, not expressed and recorded separately. Researchers are still not used to discussing knowledge as a separate object.

A third distinction between the two cultures is that the need to define what is knowledge is not as strong in the fishing community as it is on the campus. This is a question that occupies the academic mind. The traditional fishermen of Nambangan-Cumpat are used to discussing and learning technical and practical matters from each other. They found it difficult to define their knowledge. Community knowledge is embedded in the memory of the individual. Based on dialogue between individual memories, knowledge manifests itself in the form of stories, histories, habits. Stories accommodate the relay of information from the older generation to new generations, and represent what is known as traditional knowledge.

Communities acquire a lot of knowledge in their own ways. Knowledge from the Kenjeran community's perspective is linked to their daily life by the sea. For petorosan fishermen, knowing how to set up petorosan nets, diver fishermen knowing how to dive, or net fishermen determining fishing spots, is knowledge. In other words, knowledge is in the form of examples of a community's daily professional practice, such as knowledge on how to sew, how to catch a fish, when it is the season to fish, and so forth.

Usually, this knowledge is produced through the process of imitating what is practiced by the older or seniors in our societies. Knowledge within this context is in accordance with the concept of learning by doing. There are no schools or specialised knowledge institutions transmitting this knowledge within the community. No specific institutions taught Syurkon and Narwo how to fish, or how to swim. There was no specific curriculum they had to learn. Yet, the community was hesitant to define their practices, skills and beliefs as knowledge because it is not acquired in a systematic, formal way.

6   **Power Dynamics**

Discussion about community university partnership and particularly the question about the equality of power between campus and community is crucial and challenging at the same time. This is because the issue is sensitive and might provoke feelings of unease for both parties. Nevertheless, we attempted to answer this question through discussions in non-formal spaces.

We conducted our research for this case study with a community group with whom we have been associated for quite a long period of time. Yet the difficulties encountered indicate that the relationship is not a partnership; moreover, it is not an equal collaboration between the Kenjeran community and the university, UINSA. In the past, the collaborative works with the community, be it using CBPR or ABCD, have been conducted in the model of the university going to the community with an issue, researching it within the community, and then developing a program to solve the issue or optimise assets. Collaboration for this particular research under the BKC project, with research questions that evaluate the partnership with (seemingly) no intention to develop a program for community empowerment, is quite rare. Unsurprisingly, it took time and several discussions to achieve a shared understanding.

UINSA as an educational institution with knowledge and science as its core, is definitely aware that the main business of the higher educational institution is the development of knowledge. This awareness, which can be argued is the spirit of university, will have a tendency to lead efforts for creation and enhancement of knowledge through all means possible. But the campus has to be prepared to face the question regarding what is knowledge actually and how is it defined.

For the Kenjeran community, the campus-community relationship is an important one, because, in their opinion, the university is a centre for *ilmu pengetahuan* (science and knowledge). Science and knowledge occupy a strategic position in society in general, and are needed for life, such as framing laws, financial management, marketing, etc. The Kenjeran in particular need the university to optimise their assets or solve challenges and problems the community faces.

Participants in the discussions said,

> We have quite a long history of collaborations in many aspects and through various models ... We are very grateful for those and have high expectation for better collaboration in the future.

> UINSA is an Islamic university ... of course we had and always have the special bonding.

Interestingly, the university is not only perceived as a centre of knowledge, skills and expertise, it is also perceived as a centre of advantages and this includes advantages in terms of wealth or financial resources. Many community members perceive people from campus as elites who not only have knowledge and expertise but also wealth.

They emphasised the trust they have towards the university is high due to the nature of the university as a centre of education, which, according to them, will put the well-being of the community above others. In relation to this, they condemned the cooperation between the campus and companies, because, according to them, it will potentially bring risk to the community. The community expects the university to be pro-people, pro-poor advocates. Here, the university is idealised by the community as a carrier of the voices of the marginalised.

The ideal picture, in their opinion, is one where both the community and the campus need each other. Ironically, even though this is the belief, community members still feel hesitant to initiate or lead a collaboration. Therefore, most of the community engagement work is initiated and led by the university. If the university did not initiate the engagement, there would be no collaborations.

UINSA also acknowledges and appreciates the collaboration with the community, and the services performed by community leaders and religious figures.

Despite acknowledging and appreciating each other, and the advantages of the community university collaborations, there are many gaps that need improvement. The first is the issue of continuity, as many of the collaborations initiated by the university are dependent upon a program. The community expects continuous and intensive efforts at finding and implementing solutions that are not dependent upon formal scheduling or projects.

There is a perceptible shift in the paradigm – from communities merely expecting help and support from the university to becoming a partner who believes that they have the resources of their local wisdom, traditions and practical experiences to offer the university. However, further improvements are needed to generate a more natural and continuous collaboration that shifts from working for the benefit of the community to the mutual benefit of both.

7   Conclusion

The knowledge story of the Kenjeran fishing community revolves around the origins of the first village, and their traditional practices and daily life experiences. This story was built initially through observation, and then discussion.

The fishing community of Nambangan-Cumpat identifies that they are the children of Mbah Buyut Dirah. The story about the origins of the community from Mbah Buyut Dirah initially contained the routines of the character's life, but later developed into a story of noble values of kindness in the form of life lessons for fishermen, which are symbolically respected to this day. This basis for the community's noble values then influences other values, including work and professional activities.

The knowledge held by the Kenjeran community can be said to be a mixture of empirical knowledge with divine knowledge. Knowledge is learned through skills and technical practice, experimenting, trial and error, and at times questioning the knowledge held by the elders. From an academic perspective, this kind of knowledge can be termed 'inductive knowledge', as it is built from everyday realities.

Both the campus and the community produce new knowledge. Yet, in regards to the outcomes and use of that knowledge, community knowledge is usually complementary and reinforcing; it is rather difficult to find denial of old knowledge directly. For the community, discovering new knowledge is a process of continuous effort, rising from practical need to better their skills and techniques to continue to live a life by the sea. Understanding, acknowledging and appreciating such a knowledge culture can be a fundamental step in changing how the academy defines, uses and produces knowledge.

Notes

1 Tridharma is a philosophy that harmoniously integrates and aggregates the teachings of Buddhism, Confucianism and Taoism.
2 These assumptions and beliefs are not adequately supported by written evidence.

References

Coyle, M. (2016). *Model Baru Kemitraan UniversitasMasyarakat untuk Perguruan Tinggi di Indonesia*. Kementerian Agama Republik Indonesia.

Breakwell, G. M., & Jaspal, R. (Eds.). (2014). *Identity process theory: Identity, social action and social change*. Cambridge University Press.

Dalkir, K. (2017). *Knowledge management in theory and practice*. MIT Press.

Dewey, J. (2012). *Democracy and education*. Dover Publications.

Fahmi, M. (2007). *Indonesian higher education: The chronicle, recent development and the new legal entity universities*. Working Paper in Economics and Development Studies, Department of Economics, Padjadjaran University.

Farisa, F. C., & Galih, B. (2020). *Kemenkes Sarankan Dosis Konsumsi Jamu Ditingkatkan Selama Pandemi Covid-19* [in Indonesian]. Kompas.com. Accessed from https://nasional.kompas.com/read/2020/08/05/16434211/kemenkes-sarankan-dosis-konsumsi-jamu-ditingkatkan-selama-pandemi-covid-19

In 't Veld, R. (2010). *Knowledge democracy: Consequences for science, politics, and media.* Springer.

Laszlo, E. (2017). *The intelligence of the cosmos: Why are we here? New answers from the frontiers of science.* Inner Traditions/Bear.

Law of the Republic of Indonesia No. 14 Year 2005.

Lestari, H., & Widodo, A. (2021). Peranan Model Pembelajaran Nature of Sains terhadap Peningkatan Pemahaman Sains Siswa di Sekolah Dasar. *Jurnal Cakrawala Pendas* [in Indonesian], 7. https://doi.org/10.31949/jcp.v7i1.2425

Naily, N., & Mukaffa, Z. (2013). *Islam, democracy and university-community engagement in Indonesia: Learning experiences of the State Institute of Islamic Studies (IAIN).* Sunan Ampel Surabaya Indonesia.

Reijnders, L., & Boersema, J. J. (2008). *Principles of environmental sciences.* Springer.

Rosyidi, F. I. (2022). Mengenal Lebih Dekat Prodi Pengobatan Tradisional UNAIR [in Indonesian]. *UNAIR News.*

Seftiawan, D. (2017). *Menag Minta PTKIN Kembangkan Kemitraan Universitas dan Masyarakat* [in Indonesian]. PikiranRakyatCom. https://www.pikiran-rakyat.com/pendidikan/pr-01273402/menag-minta-ptkin-kembangkan-kemitraan-universitas-dan-masyarakat-392292

Siregar, Z., Lumbanraja, P., & Salim, S. R. A. (2016). The implementation of Indonesia's three principles of higher education standard towards increasing competitiveness of local universities for Asean economic community. *Social Sciences & Humanities,* 24(S).

Tan, F. B. (2008). *Global information technologies: Concepts, methodologies, tools and applications.* Information Science Reference.

Vletter, M. D. (2009). *Masa Lalu dalam Masa Kini: Arsitektur di Indonesia* [in Indonesian]. Gramedia Pustaka Utama.

CHAPTER 5

Learning with the Orang Asli Community

Experiences of the Mizan K4C Hub, Malaysia

*Mahazan Abdul Mutalib, Izawati Wook, Mohd. Dzulkhairi Mohd. Rani,
Khairunneezam Mohd. Noor, Aminuddin Mohamed,
Norhyisyamudin bin Kamil, Jufitri Joha and
Muhamad Hanapi bin Jamaluddin*

Abstract

The Mizan K4C Hub used the CBPR approach to increase understanding of the culture of the Orang Asli, indigenous communities of Peninsular Malaysia, and how the Orang Asli unique identity can be sustained and preserved. Specifically, the research aims to support the new Malaysian policy of *Wawasan Kemakmuran Bersama* 2030 (WKB) or Shared Prosperity Vision 2030, by exploring important aspects of Orang Asli cultural identity and sharing it with neighbouring local communities to strengthen community collaboration for a sustainable future for all.

Keywords

Orang Asli – Indigenous culture – Indigenous leadership – Indigenous youth challenges – community-university trust

1 Introduction

The Orang Asli are indigenous communities of Peninsular Malaysia. Their settlements in the area of Negeri Sembilan and some other states around Peninsular Malaysia are located close to local community villages. It is common understanding among the local village communities of Peninsular Malaysia, that the Orang Asli have their own traditions, customs and ways of living. Unfortunately, the Orang Asli's knowledge of the world has rarely been shared with the local communities that live alongside the Orang Asli settlements.

It is also important to note that the Orang Asli community, including the Temuan tribe of Kampung Guntur in Negeri Sembilan, have migrated to new settlement areas several times and this has caused the community to almost lose its culture and traditional knowledge (Carol Yong, 2008; Itam Wali, 1993). Although the effectiveness of social migration among Orang Asli or, in another word, resettlement of the Orang Asli, has been questioned, it has been conducted by the government to increase their social and economic status (Farah Adilla et al., 2021). However, despite the high mobility rate of Orang Asli in Peninsular Malaysia, the community is still known for their unique knowledge and culture, especially in the context of sustainable living. Preserving the Orang Asli knowledge, culture and heritage for their future generations, and sharing it with other local communities is an area that needs further exploration.

The concept of socially responsible higher education (Hall & Tandon, 2021) as well as establishing practical approaches and methods of working with the community has gained greater acceptance in the past decade. In the context of Malaysia, the encouragement for higher education to be more socially responsible is clear. This can be seen through the publication of the Malaysia Education Blueprint 2015–2025 (Higher Education) by the Ministry of Higher Education. The blueprint recognises that the impact of higher education should be clearly seen in various forms of social components, especially on student graduates, the Malaysian community, industry, and the country as a whole.

Community-university partnerships and community-based participatory research (CBPR) are recognised ways of reducing the gap between higher education institutions and communities, and to effectively address relevant issues of social development. The Mizan K4C Hub, established in 2019, has been promoting and using CBPR in its research and academic programs, and decided to use the CBPR approach to increase understanding of the culture and identity of the Orang Asli, and how it can be sustained and preserved. Specifically, the research aims to support the new Malaysian policy of *Wawasan Kemakmuran Bersama* 2030 (WKB) or Shared Prosperity Vision 2030, by exploring important aspects of Orang Asli cultural identity and sharing it with neighbouring local communities to strengthen community collaboration for a sustainable future for all.

The research conducted under the BKC project worked with several specific groups of community members in an Orang Asli village, namely, Guntur in the district of Kuala Pilah, Negeri Sembilan, Malaysia. It tried to explore methods used by the Orang Asli community to retain their culture, heritage and belief within the Orang Asli context. This includes the methods used to avoid inter- and intra-community conflicts – from how they create a community border, to how they handle social issues through effective community communication, and the vital role played by leadership and elders to maintain harmony. The research also tried to explore the approaches used by the Orang Asli to communicate their knowledge effectively within their community.

The case study presented in this chapter begins with a brief introduction to the Orang Asli community, followed by detailing their knowledge culture and connections to customary land, aspects of their indigenous leadership, and the challenges they face in accessing education and improving health and wellbeing. All of the primary information was gathered using the CBPR approach, presented in the last section.

2   The Orang Asli

Orang Asli is the original tribal community in Peninsular Malaysia or West Malaysia (Nagata & Dallos, 2001; Lye, 2011a). According to government data, as of 2010, they numbered a mere 178,197, about 0.5% of the total Malaysian population.[1] Under the Malaysian Federal Constitution, the welfare of the Orang Asli is placed under the jurisdiction of the Federal Government. The administration of their affairs is provided by the Aboriginal Peoples Act 1954 (Act 134). The legislation aims to protect the interests, autonomy and way of life of the aborigines as minorities. It provides for most aspects of the Orang Asli, including the definition of who is Orang Asli, their education and their security. The Act also establishes a specific administrative framework, i.e., the Director General of Orang Asli Affairs. This position, as an agent of the Federal Government, is assisted by a government agency, the Department of Orang Asli Development, also funded by the Federal Government.

The Orang Asli has three main groups – the Negritos, who are the smallest group; the Senoi, who are the largest group; and the aboriginal or Proto-Malays (Jones, 2009). Each of the main groups has six tribes (Department of Orang Asli Development, 2022).[2] The Negrito live in the northern part of Peninsular Malaysia close to the Thailand border, the Senoi live in the North-Central areas of Peninsular Malaysia, and the Proto-Malays live in the southern part of Peninsular Malaysia (Jones, 2009). The Proto-Malays have a long and close relationship with the locals in the southern part of Peninsular Malaysia (as well as with the Indonesians), although there are differences in terms of physical attributes. In fact, the Proto-Malays have been known to use the archaic form of Malay language. The community living in Gunturvillage, the site of this research, are part of the Proto-Malays group from the Temuan tribe.

The Orang Asli have thousands of published and unpublished manuscripts, including recorded materials, which have been noted by sociologists and anthropologists in their research (Lye, 2011a). Some of this research explores the philosophy, knowledge and wisdom of the Orang Asli, their culture, traditions, education, and their struggles from the pre- and post-independence era of Malaysia (Baer, 1999; Burenhult, 1999; Hood, 1978). Today, the issues of human rights, deforestation, peoplehood, and community legacy confronting the Orang Asli have not changed much from the first time we have information about them (Lye, 2011b).

3 Knowledge Culture of Orang Asli Community

This section presents the Indigenous knowledge culture of the Orang Asli found in the literature related to them. The literature mostly covers the customary land connections, community leadership, education, health and well-being of the Orang Asli.

3.1 Connection to Customary Land

The need for local communities, such as the Malay community, and the Orang Asli to have a strong bond between each other is based on the social development model that has been used in Malaysia, which is primarily based on the design of the social structure the country inherited from the British. It is no longer relevant to building connections between the Orang Asli and other village communities. With many of the Orang Asli and the Malays living separately in their own settlements, and attending different schools, social disparity is perpetuated. It is exacerbated by the social structure of the country which is not effective in supporting mutual understanding between communities (Benjamin, 1989; Masron et al., 2013).

The situation of the Orang Asli worsens when they are ejected from their customary land and get resettled. Their soul, traditions and knowledge are tied closely with their customary land, and loss of land acutely affects indigenous identity. Masron et al. (2013, pp. 91–92) explain:

> Traditionally, indigenous belief holds that land is not a product and consequently cannot be bought or sold. Rather, land is on loan to the people from God and it is their responsibility to take care of it. Therefore, land has spiritual and cultural values attached to it.

The Orang Asli have a close connection with the environment. They "do not take from the forest and rivers any more than they need" (Masron et al., 2013, pp. 91–92). Through these traditional beliefs and practices, the Orang Asli protect the natural environment and preserve biodiversity.

An approach that involves more participation of community leaders from the Orang Asli and other communities in all possible areas can be useful in reducing disparities, strengthening bonds, and preventing rapid deforestation that destroys the flora and fauna heritage of Malaysia.

3.2 Leadership of the Orang Asli

Every community needs strong and effective leaders and leadership in solving life-related community problems. Traditionally, the leadership of the Orang Asli community is not formal and the basis of their community leadership is to preserve community equality. There is no social structure and rank, except communal responsibilities that have been entrusted to community representatives. No community member is dominant and capable of leading. The entire community respects the customs and rules that have been established and inherited from previous generations. In the context of continuing community knowledge and skills, the Orang Asli acknowledge the wisdom of their elders.

Community members who are acknowledged as leaders are selected from among the elders who are highly respected for their knowledge, experience, skills as well as having a spirit of patience, enthusiasm, justice and tolerance towards all. The leaders normally have some specific set of skills, for example, traditional medicine, and are able to stand as mediators related to any social issue or disturbance in the community.

The traditional leadership selection process has evolved and the community now expects their leaders to have better education and knowledge to help the community face modern challenges (Nicholas, 2002). There are two ways of appointing the head of the Orang Asli community, namely, through inheritance and appointment. For example, a son can inherit leadership from his father, if the father is the headman of the community. A headman is known as 'Tok Batin', more commonly referred to as Orang Asli leader or headman.

The Orang Asli Temuan community in Negeri Sembilan practice *perpatih* and is a matrilineal society. The process of appointing descendants in this custom is based on the 'belly of the woman'. In the perpatih custom, properties are owned by the female, while customary law requires kinship or family property be transferred from mother to daughter. The perpatih society regards mothers as the most important figures. Appointment of Orang Asli leadership or batin in the Temuan community takes into account the leader's ability to understand the perpatih customs and taboos. If a batin dies or resigns, an emergency meeting led by the 'Juru Kerah' will be held. Traditionally, batin's knowledge on perpatih customs and traditions are emphasised by the 'Juru Kerah', but with the passage of time, the Temuan community has changed. The community is now more open to external influences, especially when it comes to urbanisation, globalisation, and immigration. This has resulted in changes in the leadership pattern of the Orang Asli in order to answer the needs of their community.

4   Challenges in Education

The Orang Asli are facing great challenges to retain their original community culture, language, and traditions. School dropout rate is common (Renganathan, 2016). Johari and Chab (2017) reported that only 30% of Orang Asli students completed secondary school, which is less than half the national average of 72%. Other problems reported are language barrier and existing training programs that do not adequately prepare the teachers to deal with the complexities of this community. School leaders and teachers face difficulties in helping these students, such as integrating with peers and assuring them of the importance of pursuing basic and advanced education (Zulkefli et al., 2019).

This has caused the Orang Asli community to be very vulnerable to social poverty, diminishing of rights, poor mental health, various physical illnesses and of course inability to maintain their tradition and culture for future generations. Some universities are working hard to support the Orang Asli. However, their approaches are sometimes ineffective since they focus more on the social and community rights of the Orang Asli without engaging other communities who live close to the Orang Asli settlements. This raises the question of the effectiveness of social cohesion programs undertaken by universities and other organisations.

4.1   *Health and Wellbeing*
In most countries, a large gap can be seen between indigenous peoples and non-indigenous populations with regard to socio-economic status, education and health status. Globally, the health of indigenous peoples lags behind that of the non-indigenous population (Anderson et al., 2016), and the situation is similar in Malaysia (Abdullah et al., 2021; Norhayati et al., 1998). Moreover, indigenous peoples who are undergoing epidemiological and socio-economic transition also face infectious diseases and non-communicable diseases, including obesity, cardiovascular diseases and diabetes (Harris et al., 2017).

5   Research Methodology

5.1   *Research Approach and Design*
Using the CBPR approach in this research meant engaging Orang Asli community members from the villages from the beginning. The participation of the

Orang Asli was supported by members of Malaysia Indigenous Youth Council and a Teacher's College that educates indigenous teachers. Youth from the community were supported to help with the systematic documentation of the research.

The Mizan K4C Hub has used the CBPR approach earlier when conducting community dialogues to discuss the wellbeing of the Orang Asli. However, this research is considered unique and special for our Hub because the engagement was conducted in the Orang Asli villages and the project was managed by a group of Orang Asli teachers who live in Guntur. The participation of various parties and community members in this project has caused the overall process of this research to be more robust, non-biased and inclusive.

5.2 Research Context and Setting

The location of this project is Gunturvillage located in the district of Kuala PIlah, The district could be considered an area that has strong cultural and tradition appearances and values which are visible even today. The palace of Negeri Sembilan, i.e., the Palace of Seri Menanti, is located in the district. The customs and community laws which originated from the palace are still applied, not just by the Malay community but also the Orang Asli. This includes the customs used to award community leadership status to the indigenous people (To'Siamar Menteri Hj. Ujang bin Yusop, 2001).

The historical background of Guntur includes that of the Orang Asli and the other settlements around them, such as Chergun, Tengkek and Langkap. Langkap and Chergun are considered to be Orang Asli villages, though ironically Tengkek is not. The Orang Asli argues that most of their people moved out from Guntur to live in other areas, including Tengkek, and soon assimilated themselves with the local people through marriage. There is an unspoken understanding that some of the people living in Tengkek are Orang Asli in origin, but due to economic disparity, and perhaps suspicious feelings on part of both communities, the family and historical connections of Tengkek and Guntur were hardly discussed in public in the meetings we conducted.

5.3 Data Collection and Analysis

This project used various CBPR methods, including community dialogue and the arts-based approach. Data collection relied primarily on community discussions, in which community members shared experiences, their wisdom, and observations of how the people live in their villages.

Community mapping, in which participants drew a map of their village and marked some important areas, including the village border, was the arts-based method used. The map was used to generate a discussion related to the history of the village (family relationships and genealogy), funeral traditions, Batin (leadership) system, and socio-economy (farming) of the settlement.

The data collection process was organised by six Orang Asli teachers who are residents of Guntur. Of the six teachers, three have officially worked as Orang Asli teachers while three were students at the Teacher's College. The participation of the six teachers can be said to be the most significant achievement of this study. It is perhaps the first evidence that suggests the possibility that the university and the community can work closely with each other, and with government and non-government organisations.

6   Findings

The research process allowed for the participation of Orang Asli community members and observers to interpret the findings. The data were used by the Orang Asli teachers to analyze their community's understanding of their own village.

The results are presented according to different social groups, elders, women and youth, based on the categories of respondents that we had discussions with for this study.

6.1   *Elders and Senior Citizens*

Among the elders, the original boundaries of the village drawn on the map, which showed that earlier the territory of the village was larger, generated discussion on the issue of land possession. They also shared their hopes that the government would improve the physical infrastructure and economic wellbeing of their village. They also wished for the young people to continue to be united and work together to develop the village and maintain its good name.

They were happy to have this opportunity to share their histories and hopes for the younger generation. In recounting the village's history, others in the community could begin to appreciate the uniqueness of the Orang Asli, their customs and traditions that are so inter-linked with their identity. The practices of the elders, especially the Orang Asli leadership, to communicate their beliefs, culture and traditions to all community members is one way in which the Orang Asli pass on knowledge to the next generation.

The Orang Asli face several challenges. Community leaders (Batin) help the community negotiate these challenges with the help of the community knowledge they hold. The Batin are not leaders in the sense of owning leadership authority on behalf of the community. They act as mediators for the community, linking all members of the Orang Asli toward collective understanding of how they define themselves. The Batin carry a clear trust-based relationship with everyone in the community. This leadership approach does not come with any material rewards. It is a sustainable approach that is able to protect the identity of the Orang Asli.

6.2   Women

The community dialogue involving the women also reveals the same thread and concerns shared by the elders in terms of history and traditions as well as the boundaries of the village territory. The women revealed that, in the past, there was a fight over durian trees between the communities of Guntur and a neigbouring village which led to the demarcation of the border separating them, but this has resulted in issues in the relationship between the two villages.

From the discussions, we have understood that the Orang Asli apply a harmonious and practical method to resolve inter-community conflict. Instead of confrontation, the community redefines their village border collectively. This might sound simple but it is very important for villages that are located in protected areas.

The women also spoke of issues involving schooling and the future of their children, and the village economy and infrastructure. Other issues highlighted were alcohol addiction, and common chronic diseases such as diabetes and high blood pressure. Although we did not collect data with regard to their medicinal knowledge, we found in previous literature that the Orang Asli do have knowledge with regard to indigenous medicines and foods (Hood, 1995; Mohd. Raznan et al., 2021; Tee, 1975).

The need for new houses due to the increased number of residents in their village was a particular concern for the women. They felt this should be done within the current village borders and not by relocating these families to other villages or other areas.

The women aspire to have a competent and eloquent leader who is capable enough to raise issues related to the village with government officials.

6.3   Youth

The discussion with the young people living in the villages revealed that the youth possess some knowledge on their village's history and origin of the Orang Asli people. After listening to their history from the elders, some youth later shared that they had learnt many details which they did not know earlier and were glad of the opportunity that this research provided for them to learn.

The youth highlighted several concerns, including education and health. Many children stop going to school after standard 3 (when they are 9 or 10 years old). Majority who attend secondary school, do not complete it because of insufficient money and the need to work. Some parents prefer their children to learn the traditional occupation of collecting forest products so that they can continue the tradition. Similar to the concerns raised by the elders, the youth also talked about the sustainability of their identity, culture (including their language) and heritage.

What is so special about the Orang Asli youth is their connection with their community and motivation to give back to community. Education has exposed them to various types of skills, knowledge, and opportunities, but most of them still live in the village with their parents.

Based on the issues identified by the youth, they outlined a plan of activities and programs that they think would be useful to enhance socio-economic wellbeing and unity in their community. The youth expect that these programs should be done in collaboration with various partners such as universities, schools, and youth council. These ideas could be used by the Mizan Hub to design programs for the community.

Connecting the youth with their own community, the environment and neighbouring settlements will strengthen the attachment of the younger generation to Orang Asli traditions and heritage. Sharing the beliefs and customs behind the traditions that are being practised will build understanding and knowledge among all community members.

Different groups spoke of similar issues and concerns, such as conflict in relations between the Orang Asli and other Malay communities, lack of education, poor health, land ownership and access, and community identity and integrity. Some youth and women related the way they were treated by local communities, being called names which they felt were discriminatory. The younger community members revealed their experience of being insulted by children of other ethnicities when they go to school, which affects their spirit and self-esteem.

In discussions, participants spoke of overlapping traditions between the Orang Asli and neighbouring Malay communities. They recounted an example of how the Orang Asli used to celebrate in and share a religious festival with the Malay Muslim community in Guntur. Unfortunately, in recent times, they began to be ridiculed for participating in these religious celebrations of the Malay Muslims. This has caused the Orang Asli in Guntur to no longer participate in this festival, and considers the Malaysia Independence Day as their community celebration day. They argue that celebrating independence day is more important to strengthen the spirit of nationalism spirit rather than religious festivals that are not original to their society.

7   Conclusion

The research sought to initiate discussion with the Orang Asli living in Guntur villages to understand from the community's perspectives their history, issues and aspirations. We also explored the ways in which the Orang Asli strengthen mutual collaboration among themselves and between their community and other neighbouring local communities, and build understanding among themselves on a common cultural identity.

Collective community understanding with regard to identity and aspiration is very strong for the Orang Asli despite the challenges they are facing. To maintain community culture, the Orang Asli work together closely. Their knowledge of the village history and borders is shared with everyone and they connect themselves with other villages through a traditional road. We came to understand that the knowledge held by the Orang Asli does not remain static; it is always mixed with knowledge that they derive from other communities.

The Orang Asli believes in peoplehood and maintain it through community land management. All Orang Asli villages are connected with their environment, and young people are taught to respect nature. The Orang Asli has practical knowledge about forests, including jungle 'roads', and such knowledge is considered to be community knowledge. The Orang Asli still use these roads to move within the forest, avoiding the more modern routes.

This study found that, in general, the Orang Asli have their own methods of avoiding inter-community conflicts, and apply a very practical and effective approach to communicate their beliefs, culture and traditions to all community members. Leadership of elders and women plays a vital role in maintaining harmony. Decision-making is not centralised in a specific social authority. The trust is collective.

Lastly, community ties among the Orang Asli people is solid, stronger than those of other local communities. The connection of the Orang Asli youth to their village is strong, even when they have successfully built a career elsewhere.

The participants were not shy to talk about their history and customs, and the youth were keen to listen to their elders and inherit the knowledge of their ancestors. If this knowledge transfer from one generation to another is lost, the younger generation will lose an invaluable treasure. Building knowledge of the youth to take on future leadership roles in the community people is critical, as the community expects their leaders to have knowledge, understanding regarding community traditions and history, and wisdom to resolve inter-community conflicts.

The project enriched the experience of the academics and civil society who participated. The academic and civil society members learnt the history, culture, traditions and aspirations of the Orang Asli people. It helped bridge our knowledge and awareness of community aspirations. This learning is crucial for the Mizan Hub and civil society to design future programs in which the community will want to participate as co-researchers. By involving Orang Asli community members in organising and facilitating the discussions, a level of trust between academia and society was enabled. In fact, the participatory approach helped us as researchers explore our own biases towards the Orang Asli community.

Notes

1   The Malaysia population is recorded at 32.4 million at 2018 (Department of Statistics, Malaysia).

2   The Kensiu, Kintaq, Jahai, Mendriq, Beteq, and Lanoh are the Negrito tribes. Temiar, Semai, Jahut, Che Wong, Semoq Beri, and Mah Beri are the Senoi tribes. Temuan, Jakun, Semelai, Orang Kuala, Orang Seletar, and Orang Kanaq are the Proto-Malay tribes.

References

Abdullah, M. F., Othman, A., Jani, R., Edo, J., & Abdullah, M. T. (2021). Orang Asli health and mortality in Hulu Terengganu, Malaysia. In M. T. Abdullah, C. V. Bartholomew, & A. Mohammad (Eds.), *Resource use and sustainability of Orang Asli*. Springer. https://doi.org/10.1007/978-3-030-64961-6_12

Anderson, I., Robson, B., Connolly, M., Al-Yaman, F., Bjertness, E., King, A., & Yap, L. (2016). Indigenous and tribal peoples' health. *The Lancet, 388*(10040), 131–157.

Aini, Z., Don, A. G., & Isa, N. I. M. (2019). Education development program to Orang Asli by the Ministry of Education Malaysia (MOE). *Jurnal Hal Ehwal Islam dan Warisan Selangor, 4*(1), 1.

Badariah Ismail. (1973/74). *Kekeluargaan dan Perkahwinan di kalangan Masyarakat Temuan di Kampung Guntur, Negeri Sembilan* (Latihan Ilmiah). Jabatan Antropologi dan Sosiologi [in Malay]. Universiti Malaya.

Baer, A. (1999). *Health, disease and survival: A biomedical and genetic analysis of the Orang Asli of Malaysia*. Center for Orang Asli Concerns.

Benjamin, G. (1989). Achievement and gaps in Orang Asli Studies. *Akademika, 35*, 7–46.

Burenhult, N. (1999). A bibliographical guide to Asian linguistics. *Mon-Khmer Studies, 29*, 133–141.

Carol Yong Ooi Lin. (2008). Autonomy reconstituted: Social and gendered implications of resettlement on the Orang Asli of Peninsular Malaysia. In B. P. Resurreccion & R. Elmhirst (Eds.), *Gender and natural resource management: Livelihoods, mobility and interventions*. Earthscan.

Department of Orang Asli Development, Ministry of Rural Development. (2022). *Demografi Orang Asli* [in Malay]. https://www.jakoa.gov.my/suku-kaum/

Department of Statistics Malaysia. (2010). *Population and housing census, 2010 census*. Government of Malaysia.

Endicott, K. (Ed.). (2015). *Malaysia's original people: Past, present and future of the Orang Asli*. NUS Press.

Farah Adila, A. R., Nor Hafizah, M. H., Azizan, Z., & Zarina, M. Z. (2021). Social mobility of Orang Asli: A conceptual paper. *Journal of Administrative Science, 18*(2), 249–261.

Global Peace Foundation Malaysia. (2022). *Bridging the learning gap for Orang Asli children*. https://globalpeace.org.my/2020/09/bridging-the-learning-gap-for-orang-asli-children/

Hall, B., & Tandon, R. (2021). Social responsibility and community based research in higher education institutions. In B. Hall & R. Tandon (Eds.), *Socially responsible higher education: International perspectives on knowledge democracy* (pp. 1–18). Brill Sense.

Harris, S. B., Tompkins, J. W., & TeHiwi, B. (2017). Call to action: A new path for improving diabetes care for indigenous peoples, a global review. *Diabetes Research and Clinical Practice, 123*, 120–133.

Hood, S. (1978). *Semelai rituals of curing* [Unpublished PhD thesis]. University of Oxford.

Hood, S. (1989). Bases of traditional authority among the Orang Asli of Peninsular Malaysia. *Akademika, 35*, 75.

Hood, S. (1995). *Dunia Pribumi dan Alam Sekitar*. UKM.

Itam Wali, N. (1993). *Rancangan Pengumpulan Semula (RPS) Orang Jahai: Kajian Kes Mengenai Perubahan Sosial di RPS Air Banun* [The Jahai: A case study of social change in the Air Banun Regroupment Scheme]. Anthropology and Sociology Department, National University of Malaysia.

Jaharah bte. Musa. (1973/1974). *Kekeluargaan dan Perkahwinan di kalangan masyarakat Temuan di Kampung Guntur. Kuala Pilah, Negeri Sembilan*. Latihan Ilmiah, Jabatan Antropologi dan Sosiologi, Universiti Malaya [in Malay]. http://studentsrepo.um.edu.my/12163/1/jaharah.pdf

Johari, Z. K., & Chab, N. (2017). The need for decentralization: A historical analysis of Malaysia's education system. In C. Joseph (Ed.), *Policies and politics in Malaysian education*. Taylor & Francis.

Jones, A. (2009). The Orang Asli: An outline of their progress in modern Malaya. *Journal of Southeast Asian History, 9*(2), 286–305. https://doi.org/10.1017/S0217781100004713

Lye, T. P. (2011a). A history of Orang Asli studies: Landmarks and generations. *Kajian Malaysia, 29*(1), 23–52.

Lye, T. P. (2011b). The wild and the tame in protected areas management, Peninsular Malaysia. In M. R. Dove, P. E. Sajise, & A. A. Doolittle (Eds.), *Beyond the sacred forest: Complicating conservation in Southeast Asia ecologies for the 21st century* (pp. 37–61). Duke University Press.

MAMPU. (n.d.). *Bilangan Orang Asli Mengikut Etnik sehingga Mac 2018* [in Malay]. Portal Data Terbuka Malaysia. http://www.data.gov.my/data/ms_MY/dataset/ bilangan-penduduk-orang-asli-mengikut-etnik/resource/2845394c-0e37-4b46-841a-d982boddf7ee

Masron, T., Masami, F., & Ismail, N. (2013). Orang Asli in Peninsular Malaysia: Population, spatial distribution and socioeconomic condition. *Journal of Ritsumeikan Social Sciences and Humanities, 6,* 75–115.

Ministry of Education Malaysia. (2013). *Pelan Pembangunan Pendidikan Malaysia 2013–2025* [in Malay]. Kementerian Pelajaran Malaysia.

Nagata, S., & Dallos, C. (2001). The Orang Asli of West Malaysia: An update. *Moussons, 4,* 97–112. http://doi.org/10.4000/moussons.3468

Nicholas, C. (2001). *Compromising indigenous leadership: Losing root in tribal communities–The Asian face of globalisation reconstructing identities, institutions and resources.* The papers of the 2001 The Asian Public Intellectual (API) Fellows.

Nicholas, C. (2002). Orang Asli leadership in Malaysia. *Kyoto Review of Southeast Asia.* Issue 1 (March 2002). Power and Politics. https://kyotoreview.org/issue-1/ orang-asli-leadership-in-malaysia/

Norhayati, M., Norhayati, M. I., Nor Fariza, N., Rohani, A. K., Halimah, A. S., Sharom, M. Y., & Zainal Abidin, A. H. (1998). Health status of Orang Asli (Aborigine) community in Pos Piah, Sungai Siput, Perak, Malaysia. *South East Asian J Trop Med Public Health, 29*(1), 57–61.

Ramli, M. R., Malek, S., Milow, P., & Aziz, N. J. (2021). Traditional knowledge of medicinal plants in the Kampung Orang Asli. *Biodiversitas, 22*(3), 1304–1309.

Renganathan, S. (2016). Educating the Orang Asli children: Exploring indigenous children's practices and experiences in schools. *The Journal of Educational Research, 109*(3), 275–85.

Tee O. H. (1975). Medical services of the Orang Asli (Aborigines) of West Malaysia. *The Medical Journal of Malaysia, 30*(1), 30–37.

To'Siamar Menteri Hj. Ujang bin Yusop. (2001). *Risalah Terombo Biduanda Waris dalam Konteks Pentadbiran Adat di Luak Jempol* [*in Malay*]. http://ujanglobek.blogspot.com/2012/

CHAPTER 6

Bridging Knowledge in Maternal Health Care in Rural Communities

Experiences from the Sangawari K4C Hub, Chhattisgarh, India

Reeta Venugopal, Priyamvada Shrivastava, Anuradha Chakraborty and Aniksha Varoda

Abstract

The challenge of maternal health in India are complex, especially in the tribal dominated, resource poor region where the Sangwari K4C hub is located. The hub's research investigated the link between cognitive, academic knowledge of maternal health, and the knowledge available in the community. Inter-twining academic knowledge with community knowledge can be an important partnership in achieving better maternal health outcomes, especially for rural women.

Keywords

maternal health – pregnancy rituals – nutrition – public health system – community health practices

1 Introduction

In India, as in other parts of the world, improving maternal health is a challenging task. Studies have estimated that 1.3 million Indian women died from maternal causes over the last two decades (Meh et al., 2022). Maternal mortality, or death of a pregnant woman or her death immediately post delivery, is one of the indicators of maternal health. Lower the maternal mortality ratio (that is, number of maternal deaths in a given population of women of reproductive age), better the maternal health.

India has seen a progressive decline in maternal mortality rate (MMR) in the past decade. From 167 per 100,000 live births in 2011–13, it fell to 130 in

2014–16, 122 in 2015–17, and further to 113 in 2016–18. According to the Ministry of Health and Family Welfare, India is on track to achieving the Sustainable Development Goals (SDG) of 70 per 100,000 live births by 2030. In fact, five states (Kerala, Maharashtra, Tamil Nadu, Telangana and Andhra Pradesh) have achieved the SDG target. Several other states, notably Uttar Pradesh and Rajasthan, have shown significant improvement and achieved the target for MMR set by the National Health Policy (NHP). Many others, including Chhattisgarh, continue to have high MMR (above 150). Unfortunately, MMR in Chhattisgarh has increased from 141 (in 2015–17) to 159 (in 2016–18).[1]

Maternal health refers to the well-being of women throughout pregnancy, childbirth, and the postpartum period. Maternal deaths are preventable if women have access to and receive adequate maternal health care services, which include prenatal, delivery care, and postnatal care. The World Health Organization (WHO) in its guidelines of reproductive health care emphasises prenatal care quality in order to lower the incidence of stillbirths and provide women with a smooth, healthy experience of pregnancy. These guidelines aim to promote not just a safe pregnancy for mother and baby, but also an effective transition to pleasant labour and childbirth and, ultimately, a good parenting experience by concentrating on a positive pregnancy experience (WHO, 2016a, 2016b).

The public health system in India focuses on providing comprehensive care to mother and child. The Union Minister for Health and Family Welfare in July 2020 attributed the success in reducing MMR to institutional deliveries as well as focus on quality and coverage of services under the National Health Mission (NHM) through various schemes. A major thrust of the Reproductive and Child Health Programme in India is the provision of care for pregnant women. However, a large proportion of women across the country still do not receive antenatal check-ups, even though such care can detect and treat problems and complications during pregnancy, provide counselling and advise on where to seek care if complications arise, and help the woman prepare for birth.

Chhattisgarh is a predominantly tribal state. Tribal (Indigenous) women tend to have poorer maternal health than women in general. Meh et al. (2022) found, after adjustment for education and other variables, the risks of maternal death were highest in rural and tribal areas of the north-eastern and northern states of India. As per National Family Health Survey (NFHS-4), 29.6% of rural women had a Body Mass Index (BMI) below 18.5, demonstrating persistent energy inadequacy, predominantly among tribal women (IIPS & ICF, 2017).

Public health issues are complex and the solutions to it involves not only biomedical dimensions but also biological, cultural, social, environmental and other factors (Braveman & Gottieb, 2014). Studies regarding utilization of public health schemes in India suggest that involvement of all stakeholders is necessary to improve maternal health (Mehta et al., 2018; Varoda et al., 2021; Venugopal et al., 2022). With advances in various practices in health and preventive medicine, the pattern of opportunities for partnership approaches to public health continue to arise, and academic researchers, practitioners, community members, and funders are increasingly realising the value of comprehensive and participatory methods to research and finding solutions for community problems (Altman, 1995; Argyris et al., 1985; Balcazar et al., 2004; Fals-Borda & Rahman, 1991; Hall, 1992).

The research undertaken by the Sangwari Hub under the Bridging Knowledge Cultures project is an attempt to show how participatory research approach can also be beneficial in understanding and trying to improve maternal health of rural women.

2 Knowledge Cultures in Understanding Maternal Health

Predetermined environmental and social factors tend to frame the cognitive culture in academia in researching maternal health. Inter-twining this knowledge with community knowledge can be an important partnership in achieving better maternal health outcomes, especially for rural women.

2.1 What Is Community Knowledge?

Knowledge is created and shared through social interactions among people (Berg & Snyman, 2003). In the context of this project, community is a group of people living together, who organise activities (opportunities to interact and transfer knowledge) in which all members are engaged in some or the other capacity, and these members share knowledge and learn from each other. The Sangwari Hub defines/understands knowledge in the community as collective perceptions, beliefs and values and learning derived from stories, observations and experiences of a community, and the means by which such knowledge is transferred within a community (customs, norms, ceremonies, events, rules, behaviour, instructions of the elders).

People in Chhattisgarh have strong social ties, which influence the ceremonies and practices related to motherhood and child bearing, from conception to delivery and further to post delivery. These practices, norms and events serve as the spaces in which knowledge regarding maternal health is both created and shared. Under the project, the Hub tried to document the existing community knowledge on maternal health, the knowledge gap (if any) that exists, and how sharing such knowledge can be a desirable behaviour.

3   The Sangwari Hub

The Sangwari K4C Hub in Raipur was constituted under a tripartite agreement between the Chhattisgarh State Planning Commission, PRIA and
Pt. Ravishankar Shukla University. In Chhattisgarhi dialect, 'Sangwari' means
friend, someone who walks with you hand in hand. This name of the hub sig-
nifies the concept of CBPR – academia and the community walking hand in
hand to co-create knowledge. The Sangwari Hub has chosen to focus on issues
related to SDG 5 (Gender Equality).

The National Education Policy (NEP) 2020 of India mandates that teaching, research and service activities of colleges and universities be integrated
through sustained and mutually beneficial community engagement. Socially
responsible higher education is expected to support achievement of SDGs and
provide knowledge solutions for addressing socio-economic challenges. Unnat
Bharat Abhiyan has been encouraging HEIs to become locally engaged with
rural and tribal communities.

In Pt. Ravishankar Shukla University, National Service Scheme (NSS) is an
essential component of community engagement. The NSS program has been
very active with extension activities in several villages that have been adopted.
University students camp in these villages, working with the community in the
areas of education, health, and substance abuse. The aim of the camps is to
put youth in touch with the community and work together with them to find
solutions to improve the lives of the rural population.

Using available knowledge in the public domain about maternal health
programs in India and the state, and through interactions with the community, under the BKC project the Sangwari Hub has attempted to document the
health seeking behaviour during pregnancy and after child birth of women in
rural communities in Chhattisgarh. Understanding health seeking behaviour
of women included documenting prevailing traditional practices for maternal health care, identifying the challenges in accessing maternal health care in
rural communities in Chhattisgarh, and finding the gaps in knowledge that can
be bridged to improve the maternal health care of rural women.

4   Research Partners and Community

The systematisation exercise would not have been possible without the support
of community research partners. These included members of the Panchayat
(local governance institution) and its head, the Sarpanch, Community Health

Workers (anganwadi workers and mitanins) and Traditional Birth Attendants (dais).

The community that participated in this project was the residents of 15 villages around the university (Bhatgaon, Gomchi, Abhanpur, Rajim, Amleshwar, Patan, Supebeda and Kurud).[2] The university caters to students from these villages. Some of them, like Gomchi and Supebeda, have been adopted by the National Service Scheme (NSS) of the university. The NSS involves students in problem-solving of the community, helping the students develop a sense of social and civic responsibility. In some, the Sangwari hub has been conducting CBPR projects since 2018.

5 Collecting Community Knowledge

5.1 Data Collection and Methods

To gain deeper understanding of the specific community practices, beliefs, norms and values related to maternal health, the academic researchers spoke with 120 community members using in-depth interviews, group discussions, case study documentation, semi-structured interviews, and community observation over a period of four months (September 2021 to December 2021). These conversations were held with pregnant women, women who had recently given birth, their husbands and mothers-in-law, public community health workers, and traditional birth attendants.

- In-depth interviews with 42 pregnant women and 30 women who had recently given birth, 10 husbands whose wives were pregnant or had recently delivered, and 12 mothers-in-law
- Group discussion with 30 community members
- Semi-structured interviews with 22 public health service providers, which included 12 anganwadi workers and 10 mitanins
- 10 case studies of pregnant woman, and 8 mitanins/dais
- Story narrations from 6 women

5.2 Entering the Community

The NSS program of the university facilitated the entry of the participatory researchers from the Sangwari Hub to work on the issue of health, particularly maternal health care.

We began by approaching the panchayat, through the Sarpanch. Over a couple of meetings with the Sarpanch and other panchayat members, we explained the purpose of our research and had a general discussion on maternal health. These meetings were helpful in developing rapport. It also gave us initial insights into the community's culture and practices around general health practices and of mothers and children.

The Sarpanch introduced us to the anganwadi workers and mitanins. They further introduced us to pregnant women and mothers who had recently delivered babies. All these women were registered in the anganwadi centres. We requested the women to help us have a conversation with their family members (husbands, mothers-in-law).

Initially pregnant women and their mothers-in-law were not very keen to share their experiences. Pregnant women were involved in house work and found it difficult to find the time to come and participate in the discussions. Similarly, men were engaged in farming and other work. The dais were busy making home visits and completing administrative responsibilities.

Community members thought we were government representatives who had come to collect information. They also expected the academic research team to solve their problems related to accessing health services.

As researchers we had to make several, consecutive visits, adjusting the time of our visits to the daily routine of the women and men, in order to establish a rapport, before we could conduct the in-depth interviews. It took almost three months and 25 to 30 visits to document the knowledge held in the community.

6   Community Knowledge and Prevailing Practices Regarding Maternal Health Care

In rural communities of Chhattisgarh, maternal health is preserved through various rituals and cultural norms, which include diet, hygiene and daily routines, that the mother is expected to follow during pregnancy and after child birth. Community knowledge regarding nutrition is embedded in the dishes that are cooked and eaten.

Elder women in the community told us how they include milk, apples, pulses and pomegranates in the diet of pregnant women. These foods are considered to "cool the body". Fruits like wood apple, papaya and pickle should be avoided. Such knowledge was inter-generational – these women had learnt what to eat and what to avoid during pregnancy from their mothers and grandmothers.

Food is prepared without adding coriander powder. The community members could recall pregnant women being given turmeric powder along with lukewarm ghee and hot steamed rice. In a meal, this is eaten first, followed by the vegetables and dal. A chutney made by grinding green leaves of coriander and mint along with a little sugar, salt and green chillies is also a common item.

A pregnant woman, who was happy to share her experience when we asked about her diet, said

> During pregnancy I did not eat yam, mushrooms, under-ripe papaya and under-ripe banana, because it is believed that eating these affects the health of the baby. Yam causes skin problems for the baby. Due to its sticky property, under-ripe papaya and banana constricts the uterus

Immediately after the delivery, the diet is changed. Mothers of new borns are encouraged to drink milk, have food cooked in ghee (clarified butter), and consume nuts and jaggery to regain strength and be able to breastfeed the baby. Jaggery helps in blood flow, thus cleaning up the uterus. Dried ginger powder was also included in the diet as it is believed to help dry up the body and the stitches, if any.

A dish made with drumsticks and badi(nuggets) and minimum spices is prepared to help the mother gain back strength and dry up the uterus.

Other dietary do's and don'ts include avoiding eating pineapples, tomato, curd and lemon in the post-partum period as sour food after delivery prevents the body from drying up and the stitches may develop pus.

To celebrate the pregnancy, traditional items called *rakhiyabadi*, *sadauribadi* (nuggets), and *chhattisa* (laddus prepared with dry fruits, black pepper, dried ginger powder, jaggery, ghee and medicinal herbs) are prepared by the elder women of the house. These are stored in jars/tins for the pregnant woman to eat. Eating these increases strength and helps in producing breast milk.

To increase the levels of haemoglobin, dishes with spinach and other leafy vegetables like *lalbhaji* and *chaulaibhaji* are prepared. It is a very common practice to cook in an iron vessel, also to help increase iron in the blood.

In a village, pregnancy is not considered to be a special time in the life of a woman. It is viewed as a normal part of life. Women continue to do physical work such as household chores and work in the fields. It is believed continuing to be physically active during pregnancy helps in smooth labour and easy delivery.

One mother-in-law said, "I did not allow my daughter-in-law to go out during new moon in the night". Traditional belief is that amavasya (no moon day or new moon day in the lunar month) is a harmful period for the growth of the embryo. Hence, expectant mothers avoid going out of the house on amavasya and during eclipses. Pregnant women are also advised to not to eat too much. It is believed that if they eat a full stomach, it will compress the uterus and then there will not be enough space for the foetus to grow. One participant told us: "I used to feel very hungry during pregnancy but did not eat a lot. I felt better when I did not eat too much food".

One of the women said, "During my pregnancy, I neither ate papaya nor any other fruit in spite of craving for the same". She also had cravings for saffron milk and black soil. "I followed the advice of my elders during my pregnancy, fearing that not doing so would result in bad consequences for my baby".

Another woman told us she believes that because she was not given chhattisa to eat after delivering her baby, her body is weak. She experienced body ache for several months after giving birth.

7   Institutional/Policy Knowledge on Maternal Healthcare

The researchers gathered knowledge from secondary sources on current accepted standards for antenatal care, and government public health programs that promote safe maternal health.

Maternal health care referred to as antenatal care is a sort of preventive care. Antenatal care is crucial for the health of both the mother and the unborn child. Women may learn about healthy behaviours throughout pregnancy from skilled health personnel, better understand warning signals during pregnancy and childbirth, and receive social, emotional, and psychological support during this vital period in their life through this type of preventative health care (WHO, 2014, 2015). Through antenatal care, pregnant women can also access micronutrient supplementation, treatment for hypertension to prevent eclampsia, as well as immunization against tetanus. Antenatal care can also provide HIV testing and medications to prevent mother-to-child transmission of HIV.[3] In areas where malaria is endemic, health personnel can provide pregnant women with medications and insecticide-treated mosquito nets to help prevent this debilitating and sometimes deadly disease.

There is ample literature on how pregnant woman should maintain health by eating a balanced diet and do some light exercise. From the second trimester onwards, some exercises are recommended that strengthens thigh muscles which helps during a normal delivery and also helps the developing embryo to get into the head-down position in the eighth month of pregnancy, but these should be done only on the recommendation of a gynaecologist (WHO, 2016a, 2016b).

There are several state and Central government *yojanas* (schemes) that are connected with improving health of pregnant women.

Under the Mahatarijatan Yojana, hot food (roti, rice, mixed dal and vegetables) is prepared and are served at the anganwadi centres, along with 75 grams of ready-to-eat food for six days which is home delivered by anganwadi workers to pregnant women. This service was given to the beneficiaries even during the Covid-19 imposed lockdowns.

The Mukhyamantri Suposhan Yojana emphasises locally available nutrient rich food which are important in the diet of the community to be included in the food that is provided to mothers and children, with the aim of reducing malnutrition and anaemia.

The Janani Suraksha Yojana (JSY) is a safe motherhood intervention under the National Rural Health Mission (NRHM) which aims to promote institutional deliveries. Under this scheme, females who opt for institutional deliveries receive a cash transfer of Rs 1,400 directly into their bank accounts.

The Mahatari Express Service is an emergency ambulance transport service for transferring pregnant women to the hospital for institutional delivery.

IEC campaigns, such as the Prime Minister's Safe Pregnancy Campaign, promote awareness of the need for regular ANC check-ups during pregnancies to help early detection and treatment of any issues. Pregnant women are given free antenatal checks, including ultrasounds, blood and urine tests, in their second or third trimester at government health centres.

8   Issues and Challenges in Maternal Health Care in Rural Community of Chhattisgarh

Lata Sonekar is 50 years old and has been working as a dai (traditional birth attendant) for the past 15 years. She is also trained to be a mitanin. Speaking to us, she said,

> The women who visit the anganwadi centre are not given special care in their families, as the community belief is that pregnancy isa normal part of life. Many women do not come for regular prenatal and antenatal check-ups as they have to walk 6 to 7 kilometres to reach the main road, and then there may be no transportation to bring them to the anganwadi. Even when they are given iron tablets, pregnant women are reluctant to take them as they believe the baby will grow large, making labour and delivery difficult. When they opt for institutional deliveries, they are unable to avail the Mahatari Express (ambulance service) as it is very difficult to connect to the help line number due to poor mobile network in many villages. Often family members have been known to climb tall trees in order to catch a signal to make the phone call.

These were some of the challenges shared by mitanins and dais in a group discussion to understand the barriers in implementing the government's maternal health schemes.

Conversations with husbands revealed that most men were not involved or interested in maternal health care. They said that they accepted what their parents, especially their mothers, decided was good for their pregnant wives. When asked if they care for their wives during pregnancy, one husband said, with hesitation, "I am not involved in this matter. It is none of my business, and I advised my wife to follow whatever instructions were given by my mother". They often could not visit the health centre where their baby was born. They said it becomes difficult to reach the hospital as it is far away and they have work to do, so cannot take the time off.

Challenges with accessing institutional and public health services get compounded with over-reliance on traditional beliefs that can put a pregnant woman at risk. One woman told us how she "was confined to [her] house during eclipses" and was advised "to apply cow dung on [her] stomach to protect the baby inside the womb".

Pregnant women said that they follow whatever advice their elders give during pregnancy as they fear something may go wrong with their baby if they don't follow the traditional practices. Several spoke of cravings they had, such as for spicy food, but did not indulge because it is forbidden. On hearing this, one woman narrated with a smile,

> "I had cravings for foods that are usually avoided during pregnancy. I ate 'cold food' – curd, cold fruits and milk apart from regular khana (the staple food, rice). I did not eat 'hot foods' even after my delivery, which is generally recommended by family elders". She further added, "I think a person should eat as per their cravings or what suits them. We are told not to eat tuma (bottle gourd) and kochai (taro) and phuttu(mushrooms) during pregnancy as eating them may lead to the child having scars at birth, or not to eat spicy food because the child may be born without hair. But I did not follow this during my pregnancy and had none of these issues my elders had described".

9   Institutional/Policy Knowledge vis-a-vis Community Knowledge

It was not a surprise that some of the community practices tied in with institutional knowledge to promote maternal health. Drinking alcohol during pregnancy is not recommended and is also considered a taboo by the community. The practice of *sadauri* (baby shower) for the mother and the foetus and the food served during the event time has great value in the context of a mother's nutrition. Community practice is to keep the baby and mother in isolation for six days after delivery. This is useful for avoiding infections. Institutional deliveries also recommend that baby and mother remain isolated for several days post birth.

Experiences recounted by public health officers and pregnant women nonetheless reveal a knowledge gap between medical/scientific information that promote a healthy pregnancy and community practices that women have been traditionally following for generations. Some of these gaps are given in Table 6.1.

Understanding these gaps can be useful in formulating new policies and making changes to existing schemes so that communities can adopt scientific health practices along with traditional practices for the overall improvement in maternal health indicators.

10 How Maternal Health Care Knowledge Is Bridged in Rural Communities of Chhattisgarh

Mitanin in Chhattisgarhi means friend, a female friend. In most parts of Chhattisgarh, there exists a traditional custom that a girl of one family is bonded to a girl of another family through a simple, enchanting ritual ceremony, and after this ceremony they become mitanins to each other. It is this custom that was built upon to create a new type of mitanin – the Swasthya Mitanin, or a friend of the community for their health care needs. The Swasthya Mitanin in Chhattisgarh's public health outreach is a crucial link in bridging knowledge between communities and institutions. She is a paramedical professional employed by the government, responsible for raising awareness in the community to use government health services.

Dais are also an important link in the chain of supporting women to opt for deliveries in sterile and hygienic conditions. By dropping oil on the abdomen to assess uterine contractions, dais can predict the time of delivery. One of the dais told us that in tribal areas of Chhattisgarh the delivery room is prepared by cleaning it and plastering with a freshly prepared mix of cow dung and mud. Neem leaves, which are known to have anti-infective properties, are burned to raise the room temperature and repel mosquitoes. Women usually deliver in a squatting position.

TABLE 6.1   Community knowledge vis-à-vis institutional/policy knowledge

Community knowledge	Institutional/Policy knowledge
Community believes that medical attention is not required as soon as pregnancy is detected. Rural communities in Chhattisgarh do not register pregnancies with the anganwadi until the second trimester.	Medical check-up is essential as soon as the woman thinks she may be pregnant. Early registration of pregnancy can help detect complications, if any.
Regular check-ups are not necessary.	Regular check-ups help track the development of the foetus.
Following elders' advice, pregnant women consume seasonal fruits that are locally available along with rice, curd, chattisa, and various types of decoctions prepared with local medicinal herbs. They think this is sufficient, as their traditional diet includes green leafy vegetables that are rich in iron. They avoid taking additional IFA supplements.	Regular, balanced diet is desirable, for general health. During pregnancy, however, additional amounts of micronutrients, vitamins, and iron is required, which can be provided through supplements.
It is best to avoid certain foods.	Biomedical evidence does not support avoidance of food items. Biomedical recommendations conflict with some of the traditionally avoided foods such as wood apples and papaya (they are high in nutrients such as vitamin A and vitamin C).
It is better for a pregnant woman to eat less, keep her stomach light.	One should eat well during pregnancy to meet the additional nutritional requirements of mother and baby.
A pregnant woman should work until she is in labour. Pregnancy is part of a woman's life; it is nothing special. She should continue to do the household chores and work in the fields, as this facilitates smooth labour.	It is advised to avoid doing heavy work during pregnancy. Light exercises are recommended to facilitate positioning of the foetus.
In earlier times, women did not feed colostrum (the first milk a woman's body produces) to the new born.	Colostrum should be fed to the new born as early as possible. Nowadays, due to higher institutional delivery and awareness, women have begun giving colostrum to their new born.

Knowledge is transferred inter-generationally and through formal training. Reena Patel has been working as dai for almost 30 years. She learnt the delivery process from her mother, who was also a dai.

> I had no formal training of maternal care but gained knowledge from my mother and from the experience of assisting her with deliveries. I gradually picked up the techniques of ensuring safe labour. As my mother grew old, she stopped going for deliveries and it became my job to carry on helping the community.

> I underwent a formal training in 1995 in a Community Health Centre. Before my formal training, we used to bathe the new born in lukewarm water immediately after birth and it was common for new born babies to catch pneumonia, especially babies who were born during the winter and monsoon months. As we were not equipped to treat such cases, it was difficult to save the life of the new born. As a result, we had many failures and several infant deaths. There was no child specialist or incubators in the health centres.

> After I received formal training, we changed our care process of the new born. Now, we do not immediately bathe them. Instead, we clean them with duly washed and sundried cotton cloth, and thereafter wrap then in clean cotton clothes and woollen shawls. We also learnt to hold the babies in our arms close to our bodies to keep them warm. This procedure has been very effective in saving the lives of the newly born. This is how we can reduce infant mortality rate to a great extent. We also have well equipped government and private hospitals in Raipur. In case of any emergency, we seek medical care in these institutions.

The Sangwari Hub can empower communities by sharing knowledge back with them and creating awareness of existing government schemes and programs. Regular communication and interaction can promote the necessity of taking supplements, ANC check-ups, especially in light of the anaemia among women and children, and overcoming misconceptions about caesarean delivery.

Maternal health care knowledge for the community can be bridged through the community health professionals, and regular community-university engagement. Ultimately, knowledge is bridged through interactions. Socialization is at the core of knowledge creation (Nonaka, 1994). People's interaction gives the platform for communities to share and create new knowledge.

11   Conclusion

This was a unique experience for the Sangwari Hub research team to understand how to work with rural communities. The Hub team was prepared from the beginning to give recognition to and learn from the community. In building partnerships with community members, we were able to use community knowledge and skills to strengthen our own understanding of maternal health. The community health personnel and panchayat members were a powerful source of information as well as help in connecting with the community and fostering trust.

The community members, in sharing their knowledge, have trusted us to pass on this information to policy makers, to advocate for local practices to be accommodated in maternal health schemes, for example, supplementary food provided by the government can be modified by including community nutritional practices and food items. This will help validate and legitimise community knowledge, along with formal academic publications as sources of valid knowledge.

As knowledge culture enablers, the Hub should continue to collaborate, adapt and develop trust so as to co-create knowledge with the community.

Notes

1   Ministry of Health and Family Welfare, Government of India: https://main.mohfw.gov.in/sites/default/files/5665895455663325.pdf
2   For the study, data was collected from the villages of Bhatgaon, Gomchi, Abhanpur and Rajim in Raipur district, within 15 kilometres distance from the university; Amleshwar and Patan in Durg district, at a distance of 30 kilometres distance from the university; Supebeda in Gariaband district, at a distance of 90 kilometres distance from the university; and Kurud in Dhamtari district at a distance of 90 kilometres.
3   UNICEF: https://data.unicef.org/topic/maternal-health/antenatal-care/
    https://www.unicef.org/india/what-we-do/maternal-health
    Population Reference Bureau (PRB) https://www.prb.org/resources/maternal-care-in-india-reveals-gaps-between-urban-and-rural-rich-and-poor/
    World Health Organization (WHO): https://apps.who.int/iris/bitstream/handle/10665/250796/9789241549912-eng.pdf

References

Altman, D. G. (1995). Sustaining interventions in community systems: On the relationship between researchers and communities. *Health Psychology*, 14(6), 526–536. https://pubmed.ncbi.nlm.nih.gov/8565927/

Argyris, C., Putnam, R., & Smith, D. M. (1985). *Action science: Concepts, methods, and skills for research and intervention.* Jossey-Bass Publishers. https://actiondesign. com/assets/pdf/ASintro.pdf

Balcazar, F. E., Taylor, R. R., Kielhofner, G. W., Tamley, K., Benziger, T., Carlin, N., & Johnson, S. (2004). Participatory action research: General principles and a study with a chronic health condition. In L. A. Jason, C. B. Keys, Y. Suarez-Balcazar, R. R. Taylor, & M. I. Davis (Eds.), *Participatory community research: Theories and methods in action* (pp. 17–35). American Psychological Association. https://doi.org/ 10.1037/10726-001

Barbara, A., Israel, A., Schulz, J., Parker, E. A., & Becker, A. B. (1998). Review of community-based research: Assessing partnership approaches to improve public health. *Annual Review of Public Health, 19,* 173–202.

Berg, H., & Snyman, M. M. M. (2003). Managing tacit knowledge in the corporate environment: Communities of practice. *South African Journal of Information Management, 5*(4).

Braveman, P., & Gottlieb, L. (2014). The social determinants of health: It's time to consider the causes of the causes. *Public Health Reports, 129*(2), 19–31.

Chakravarty, M., Venugopal, R., Chakraborty, A., Mehta, K. S., & Varoda, A. (2022). A study of nutritional status and prevalence of anaemia among the adolescent girls and women of reproductive age of Baiga tribe accessing antenatal clinic in public health sector in Chhattisgarh, India. *Research Journal of Pharmacy and Technology, 15*(2), 598–604.

Chokshi, M., Patil, B., Khanna, R., Neogi, S. B., Sharma, J., Paul V. K., & Zodpey, S. (2016). Health systems in India. *Journal of Perinatology, 36,* S9–S12. https://doi.org/ 10.1038/jp.2016.184

Fals-Borda, O., & Rahman, M. A. (1991). *Action and knowledge: Breaking the monopoly with participatory action research.* Apex Press. https://www.worldcat.org/title/ action-and-knowledge-breaking-the-monopoly-with-participatory-action-research/oclc/623516546

Hall, B. (1992). From margins to center? The development and purpose of participatory research. *The American Sociologist, 23,* 15–28. https://link.springer.com/article/ 10.1007/BF02691928

International Institute for Population Sciences (IIPS) & ICF. (2017). *National Family Health Survey (NFHS-4), 2015–16.* IIPS. https://dhsprogram.com/pubs/pdf/FR339/ FR339.pdf

Koblinsky, M. A. (2003). *Reducing maternal mortality: Learning from Bolivia, China, Egypt, Honduras, Indonesia, Jamaica, and Zimbabwe.* https://openknowledge.worldbank.org/handle/10986/15163

Lakshminarayanan, S. (2011). Role of government in public health: Current scenario in India and future scope. *Journal of Family and Community Medicine, 18*(1), 26–30.

Meh, C., Sharma, A., Ram, U., Fadel, S., Correa, N., Snelgrove, J. W., Shah, P., Begum, R., Shah, M., Hana, T., Fu, S. H., Raveendran, L., Mishra, B., & Jha, P. (2021). Trends in maternal mortality in India over two decades in nationally representative surveys. *BJOG: An International Journal of Obstetrics and Gynaecology, 129*(4), 550–561. https://doi.org/10.1111/1471-0528.16888

Metha, S., Chakravarty, M., & Venugopal, R. (2018). Nutritional status and utilization of antenatal health care services among the Baiga women of Chhattisgarh. *International Journal of Research in Social Science, 8*(9), 200–206.

Minkler, M. (2004). Ethical challenges for the 'outside' researcher in community-based participatory research. *Health Education & Behavior, 31*, 684–697.

Nonaka, I., & Konno, N. (1998). The concept of "Ba": Building a foundation for knowledge creation. *California Management Review, 40*(3), 40–55.

Park, K. (2021). *Preventive and social medicine* (26th ed.). Banarsidas Bhanot.

Pathmanathan, I., Liljestrand, J., Martins, J., Rajapaksa, M., Lalini C., Lissner, C., de Silva, A., Selvaraju, Singh, S., & Joginder, P. (2003). *Investing in maternal health: Learning from Malaysia and Sri Lanka.* In *Health, nutrition, and population.* World Bank. © World Bank. https://openknowledge.worldbank.org/handle/10986/14754

Pillai, G. (1993). Reducing deaths from pregnancy and childbirth. *Asia Links, 9.* https://pubmed.ncbi.nlm.nih.gov/12159274/

Ronsmans, C., Graham, W. J., & Lancet Maternal Survival Series Steering Group. (2006). Maternal mortality: Who, when, where, and why. *Lancet, 368*(9542), 1189–200. https://pubmed.ncbi.nlm.nih.gov/17011946/

Varoda, A., Chakravarty, M., Venugopal, R., & Kumar, A. (2021). Prevalence of anaemia among adolescent girls of Baiga (PVTGs) of Chhattisgarh, India. *Human Biology Review, 10*(2), 129–139.

World Health Organization (WHO). (2005). *Health and millennium development goals.* World Health Organization. http://apps.who.int/iris/bitstream/handle/10665/43246/9241562986.pdf?sequence=1

World Health Organization (WHO). (2014). *Trends in maternal mortality: 1990 to 2013. Estimates by WHO, UNICEF, UNFPA, The World Bank and the United Nations Population Division.* https://apps.who.int/iris/bitstream/handle/10665/112682/9789241507226_eng.pdf;jsessionid=BCFB4FF2B22284832916900CBD72304C?sequence=2

World Health Organization (WHO). (2014). *Maternal mortality: Fact sheet.* https://apps.who.int/iris/handle/10665/112318

World Health Organization (WHO). (2015). *Trends in maternal mortality: 1990 to 2015. Estimates by WHO, UNICEF, UNFPA, World Bank Group and the United Nations Population Division.* https://www.unfpa.org/publications/trends-maternal-mortality-1990-2015

World Health Organization (WHO). (2016a). *Maternal mortality.* https://www.who.int/
health-topics/maternal-health#tab=tab_1
World Health Organization (WHO). (2016b). *New guidelines on antenatal care for a positive pregnancy experience.* https://www.who.int/publications/i/item/9789241549912

CHAPTER 7

Understanding Community Waste Management through Service-Learning

Experiences from the Manipal University Jaipur K4C Hub, India

Madhura Yadav, Minali Banerjee, Siraz Hirani and Manish Sharma

Abstract

The MUJ K4C hub research reflects on the power inequalities, biases and institutional challenges in building effective knowledge relationships with the communities living around Manipal University Jaipur. They use the issue of waste management to illustrate how communities also have and use knowledge, and a community's expectations from academia to solve their day-to-day challenges of accessing municipal services. The role of community based organisations in facilitating community linkages to build trusting community university relationships is also highlighted.

Keywords

sanitation – Swachh Bharat Mission – waste management – institutionalising CURP – service learning

1   Introduction

Knowledge creation in university settings is usually through research (Marks, 2014) that is restricted to the conventional methods that are generally believed and followed by academicians. In contrast, knowledge creation by communities is open, far from the limitations of any conventional rules. Here, it evolves through years of experiences and is disseminated through family stories (Norrick, 1997; Stone, 1988). "The traditional knowledge acquired from their ancestors is freely transferred within the family" (Panghal et al., 2010, p. 6).

Knowledge can be used as a source of power. Exercise of power through control of knowledge – how it is produced, who owns the knowledge that is produced, how it is disseminated, and how and for what purposes the knowledge is used – is made possible through professionalism and monopoly over means of communication and learning (Tandon, 2002). Limiting and devaluing knowledge of the ordinary people is influenced through the control and use of this power (Gaventa, 1980). Devaluing popular (people's) knowledge is connected with the rise of modern, professional, knowledge-producing enterprises such as universities and the growth of the knowledge economy.

This chapter aims to understand the differences in knowledge creation between universities and communities. Specifically, it aims to understand whose knowledge counts and who validates what is knowledge? The authors argue there is an asymmetry in who controls the use and validation of the knowledge that is generated through community-university partnerships. They use a waste management case study to explain existing inequalities of knowledge ownership, use and validation in the Indian context.

The MUJ hub considered the case of waste management as an ideal example to understand how community knowledge can be valuable in managing the persistent solid waste management in India's cities given the limited financial resources of municipal authorities to reach every household for waste collection. Moreover, the Swachh Bharat Mission (Clean India Mission), launched by the Government of India in 2014, made waste management a priority for the government as well as to the community. To help every household protect their health and well-being, Swachh Bharat Mission (SBM) developed measures for improved sanitation and waste disposal (Singh et al. 2018; Swain and Pathela 2016). But these measures rely heavily on resources of local bodies and public engagement and support. Furthermore, Indian communities have traditionally been sustainable and sensitive towards waste management by recycling and reusing waste. Hence, the MUJ K4C hub chose to learn from the past (specifically local knowledge used by resource poor communities) to understand how academia can contribute to resolving the issue and support municipal efforts in managing waste.

The authors believe that partnership is essential in knowledge creation and knowledge sharing. A university can work as a partner between government and communities to jointly identify solutions to implement developmental goals in a way that is acceptable to the community as well as make this knowledge freely accessible for all communities to use.

2   The MUJ Hub and Service-Learning

Manipal University Jaipur (MUJ) was established in 2011. In 2018, the MUJ K4C Hub began as a collaboration between MUJ and Society for Participatory Research in Asia (PRIA). Currently, Mahila Housing Sewa Trust (MHT), a local civil society organisation, is the community partner for the hub. MHT has been active in Rajasthan since 2005. MHT's mission is to strengthen grassroots collectives of women in the urban informal sector to advance constructive dialogue and action on improving their housing, living and working environments. The organisation been instrumental in motivating communities in Jaipur to segregate and use community bins for disposing waste, rather than throwing waste in and littering unoccupied land parcels. MHT has empowered communities by providing technical know-how to make organic manure from kitchen waste.

MUJ practises service-learning to promote community engagement. Service-learning refers to activities organised for the students to interact and work with the communities to solve their issues (Bringle and Hatcher, 1996). Through service-learning, students apply their knowledge to the natural settings of society. By making students partner with the community they are living in, they develop problem-solving competency.

Service-learning has always been an integral part of the Indian education system. The gurukul system believed in knowledge creation and sharing where the student used to live with the teacher (the Guru) (Selvamani, 2019) and practise the gained knowledge through service to the people (Kashalkar & Damodar, 2013).

In universities, service-learning is generally presumed to be 'community engagement', 'extension' or 'social connect' (NAAC resources, 2006). The university-community relationship in service-learning is uni-directional and cannot commonly be referred to as 'community-based participatory research' (CBPR). But, for the purpose of this case study, we use service-learning to mean some form of community engagement and community-based research. This study defines community as a group of individuals following similar beliefs, sharing a geographical location, and facing common issues.

3 Knowledge Society in Contemporary India

Civilisationally, the goal of knowledge in India has been to enhance mental and physical well-being of all. But, in the 21st century, with every nation trying to become a leader in the creation, application and dissemination of knowledge (Law, 2010), we have also seen some paradigm shift in the purpose of knowledge. Now creation of new knowledge principally depends on strengthening the academic institution, promoting research and innovation in laboratories and tapping foreign sources of knowledge. The important aspect of learning from the local community has slowly disappeared.

National Knowledge Commission of India has identified access as one of the most fundamental issues in a knowledge society (Law, 2010). Even if universities, research institutions and laboratories produce large amounts of knowledge, it will be of little use until the majority of the population actually possesses adequate means to acquire, absorb and communicate this knowledge.

Recent policy developments like India's New Education Policy 2020 and the Unnat Bharat Abhiyan program of the University Grants Commission lay emphasis on university-community partnerships in which students engage with communities to solve local problems through local solutions. The emergence and wider acceptance of community based participatory research (CBPR) has also helped to address the issue of making knowledge more accessible and useful, wherein knowledge is created and owned by both the community and university.

4   Case Study Context

MUJ is surrounded by rural areas. The MUJ Hub, quite naturally, began to engage with the communities living in the villages and slums around the university. As a part of the studio hours, students have designed and executed the transformation of a public space in the community, taking lessons and feedback from the users.

Initial engagement for the BKC project involved visits to houses in these villages by university faculty members, along with students. Local representatives (ward members) supported and accompanied us during these visits, assisting with the interactions.

We began to understand how communities produce and use knowledge that enables them to live their daily lives. This was different from how we, as academics and university students, were producing and consuming knowledge, and the purpose for which it was being used.

These initial interactions gave us a sense of how communities view the university. The locals viewed academia as an isolated entity, unconnected to their daily lives.

The gap in how knowledge is generated and consumed relates to how the current community-academia partnership is inherently unequal.
– The authoritative status enjoyed by academia by virtue of the university's formal recognition in the education industry and financial strength. University curricula is guided and validated by the education system through accreditation bodies and government policies. Formal employers only recognise the degrees granted through this structured education system.

- The knowledge coming from a community does not enjoy the same status as the university knowledge even in the general society itself.
- There is no integration of community knowledge into the knowledge that the university is imparting to its students.
- In terms of having knowledge, locals are considered ignorant, raw and unrefined by the academia.
- There is no platform to facilitate exchange of knowledge between locals and academia, both at the one-to-one (household) level and institutionally.

The BKC project gave us the opportunity and incentive to study these inequalities in greater detail. Specifically, through documenting the case study on waste management practices, we aimed to understand:

- How community knowledge is created, shared and validated – both in the community and by the university
- Identify and illustrate the power inequalities that exist between universities and communities
- How can these existing inequalities between the university and the community be bridged

The case study documents the waste management practices in two adjoining villages (Thikaria and Sanjhriya) and two slum localities in the city of Jaipur. The two villages are located in the fringes of Jaipur city. One slum (Kalakar Basti) lies within the city boundaries, while the other slum (Sarai Bawari) lies beyond the municipal limits.

According to the 2011 census, Jaipur is the 10th most populous city in India, with a population of 3.05 million. Jaipur region covers a total area of 2940 sq. km, consisting of 725 villages, one Municipal Corporation and two Municipal Councils, out of which the municipal area covers 484 sq. km. The Panchayat Samitis and Gram Panchayat are part of the rural administrative setup, while Nagar Nigam and Nagar Palika are part of urban governance (Jawaid et al., 2017).

There are 190 listed slums under Jaipur Nagar Nigam and 47 listed slums under the Jaipur Development Authority, out of which 56.13% are without drinking water access, and 19.0% are without access to sanitation facilities (Census Department of India, 2011). The existing sewerage network covers only 60% of the total population of Jaipur city.

The Public Health, Public Works and Mechanical (Garage) departments of Jaipur Nagar Nigam are jointly responsible for municipal solid waste management in the city. The city generates approximately 1831 metric tons/day of solid waste with an average of 0.460 kg of solid waste, per capita, per day, where per capita solid waste is expected to grow at the rate of 1.5% annually. The current capacity of sewerage treatment plants in the city is only 89.5 MLD, against the requirement of 272 MLD.

Only 50,000 households confined in eight wards have house-to-house waste collection facilities. The waste collection data from Jaipur Nagar Nigam suggests a collection efficiency of only 48%. Also, most of the collection sites are open collection sites (Jawaid et al., 2017).

The main causes of land pollution in Jaipur are poor sewerage systems and solid waste management systems. A huge number of unlined septic tanks, indiscriminate garbage dumping, and the absence of a sanitary landfill site are some of the reasons for land pollution in the city.

5   Methodology

The waste management practices in the two villages and two urban slums were documented to understand how knowledge in a community is created, shared and validated. To document these practices, the MUJ Hub research team visited houses and conducted personal interviews. Data collection was based on a structured questionnaire containing both open and closed-ended questions.

The data collected from the households was shared with various stakeholders, including academic institutions, administrators and other social actors like non-governmental organisations working on the issue of sanitation and waste.

Interviews were also conducted with university administrators and faculty. This was aimed to seek information about knowledge creation by academia and extent of co-creation of knowledge with community. This spotlighted the existing power inequalities in the sharing and validation of community knowledge by the university.

Analysis of the community practices and the university practices around knowledge creation and sharing helped identify the gaps in university-community partnership and suggest a way forward on how the two knowledge systems can be bridged.

Trained Community Action Group (CAG) women members supported the Focus Group Discussions (FGDs) that were held with community women and local ward councillors.

In the sections below, specific quotes from participants have been anonymised to protect identities of individuals.

FIGURE 7.1   Interview sessions with university administrators

FIGURE 7.2   Community interaction with the project team on site

FIGURE 7.3   Women who participated in the FGDs along with the community facilitator

FIGURE 7.4   FGD with ward representatives and community members

6   Community Knowledge: Creation and Validation

Our forefathers have taught us that vegetable peels are good for animals. (Community respondent 4)

My son knows the waste disposal technique because we have taught it to him. (Community respondent 5)

I, my family and my elders validate the knowledge and the same will be disseminated to our children. (Local leader 1)

No school or university can validate or teach the knowledge that parents provide to their children. (Local leader 2)

In response to the questions regarding management of solid waste at household level, the Sarai Bawari community proudly mentioned their traditional practice. For ages, the community has segregated kitchen/vegetable waste and fed it to animals.

It was very clear from the discussions that those who have been managing waste locally through traditional practices are happy and proud of it. However, with launch of SBM, a system of waste segregation at source was introduced without any consultation with the local community. A new system was imposed on them – that of giving their segregated waste to the garbage collection van. They are hesitant to accept it as an alternate practice to their traditional practice of waste management, and replace their knowledge that has been validated in the community over a long period of time.

The community was using dry waste as fuel and were aware it causes pollution, especially the burning of polythene. But they were not aware of how it can be safely disposed.

In the absence of the mandated government waste collection mechanism being effective, communities find their own solutions that solve their contextual problem (*necessity being the mother of invention*). They usually dispose of their domestic waste on a vacant piece of land. This is unsustainable but considered a more straightforward, less time consuming alternative, instead of learning sustainable solutions such as producing less waste, or using specific material waste for creating household articles (glass bottles can be converted to light fixtures, etc).

Acceptance and learning of new methods to reduce and manage waste is higher when mediated through trusted community based organisations and leaders. Approximately 220 households live in Kalakar Basti. Despite being under Jaipur Municipal Corporation jurisdiction, most households did not have access to essential services like water, sanitation, and solid waste management until 2017, when MHT started a project in the slum. As part of its intervention, MHT facilitated the formation of a Community Action Group (CAG). CAG members were trained on various aspects such as the importance of collective leadership, structure of the local municipal corporation, entitlements and government schemes for urban poor and slum development, etc. Training provided by MHT played a pivotal role in the dissemination of knowledge which was then leveraged by the community to access various entitlements and services. The CAG managed to get legal water connections for almost all households, thus improving the overall water, sanitation, and hygiene conditions in the slum.

Learning about organic decomposition of solid waste, its benefits and ease of implementation from MHT, the community jointly agreed to dig a pit in which households could dump their wet waste, cover it with sand, and within a few months this would get converted to manure which could then can be used to grow trees. MHT helped set up the pit in their slum. Once the pit was constructed, responsibilities were assigned to members of the community to ensure that waste is collected in the pit and the pit was properly maintained. Once a few households start doing it, it was quickly adopted by other households when they saw the benefits. The community was willing to learn new knowledge/adopt a new solution, and validate the knowledge into the community, because the solution provided a benefit (manure) that was useful to them locally, was created in consultation with them, and one they could practice without any support from outsiders or the government.

7 Is Community Knowledge Valued in the University?

We know that communities possess great knowledge, but we cannot rely on them only. (University administrator 1)

There is no significant proof of their knowledge as correct so it will not be possible to include it in the daily teaching-learning. But yes, we may provide them with a lot of validated and correct knowledge and that is why we do outreach activities. (University administrator 2)

Students are sent to the local communities to have a practical application of the theories learned in the classroom. (University administrator 3)

From the interviews conducted with the MUJ academic staff and administrators it emerged that Indian academics believe the university must co-exist with the local community and the university does have an important role to play in developing solutions to the issues that a community faces. They do desire to conduct community-based teaching-learning and research, but lack the necessary direction and institutional support.

The institution is generally weak in community-based teaching and research. Lack of knowledge about effective community engagement methods, institutional policies that don't go far enough to support such engagement, and inadequate allocation of funds to try new methods emerged as the primary reasons behind limited efforts currently being made to co-create knowledge with the community. Universities engaging in community-university partnerships ... can benefit from a realistic consideration of university readiness prior to the formation of [community] partnerships (as well as during later stages when considering institutionalisation (Curwood et al., 2011).

It is also evident from the interviews that the primary purpose of service-learning in MUJ is not the co-creation of knowledge but to give students an opportunity to assert and validate the theoretical concepts learned in the

classroom to the community. It is uni-directional, and there is little engagement with the realities of how the community actually lives, and then use the
theory or knowledge acquired in the classroom to co-create a solution that is
acceptable to the community.

University staff also felt that communities are not very open to partnering
with them. The main reason for this is because university efforts to engage
with the community are sporadic and generally on a project-to-project basis.
Such temporary engagement does not allow trust to be established between
the two parties, which is pre-requisite for knowledge partnerships.

The academics we interviewed in MUJ are aware that knowledge does exist
within the local community. They have often learnt such knowledge during
a project when a community member has shared it with them (for example,
community practice of reusing kitchen/wet waste as garden manure). However, they are hesitant to validate such practical knowledge by including it in
the university syllabus.

Practical community knowledge is occasionally valued by academics; at
times may even be given value above academic knowledge as the community practice may be found to work better than textbook solutions. However,
including this knowledge from the community in the formal academic framework requires validation from the academic and research community (through
publications, for example), which takes time. Where community knowledge
and academic knowledge converge, it becomes easier to accept community
knowledge. For example, the CAG member from *Sarai Bawari* mentioned using
vegetable peels as animal feed and to make organic manure. Academics accept
this practice as sustainable, because formal research has validated it as a way
of discarding waste to reduce dependence on cultivated fodder and replacing
artificial fertilizers with organic manure.

Learning from the community has mixed acceptance. Though academics
value the utility brought by community in terms of undertaking community-
based research studies, or implementing pilots, accepting community recommendations and incorporating it in research does not have generalised
acceptance. The usefulness of community knowledge (i.e., validating it by
including it in the research process) is seen to be project specific and contextual.

8   Power Inequalities

There is no doubt inequalities exist in the value put to the knowledge generated in the villages around/in the slums of Jaipur vis-à-vis that created
within the university system. Knowledge, for the university, is in the books

and academic papers that are updated through research as per requirements of the higher education administrators and the policymakers, and as verified by policy-making organisations like National Assessment and Accreditation Council (NAAC) and University Grants Commission (UGC).

The current knowledge culture at MUJ considers knowledge 'correct and valid' when it goes from the university to the community through the service-learning process. Inequality is affirmed in the service-learning component wherein the university/student need is the priority for which community engagement is forged. The project or issue for which the students go to the field may or may not necessarily address the needs of the community. And, most importantly, academics do not consider the possibility that students can learn from the community. Knowledge successfully practised by local communities for generations, which the students may learn during the service-learning engagement process, is not considered useful in itself, and needs to be verified with other sources, such as published research.

In the discussion with university faculty we learnt that the findings emerging from the research done in the community is rarely shared back with the community. This is primarily because the academics believe 'research results' are supposed to be used only for academic purposes. Hence, community continues to be treated as 'subjects' – to collect information and data from, to test new or existing ideas on – but are rarely the beneficiaries of the research project.

There is a lack of trust between the university and community. Sporadic engagement from the university doesn't help to build lasting relationships of trust. The MUJ Hub research team carried out FGD at the Kalakar Basti to capture the community's viewpoint regarding knowledge partnerships between community and academia. One of the key findings that emerged was that the community is only willing to partner with the university (or any other organisation) if they know them well and the project intends to address issues relevant to them.

Differences in how knowledge is dispersed widens the inequality. The university focuses on academic publications, conferences, books, etc, to meet global standards. Additionally, language widens the inequality. Academic publications are usually not in the local language (Hindi). This makes it inaccessible to the community. The community shares knowledge through stories and inter-generational hands-on practice, which is often shared orally in the local language and not documented.

The MUJ Hub researchers took care to translate the questionnaire into Hindi, and hold discussions with the community in Hindi. This made the community participants feel more connected and be open with the researchers.

Some respondents, especially women, are not comfortable (in Hindi) as they were monolingual, and prefer to speak in their local dialect (Doshi and Purohit, 1968). Community leaders (the CAG members) accompanying the researchers stepped in to help translate as they were familiar with the local dialects.

9   Bridging the Divide

We have never thought about it (university role). (Community respondent 1)

They (university) are literate; they know everything ... why will they come to help us? (Community respondent 2)

How can one question our techniques. It is developed through experience. Not every knowledge requires validation from government or universities. (Community respondent 5)

How will a university help in this. Can they come here and collect waste? It is only government who can help us. (Community respondent 5)

There are many big universities in Jaipur but they even don't teach waste disposal much. (Community respondent 6)

Universities can find out new waste management methods, but they will do so only when government asks them to do it. Nobody works without an incentive and the government does not have money to incentivize universities for such petty things. (Multiple community respondents)

Universities are concerned about marks and degrees. (Community respondent 5)

Everyone is interested in earning (money). They (university) never think of the poor. (Community respondent 3)

The above statements were made during the FGD MUJ Hub researchers held with the community to understand their perspectives regarding the role MUJ can play in creating knowledge with them, and for them.

From the discussion it emerged that the communities were unable to envisage how MUJ may help them with waste management. They believed that universities possess knowledge on everything, so they might have some knowledge on waste management as well, but they were not confident that MUJ would come to the community and solve their specific problems related to waste. If the university is pushed by the government, it may try and find solutions.

Lack of trust emerged as a major issue. Why would the university help them? They believe that universities are only interested in making money, and awarding degrees. They have never in the past seen any university helping poor communities to solve their issues.

Bridging the divide then appears to be difficult. But there is common ground – both the community and academia want sustainable waste management practices. Community wants a solution to this persistent problem which causes health issues, while academia wants to identify *indigenous* solutions that can work in the Indian context and thereby help spread sustainable practices.

This can be the impetus needed to improve collaboration between MUJ and the village and slum communities. Solutions to convert kitchen waste to manure, waste segregation, use of plastic, etc are some of the areas for collaborative solutions. Solutions should value and consider existing practices and approaches in different communities. For example, we found some households already avoid plastic bags and use cloth carry bags to fetch articles. Other households collect the plastic bags to return them to the local vegetable vendor. Some households segregate organic, paper and plastic waste, and use organic waste for manure and cattle feed. This was overlooked by the municipal waste collectors, and they encouraged households to use single bins for throwing waste. This meant less work for the waste collector, but disregarded existing sustainable waste management practices in the community.

Setting up community bins in locations considered accessible and safe by community members, time of waste collection (in congruence with the working hours and availability of community members), waste disposal by small-scale commercial establishments like local food stalls, and frequency of waste bin replacement can be determined along with the community. Valuable insights and experiences in implementing the community-based solutions and training of waste collectors can be shared by the university using its considerable resources and modes of communication. The university can also work to fulfil the need to train waste collectors to understand current community practices.

10   Conclusion

The study concludes that power in knowledge generation, use and validation is skewed in favour of MUJ. This is seen is how the service-learning process is structured to benefit the students, and how information/data collected from the community and research findings are not shared back with them, even though universities possess significant resources to do so.

The research conducted by the MUJ Hub shows the academic's role in knowledge generation is considered primary. Though some academics do accept the ability and contribution of the community in generating knowledge, they find it difficult to embed it into the 'formal knowledge' system of the university without scientific validation. Community based research is gaining traction, but to make inroads into the wide-networked research and academic world, gradual enhancement in acceptance of local knowledge in tackling social problems is necessary (Hall & Tandon, 2017).

Knowledge intermediation by a community-based/civil society organisation that the community trusts to identify needs and priorities and support the co-creation process becomes helpful. In our research the support of MHT community facilitators and the community leaders trained by them was invaluable.

Though this initiative helped reduce the boundaries between the communities and MUJ (before this study, these communities were unaware of how MUJ could help them with waste management), the existence of a partnership between MUJ and these communities is missing. The communities remain unaware of the social responsibility role of universities like MUJ in solving their day-to-day problems.

There is a need to strengthen academics' capacity to encourage, promote, regulate and sustain research partnerships with the community. Given the static culture of universities and the longstanding tradition of independent scholarship, it is essential to ask whether universities are genuinely ready to contribute appropriately to initiatives that move away from a short-term charity model of community service to fulfil the potential of long-term social justice initiatives through community research collaborations (Marullo & Edwards, 2000; Ostrander, 2004).

It is evident from the study that as long as a consistent relationship is missing, the co-creation of knowledge is difficult and bridging knowledge cultures remains impossible. Sustainable partnership characterised by regular meetings and discussions between MUJ and its surrounding communities is vital to bridge the knowledge inequalities that exist.

References

Bringle, R. G., & Hatcher, J. A. (1996). Implementing service learning in higher education. *The Journal of Higher Education, 67*(2), 221–239.

Census Department of India. (2011). *Census 2011.* Ministry of Home Affairs, Government of India.

Curwood, E., Susan, Munger, F., Mitchell, T., Mackeigan, M., & Farrar, A. (2011). Building effective community-university partnerships: Are universities truly ready? *Michigan Journal of Community Service Learning, 17*(2), 15–26. https://www.academia.edu/32956998/Building_Effective_Community_University_Partnerships_Are_Universities_Truly_Ready#:~:text=Building%20Effective%20Community-University%20Partnerships%3A%20Are%20Universities%20Truly%20Ready%3F,research%20necessitate%20the%20development%20of%20strong%20community-university%20partnerships

Doshi, S. L., & Purohit, D. S. (1968). Social aspects of language: Rajasthan's multilingual situation. *Economic and Political Weekly, 3*(38), 1441–1444. https://www.jstor.org/stable/4359082?seq=1

Gaventa, J. (1980). *Power and powerlessness: Quiesence and rebellion in an Appalachian Valley.* Clarendon.

Hall, B., & Tandon, R. (2017). *Mobilizing community and academic knowledge for transformative change: The story of the UNESCO chair in community based research and social responsibility in higher education.* Canadian Commission for UNESCO's IdeaLab.

Jawaid, M. F., Sharma, M., Pipralia, S., & Kumar, A. (2017). City profile: Jaipur. *Cities, 68*, 63–81.

Kashalkar-Karve, S., & Damodar, S. N. (2013). Comparitive study of ancient gurukul system and the new trends of Guru-Shishya Parampara. *American International Journal of Research in Humanities, Arts and Social Sciences, 2*(1), 81–84.

Kumar, C. R. (2013, March 20). Still not in a class of their own. *Hindustan Times.*

Law, D. (2010). *National Knowledge Commission (NKC) of India: An overview.* Governement of India. http://eprints.rclis.org/7462/1/National_Knowledge_Commission_Overview.pdf

Marks, S. P. (2014). Challenges of knowledge creation for Indian universities. In C. Raj Kumar (Ed.), *The future of Indian universities: Comparative and international perspectives.* Oxford.

Marullo, S., & Edwards, B. (2000). From charity to justice: The potential of university-community collaboration for social change. *American Behavioral Scientist, 43*(5), 895–912.

NAAC Resources. (2006). *Community engagement case presentations.*
    http://naac.gov.in/docs/Best%20Practices/Best%20Practise%20in%
    20Community%20Engagement.pdf

Norrick, N. R. (1997). Twice-told tales: Collaborative narration of familiar stories.
    Language in Society, 26, 199–220.

Ostrander, S. A. (2004). Democracy, civic participation, and the university: A compara-
    tive study of civic engagement on five campuses. *Nonprofit and Voluntary Sector
    Quarterly, 33*(1), 74–93.

Panghal, M., Arya, V., Yadav, S., Kumar, S., & Yadav, J. P. (2010). Indigenous knowledge
    of medicinal plants used by Saperas community of Khetawas, Jhajjar District,
    Haryana, India. *Journal of Ethnobiology and Ethnomedicine, 6*(1), 1–11.
    https://link.springer.com/content/pdf/10.1186/1746-4269-6-4.pdf

Rubin, V. (2000). Evaluating university-community partnerships: An examination of
    the evolution of questions and approaches. *Cityscape, 5*(1), 219–230.
    http://www.jstor.org/stable/20868505

Saranya Kumar, S. R. (2016). Gurukula system of education in ancient times. *Business
    Sciences International Research Journal, 4*(2), 44–45.

Selvamani, P. (2019). Gurukul system: An ancient educational system of India.
    International Journal of Applied Social Science, 6(6), 1620–1622.

Singh, S. L., Kunwar, N., & Sharma, A. (2018). Impact of Swachh Bharat Abhiyan in
    Indian society. *International Journal of Home Science, 4*(1), 215–219.

Stone, E. (2004). *Black sheep and kissing cousins: How our family stories shape us.*
    Transaction Publishers.

Swain, P., & Pathela, S. (2016). Status of sanitation and hygiene practices in the con-
    text of "Swachh Bharat Abhiyan" in two districts of India. *International Journal of
    Community Medicine and Public Health, 3*(11), 3140–3146.

Tandon, R. (2005). Knowledge as power. In R. Tandon (Ed.), *Participatory research:
    Revisiting the roots* (pp. 40–53). Mosaic Books.

CHAPTER 8

Engaging in a Movement of Cognitive Justice at the Gulu University K4C Hub, Uganda

David Monk, Gloria Aber, Alice Veronica Lamwaka, Martin Odoch and George Openjuru

> Let us come together to create that unique moment when the inner voice of disenfranchisement meets the outer voice of empowerment; When the inner cry for self-determination meets the warm embrace of co-determination.
>
> CATHERINE ODORA HOPPERS, 2021

∴

Abstract

In this case study, the Gulu University Knowledge for Change Hub located in Northern Uganda reflects on the possibilities of knowledge pluralism, relationships and power in the work done by the hub, and shares some lessons that were learnt from engaging in a movement of cognitive justice. The research for this case was conducted using a collaborative community-based approach that included active participation of all hub members in the formulation of research questions, data collection, and analysis. In this type of approach, the documentation of the process and dissemination activities becomes part of the data collected, which is then used to inform future direction and activities for the hub. The research therefore fits into the reflexive and ongoing process of the hub, and is useful for improving the praxis and goals to further knowledge democracy and solve local problems through community-based research.

Keywords

cognitive justice – knowledge pluralism – process documentation – research dissemination – knowledge communication

1   Introduction

The Gulu hub is an initiative of the Gulu University under the Knowledge for Change (K4C) initiative of the UNESCO Chair in Community Based Research and Social Responsibility in Higher Education. The hub's work is linked to the university's mandate "for community transformation" oriented toward serving the geographic space of Northern Uganda. It is a somewhat unique hub, because it does not have formal space within the university, and most of the hub's activities are generated through informal community partnerships and networks.

The Gulu hub's partners are defined by parameters of social and epistemic justice (Monk et al., 2020). That is, the hub works with organisations in Northern Uganda, including Gulu University, that have an interest in promoting social justice and authentic participation in decision making processes. Another layer of community partnerships for the Gulu hub includes a broader network of intellectuals both within Uganda and internationally that are committed to promoting and learning from Indigenous Knowledge Systems (IKS).

Placing relationships first is at the core of the Gulu hub's multi-layered sense of community and research. The academic members of the hub use relationships with the community to advocate for a participative culture of research and learning within the university. Linked to this is the university's efforts to create enabling institutional policies for community engagement. The university promotes IKS through program development and using IKS as the foundational culture of Community University Engagement (CUE). This knowledge distinction is important to note in the context of community engagement by the Gulu hub, because the Gulu community is diverse, with influences from both IKS and Ameripean (Ndawula, 2017)[1] epistemic paradigms. An example of this is in the herbal medicine program described in this chapter.

An IKS-based understanding of community engagement positions the university as one (important) actor within a learning ecosystem – an important departure from objective and linear understandings of research and the role of universities, which typically centre the university or position it as the only ("uni") actor (Visvanathan, 2006). Odora Hoppers (2021) explains that universities (generally) associate knowledge production with university experts and thus purposefully separate the university and its research from the lifestyles and lifecycles and cosmologies of the communities in which they are embedded. This separation fractures relationships and isolates universities. In contrast, IKS based research and community engagement is relational and relies on shared experiences, transdisciplinarity and mutuality (Ndawula, 2017; Odora-Hoppers, 2021). IKS recognises research and knowledge production as a shared community responsibility emerging from deeply entangled

FIGURE 8.1   Gulu university Inter-Nation gathering at the Pharmbiotrac Village, Gulu City,
Uganda
PHOTOGRAPH: DAVID MONK

relationships based on respect and reciprocity with all species, both now and
in the future. Thus, using IKS as a framework for CUE repositions the university
as "multi" rather than "uni", with a focus on relationships, participation, and
actively seeking to promote cognitive justice.

This sense of interconnectedness provides a continuity of shared experience
whereby the traditionally separated knowledge generation, validation, and diffusion, are entangled and shared as part of a longer term project of community
wellbeing. Finding ways of integrating the useful technical elements of this
'conventional' research regime into a paradigm of democratic knowledge culture requires careful interpersonal and intercommunity communication. The
Gulu hub, and the research it has done under the BKC project, exists in this
context of promoting a culture of IKS as both a method for CUE and an activity
of cognitive justice.

In the sections that follow, the authors expand on literature about epistemic
injustice, cognitive justice and the Afrikan Indigenous Knowledge Systems
(AIKS), thereby to providing a theoretical framework to describe the context and
composition of the research undertaken by the Gulu Hub. They go on to elaborate the research processes, identify some learning themes, critically reflect
on these themes, and conclude with some general insights on the implications

from this research on bridging knowledge cultures. The titles of the sections in this chapter are a deliberate attempt to shift away from language and writing that we feel separates us from the participative nature of the research process.

2   Epistemic Injustice and Cognitive Justice

Miranda Fricker (2007, as cited in Tuana, 2017, p. 132) defines epistemic injustice as "the injustice of having some significant area of one's social experiences obscured from collective understanding owing to a structural identity prejudice in the collective hermeneutical resource". Pohlhaus (2017) explains that epistemic injustice is a function of silencing individuals and groups of people's ability to authentically contribute to social pools of knowledge. Medina (2017) elaborates that epistemic injustice is often structural and socially constructed to the extent that entire groups of epistemically oppressed people are taught – and often believe – that they do not know. Patricia Hill Collins (2017) explained that the accreditation of theoretical knowledge over embodied knowledge is a core function of "othering" marginalised people(s). Collins (2017) frames the silencing as violence that functions to maintain and reproduce privilege, through *epistemic gatekeepers* who carefully construct narratives and contexts that decide what knowledge counts.

Visvanathan (2006) explains that cognitive justice is the right of all forms or traditions of knowledge to co-exist *in public* without duress. Odora Hoppers (2009, 2021) provides depth to this definition of cognitive justice through her work on IKS. Odora Hoppers emphasises that cognitive justice requires authentic respect and dialogue across knowledge cultures. She centres cognitive justice as a fundamental human right and precondition to developing equal societies. Both Visvanathan (2006) and Odora Hoppers (2021) stress the importance of IKS for planetary survival because it is based on ontological foundations of intersubjectivity and continuity of relations beyond the human lifeworld and human life-time. It therefore promotes transdisciplinarity and allows for a deeper connection to the non-visible and subconscious realms of knowing. In the next section, we offer some literature about IKS in the Ugandan context.

3   Afrikan Indigenous Knowledge Systems

In the poem entitled *Wer pa Lawino*, the poet p'Bitek (1984) asserts that Afrikan culture and values need not emulate European standards in order to be recognised. The poet's work is filled with the recognition that indigenous knowledge systems are fighting a losing battle in the face of modernization. The section of the poem, "The graceful giraffe cannot become a monkey", highlights the differences between the Whites and Africans, and the pride of an Acholi woman in her culture and identity amidst colonial attacks on it. In general, the feelings in the poem are more of pride, pity, protest, anger and boldness.

By moving away from defining knowledge within the strict confines of how the Western epistemology recognises knowledge, authors are faced with the task of refining the concept of what is considered knowledge within the African Indigenous Knowledge Systems (AIKS). Odora Hoppers (2021) points out that the value of AIKS is located in its understanding that culture is knowledge. She gives the example of Ubuntu, which is a philosophy derived from traditional ways of living, emphasising interconnectedness as the key element for understanding human behaviour and thinking.

Elements of AIKS, this way of knowing are revealed in the relationship between indigenous communities and their ecosystems. Among several communities within Uganda, designated forested areas were not subjected to firewood gathering or timber logging. This was primarily due to the belief that spirits of the ancestors/gods lived within these large trees and cutting them down would infuriate the ancestral spirits, which in turn would rage against the community's crops and livestock. This knowledge system, like several others, was challenged by the arrival of the church missionaries into Acholi land. The missionaries were offered such gazetted forest areas in the hope that once they cut the trees during their settlement process, they would be struck down by the spirits. When this did not occur, the resultant doubts among the community of their spiritual leaders appears to have accelerated condemnation of indigenous knowledge. They did not wait long enough to see the impact. However, indigenous knowledge began to be devalued also due to the application of a missionary framework of (ignorant) interpretation, criticized by p'Bitek. What if the message in regard to the trees was not to do with disturbing the spirits but more about conservation? For example, the Acholi had a saying that you do not defecate on the river banks, otherwise the mother of the river will twist your intestines and cause you to die. Other sayings state that you do not sit on the grinding stone, otherwise your mother will die. These teachings appear aimed at ensuring hygiene behaviour of children within the community. Defecating on the river banks would disperse human waste into the river system, affecting downstream communities. A young child with an uncovered bottom would pollute the grinding stone, used for processing the family meal. When looked at from this perspective, it is difficult to discount these knowledge systems which are connected to the practical needs of daily life.

Much indigenous knowledge is created and shared using all of the senses based in a relational ontology, which interprets and creates knowledge multi-modally and together with the non-human world within a non-linear temporal perspective (Odora-Hoppers, 2009; Visvanathan, 2006). Translating embodied, tacit knowledge into text is a difficult task because it requires translations of feeling, intuition and sensory experiences. Knowing and interpretation of knowledge is often embodied and moves beyond rationalisations, intertextual and inter-language experiences and, therefore, as p'Bitek warns, cannot be understood through a European lens.

4   The Gulu K4C Hub

The Gulu K4C hub was founded in 2018, under the leadership of the Vice Chancellor of Gulu University. Gulu University is a leading public university established in 2003 in Gulu City, which is a rural city in Northern Uganda, in a period of dynamic transformation following 20 years of civil war ending in 2007. The hub conducts training in participatory research processes, with emphasis on art-based inquiry, particularly in photo voice, poetic inquiry, paint-based inquiry and theatre inquiry. The arts facilitate embodied and nonlinear connections and relationships which help connect deeply with the world (Monk, de Oliveira & Salvi, 2019). The hub has initiated its efforts in community settings, working mostly with youth on a variety of research and community projects, and sharing the informality of learning and doing in the community. The hub intentionally takes the time to listen and share through authentic participation, developing strong partnerships and relationships by working with the community through hub partners. Shared projects include a youth-initiated program to plant trees on all the streets of Gulu, ongoing participation in street-based art groups, and research with a Community Based Organisation (CBO) on waste management in Gulu. The hub has no core funding, so projects are based on voluntary work and disparate grants sought out in partnership with community organisations. Current active partners include:
– Gulu University: Faculty of Agriculture and Environment, Faculty of Medicine (Public Health and Herbal Medicine program), Faculty of Education and Humanities
– CEED Uganda: Youth empowerment CBO with a focus on gender and environment
– Partners for Community Development: Grassroots political and environmental activist organisation
– Kijani Trees: Private enterprise involved in sustainable agroforestry
– Afrigreen Sustain: Environmental CBO

- Starface CAMP (Youth group): Focused on multiculturalism and developing pathways in the arts
- Loremi Tours: Social enterprise focused on environmental and cultural tourism
- Taka Taka Plastics: Private environmental enterprise that makes building materials using recycled plastics. It is also a strong force in the environmental movement in Gulu.
- UNESCO Chair in Lifelong Learning Youth and Work (hosted at Gulu University)

Building on these networks and informal partnerships, the hub has begun to engage with the university through Memoranda of Understanding with the faculty of agriculture and environment and with the herbal medicine and indigenous knowledge programs, launched in 2018 in the Faculty of Medicine.

The herbal medicine and indigenous knowledge program uses an IKS framework of transdisciplinary learning that integrates chemistry, biology, pharmacy, agriculture and spirituality. The program delivery uses some classroom lecture sessions; however, it is mainly based in a collaborative and experiential learning model that relies heavily on the prior learning of herbal medicine practitioners. It revolves around validating the experience and knowledge of the practitioners, preserving biodiversity and culture, integrating business and marketing, as well as medical research and copyright procedures to meet the licensing demands of the National Drug Authority. Gulu University has a laboratory that is used to test new products, but much of the research and learning is done through ceremony, dreams, dance and food around the traditional learning space – the campfire. The hub has also led a series of inter-nation gatherings of indigenous knowledge holders from the Bunyoro kingdom, Buganda kingdom, Busoga kingdom and Acholi chiefdom. There is a strong focus on bringing Acholi elders together to inform and lead these inter-nation gatherings, particularly in partnership with the deeply community ingrained herbal medicine practice and activism of Alice Lamwaka. Regular gatherings of elders are essential to the process of relationship building and connecting to the ongoing nature of knowledge production that is fractured by modernist universities. Gulu University has created a space on campus to host these gatherings in a village-like setting so that elders feel comfortable. The space is a location where herbal doctors can experiment and share their remedies, preserve biodiversity and treat people. The location is next to a Gulu university laboratory where they can also perform tests such as phytochemical analysis. More recently, a university committee has been formed to integrate IKS in all programs at Gulu University, in which the hub is also participating.

5   Research Processes

This research is underpinned by an ontological understanding of intersubjectivity and interdependence of all species (Monk et al., 2020; Odora Hoppers, 2009; Visvanathan, 2006). Briefly, this means that we interpret the world as being a mix of diverse species that are reliant on each other for survival. Following from this, we value diversity in experience as we seek to understand our world. The research has been a collaborative process between hub members, and as a result it has used multiple forms of learning together including dance, ceremony, food, storytelling, energy sharing, interviews and focus group discussions. Two research assistants were hired from within the hub and worked with the research lead to facilitate the research. It is an ongoing process of reflection, participation, analysis and action. Not all of the learning can be translated into written expression, but we do our best to share the written representations which deepen understanding of the overarching research question.

The particular research direction and questions were developed cooperatively in a meeting with all hub members at the outset of participation in the BKC research project in 2019. The hub decided that the process of conducting this research should also contribute towards developing the strategic direction of the hub, as expressed by one of our advisors, Professor Catherine Odora Hoppers, when she asked us in a reflection session: *How can we uncover and support what has made resilient societies worldwide, and find out whether we have something different to say to them?* To this end we used a mix of research mechanisms including storytelling and interviews. The focus of the research was on relationships that are being developed, the knowledge cultures being brokered, and the resulting type of action and community impact. This was informed by an initial report led by one research assistant, analysing the indigenous knowledge cultures in Uganda, which informs the IKS literature shared earlier in this chapter. Briefly, the report emphasised the cultural and spiritual dimensions of Acholi knowledge making a framework for knowing that cannot be analysed or translated using a European lens. The knowledge making mechanisms include a spiritual understanding that goes beyond the human lifeworld but are practically located in efforts of life arrangements oriented towards peaceful coexistence.

The sub research questions we set as a team were oriented towards understanding power dynamics within the hub:
–   What kinds of knowledge bridging partnerships exist in our hub?
–   What are the power dynamics between the knowledge making partners and how can they be improved?

- What are the core components needed for authentic and equal knowledge making partnerships?
- What are some of the difficulties involved in community university partnerships and how can they be overcome?
- What is the viability of a sustainable centre for community-based research at Gulu University, and what is required?

6   Learning

Learning occurred through participation and reflection on hub activities, interviews, and focus group discussions.

6.1   *Focus Group Discussion*
A series of reflection sessions among hub members were facilitated throughout the research process using different approaches. For example, riddles, dance therapy, medicinal practice demonstration, food sampling, ceremony and storytelling were used in the learning circles around the fire at the Gulu University biodiversity and cultural preservation centre. We loosely refer to this as a type of focus group discussion, though these sessions were led by elders, and documentation involved observation and deep sensory experiences, some of which simply cannot be translated here. We also facilitated an inter-hub gathering (organised in partnership with the West Virginia K4C hub) with K4C hubs in South Africa based at Durban University of Technology, Rhodes University, and University of the Free State, which took place over two days and involved deliberation on the research questions. The video recording, presentations and shared notes were reviewed as a component of the research.

Another focus group discussion used art-based inquiry with hub members to enter more deeply into the power dynamics of the hub and its affiliated networks. In this particular form of inquiry, we asked members to draw pictures on sticky notes in response to the research questions – a separate drawing for each sequential research question. The members then placed their pictures on a power matrix drawn on poster. The power matrix was a simple matrix with four quadrants – the vertical axis representing power hierarchies and the horizontal axis representing power distribution. The top left quadrant represents considerable hierarchical power that is not shared. The bottom left represents little power, also not shared. The bottom right is little power with more sharing, and the top right represents high power that is highly collaborative.

Participants placed their picture in any quadrant according to how they thought their response represented power dynamics and decision making, and

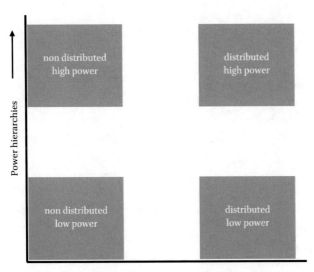

FIGURE 8.2   Power matrix

FIGURE 8.3   Focus group discussion with hub partners using power matrix
              PHOTOGRAPH: DAVID MONK

explained how their pictures represent answers to the question as well as why they selected that location on the power matrix.

6.2   *Key In-depth Individual Interviews*
Interviews were conducted with traditional herbalists, project leaders, community based organisations, Gulu University Herbal Medicine lecturers, the office of community university engagement and some hub members.

6.3 Participant-Observation

Learning also included observing participants in hub activities, which included – (1) inter-nation gatherings of indigenous knowledge holders: an assembly of elders from different nations in Uganda (with analysis of the planning meetings and reports of the gatherings); (2) Wang OO (elders' fire of wisdom, the traditional classroom); (3) Two (annual) Traditional Medicine weeks, and (4) training of Traditional Herbalists. The researchers observed the process from making of herbs to the final product in quality conditions. Ethical considerations were adhered to include protection of Intellectual Property Rights of herbal practitioners, particularly the Covilyce-1 remedy to COVID 19, which is an innovation of the herbal medicine program and is undergoing clinical trials in order to translate validity into Ameripean science paradigms.

6.4 Critical Reflection

Learning was collated and analysed in ongoing cycles of reflection throughout the research among all hub members. Participatory research processes recognise participants as expert knowledge holders and therefore include them in the entire research process (Tandon et al., 2016). In this process, the analysis itself becomes another source of learning, in an ongoing cycle of reflection and action (Hall, 1985). In the reflection sessions, hub members were asked to reflect on the discussions and identify themes and their implications. Their inputs became a component of the learning.

To delve deeper into the initial broad areas of inquiry, the two research assistants and the research lead coded the interviews and personal observations, first independently identifying additional emerging themes and then comparing and discussing them together. This was presented to the hub members for further reflection before collaboratively taking a final decision on how to present them. Partners and participants names are included, where requested by them. All participants are members of the Gulu Hub network, and there is deep bias ingrained in the research and this report. Acknowledging that this is a learning endeavour in which we are all intertwined aligns with our ontological understanding of intersubjectivity and interdependence. Epistemologically speaking, this connects to learning as being interpreted, and meaning being made through applying our diverse experiences to situations that we are part of, not removed from. We hope that our open and reflexive collective voice can share some of the emotion and passion we have in a deeper intertextual shared sensory experience with the reader. We therefore try to bring in longer quotations. We consider this to be important for translating those aspects of the sensory and emotional knowledge that we have gained and is difficult to express within the limits of written text.

FIGURE 8.4   Gulu university Wang OO bonfire where elders provide knowledge, vision,
              wisdom and understanding of indigenous knowledge and Indigenous Knowledge
              Systems
              PHOTOGRAPH: DAVID MONK

7   Learning Themes

In what follows we share the findings according to the core themes that
emerged to better understand knowledge bridging relationships. We draw on
the literature related to cognitive justice which emphasises reciprocity, respect
and dialogue. The findings are framed in the power dynamics (based on the
reflections) and attempts to bridge the structural limitations to validating and
respecting the contributions of IKS to the general pool of social knowledge
making.

A vital point to understand in the interpretation of the findings is
that the hub, while considering ongoing work moving forward, does not lay
claim to developing the associated work of our affiliated partners, such as
those of the herbal medicine program, which have been built over considerable time and with considerable effort. As participants in our hub, some of
the members have chosen to share their experiences in developing partnerships, and we include this in the research, as by extension we are involved in
shared activities and vision. In terms of bridging knowledge cultures, we are

moving forward and learning together as we reflect on the different partnerships and networks that we have. In the presentation of members' perspectives, we hesitatingly differentiate between the background of the members
(community, university, teacher, herbal doctor, etc), to provide some insight
into how the hub is composed; however, identities and roles of the members are fluid and are not solely represented in the titles we have associated
with them.

7.1   *Theme 1: What Healthy Relationships Look like*

In terms of bridging knowledge cultures, the participants emphasised that
centring healthy and balanced relationships, rather than individual short term
research projects, was important. This is a major theme because it re-visions
research as an ongoing process that emerges from community contexts among
partners with similar learning interests. This re-centring shifts traditional sep-
arations of the researcher and the researched. One university partner reflected
on this shift:

> As a researcher, as soon as I entered her house I entered a relationship.
> She was not interested in my particular research questions, she was inter-
> ested in sharing her story. She invited me into her life by sharing her story.
> She served me food, I met her family and neighbours. I am not a stranger,
> I am a trusted friend worthy of sharing food and discussing a common
> issue. That conversation provided far more insight than if we had met as
> strangers. But she is now part of this research, and I am bound ethically
> to continue to work on this issue and other issues that come up in that
> community – not just on my terms. I am no longer other, and that comes
> with responsibility. Research is about people's lives – real people – not
> objects. It is serious".

Beyond the ethical implications observed above, centring relationships
muddles the whole idea of research as being bound by time and questions.
It entangles conventional linear research paradigms of knowledge generation, validation, diffusion and use into an ongoing process of transdisciplinary meaning-making in a world that is ongoing and emergent. Relationships
enhance an intrinsic drive for learning, personal contentment, peer recognition and self-actualization. This is reflected on by a university partner: "What
K4C Gulu Hub needs is a diverse and multifaceted knowledge system in which
techniques are continuously updated to reflect current understanding and
needs". Likewise a community partner reflects on the importance of bringing
together diversity, and not thinking of community as homogenous:

There was initial interaction with the community, institutions and even the communities themselves, the people in the community to guide how the research should be done. So, I think that was really, really nice work. And it kind of brought that togetherness between the community and the university, also giving opportunity for the youth to air out their thoughts.

A community partner described a picture of a tree they drew that represented healthy relationships as, "a form of empowerment. So, for me, I looked at that" [picture of a tree] "as symbolising birth, power; life, and politics changes the community". This reorients research as a broader conceptualisation of a flourishing community, as one academic partner suggests: [We have to think] "what are the reasons for research and knowledge we are trying to build in these communities? For me, it's around environmentally sustainable futures for everything, for people and the planet".

The hub partners all felt that building relationships required meeting regularly, not only for research purposes, but as an academic partner observed: "We are developing some important networks nationally and internationally ... that engage people in different ways but are all very important ways of staying connected to each other". Likewise, a community partner explained that meeting regularly de-centres the university and builds "a common ground, and acknowledges both power dynamic and fully equal participation of the community".

Another community partner reflected how their organisation uses a "group of community called reflection action groups" in their own practice. They explain that these are fundamental to setting the organisation's work because the reflection action groups, "will sit and discuss what is wrong for them".

Creating spaces and concerted action to understand the full ontological underpinnings of different traditions of knowledge was seen as essential. Simply listening or letting people speak is not sufficient for understanding, though it is seen as a starting point as one community partner suggests: "bridging knowledge cultures can be improved by recognising the voice of all and to understand that boundaries are fluid ... thus knowledge and values will always interface with another".

In terms of bridging knowledge cultures, relationships open up an opportunity for what Odora Hoppers (2021) refers to as inter-personal and inter-community communication and understanding. We will finish this theme on healthy relationships with a quote from one of the academic partners, which sums up their value: "Essentially, CBR builds on the way that engagement between practitioners/communities and researchers generates opportunities to bring very diverse resources to understanding causes of, and solutions to, wicked societal problems".

7.2 *Theme 2: Barriers to Healthy Relationships*

Most of the hub reflections are oriented towards challenging the traditional university approach towards knowledge and research. This is because the current paradigm of knowledge production is dominated by Ameripean approaches. Hub partners reflected on the power imbalance and ways to promote IKS.

Broadly speaking, the core problem that stakeholders observed was that community has little agency when it comes to relationships. An academic partner explained,

> The community has been ignored for a very long time. And yet, there is a lot of knowledge down there, which is not disseminated. So, I feel that this is because the decisions are normally made from the top ... ignoring the other one. And then when somebody talks, and you get a very important finding, even when you know that the knowledge was got from there, there's no recognition. It remains up. And it's usually [remains] like that.

A community partner reflected on a research project they were in, where they felt objectified and excluded:

> the decisions were made by researchers or the lead team. Once you have made up your mind, you don't want to listen to anyone, no one wants to listen, she needs to say yes, I've got it, it's me, it's me who has this, it's me who got the money, we will have this so you don't listen to anybody else. So we lose out a lot on that.

An university partner agreed that power is often unbalanced in research and adds that it is often defined by funders' requirements:

> Top down, we had the power. Gulu University now, we did a lot of formal traditional research. So we went to stakeholders, and we would ask them, approach them to do focus group discussions and interviews. That's very top-down. You know, we decided based on what other people [wanted from us].

Reliance on funders and their associated demands and expectations is challenged as a structural problem that has created a dependency on money and consequent control by the people who own the structures we buy into. A community participant reminds us that,

money is a perceived challenge and we are chasing it a little bit always ...
we think that we can't bring our community together without money.
Time is also a resource that we measure in a very linear way and we have
our lives that we are measuring, so we are doing lots of things. Community
often changes with very little budget and often no budget.

7.3   Theme 3: Focus on Community and IKS

As explained in the introduction, the Gulu hub and Gulu university attempts
to use an IKS framework to interpret and build relationships in the community. It is therefore not surprising that this emerged as a theme.

One participant from the university explained, "Often the most important
resource is forgotten: The knowledge and power of working together". This is
an important point when it comes to building IKS which relies on the ontological assumption of shared experience and values the diverse skills and
knowledge that exist in the community. Relying on money as the only conceptualisation of wealth demeans community knowledge and plays into the
carefully constructed hierarchies of knowing and the narrative of Ameripean
universality that permeates the traditional university. A community member
recognises that reorienting and rebalancing relationships requires finding a
more balanced sharing of all wealth, including money: "The element of trust
plays a big role in engagement and we start with probably the youth group,
this means money is coming into it unless people can come up with things".
Devaluing culture and other ways of knowing also reduces the financial contributions back to the community.

Legal rights were also a core concern related to valuation of herbal doctors.
In developing processes for drug certification, this was especially relevant.
There have been many experiences of researchers coming and taking information, transforming it, and claiming it as their own. Herbal doctors were
therefore afraid of people stealing their cures. Odora Hoppers (2009) has
elaborated on how this happens in the pharmaceutical industry. However,
this is not isolated to herbal medicine. Denigrating people to objects and
claiming knowledge superiority lies at the centre of colonisation and the jus-
tification of exploitation (Ndawula, 2017; Odora Hoppers, 2021; Visvanathan,
2006).

The community partners working in indigenous science emphasised a feeling of not being accepted by society, because the communicative structures
on the part of the dominant paradigm of knowing are unable to interpret or
understand the different knowledge systems. One practitioner explained that,
"the population still shuns traditional medicine and associates it with witch-
craft/ being evil ... thus mindset is a limitation to knowledge culture".

Indigenous knowledge holders were seeking ways of opening the channels of communication, by packaging their products in ways people can understand. Two traditional healers from the Pharmbiotrac project were of the view, "that the traditional set up of the structures is not conducive and doesn't attract those seeking traditional and contemporary health service".

Challenging the epistemic narrative that separates culture from knowing, and knowing from certain communities, is therefore a foundational activity in the search for cognitive justice and any attempt to bridge knowledge cultures requires efforts to include meaningful epistemic dialogue and reciprocal relations which equally value different contributions (financial or otherwise) to a flourishing society.

7.4   Theme 4: Research Solutions

Developing more balanced research partnerships and overcoming cultural hierarchies has partially been discussed in the theme of relationship building. However, hub participants also reflected on the particularities of reconciling research methods within relationships. This comes back to the purpose of research and the related outcomes.

A partner from a CBO explained that research needs to be more of a cyclical process because: "R&D is used for the communities, which will then go back to the communities and work with them ... a kind of relearning, which then puts it more towards the community based research".

A university partner emphasised that inclusion can take time, which is conceived of differently by the university and the community, but it is important to respect this. "I think we also need to let them give us their view, so that we can move together without leaving anyone behind". The same partner elaborated that knowledge dissemination has to be done differently as well so that "the community fully understand and also disseminate this knowledge locally".

A different university partner reflected on a research program that shifted this power dynamic:

> like this formulation lab, right, where we put some space more in the hands of the community ... a little bit more ... I'm thinking about when we did the talk with the elders. So that was a component of where we were trying to build and connect with things in a more open way where we weren't going to, we weren't deciding how things were being done.

Likewise, a community partner reflected on a different project: "We went to the youth group, and they decided the questions that we were going to ask and where we were going to do it and how we were going to do it".

Creating spaces of epistemic equality requires valuing the entire research process, not just deciding what questions to ask. An academic partner emphasised that this is especially true in the case of "peer review and validation of the research or work rather than the traditional peer review so that the community accepts it".

Furthermore, sharing in the benefits of the research is crucial for equal and healthy relationships. Participants reflect on instances of shared impact across the community. For Gulu University Vice Chancellor, Openjuru, the relationships that Gulu University has fostered with the community,

> has led to numerous achievements like the innovation of Covilyce-1 herbal remedy for Covid-19; agri-business entrepreneurship; Mango Enterprise by Faculty of Agriculture; water drillings; and contribution to peace restoration. Testing of the entire town of Gulu by Gulu University has also improved more engagement and participation in the vaccination [effort], and has strengthened engagement both nationally and internationally.

Another example is given by a teacher in the herbal medicine program. They explain that the students trained in the herbal medicine program (Pharmbiotrac), "are helping out in the various communities like Omoro, Teso, Lira in managing diseases using indigenous knowledge and culture".

A practical example of social contribution comes from a traditional herbalist doctor:

> Now it is those who can afford and look at modern treatment as the best treatment. However, those that cannot afford, go to herbalists for healthcare. The relationship we have with Gulu University, Pharmbiotrac has created access to healthcare for the disadvantaged.

Reconceptualising research impact without borders of time or particular orientation was seen as important, as one community participant inquired: "So how impactful is a two-year project that eventually goes away or a one-year project? What impact are you going to leave there and how sustainable are our projects"?

All of these instances demonstrate that social impact is a core component of authentic and reoriented paradigms of research partnerships. The empowering nature of the research opens up potential for deep community change.

7.5   Theme 5: Future Directions

Bridging knowledge cultures is not a small endeavour, it requires reorienting an entire paradigm of living, within which the university, as an acknowledged knowledge producer, must play a significant role. In this final theme, hub members reflect on the practical and strategic role the hub can play to further knowledge democracy and cultural plurality in the Gulu community.

A core strength of the hub is recognising that it is a network of differently abled and differently interested people, with different cultural and knowledge backgrounds. An academic partner explains that, "Appreciating and redesigning community solution in partnership gives us an opportunity, because we all have different expertise on how best we can redesign the solutions ... the community has these solutions but it is a dream, not yet modified".

A community partner suggested that this is effective both in terms of funding, but also in developing a transdisciplinary understanding of community:

> We have effective partnerships and networks and what we have been doing is building on the momentum of the different partners and different projects that come in so there is money, research projects that come here with this money and we need to integrate this research with [our] research.

Our hub could do better in coordinating the disparate parts of our networked efforts. A university partner reflects:

> We need to coordinate, we need to share perspective for us to be effective ... as said earlier, the different projects have to contribute to the centre. Finding sustainable local solutions to global societal challenges requires the active engagement of a variety of stakeholders. We need to know about how wide our branches going to the community are to make sure that at least everybody is aware about something, about what we are doing, about the research.

Expanding personal and community learning and embodied practice is seen as the most essential work needed. One university partner suggested this can be done through:

> inductive training of all decision makers like K4C Gulu Hub and its partners on how to find research evidence in relation to indigenous knowledge, for instance in education, agriculture. Initial training, however, is effective only if it is supplemented by refresher sessions. For instance, it is advisable for every decision maker to do a search and review it with a skilled searcher several times a year. And skills of appraisal in K4C activities need to be developed during training.

A community partner felt that there

> is a need for creation of modules for informal education to build Acholi
> culture especially during the Wang OO in the forest that will build on
> children, youths' morals and character. Through this, the indigenous
> knowledge will continue spreading and remain intact in memory and
> transcribed in books.

These future directions point back to the rest of the themes, which are all
oriented towards understanding and integrating IKS into practice. Shifting
habits of research from objective to relational, knowledge cultures from linear
to complex, and advancing cognitive justice takes time and requires an epistemic social movement. The Gulu hub has the goal to support this movement.
Certainly, Gulu University as an institution is taking strides to be a leader in
cognitive justice by establishing more equal partnerships with community and
emphasis on integrating IKS.

8   Bridging Knowledge Cultures in Practice

Okot p'Bitek warns in his poems against using European frameworks to interpret Acholi life. He explains that it cannot be translated, but rather needs to be
understood in Acholi, because the meanings are foundationally different. This
forms the core point in our research findings. In our hub's very first meeting to
discuss the research for this case study, members agreed that you cannot take
the knowledge innovations and leave the Cen (spirts), dreamers, and rainmak-
ers, because they are the scientists. Acholi scientists are able to communicate
and interpret phenomena along dimensions that the Ameripean Knowledge
Systems are not capable of. This comes from a relational understanding of
time and being beyond human life-times. Much Acholi science comes from
understanding vibrations and energies. Acholi scientists are able to communicate using vibrations to, for example, hold off rain or shift the landing location of locusts. The learning process is based on longstanding relationships
and learning to communicate with the human and non-human world in a
non-transactional, embodied way beyond the four dimensions perceived by
Ameripean science.

Visvanathan (2006) suggests that the current crises of war and climate are
related to a dominant paradigm of science which has fractured relationships
to each other and to the world in which we live. A massive paradigm shift is

essential, not just for cognitive justice, but for the survival of the planet. This requires a shift in habits of perception and (re)learning how to "be", using more of our senses and keener atunement with phenomena, and recognising that seeing, hearing, smelling, feeling are more than what is visible or physical. In other words, we all need to become less ignorant, and this requires learning and interpreting differently.

The reflections that we have shared above point towards a reconceptualisation of research as embedded in a complex field of diverse and interdependent communities. In this section, we will deepen this learning from our research and convey impressions and insights from participant observations (made during inter-nation gatherings and herbal medicine week). We attempt to relay the significance and impact of bridging knowledge cultures in practice to the best of our ability in this written forma.

First, there are two very essential points we would like to make clear. For one, diversity and plurality of knowledges and cultures are essential to make meaning of our world (Hoppers, 2021; Husserl & Merleau-Ponty, 2002). The difficulty is that repression of knowledge systems (epistemic injustice) are used as a tool for colonisation and a rationalisation of violent oppression (Hill Collins, 2017). Second, great efforts must be made to understand and learn different approaches towards learning and living, including different knowledge systems. This requires broadening the scope of our shared hermeneutical resources, and trying to make meaning of differences that we do not have words or cultural capacities to fully understand.

The research we have conducted demonstrates just how important and difficult it is to communicate across knowledge (making) cultures. When it comes to knowledge production processes, our findings show our attempts to listen, learn and practice. Creating spaces for intra-cultural and inter-cultural dialogue and shared learning is what emerges as a good example at Gulu University. Inter-nation gatherings and herbal medicine awareness week are an important representation of the priority areas of the Gulu hub: building a public movement for IKS. These events also illustrate the difficulty involved in translating knowledge cultures. Representing the rich embodied intellectual work of all the senses is difficult to reduce to an Ameripean conception of learning. In her 2012 book, *Borderlands,* Gloria Anzaldúa explains how the Spanish colonisation process of Mexico, which involved stealing ancestral and cultural artefacts, removed the spiritual ceremonial power from these materials and reduced them to mere European artefacts. It is the same in other knowledges which, as Odora Hoppers (2021) explains, cannot be separated from culture.

Deep spiritual sensitivities and connective healing energies that comes from listening and attuning the senses to the land and energies around us occurred among the delegates sitting around the Wang OO, learning about how to set the fire according to the position of the moon, which wood to use, and the healing power of the fire. There are some things that we learn through sensory experience – without words we learnt many things and communicated at these gatherings.

Food and dance were integral to the entire process. Two full days were spent on learning about the medicinal value of different plants, food combinations and their preparation. Plants and knowledge were shared and exchanged between visiting chiefdoms and nations. Likewise, different dances were shared, including a dance therapy session that demonstrated through an intricate process of dance and drumming, a deep spiritual healing process where participants in the therapy were clearly in a trance and fully engaged with their deepest demons which were enticed out by skilful psychiatrists. The events brought together not only local participants (open to the public and publicly open), but also indigenous academics and leaders from different parts of Uganda and the world using digital technologies.

Reflecting from a meta perspective in terms of the power relations that this process embodied, it is clear that the elders took over and owned the entire process. The rich process of sharing knowledge and healing practices was a traditional academic activity. Elders taught traditional values and observed strict cultural protocols.

The social impact of these gatherings and the integration of knowledge was remarkably rich. First, the gatherings were connected to the herbal medicine, biodiversity preservation and cultural centre. The centre sits on land owned by the university. The space was developed according to a traditional Acholi *paco* (village). Youth who work with our hub in other contexts were recruited to build two large houses, outhouses, a granary, and clear the land for farming, thus engaging younger generations in the embodied cultural learning. A location for a shrine was set up and appropriate spiritual cleansing was done for the space.

The significance of these events cannot be understated. The Acholi chiefs and their parties heralded this shift at the university and took over the space. They saw it as a space for historical alignment and networking among indigenous knowledge keepers from the disparate nations. They host quarterly meetings in this space. Delegates from other nations commended the leadership of Gulu University to carry the epistemic momentum forward.

The early inter-nation gatherings catalysed discussion about herbal remedies for Covid-19 that were being used in different locations, which eventually resulted in the development of Covelyce-1. With. A unique time and space has opened up, as the creation and clinical trials of Covelyce-1 challenge the colonised and capitalised research processes. Covelyce-1 has resulted in a series of activities with the National Drug Authority, National Council for Science and Technology (NCST), and the Ministry of Health (MoH). The President of Uganda is a strong supporter of developing IKS and has been a leader in initiating both public discourse and a mandate for the NCST and MoH to explore indigenous validation mechanisms and intellectual property rights of indigenous pharmacology. In turn, possibilities emerge for dialogue in other areas of indigenous science, not limited to indigenous knowledge in Acholi land, but broadly within the traditional academy.

Having Gulu University participate and lead in this process was essential in opening an academic dialogue that validates a different knowledge culture. The university is seen as a space of higher knowledge, and often a representation of and reproduction of colonial hierarchies and epistemic injustice. Crossing these boundaries at the university is an essential for breaking down fallacious epistemic hierarchies.

9   Conclusion

The goal of this chapter has been to reflect on the possibilities of knowledge pluralism and share some lessons that we have learned as we engage in a movement of cognitive justice. The Gulu Hub's pursuit of translating knowledge cultures is made possible largely through its informality and broader university vision and leadership, which itself is integrated and participating with(in) the wider community. The hub does not lay claim or seek ownership of community university dialogue or knowledge democracy. Rather, it is focused on developing relationships and networks among a vibrant community of existing initiatives which are bridging knowledge systems and promoting knowledge democracy. The main work of the hub is finding spaces to support and partner in a growing movement to include IKS in community development and improve dialogue across knowledge making cultures.

The power dynamics of the hub's work are more distributed because of this participative and supporting (rather than initiating) role. This forms one of our essential learning points. The other learning point is the creation of a distinct space for the practice of AIKS. The university provided space, built a traditional village on the university campus, and developed an integrated herbal medicine program which supports AIKS academic pursuits and publicly validates AIKS. This is also a space of (and for) knowledge brokering – lecturers and the public cannot help but come and learn a little when the campfire is lit. Likewise, the indigenous practitioners are making good use of the university labs and expertise in branding and marketing. They also have a location to share their products in a place where the general public is comfortable to visit.

We would like to end this chapter on a cautionary note. The history of colonisation and epistemic injustice is based on a zero sum power game that suggests universality and ownership of truth. In his novel *Things Fall Apart* Chinua Achebe comments on the flexible nature of the oppressor, to always be lingering and ready to adapt to transformations and subversively return to oppress. In the pursuit for knowledge democracy, we see universities as places which need to change, and develop a stronger sense of mutuality and communication across knowledge systems in an effort to better meet the needs of society. However, universities are themselves colonial institutions and extraordinary spaces of epistemic injustice (de Sousa, 2015). From a broader social perspective, we draw on the warning of Achebe to caution against relying too much on the university as an institution and structure of knowledge plurality and a universality of knowledge cultures. Rather, as we seek out spaces for survival, flourishing and living together, we need to perhaps recognise and validate a plurality of spaces where this can happen differently, with toleration, respect and dignity.

Note

1   Ndawula uses 'Ameripean' to reflect the shared hegemony of White European and American epistemic cultures.

References

Achebe, C. (2013). *Anthills of the Savannah*. Penguin UK.

Anzaldúa. (2012). *Borderlands: la frontera : the new Mestiza* (4th ed.). Aunt Lute Books.

de Sousa Santos, B. (2015). *Epistemologies of the South: Justice against epistemicide*. Routledge.

Hall, B. (1985). Research, commitment and action: The role of participatory research. *International Review of Education, 30*(3), 289–299. https://doi.org/10.1007/BF00597906

Hill Collins, P. (2017). Intersectionality and epistemic injustice. In *The Routledge handbook of epistemic injustice* (pp. 115–124). Routledge.

Husserl, E., & Merleau-Ponty, M. (2002). *Husserl at the limits of phenomenology.* Northwestern University Press.

Medina, J. (2017). Varieties of hermeneutical injustice 1. In *The Routledge handbook of epistemic injustice* (pp. 41–52). Routledge.

Monk, D., Openjuru, G., Odoch, M., Nono, D., & Ongom, S. (2020). When the guns stopped roaring: Acholi ngec ma gwoko lobo. *Gateways: International Journal of Community Research and Engagement, 13*(1), 1–15.

Monk, D., de Oliveira Jayme, B., & Salvi, E. (2019). The heART of activism: Stories of community engagement. *Engaged Scholar Journal: Community-Engaged Research, Teaching, and Learning, 5*(2), 61–78.

Ndawula, W. (2017). *The first Afro Native American Summit: At the source of the Nile.* Inclusion Press.

Odora Hoppers, C. A. (2009). From bandit colonialism to the modern triage society: Towards a moral and cognitive reconstruction of knowledge and citizenship. *International Journal of African Renaissance Studies, 4*(2), 168–180.

Odora Hoppers, C. A. (2021). Research on Indigenous knowledge systems: The search for cognitive justice. *International Journal of Lifelong Education, 40*(4), 310–327.

p'Bitek, O. (1984). *Song of Lawino & song of Ocol* (No. 266). Heinemann.

Pohlhaus, G. (2017). Varieties of epistemic injustice 1. In *The Routledge handbook of epistemic injustice* (pp. 13–26). Routledge.

Tandon, R., Hall, B., Lepore, W., & Singh, W. (2016). Training the next generation. In R. Tandon Tandon, B. Hall, W. Lepore, & W. Singh (Eds.), *Knowledge and engagement: Building capacity for the next generation of community based researchers* (pp. 7–39). University of Victoria and PRIA. http://unescochair-cbrsr.org/pdf/FINAL_Training_the_Next_Generation_2016.pdf

Tuana, N. (2017). Feminist epistemology: The subject of knowledge 1. In *The Routledge handbook of epistemic injustice* (pp. 125–138). Routledge.

Visvanathan, S. (2006). Alternative science. *Theory, Culture & Society, 23*(2–3), 164–169.

CHAPTER 9

Developing an Understanding of Traditional Maasai Water Practices and Technologies

Experiences from the Nyerere K4C Hub, Tanzania

Mwemezi Johaiven Rwiza, Haikael D. Martin and Ahmad Kipacha

Abstract

The African traditional knowledges and knowledge systems are on the brink of extinction. The indigenous knowledge of Africa has not been extensively studied and documented. In sub-Saharan Africa, the supremacy of colonial education in higher learning education has been responsible for erasing traditional knowledge. It is against this backdrop that a team of researchers from the Nyerere Knowledge for Change (K4C) Hub set out to investigate how traditional knowledges and modern, mainstream ways of knowing can be bridged. The study we report on was conducted in collaboration with the Maasai village leaders of Nduruma Village in Arusha, Northern Tanzania. Village committee meetings, interviews, group discussions, photograph taking, video recording, voice recording, and direct observation were among the methods used to gain knowledge on the Maasai traditional technologies of water management. The information gathered and shared in this case study contributes to building mutually beneficial expert-community partnerships.

Keywords

Maasai communities – Indigenous knowledge – knowledge cultures – decolonisation of knowledge – CBPR methods

1   Introduction

Currently led by the Nelson Mandela African Institution of Science and Technology (NM-AIST) in Arusha, Tanzania, the Nyerere Knowledge for Change (K4C) Hub is part of the Global K4C Consortium. The goal of the Nyerere Hub is to build community-based participatory research capacity to address the United Nations Sustainable Development Goals (SDGs), with a focus on

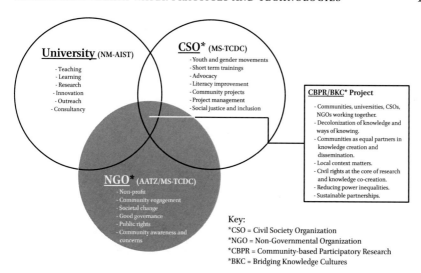

FIGURE 9.1   A pictorial representation of the diversity of the partners in the Nyerere Hub consortium and how the Bridging of Knowledge Cultures Project comes in

SDG4-6 and SDG13. This is done by designing and conducting educational programs aimed at developing research capacity for the co-creation of knowledge through collective action by professionals, community-based researchers, community groups, and academics.

The partners in the Nyerere Hub consortium form a university-advocacy-community triangle (Figure 9.1). The objectives, interests, and organisation culture within the consortium, although intersecting, may vary. For example, civil rights and advocacy, although important, are not the core business of the NM-AIST, which is a higher learning education (HLE) entity; but civil rights and advocacy form a core business for both the MS-Training Centre for Development Cooperation (MS-TCDC) and ActionAid Tanzania (AATZ). It was this variation in the Nyerere Hub consortium that fuelled the idea to research how traditional knowledge cultures, in this case the Maasai knowledge cultures, could reshape the mainstream thinking in HLEs, civil society organisations (CSOs), and non-governmental organisations (NGOs).

The NM-AIST is a typical colonised-education university characterised by a teacher-centered pedagogy rooted in Western science (le Grange 2019). Higher learning pedagogy rooted in postcolonial teaching and learning style has been shown to be less effective in the African learning context (ibid). For example, to date, six decades after independence, it is still rare for a Tanzanian, Mozambican, or Malawian construction company to win a contract of a multimillion-dollar road construction project. The curriculum at the engineering school the Tanzanian, Mozambican, or Malawian engineer has studied in is not directly tailored to their context, thus hindering effective practice (Blom et al., 2015; Kaplinsky & Kraemer-Mbula, 2022; Kithiia & Majambo, 2020; Sherratt & Aboagye-Nimo, 2022). In most cases, in sub-Saharan Africa, what people grow up learning in their local community is usually detached from what they come to learn later in school and university settings (Seehawer & Breidlid, 2021). Therefore, universities and research institutions in Tanzania, and in most of the sub-Saharan Africa, still struggle when it comes to university-community linkages. For economic and social development, education that takes into account the culture and values of the community may help to avoid a mismatch between the missions and visions of education institutions and community problems (Coman, 2016; Ponnuswamy & Manohar, 2016; Tierney, 1988).

The Nyerere Hub is generally embedded in a postcolonial knowledge environment characterised by walls and fences in which the co-creation of knowledge is difficult (Seehawer & Breidlid, 2021). The NM-AIST has a motto: "Academia for Society and Industry". However, NM-AIST trains its scholars using colonial tools and facilities, and the inclusion of 'society' has been questionable. MS-TCDC is, by design, an NGO (ActionAid – Denmark) and a CSO at the same time. The principles of community-based participatory research are key to the success of multipurpose and multicultural organisations such as MS-TCDC. The NGO culture is characterised by aid, donations, community involvement, empowerment, and advocacy, and this approach could serve communities better than the practice in higher learning education. However, emphasis on 'management for results' may mean that NGOs are more results-oriented than community-based (Claeyé, 2014). Furthermore, most NGOs are under pressure to operate as a 'business-like' organisation. This may pose some limitations on how NGOs deal with community problems. NGOs that use community-based approaches are known to be more successful compared to those that ignore the local contexts and community participation (Selman, 2004).

Rural communities of sub-Saharan Africa have an untapped wealth in the form of indigenous knowledge (Thakur et al., 2020), though this knowledge and associated practices ingrained in the local communities is gradually but steadily eroding and may even be lost in the next generations (Lwoga et al., 2010). The Nyerere Hub chose Maasai community water practices to learn how to better engage with community, consider prioritising research and projects that involve the community and action, and in doing so bridge the existing gaps between community knowledge and expert knowledge. The topic of water management addresses a multidimensional problem (ethics, rights, access, and management). The goal of the case study was to learn how universities and advocacy groups, CSOs and NGOs can work with communities on equitable terms. By analysing how a Maasai community manages its community water project, we explored the Maasai knowledge culture. Hub partners and Maasai village leaders narrated and co-investigated their different knowledge cultures. By mapping differences in the two knowledge cultures we aimed to better inform delivery of educational and other services which do not neglect inclusion and co-creation with indigenous knowledge, and help establish more egalitarian and resilient expert-community relations. The knowledge systems within the hub and the knowledge gathered in this case study will help establish more.

Beginning with an overview and general background of the hub members, this chapter moves on to the methodology used in the research and how the data was analysed. The section on findings discusses key lessons learned. The chapter concludes with some of the hub's plans to bridge the Maasai knowledge cultures with the work of the hub.

2 Study Area and Participants

This study was carried out in Nduruma, a village 40 km from Arusha city, Tanzania (Figure 9.2). The village has a population of 12,000 (National Census, 2012) and an average family size of 5. The main economic activities in the village are agriculture and livestock keeping.

In this case study, participants were of two types: (1) village leaders, elders and (2) representatives from the hub partners. The village leaders/elders

FIGURE 9.2   Learning with the Nduruma village water committee leaders

represented the people of Nduruma while the hub representatives were the researchers (experts). One of the hub partners had previously worked in this Maasai village on a different project. This prior engagement led to the selection of Nduruma village for the BKC case study.

All pictures used in this chapter were taken with consent from the participants.

3   Methodology

Structured and nonstructured interviews were used to initiate a community conversation with the Maasai village leaders. The interviews focused on how the traditional knowledge about furrow maintenance, water distribution, and irrigation management was acquired, retained, and transferred. For example, how do the Maasai communities come up with new irrigation technologies? Researchers also performed onsite observation by participating in the village committee meetings and taking notes of how the meetings are conducted. Through observation we gained information on leadership patterns in Maasai communities.

3.1   *Data Collection*
An introductory session preceded the village meetings. Facilitators kicked off the meeting by briefly introducing the role of community-based research in the decolonisation of knowledge (Figure 9.3), explaining that in community-based research there are no experts and laymen – we are co-learners and knowledge co-creators. The host villagers were excited to hear that their knowledge was valued and that not having formal education did not make them illiterate.

For triangulation purposes, different data collection tools were used. Also, different methods fit different environments better than others. Standard data collection methods such as interviews, observations, and focus groups were used. Participatory methods such as community mapping, photography, video recording, resource mapping, and story-telling were also used. A village leaders' workshop at NM-AIST was planned, but this was not possible due to time and budget constraints. The university was still determined to conduct at least one traditional knowledge workshop with the Maasai leaders. With signed consent (release letters), the village and the meetings were (1) recorded (voice), (2) filmed (video), and (3) photographed (pictures). As the meetings progressed, participants from the university and NGOs took notes in their notebooks. Voice clips, video clips, and pictures were taken using mobile phones. Maasai village leaders led the mapping of water and infrastructure resources by drawing on flipcharts. The flipcharts and marker pens were

FIGURE 9.3   The Nduruma water canal that serves Olmaroroi, Nduruma-Kati, and other subvillages in Mlangarini village. The canal passes through a largely semi-arid landscape of the Arusha region in Tanzania (Photo taken onsite)

brought in by the university participants. The interviews and discussions were held in Kiswahili (Swahili). Table 9.1 indicates how some of the methods were used during the study.

3.2   *Analysis*

The data collected was investigated by the hub team to consolidate lessons relevant to the BKC project. The hub team also reviewed the pictures taken in the field to identify the ones to use in this chapter. The videos were watched by the hub members to augment the lessons learnt from the discussion notes. Likewise, the voice recordings were played to ensure key messages were not getting missed. The messages were synthesized in a report under the following heads: (1) Village lifeline: the water canal; (2) Water resource sustainability: a living classroom; (3) Maasai knowledge system and knowledge culture; (4) Canal history: the water heritage; (5) Not agricultural, but pastoral: the leadership heritage; (6) Water governance; (7) Cultural modernization; and (8) Age-set system, democracy, and culture.

As a dissemination strategy, a summary of the report was printed and shared with the Maasai village leaders in a workshop. The printout summary and the presentation were in Kiswahili. This was done to ensure that all participants understood the content of the report. The hub partners led the discussions. Whenever disagreement occurred, the village chairman (Maasai elder) would intervene to narrate the correct information that should be included in the report. This has a bearing on in-hub power relations. Like in any other formal organisation, the Maasai have a leader who comes in to settle disputes. Unlike

TABLE 9.1   A summary of the methods used during the study

No.	Method/Tool	Procedures
1.	Interviews	The interview schedule with open-ended questions was prepared by the hub members. One hub member was selected to lead the question-and-answer session with other hub members allowed to join in the discussion by asking follow-up questions and/or giving clarification to enrich the discussion.
2.	Observation	The hub members accompanied by the Maasai elders walked around the village. During the walks, different features of the village were recorded by either taking photos or by jotting down what was being discussed in the notebooks. The purpose was to gain more understand of what the day-to-day life in a Maasai village setting is like.
3.	Focus group	Apart from the discussions that resulted from the interview questions, there were sessions that were led thematically, e.g., leadership practices, water resource management, the importance of indigenous knowledge, etc. This was done with a few selected elders to gain a deeper understanding of how systems work in the Maasai knowledge culture.
4.	Community mapping/resource mapping	We asked the elders to draw maps indicating natural resources and settlement arrangement with a focus on water resources distribution. This encouraged rich discussions about indigenous natural resource management among the Maasai.
5.	Photography/ video recording	The hub members were accompanied by a Maasai warrior (youth) who used a smartphone to take pictures in the village walks and during the meetings. During the introductory visits, the hub members helped the Maasai warrior learn how to take good pictures and videos using a smartphone.
6.	Storytelling	The village elders have a culture leader for their village who was also part of our field meetings. This Maasai elder narrated historical events relating to changes in climate and the changing of Maasai livelihood strategies. We also heard stories about how knowledge is transferred from one Maasai generation to another.

TABLE 9.2   A comparison of the Maasai traditional knowledge culture and higher learning education cultures

No.	Maasai knowledge culture	HLE knowledge culture
1.	Characterised by collective learning to improve the livelihoods of the whole community.	Individualistic and driven by personal achievements.
2.	Learning-intensive.	Teaching-intensive.
3.	Dominated by daily practice.	A mix of theoretical and practical components. In Africa, the theoretical component supersedes the practical component.
4.	Skills more important than achievements.	Importance laid on program completion and timely graduation with high grades.
5.	No accreditation bodies required.	Local and international accreditation an important feature.
6.	Gender segregation dominant.	Highly inclusive.
7.	Social values and age seniority over democratic practices.	Knowledge and democracy are compatible.
8.	High knowledge democracy. Knowledge acquired in an open community setting.	Operated under colonial principles. Knowledge walled in campuses, libraries, and auditoriums.
9.	Knowledge is a community property.	Copyrights and intellectual properties.
10.	Knowledge and skills are intergenerational and governed by culture and traditions.	Highly influenced by market forces. Demand-driven curricula.

in formal organisation settings, the Maasai leader must be a respected elder. Furthermore, in one of the focus group discussions, the village leaders were asked to compare the Maasai knowledge system against the formal education system. Their views were organised and are presented in Table 9.2.

4   Discussions

In the following discussions, the excerpts are transcriptions from the audio-video recordings of the village meetings.

4.1   *Lesson 1: Village Lifeline – The Water Canal*

We manage a water canal for livestock watering and irrigation purposes
(Figure 9.4). The water canal serves two sub villages of Nduruma-Kati and
Olmaroroi. But the canal goes as far as the neighbouring Mlangarini village. The water canal brings the village communities together to manage
the water in the canal as 'canal members' come from the two sub-villages
that were mentioned before, and from sub-villages in Mlangarini village.
However, the water canal is owned by the Olmaroroi sub-village. (Village
leader)

To us, the experts, and for the BKC project in particular, this was eye-opening.
The fact that a natural resource brought the community together through
shared knowledge on water management, led us to think can a resource and
knowledge that is at risk bring the hub partners together? As a follow-up, the
hub will run workshops in which the Maasai elders will be co-facilitators and
co-trainers – focusing on traditional natural resource management and fostering of indigenous knowledge. A recent study conducted in the indigenous
communities of Australia found that indigenous land and sea management
promoted knowledge exchange, and generated opportunities for both learning
and sharing to enhance the quality of life (Jarvis et al., 2021).

FIGURE 9.4   Preparation for a living classroom between formal education leaders and
traditional Maasai water canal leaders

4.2   Lesson 2: Water Resource Sustainability – A Living Classroom

This [the canal] is not just water; it is water for this and future generations. We are water stewards. There is a difference between wealth heritage and knowledge heritage. These are different. Our ancestors, the Maasai ancestors, made us inherit knowledge, not wealth. They did so with a purpose: they knew that by making us inherit good knowledge, we will definitely find wealth. This inheritance process works by ensuring that the Maasai child stays close to their father as the father performs his day-to-day duties. [*Note: the Maasai culture is predominantly patriarchal*]. As the child stays close to the father and sees his father working, they acquire knowledge, this is practical knowledge. But these fathers and grandfathers also acquire knowledge from their children and grandchildren. The children do not passively watch their elders to learn. These children work alongside their fathers and grandfathers. But, you know, children invent things. So, it is a living classroom for both groups – knowledge exchange between elders and the younger generation. (Maasai elder 1)

For sustainable university-community partnerships, the hub partners need to develop community-based curricula that has a large proportion of hands-on activities. As research by Bodorkós and Pataki (2009) indicates, for universities to sustainably work with communities, a possible methodology would be conducting participatory action research. This, they argue, would facilitate bottom-up sustainable planning and development in socio-economically disadvantaged rural communities. To this end, the hub members plan to work with communities on common research topics to address a community problem.

4.3   Lesson 3: Maasai Knowledge System and Knowledge Culture

Our knowledge system, unlike the [post-colonial type, colonized] classroom, is highly dynamic. Our knowledge system is based on values. Younger generations must respect older generations. We have a highly strict ethical system. We cannot separate values and ethics from knowledge. They go together. For example, the value we place on cattle is almost religious [laugh]. Your cattle, your life – we say. We almost look at our herds the same way we look at our fellow humans [laugh]. No cattle, no Maasai. We do not have [commercial] banking systems. Our livestock is our bank and our economy. Our traditional water management practices are somehow better than what is usually taught in formal [engineering] classes. We have had educated villagers come to our village with their classroom knowledge; very boastful. In most cases their classroom practices have failed, and these educated people end up getting frustrated. However, we have also had some educated people who came to live in our village, and they listened to us [we taught them how things work] and they live with us happily. We may not have received a formal education, but we know how life works here in the semiarid lands. We research, learn, and acquire knowledge while working. You fail, you do it again, until you pass. (Maasai elder 2)

The post-colonial, non-participatory, and teacher-centered model in higher education has largely failed Africa. A recent study of the Maasai students' experiences and their perception of the education process in Tanzania revealed that formal (post-colonial) education was challenging in a way that it was difficult for them to reconcile the requirements of their traditional life with those of formal schooling (Pesambili & Novelli 2021). It seems to us, that experts need to develop curricula that suits the needs of the community. In doing so, the bridging of knowledge cultures is inevitable. Curriculum design, development, and review must consider the needs of the immediate beneficiaries – the neighbouring community. Needs assessments, therefore, have to be community-based.

Community knowledge, handed down over generations, is not antagonistic to expert knowledge. The production, use, validation, and dissemination of community knowledge may revitalise university-community linkages by promoting local participation in higher education initiatives to counter the power asymmetries that usually hinder engagement with communities (Fernández-Llamazares & Cabeza, 2018). Social responsibility in higher learning requires academic and research institutions to open up to society's real problems, narrowing the expert-community power inequalities that exist (Bodorkós & Pataki, 2009). By borrowing experiences from local communities on how knowledge is generated and handed down from generation to generation, hub members may gain insights on how to practice a locally-relevant pedagogy. Our hub is currently not practicing this. The Nyerere hub will work with the neighboring Maasai communities to run workshops and informal classes for indigenous knowledge transfer.

4.4   *Lesson 4: Canal History – The Water Heritage*

This water canal was established a long time ago by our forefathers. They built it from scratch. This was during the colonial era [before

1961]. At that time, there were no established villages – the Maasai were living freely, there were no maps, no delimitations, no modern land use planning, etc. The water canal was a private property owned by two Maasai elders [late]: Toviwo and Elkeleyoni. There was no need for a village water committee because the canal was privately owned by the two elders. If someone wanted a portion of this water, they would bring a token (a bag of sugar or a goat) and request to be permitted to use the water. These were very powerful elders. People feared them. In the past [pre-independence], this village was not as arid as today. There used to be rivers [points to a nearby gully]; and from these large rivers, our elders dug trenches to transfer water to their pasturelands. It is dryer these days. So, this canal is even more important today than it used to be in the 1960s. (Village water canal supervisor)

This is a great lesson to the universities in Tanzania and the hub members, in particular. We can see how the Maasai communities have been changing their practices to respond to socio-political and socio-economic changes. The canal started as private property and later, as the circumstances changed, ownership of the canal became communal. We can also see that water canal management in the beginning was nondemocratic, but over time a more democratic natural resource management system was introduced. Unlike the general perception of many African elites, the traditional systems are not conservative and static. Instead of criticizing rural communities for not being progressive, the hub members need to work collaboratively with communities as they grapple with changing environments, including climate change (Mapfumo et al., 2013). For the Nyerere Hub members, this would mean that we visit communities when writing research projects, to co-generate project concept notes and write proposals that address the community's problems.

4.5   Lesson 5: Not Agricultural, but Pastoral – The Leadership Heritage

You may think that this canal was built to bring water to the village for irrigation. However, remember that the Maasai are traditionally pastoralists. Therefore, in the beginning, this water canal was made in order to bring water to the herds. Irrigation and smallholder farming came later, probably as a means to cope with the changing environments. Farming is new and when it started, most farmers depended on rains. When the rains became unreliable, these smallholder farmers began to ask for a portion of the canal water to irrigate their farms. Farming practices in our Maasai communities are, in themselves, a community classroom for knowledge production, sharing, and usage. This is something we are learning. It is a very practical classroom. We have no teachers, we teach ourselves. And we are learning from each other. When a neighbour fails, you learn from their mistakes and do something different. [Because of the changing climate and increasing population], the implementation of water canal management was necessary to avoid disputes and conflicts over water use. The Maasai knowledge system is a continuously evolving living classroom [or laboratory]. As we speak, we have formal leadership for our canal water distribution and management – since the late 1980s. We conduct whole-village meetings to elect leaders. (Village chairman)

This is a situation referred to by Brock-Utne (1996) as coming "to terms with the situation in which even the social construction of a people's reality is and has been constantly defined elsewhere" (p. 335). The African university (expert knowledge) is too 'westernised' to respond to the needs of Africa. African experts need to find its eyes in the eyes of her elders – in the rural 'unlearned' communities. The Nyerere Hub will advocate for a community-inclusive curriculum. Currently, stakeholders in curriculum development exclude the village and rural marginalised communities. Through our collaboration with the Maasai communities, the hub will seek community members' participation during curriculum development and review stages. The NGO and CSO hub members will initiate campaigns for community-inclusive curricula; the university hub member will create the modalities through which community voices can be tapped during development and review of academic and research curricula.

4.6   *Lesson 6: Water Governance*

In the beginning, there was no government interference with the village water committee leadership. The canal was managed according to the Maasai 'age set' system. Although the village government has a hand in the management of the water canal, the canal is still largely managed using traditional means. The elders are passing on the skills, knowledge, and culture of water management to the younger age groups. The elders are mentors, trainers, and teachers. The culture of water canal management is inheritable. It is passed on from one generation to another. The Maasai culture is a heritage one: one may go to formal school, but the governance structure is usually traditional. We listen to elders and prioritise herds over agriculture. It will probably always be that way. (Village chairman)

It would be of interest to the hub partners in the future to study the role of the Maasai age-set system on natural resource management in order to bridge the gap with indigenous knowledge cultures. In search for literature reflections on the Maasai age-set system and the role it plays in natural resource management, it was difficult to find published information on this subject. Bruyere et al. (2016) came close to decoding the role of the Maasai elders in transmitting knowledge to younger generations, recognising the scarcity of literature that explains traditional Maasai knowledge and how it can be passed on to future generations for sustainable environmental management.

4.7   Lesson 7: Cultural Modernization?

> The Maasai culture that used to be strict and strong, is gradually changing. The younger generations are slowly learning that farming can be equally profitable. They are learning from their non-traditionalist neighbours that having a smaller but well managed herd could be more profitable than having bigger but degraded herds. (Maasai elder 3)

In this change to more modern practices, there is a danger – the loss of traditional knowledge. Authors such as Bruyere et al. (2016) have said that

> Communities have shifted to alternative modes of traditional knowledge transmission when the historically familial modes are weakened, or as more viable alternatives develop. These new and non-familial avenues for knowledge transmission have often emerged when communities undergo social and economic changes. (p. 3)

The Nyerere hub, by working with the Maasai communities, will look for funding to establish the 'Maasai indigenous knowledge bank' to prevent valuable knowledge from getting lost.

4.8   Lesson 8: Age-Set System, Democracy, and Culture

> We vote to get village leaders. Voters vote for people who they think will uphold our Maasai traditions. In the past, it was impossible for the younger members of the community to be voted to lead because that was against the traditions. However, that is changing. We have young leaders, but the elders were satisfied that these young ones were cultured enough before they were elected. The elders were satisfied that the young leaders would follow the traditions. The Maasai age-set system is nonetheless

still respected. Without the age-set system, there will be no values. The age set system is basically a value system. The age-set system is traditionally highly-coded – a group of young men who went for circumcision during the same period, have a specific name that refers only to them. A mention of the age-set name is loaded with information – of the year that this group of people attended the circumcision rituals, definitely of an approximate year that this group of people were born. The name of that particular age-set also carries a meaning – heavy rains, disaster, plentiful harvest, droughts, etc. "Korianga", "Nyanguro", "Seuri", and "Makaa" are some of the Maasai age-set names, and they all have a meaning. The age-set names are made by a group of respected elders (the Laigwanans). They are not just random names. These names have a history imbedded in them. In our Maasai traditional (cultural) meetings, all age-sets participate. It is in such meetings where old-age knowledge is passed on from the very old generations to the younger generations. In such meetings, it is mostly the elders (the "Laigwanans") who lead the conversations; the younger age-sets sit and listen. The wise elders (the Laigwanans who are knowledge specialists, the) have a special name, they are also the clan leaders. The Laigwanans are more or less like presidents. (Maasai elder 4)

The strict Maasai age-set system draws many controversies. Some scholars have argued that the Maasai age-set system is incompatible to the modern education system and may lead to increased illiteracy among males in the Maasai communities (Rohoh et al., 2010). Other scholars have argued, however, that the introduction of modern schooling system into the traditional Maasai age-set system has empowered Maasai girls who, customarily, would have been relegated by the age-set system to domestic duties; modern education could then be a useful tool in the preservation of the Maasai culture (Archambault, 2017). The tensions that exist between the Maasai age-set culture and how these can be reconciled by bridging knowledge cultures is still subject to research. The Nyerere Hub will encourage conversations around gender inclusivity in meetings with the Maasai communities; the hub will also run conversations with the Maasai community on the role of inclusive education for community development.

5   Water and Other Resources Mapping

The Maasai conversations was followed by the water and other village resources mapping. A flipchart was hung on a sycamore fig tree by the water canal, and the Maasai leaders held marker pens to draw the village resources (Figure 9.5).

In the resource mapping session, the visiting researchers were surprised by how highly knowledgeable their village counterparts were. The completed resource map was excellent (Figure 9.6). The quality of the map was almost comparable to the Google map in Figure 9.2. This indicated that traditional knowledge and modern knowledge can be bridged to yield great results – although the Maasai elders did not go to a formal school to learn map drawing, they still could draw a good map, meaning that traditional knowledges and academic knowledge are synergistic. The question that is still bothering the research participants is: Why have African universities, to a large extent, ignored traditional knowledge? What we have included in Table 9.2 indicates that the postcolonial model university may not the 'only' best fit for African education. African scholarship needs to rethink the postcolonial knowledge model by embracing participatory approaches. The renewed movement for the decolonisation of the African university should be started by African scholars. The marginalization by postcolonial education of the cultural uniqueness of different African societies and the consequences this marginalisation carries cannot be overemphasised (Prempeh 2022).

After the resource map, the villagers drew the leadership pattern for their village, i.e., the village water leadership organogram (Figure 9.6). The organogram

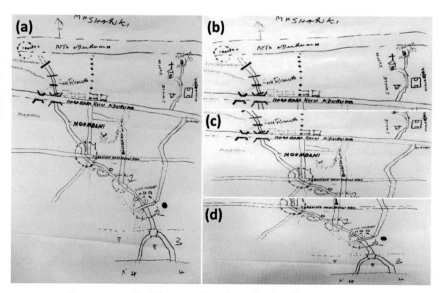

FIGURE 9.5   Resource map for Nduruma village drawn by the village water committee leaders – (a) the whole-village map, (b) to (d) zoom-in crops of the whole-village map

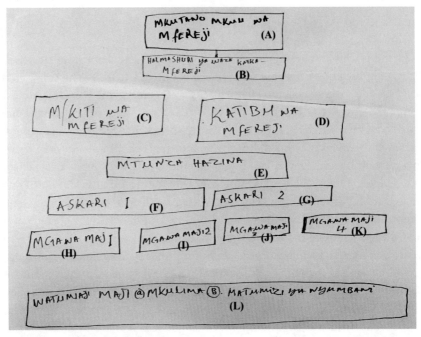

FIGURE 9.6   Village water canal leadership drawn by the water canal members of Nduruma
              village – (A) Village water canal general meeting; (B) The advisory council of
              elders; (C) Water canal chairperson; (D) Water canal secretary; (E) Water canal
              treasurer; (F) and (G) Water canal guards; (H) to (K) Water distribution persons;
              and (L) Water users

was simple and self-explanatory. The village water committee leaders did not
include lines or arrows to join the boxes. Power relations and power dynamics are interpreted. Apart from organised leadership, the Maasai follow the
culture-based traditional leadership that is difficult to draw – parallel to the
formal water management system there is a complex age-set system playing
in the background. This could be a reason why the village water committee
leaders avoided drawing lines and arrows in the water canal leadership organogram. The village water canal management practices were well organised, and
they were amicably optimised by the embedded culture and traditions. This a
good lesson to university hydrologists and water resource management professionals. It is also a lesson for NGOs and CSOs working in rural areas to ensure
access to safe and clean water for all. What the Western (North) literature
identifies as underdevelopment in Africa is probably replicated in the African
scholars' mindset (Chokor 2004; Njoh & Akiwumi 2012). Participatory research

methods could be used to mitigate the effects of the damaging colonial legacy in African HLE systems.

6 Maasai Knowledge versus Hub's Knowledge Systems: Bridging the Two Cultures

1. In Maasai traditional settings, knowledge is handed down over generations through storytelling and hands-on practice in which the younger generations learn from their elders. In the hub setting, knowledge is generated through scientific research, validated by reviewers, and shared through print media, videos, pictures, policy briefs, dissemination meetings, etc. By working together, methods such as storytelling, elder-youth engagement, practical skill impartation, whole-village meetings, and communal leadership used by the Maasai community to generate, validate, and transmit knowledge can be tapped by the hub members. Similarly, scientific technological methods such as observation, geo-mapping, photo-taking, and videography that are compatible with the Maasai culture may be transferred to the Maasai community in order to record and preserve their practices.

2. The hub members face difficulties relating to organisational change. The Maasai, although traditionally pastoralists, have managed to acquire and apply skills in agriculture and water management and transition into a pastoral-agricultural livelihood strategy. By working together, community knowledge on how to transition into a different business model may be beneficial to the hub members, who are accustomed to the NGO, CSO, university culture, i.e., the experts need to be less rigid to change, and learn to transition and operate in a way that is compatible for mutual understanding and enriched community engagement. The hub members should feel that it is their social responsibility to reach out and work with the Maasai community to document the livelihood transitions that the Maasai, have made in response to climate change and population growth.

3. Some cultural aspects of the Maasai culture are difficult (or so we felt) to bridge with the hub practices. While the age-set cultural aspect of the Maasai traditions is good for them, we felt that it marginalises women and girls and portrays elderly men as dominant figures in the community. The hub believes that the Maasai age-set system and its rigid structures will change as a result of community-CSO-NGO-university engagement.

4. The Maasai culture is loaded with power asymmetries, i.e., the position of the Laigwanans on social matters cannot be challenged. The Laigwanans are the community guardians whose word is final. Our hub strives for excellence in social and gender inclusivity. We acknowledge that there are some aspects of the Maasai culture that cannot be democratised. In the hub, we believe that as expert knowledge will gradually start change in response to including community knowledge, the same will happen in the Maasai community – and power inequities with also change.

Mutual change is essential for bridging knowledge cultures. Through co-generation, co-validation, and co-dissemination of knowledge, we hope the two knowledge systems will impact each other in a positive way. There are knowledge culture aspects such equal opportunity and gender-inclusive practices that the Maasai communities can acquire from HLE institutions and CSOs to positively complement their traditional practices. There are also many knowledge culture aspects such as skill-based practices, learning by doing, intergenerational handing down of knowledge, etc., that HLE institutions, NGOs, and CSOs can acquire from the Maasai knowledge culture. This is not only limited to water management practices and technologies but also to the learning environment, mode of teaching, value system, knowledge democracy, etc.

Acknowledgements

The research team would like to acknowledge the UNESCO Chair in Community Based Research and Social Responsibility in Higher Education for support and guidance. Many thanks to the Social Sciences and Humanities Research Council of Canada (SSHRC), Canada, for financial support. We would like to thank the Nelson Mandela African Institution of Science and Technology (NM-AIST), the MS-Training Center for Cooperation Development (MS-TCDC, ActionAid Denmark), and ActionAid Tanzania (AATZ) for supporting and hosting the Nyerere K4C Hub. The hub mentors are all appreciated. We, authors would like to thank the following village leaders and community members: Petro Toviwo Mollel, Mejool Toviwo Mollel, Elibariki Ng'idare, Alex Toviwo ole Merinye, Lucas Abraham, Mesiaki Mungaya, Sangau Toviwo Mollel, Peter Gombo, Thobias Ng'dare, Tayai Sumlei, and Jackson Lamiani. Many thanks to the then staff members at MS-TCDC and AATZ: Nkatha Mercy, Redimna Ginwas, and Zahra Mansoor.

References

Archambault, C. S. (2017). The pen is the spear of today: (Re)producing gender in the Maasai schooling setting. *Gender and Education, 29*(6), 731–747. https://doi.org/10.1080/09540253.2016.1156061

Blom, A., Lan, G., & Adil, M. (2015). *Sub-Saharan African science, technology, engineering, and mathematics research: A decade of development.* World Bank Publications.

Bodorkós, B., & Pataki, G. (2009). Linking academic and local knowledge: Community-based research and service learning for sustainable rural development in Hungary. *Journal of Cleaner Production, 17*(12), 1123–1131. https://doi.org/10.1016/j.jclepro.2009.02.023

Brock-Utne, B. (1996). Globalisation of learning: The role of the universities in the South, with a special look at sub-Saharan Africa. *International Journal of Educational Development, 16*(4), 335–346. https://doi.org/10.1016/S0738-0593(96)00055-7

Bruyere, B. L., Trimarco, J., & Lemungesi, S. (2016). A comparison of traditional plant knowledge between students and herders in northern Kenya. *Journal of Ethnobiology and Ethnomedicine, 12*(1), 48–48. https://doi.org/10.1186/s13002-016-0121-z

Chokor, B. A. (2004). Perception and response to the challenge of poverty and environmental resource degradation in rural Nigeria: Case study from the Niger Delta. *Journal of Environmental Psychology, 24*(3), 305–318. https://doi.org/10.1016/j.jenvp.2004.08.001

Claeyé, F. (2014). *Managing nongovernmental organizations: Culture, power and resistance.* Routledge.

Coman, A. (2016). Organizational culture in higher education: Learning from the best. *European Journal of Social Science Education and Research, 3*(1), 135–145.

Fernández-Llamazares, Á., & Cabeza, M. (2018). Rediscovering the potential of indigenous storytelling for conservation practice. *Conservation Letters, 11*(3), e12398.

Jarvis, D., Stoeckl, N., Larson, S., Grainger, D., Addison, J., & Larson, A. (2021). The learning generated through indigenous natural resources management programs increases quality of life for indigenous people: Improving numerous contributors to wellbeing. *Ecological Economics, 180*, 106899. https://doi.org/10.1016/j.ecolecon.2020.106899

Kaplinsky, R., & Kraemer-Mbula, E. (2022). Innovation and uneven development: The challenge for low- and middle-income economies. *Research Policy, 51*(2), 104394. https://doi.org/10.1016/j.respol.2021.104394

Kithiia, J., & Majambo, G. (2020). Motion but no speed: Colonial to post-colonial status of water and sanitation service provision in Mombasa city. *Cities, 107*, 102867. https://doi.org/10.1016/j.cities.2020.102867

le Grange, L. (2019). Rethinking learner-centred education: Bridging knowledge cultures. *Africa Education Review, 16*(6), 229–245. https://doi.org/10.1080/18146627.2018.1464642

Lepore, W., Hall, B. L., & Tandon, R. (2021). The knowledge for change consortium: A decolonising approach to international collaboration in capacity-building in community-based participatory research. *Canadian Journal of Development Studies/ Revue canadienne d'études du développement, 42*(3), 347–370.

Lwoga, E. T., Ngulube, P., & Stilwell, C. (2010). Managing indigenous knowledge for sustainable agricultural development in developing countries: Knowledge management approaches in the social context. *The International Information & Library Review, 42*(3), 174–185. https://doi.org/10.1016/j.iilr.2010.07.006

Mapfumo, P., Adjei-Nsiah, S., Mtambanengwe, F., Chikowo, R., & Giller, K. E. (2013). Participatory Action Research (PAR) as an entry point for supporting climate change adaptation by smallholder farmers in Africa. *Environmental Development, 5*, 6–22. https://doi.org/10.1016/j.envdev.2012.11.001

Njoh, A. J., & Akiwumi, F. (2012). Colonial legacies, land policies and the millennium development goals: Lessons from Cameroon and Sierra Leone. *Habitat International, 36*(2), 210–218. https://doi.org/10.1016/j.habitatint.2011.08.002

Pesambili, J. C., & Novelli, M. (2021). Maasai students' encounter with formal education: Their experiences with and perceptions of schooling processes in Monduli, Tanzania. *International Journal of Educational Research Open, 2*, 100044. https://doi.org/10.1016/j.ijedro.2021.100044

Ponnuswamy, I., & Manohar, H. L. (2016). Impact of learning organization culture on performance in higher education institutions. *Studies in Higher Education, 41*(1), 21–36.

Prempeh, C. (2022). Polishing the pearls of indigenous knowledge for inclusive social education in Ghana. *Social Sciences & Humanities Open, 5*(1), 100248. https://doi.org/10.1016/j.ssaho.2022.100248

Rohoh, A., Chiuri, L., Matheka, R., & Bor, E. (2010). Effects of Murran system's indigenous knowledge on Maasai youth's school attendance in Narok District, Kenya. *African Research Review, 4*(3). 1–23. https://doi.org/10.4314/afrrev.v4i3.60212

Seehawer, M., & Breidlid, A. (2021). Dialogue between epistemologies as quality education: Integrating knowledges in Sub-Saharan African classrooms to foster sustainability learning and contextually relevant education. *Social Sciences & Humanities Open, 4*(1), 100200. https://doi.org/10.1016/j.ssaho.2021.100200

Selman, P. (2004). Community participation in the planning and management of cultural landscapes. *Journal of Environmental Planning and Management, 47*(3), 365–392.

Sherratt, F., & Aboagye-Nimo, E. (2022). Decolonizing occupational safety management: The case of construction site safety culture in Ghana. *Safety Science, 151,* 105732. https://doi.org/10.1016/j.ssci.2022.105732

Thakur, R., Rane, A. V., Harris, G., & Thakur, S. (2020). Future prospective and possible management of water resources in respect to indigenous technical knowledge in South Africa. In P. Singh, Y. Milshina, K. Tian, D. Gusain, & J. P. Bassin (Eds.), *Water conservation and wastewater treatment in BRICS Nations.* Elsevier.

Tierney, W. G. (1988). Organizational culture in higher education: Defining the essentials. *The Journal of Higher Education, 59*(1), 2–21.

CHAPTER 10

Bridging Knowledge Cultures in Rural Health Education

The Trompsburg Project at the South African (North) K4C Hub

Lesley Wood, René Walter Botha, Beatrix (Bibi) Bouwman,
Hendri Coetzee, Alfi Moolman and Karen Venter

Abstract

Devaluing African indigenous knowledge during the apartheid years has implications for how the still marginalised populations that the Trompsburg Project works with in service-learning and community-based research respond to, and behave within, a working partnership. Using the Interprofessional Health Education (IPE) project, in which students from various health professions engage with a rural community to improve local health outcomes, the authors of this case study explore the different knowledge cultures and how they contribute to the power differentials between university and community partners, interrogating concepts of democratisation of knowledge, knowledge validation and dissemination of knowledge, to help understand how universities can begin to change perceptions and behaviour within CURPs.

Keywords

health – knowledge democratisation – levels of knowledge – structure of knowledge – power differentials

1 Introduction

International literature positions community engagement (CE) as an essential feature of the contemporary university (e.g., Farner, 2019; Hall & Tandon, 2021; Welch & Plaxton-Moore, 2017), with many South African researchers also contributing to the debate (e.g., Musesengwa & Chimbari, 2017; Mtshali & Gwele, 2016; Smith-Tolken & Bitzer, 2017). For over twenty years, policy (Department of Education, 1997) in South Africa has stipulated community engagement as one of the three core activities of public universities. Most South African universities now boast elaborate policies to govern CE within their institutions and require academics to integrate it into their core activities. Moreover, institutions are obliged to deliver an annual report on their social impact to the Ministry of Higher Education and Training (Higher Education Quality Committee, 2004). To increase their social impact, engaged researchers can build mutually beneficial community-university research partnerships (CURP) to enable service-learning and community-based research. Such partnerships are necessary to generate knowledge that is useful, relevant and responsive to local social issues and needs (Wood, 2022) and to inform research agendas and CE strategy. However, this is easier said than done as it requires a drastic paradigm shift on the part of both university and community partners. Specific ideas within the academy about the ownership, validity and purpose of knowledge have been built up over centuries and are not easily discarded. These ideas can be summarised as a specific academic knowledge culture (Travica, 2013). Likewise community partners also have their own knowledge cultures. The aim of this chapter is to indicate what these differences are in the field of Health Education through referring to a case study of an existing community-based education project. The ultimate aim of generating an improved understanding of the different knowledge cultures is to reduce power inequalities between the different partners so that they can converge them to more effectively and sustainably address relevant development goals. Five of the authors of this paper are members of the South African (North) Knowledge for Change (K4C) hub, part of an international network co-ordinated by the UNESCO Chairs for Community-based Research and Social Responsibility in Higher Education. This hub is a collaboration between North-West University and University of the Free State. First, we position our discussion of knowledge environments within the context of South African society.

2   The Historical and Political Knowledge Environment in South Africa

In countries with a colonial history, such as South Africa, indigenous knowledge was basically eradicated through legislation and practices designed to favour the dominant minority. De Sousa Santos (2014) coined the term *epistemicide* to describe the process of gradual devaluation and extinction of local knowledges. The legacy of colonialism still negatively impacts on education and development in the African continent. In South Africa, however, the situation was compounded further by nearly 50 years (1948–1994) of apartheid rule following independence from the United Kingdom in 1910. The years between 1910–1947 saw the introduction of legislation that increasingly restricted the rights of non-Whites in the country. Christian National Education (CNE), the curriculum adopted by the Afrikaner regime, aimed to "[indoctrinate] all children in Nationalist ideology from the nursery school right through beyond the university or technical college" (Van Henyningen, 1980, p. 50). Nationalist ideology viewed the world through the lens of the doctrine of the Dutch Reformed Church and any deviation from this way of thinking and being was condemned as sinful and wrong. Racial separation was justified by scriptural injunction, reducing non-Whites to the level of children who should consent to be cared for by their wiser and more morally upright White counterparts (Dubow, 1992). Indigenous culture was regarded as barbaric, and this ideology suggested that non-Whites needed to be educated to think and behave in accordance with nationalist doctrine or, if they wanted to continue with cultural practices, they should move to designated homelands, which were undeveloped and underserved rural areas. CNE thus determined what should be learnt and by whom, and such epistemological brainwashing naturally takes years to eliminate. Harper (2012) explained how this knowledge dominated and manipulated the minds of all, causing Whites to believe they were superior and Blacks (particularly those of African origin) to feel inferior. It is known that the oppressed learn to assimilate the knowledge and behaviours of the oppressor in a bid to raise their social standing and feel better about themselves (Fiske & Ladd, 2004), and thus indigenous knowledge and practices are further devalued by the indigenous groups themselves. The education system was thus impacted by this knowledge environment.

3   Knowledge Environment of the South African Education System

Mandela (1994) is often cited as saying that "Education is the most powerful weapon which you can use to change the world", but of course it depends on what epistemological foundations that education is based. Education systems are rooted in a specific philosophy, which in turn creates a knowledge culture. A racist ideology thus creates a hegemonic knowledge culture that represses the production and dissemination of any paradigm rooted in a culture of universal human rights; it validates its own knowledge culture through indoctrination, oppressive legislation and systematic disempowering of other race-groups. Apartheid used education to promote the "strategic dehumanization" (Memmi, 2013, p. 23) of the majority of the South African population through racial segregation, differing curriculums and unequal distribution of resources at both school and tertiary level.

Thus, transformation of education has been the focus of post-apartheid education policy. It is important to know this history because it has implications for how the still marginalised populations that we work with in service-learning and community-based research respond to, and behave within, a working partnership. Longstanding social and economic inequalities have not reduced despite progressive legislation. Poverty, unemployment, crime, health disparities have risen in recent years (Francis & Webster, 2019), and it is within this context that the gap between university and community knowledge cultures has also increased. Moreover, the predominant ivory tower image and paternalistic approach to knowledge sharing between higher education institutions and communities further propagates the devaluation of community/ indigenous knowledge. Community engagement is one of the key approaches to bringing about change at tertiary level to shatter this ivory tower and promote collaboration for knowledge production between university and community.

For successful establishment of working partnerships for knowledge creation between the university and community, there is a need to dispel the "epistemic disjuncture" (Hall, 2010, p. 3) between how knowledge is respectively created, structured and validated in universities and communities. Policy may mandate the university to be more socially responsive and work with community partners to co-create knowledge, but as Delport (2005) has pointed out, accompanying paradigm shifts in the stakeholders implementing the policies is a slower yet essential process for real transformation to occur. Likewise, community partners have to learn to believe in their own ability to make valuable contributions to the generation of new knowledge (Wood & Zuber-Skerritt, 2021).

4   Institutional Knowledge Environments of the Universities Involved in the K4C Hub

University of the Free State and North-West University were both formerly Afrikaans institutions,[1] whose curriculum and culture reflected the nationalist ideology and Calvinistic theology. Both universities have since merged with formerly Black institutions to form multi-campus organisations. The unitary culture and alignment have taken place slowly over the past few years. Both institutions are driven by the values contained in the South African constitution, especially human dignity, equity and freedom. Their constitutions promote tolerance and respect for all perspectives and belief systems to ensure a suitable environment for teaching, learning, research and community engagement. The allocation of bursaries, funding projects and loans are used as a mechanism to make higher education accessible to historically disadvantaged students. However, successful completion of programmes among this demographic remains significantly lower than their historically advantaged counterparts, with more than 30% of non-White students dropping out before completion (Council on Higher Education, 2018).

Notwithstanding the still unequal outcomes, concerted efforts over recent years indicate the commitment of higher education to adopt an engaged approach to scholarship (Beaulieu et al., 2018) to be more responsive to societal needs. Community engagement is an umbrella term that is used by universities to include engaged research in mutually beneficial partnerships with diverse communities and engaged teaching and learning which is delivered through service-learning or work integrated learning. Both universities also subscribe to contributing to the scholarship of engagement and therefore all CE activities have a strong engaged research approach. One of the recent initiatives is the creation of a Knowledge for Change (K4C) hub that spans both universities. The current mentors in our K4C hub come from the disciplines of education and health sciences, as well as from institutional directorates of community engagement, with memoranda of understanding with local community organisations. The mission of the hub is to enable the university to become more socially responsible through conducting community-based teaching, learning and research. Yet, although in theory there is a growing acceptance of the need to embrace indigenous and local knowledge to address the many societal problems that hinder attainment of the United Nations' Sustainable Development Goals (SDGs), and an awareness that modern science may not have all the answers (Diaz et al., 2018), in practice traditional 'scientific' views of knowledge still tend to prevail, and community knowledge is not yet sufficiently valued (Wood, 2020).

Exploration of the different knowledge cultures and how they contribute to the power differentials between university and community partners is thus necessary and justified to help us understand how we can begin to change perceptions and behaviour within CURPs. This paper reports on findings from research undertaken to interrogate concepts such as the democratisation of knowledge (e.g., who has the right to create knowledge), the validation of knowledge (e.g., who decides if knowledge is valid, useful, etc.) and the dissemination of knowledge (e.g., who will have access to the knowledge and how will those in the know gain access). We also analyse complex issues such as the level of knowledge (e.g., whether knowledge is entrenched or superficial), the generality of knowledge (e.g., whether knowledge can be simplified and/or made understandable for people who struggle to access it), the level of atomization of knowledge (i.e., uptake), the modality of knowledge (i.e., what form it takes – written, oral, visual etc.), and the structure of knowledge (i.e., conceptual, declarative, procedural). We chose as the case study a project within the Faculty of Health Sciences at the University of the Free State, where students from various health professions engage with a rural community to improve local health outcomes. The programme is known as the Interprofessional Health Education (IPE) project. We now explain some of the key concepts underpinning our theoretical framework for CE.

5   Knowledge Cultures

In the literature, knowledge culture usually refers to how knowledge is managed in organisations (Travica, 2013). In the context of this paper, we conceptualise it as the way knowledge is respectively created, validated and disseminated in and by the university and in and by community. Knowledge creation within the university has traditionally been a result of rational, cognitive and technical procedures undertaken by 'accredited' academics (Cetina, 2007). The validity and usefulness of this scientific knowledge was not questioned so long as peers judged it to adhere to strict academic conventions. This understanding of knowledge is on the opposite end of the continuum from practical or experiential knowledge, whose validity is tested not by some predetermined criteria, but by how well it solves the problem at hand (Travica, 2013). The creation of so-called scientific knowledge is separate from the creator. Objectivity is key, and the foremost aim is to contribute to theory, rather than be of practical use.

In terms of public health professionals, the focus of our case study, scientific knowledge is akin to factual information, such as knowing how to avoid transmission of HIV. It does not take into consideration the life circumstances and beliefs of the target population and assumes that if people know the biomedical facts, they will adjust their behaviour accordingly. Of course, we know this is not so since cultural beliefs and practices tend to wield more influence over people's behaviour, as the persistent high rate of HIV infection in South Africa shows (Kilburn et al., 2018). It is therefore important that health care professionals understand the cultural beliefs and knowledge systems of those they serve, since these influence the uptake and impact of health education. Although both parties may have a shared goal – improved health within the community – the various knowledges that they hold can either work for or against positive health outcomes (World Health Orgnisation, 2020). Thus, it is imperative to identify the differences between these diverse knowledge cultures to bridge them for mutual benefit.

The aim of service-learning and community-based research is to create a space where knowledge can be democratically generated for the purpose of reducing social injustices, such as health inequities, and improving life for all (Hall & Tandon, 2015; Kemmis, 2010). Knowledge democracy embraces epistemic diversity where the "intellectual colonialism" of the traditional academy is replaced by an "ecology of knowledges" (de Sousa Santos, 2017, p. 7) in which diverse types and representations of knowledge are welcomed and acknowledged as being equally valuable and valid. Unlike in traditional, theory-driven research or philanthropic approaches to service-learning, in community-based research participants reflect on power relations to reduce them so that everyone can contribute what they know and determine how they want that knowledge to be used. In other words, diverse knowledge cultures converge to form a knowledge democracy, with the aim of bringing about sustainable improvement in the lives of all. In the next section, we explain the context of the study.

6   Context of the Case Study

The University of the Free State (UFS) Trompsburg community-based IPE and rural health project, conducted in the Xhariep District of South Africa's Free State Province, was considered as a unique context for an in-depth exploration of the participants' subjective experiences to identify knowledge differences/gaps and recommendations to bridge them. The Trompsburg community lies just off the main N1 motorway about an hour's drive from Bloemfontein, the capital city of the Free State. According to the 2011 census (most recent available to the public), it has a population of 1,880 (Black 37.8%; Coloured 41.3%; White, circa 18.7%; 2.2% others). The dominant language is Afrikaans (68%), with Sesotho as the other main language. Although a rural area, due to its strategic geographical location, it boasts a well-equipped hospital. Apart from the hospital, the main employment is on local farms and shops that serve the community. The unemployment rate in 2011 was 7% but one can suppose it is now higher in line with the national increase.[2] Most households have running water and electricity, but many of them also live close to the poverty line (Department of Corporate Governance and Traditional Affairs, 2020).[3]

The engagement initiative established in the Southern Free State includes collaboration and knowledge sharing between groups of individual community members diagnosed with diabetes mellitus and IPE student groups (nursing, nutrition and dietetic, occupational therapy, physiotherapy, medicine and biokinetics). The aims are to improve health outcomes by establishing Lifestyle Groups (LG) to enable sharing of health information among participants, and thereby encourage sustainable, accountable lifestyle practices. The engagements with these LGs include home visits by students, accompanied by community healthcare workers, to conduct holistic screenings, as well as two-hour weekly LG meetings to discuss topics proposed by the LG members, facilitated by IPE student groups. During the Covid-19 pandemic virtual engagement in this low technology environment included telephonic discussion between students and LG members, the distribution of pamphlets themed around feedback from surveys regarding the current needs of group members, low contact shortened home visits, and the loan of university equipment to enable LG members to self-monitor their sugar levels and blood pressure. These student-community engagements are supervised and monitored by academic personnel. The methodology we adopted in this case study will now be discussed.

7   Methodology

We adopted a qualitative design (Nassaji, 2020) to understand how participants perceived the different facets of knowledge generation, use and dissemination within the community-based initiative. The co-ordinator of the project invited students, academics and community members involved in the IPE programme to participate, after explaining to them the purpose of the project and what was expected of them. The interviews with academics and students were conducted on the university campus but since some of these participants requested online sessions, we decided to conduct semi-structured interviews rather than use more participatory strategies for data generation. Semi-structured interviews meant that the six interviewers (authors of this paper) could use the same questions for all participants, with some latitude to probe (Segal et al., 2006). This would help to ensure that the data from all the interviews would be comparable and useful for answering the research questions guiding our case study. Six IPE students, five academic staff involved in the programme and ten community members who attended the LGs run by the students agreed to participate in the study in response to a general invitation to all. Due to Covid-19, the regular LG face-to-face sessions had been suspended for some time but we provided transport for the community members to come to the facility where they normally had their sessions. We provided refreshments for them as a token of gratitude for their time, in line with acceptable ethical practices in community-based research (Wood, 2020). Interviews were conducted in either English or Afrikaans, depending on the choice of the participants. Unfortunately, we were not able to accommodate Sesotho, but all participants were fluent in at least one of the two languages mentioned and no interpreter was necessary.

The questions asked are listed below and where necessary, the interviewers rephrased them to aid understanding.

- Do you think that the knowledge you bring and create within a research partnership matters? Explain why or why not.
- How do you think you can best partner with the university/community to ensure the democratisation of knowledge? (i.e., that all can generate knowledge, not just university researchers).
- Who has the right to create knowledge and who should own it within the partnership?
- What are the best methods to generate knowledge in community engaged research/education?
- What kind of knowledge is valid and useful to you as a community member/ educator?
- How can the knowledge be generalised (made more understandable) to enable more people to access it?
- How should knowledge be disseminated/mobilised for the greatest impact?

The audio-recorded interviews lasted between 30–60 minutes each and were transcribed verbatim by an independent person. The transcriptions were done in the language of the interview. The members of the research team then analysed the transcripts to identify themes (Creswell & Creswell, 2017) that spoke to the knowledge cultures of the respective participants and the existing power relations that guided their interaction. After individually identifying the themes, the team met to validate them and make changes where necessary. We are aware that this rather one-sided method of data generation and analysis is not in line with the principles of community-based research but, given the Covid-19 restrictions which had prohibited us from doing any research for several months, this was the most efficient and safe way to conduct the research in the limited time available. Trustworthiness of data was ensured by triangulation of data sources (three sets of participants), peer debriefing of the research team after the interviews, avoidance of inferences and generalisations, avoiding the selective use of data, as well as independent re-coding by different team members before coming together to reach consensus (Flick, 2018). The usual ethical considerations applicable to qualitative research (Neuman, 2011) were employed and the study received ethical clearance from both universities involved (NWU-00782-18A2/UFS-HSD2021/1063/3108) attesting that it adhered to their stringent ethical requirements.

8   Findings

We now present the findings in relation to the main questions outlined in the introduction to this paper: Who has the right to create knowledge? Who decides if knowledge is valid? Who will have access to the knowledge? The findings are supported by verbatim quotes from the participants who are identified by the following codes: A*n* (academics); S*n* (students); CM*n* (community members). Findings are also controlled against relevant literature. In each theme we explore the power relations within the partnership in relation to the respective knowledge cultures.

8.1   *Theme 1: Knowledge Creation and Sharing*
The nature of the engagement determined to a certain extent the kind and level of knowledge that was created and shared within the partnership. Since the instigator of the relationship was the university, to meet their need of providing practical experience for the students and services to the community, the knowledge shared with the community was initially pre-determined and based on biomedical science. However, as reported below, the community also created and shared knowledge with the students within the LGs. The Trompsburg project enables the university to research the changing process of engagement via a service-learning and community-based education programme, and it was thus ideal as a case study to explore the mutually beneficial partnership that has been established over recent years.

An important part of the relationship was sharing, rather than creating, knowledge with the community about how to live a healthier lifestyle and manage/reduce their level of lifestyle-related disease since this project was conceived as community education, with a focus on teaching and learning, rather than a research partnership. Students had little choice in whether they want to be part of the partnership or not, as it is an integral component of their course. As A4 indicated, the "work is outcome driven, guided by what the students need to achieve".

Feedback from one academic indicates that the university tended to take the lead in terms of research, determining what services are rendered and who benefits from them since they control the funding. The university sourced the funds to implement the rural community initiative and has the fiduciary responsibility to the funders to manage them well and in accordance with the funder's criteria for use. Only one academic mentioned the power accorded to the university in this respect, which implies that extant power relations tend to deter any questioning about how funds are spent, even although the needs of the community might warrant the funds to be spent in other areas than those determined by the university:

> So, this whole was initiated and driven by the university, which is correct. They arranged money and sponsorship, and so the university attempted to provide that service, which, which I think is great ... the problem, the underlying problem is that the university is dependent on sponsorship research money. And so, they can initiate things if they give them money for that. (A1)

The above remark implies that the university is also vulnerable as it relies on outside sponsorship which could be withdrawn at any time, which may force the services they render in the community to come to an end. The institutional knowledge environment thus influences the relationship with funders, who could be seen to dictate what research is conducted and how. Universities often rely on financial investments from corporate donors (stock exchange listed companies) that have to spend corporate social investment (CSI) funding to contribute to the development of the country. These industry partners have developed various sets of rules in terms of how they wish to see return of investment of their donations in order to be able to report to their shareholders and to determine the impact that was made by their donations. Funders have to comply with the legislation and guidelines of King IV on corporate governance (King, 2016) and the Inyathelo guidelines for social investment (Next Generation, 2021). Unfortunately, pervasive corruption has dominated all spheres of public and government life in South Africa and this situation has forced private sector funders to apply very stringent controls over how and where their CSI funds are spent (Patel & Govindasamy, 2021).

In terms of the reciprocity of knowledge sharing, the perceptions of the academics were mixed, with some thinking that the students learnt a lot from the community about what life is really like in contexts of poverty and how resilient community members can be, which they would not otherwise learn from their lecturers. "Everyone learns from everyone ... so yes, I think knowledge is being conveyed from one group to another, and vice versa" (A3) and others saying that it was the university who provided the information "with knowledge that we can give them" (A2). The students were aware of the need "to learn from the community" (S4), as knowledge creation should be "an equal partnership" (S4). The knowledge that the community provided was less medical, and more about context, e.g., how difficult it was to afford more healthy food options. This does not make it any less valuable, as uptake of medical knowledge is very context dependent (Kressin et al., 2019). The community members themselves regard the medical knowledge shared by the IPE team as valid ("And we have to do what we hear, we have to do it. We cannot just do our own thing" – CM5; "We learned a lot from them, you cannot tell them anything about diabetes" – CM2). At the same time, community members enjoyed it "when they listen when you tell them something no, so, not so" (CM3). This community member was proud of the fact that she "taught" the student about how drinking water can help to improve vision. She said she knew this, because she had experienced this benefit herself. On the whole, the community members felt they "were part of the team" (CM10) when it came to making decisions about what knowledge was important to be shared as they were asked each week what they would like to talk about the next time. Community members also conveyed their knowledge through storytelling, which is a form of knowledge sharing embedded in traditional African culture ("A grandma teaches you with stories, she sits with you, teaches you, tells you that story to allow you to understand" – CM6). Some community members indicated that they enjoyed learning through visual and participatory methods but that this was only used on occasion by the students.

The findings also indicate that both university and community can take the lead in knowledge management. As far as ownership of knowledge goes, there was agreement that it belonged to everyone, that it should be "shared and not owned" (A5) and that "the shared knowledge belongs to all of us" (CM10). One student even referred to experiential knowledge (as opposed to research-based knowledge) as "expert knowledge" created by people "who all see things differently" (S1). The academics who facilitate the programme recommended that local facilitators should be used to harness local knowledge and equalise power relations: "In my perception of primary health care, about a third of the educators of that programme should actually be local people" (A2).

There are some local educators at present, but they tend to be highly qualified people who live in that area, rather than grassroots community members who could share their experiential knowledge of living in challenging circumstances and trying to live healthily.

Even if the current knowledge cultures tend to skew power relations in favour of the university, there was acknowledgement by academics that this needed to change and that it should not be "a top down approach ... for me it is a partnership ... a partnership between me and the community to thereby transfer and share knowledge" (A2). Another commented that they needed to engage community at all levels of the project to make it a truly collaborative effort:

> I think, definitely the community can be there to generate knowledge, not just that we come here and make them guinea pigs, but ... they must form part you know, in terms of like, active research that they form part of the whole process and actually from the get go, that they must also give their input and that we must ensure that where they buy in that they feel part of this whole knowledge creation. (A5)

Another academic insisted that the community should be "asked what they need, or make sure that we don't just go there and put info in their heads, which does not matter to them" (A3). These opinions indicate that the academics working on the programme realise the importance of reciprocal relationships but that perhaps the programmatic bureaucracy of the university system has not allowed them to practice true collaboration. From the perspective of true collaboration and equal power relationships, the context of the programmatic bureaucracy of the university system does limit the control over some of the community needs that are currently addressed. The obvious example is the needs that are addressed are not only influenced by the IPE, but also by the funders of the programme and what the funds are purposed for. Funders in general are from the private sector and require strict reporting and seek a good return on investment for their shareholders. Students too felt it important to involve the community in an analysis of their needs and then tailor the health intervention to suit, rather than just deciding for them (S5). Currently the students and academics do listen to the needs of the community in terms of what they want to learn and attempt to meet those needs, but to a greater extent it is still a matter of students providing the information to community, rather than community being completely involved in meeting their own needs.

It does appear that academics learn from the community about things other than just medical issues ("my knowledge broadens and I get a new perspective on life every time I go" – A3; "making food here, how I test myself, and how if I don't have it, I can use another way" – A2). Also, what the students learn from the community members they interact with contributes to their development as professionals as they "understand the circumstances and the role that these circumstances play ... their impact from a community perspective" (S1).

The relationship with the students also enables community members to access additional information, rather than just treatment.

> I could see that the people are hungry for knowledge, they crave for what we can give them. They made it clear that they need this knowledge because they don't always get it from the clinics because the clinics don't always have the time to pay attention to their search for knowledge. Attention is only paid to their immediate physical, medical needs, but not to what else they want to know. (S2)

In summary, although the knowledge shared with the community was mostly controlled by the university, it is also clear that the community valued this knowledge and adapted it to their own needs. University academics involved in the project appeared to value the knowledge brought by the community, but it is doubtful if this is the general attitude within the university, indicating the need for capacity building in this area. What knowledge is considered valid, is thus an important aspect to interrogate.

8.2   Theme 2: Knowledge Validation

Academics are also open to indigenous knowledge, or knowledge passed down over the generations ("and that [indigenous knowledge] is also a form of knowledge creation" – A5). Students agreed and thought this type of lay knowledge should be explored ("If they found that this was actually working much better then it might be something we need to explore" – S5). However, that knowledge could not be validated until it was then "scientifically proven" (S4) through research by the university. For example, one community member shared how they lick the molasses given to cattle, as it contains specific vitamins and minerals that help to combat against disease (CM1); another explained how they use cannabis tea to lower blood pressure (CM7). However, it was interesting that community members did not always consider this type of knowledge as valid and worth sharing with the students. As C3 said, "We licked it as children but did not know that it was medicine. Now we realised it is iron. We did not share it with the students".

Community members also have the capacity to work out how best to treat specific illnesses, as one student was surprised to learn when a community member "figured out what to do for her diabetic foot" (S5) on her own before an appointment could be made with the physiotherapist. A novel suggestion for a "community review" (S4) stressed the need to conduct ongoing community-based research within the partnership so that both parties can learn how they need to improve their collaboration in their mutual quest to improve health outcomes. Another aspect that such dialogue could cover is how the knowledge is shared and used in the wider community.

Although we did not interview the primary health care workers (PHCW) that the students work with on a daily basis due to the Covid situation (they were not available at the site), it appears that students in general respected them, unlike some specialist doctors who felt their knowledge was superior to that of the PHCW and that they had nothing to learn from them. This issue was regarded as a serious one by one of the academics, as they are also local people who hold contextual knowledge that will influence diagnosis and treatment options:

> Well, he (primary health care worker) understands the context of the disease he treats. So if I'm a young person and I go straight into my speciality, I will disregard health workers in the primary care because I am a specialist and much more important. I actually know everything and the stupid community just can't do their thing. And that gap is, is a big problem. (A1)

In other words, by excluding the knowledge of the community-based health workers, it negated its value. This highlights the importance for the principles and paradigm of community engagement to be part of the training of all health professionals so that they begin to understand the value of listening to local people to learn how the community lifestyle and circumstances affect the prevalence and treatment of disease. This would include local professionals who were seen to have valuable insights to share to guide the university team in their decision-making about what knowledge to share and how to share it (S1).

8.3   Theme 3: The Dissemination and Use of Knowledge

Students and academics thought that the language used for sharing health information should be in "layman's terms" (S1) and "available in terms of the language of the people" (A5). Students also realised that they had to communicate on the level of the community ("I think the first thing is to ... make the community feel like okay, I am not above you I am here ... on your level" – S6). However, students could not always communicate in the language of the community members and this presented a barrier (S1). This speaks to the importance of having a diverse team so that interpreters can be called in if needed.

Another interesting point made by community members is that the relationship with the students enables them to access information that they would not have got otherwise as they are reluctant to visit the clinic to seek treatment for what they perceive to be minor issues:

> when you maybe have a wound, then the student tells you that you must go to the clinic, they will take you. We did not work like that. We always thought we had to wash that wound with hot water and salt. (CM1)

They also perceive that the knowledge they gain enables them to control their own health, thus imbuing them with personal power ("We believe in the knowledge we get from the students. Now that is what we take and we use it" – CM1). Knowledge gained by students on home visits pertaining to specific patient's home circumstances is shared with the health care professionals at the clinic and hospital so that they have a better idea of how the lived experiences of the patient might impact their health or treatment of ailments ("This information is shared with the local clinic, who in turn use the information to make decisions or to compile basic stats" – A2). Regarding sustainability of improved health outcomes, both students and academics thought it was important that "the community, when we are not there anymore, the community must still continue" (A4). This implies that community must be enabled to disseminate knowledge and become community educators who can run their own education sessions.

Currently, knowledge sharing is more on a one-to-one basis by community members and limited to repeating what they learned by participating in the LG ("And when I have guests that also have diabetes, I talk to them and share what we learned at the Lifestyle Group" – CM2). One community member (CM5) collated information from pamphlets supplied by the students into a book to enable her to share it with others and use it as a reference when community members needed help with a particular ailment. In general, community members reported improved physical health because of the interactions with the student groups. One aspect that hindered uptake was the fact that most of the community members live on a limited income and struggle to purchase the healthy food recommended by the students to improve their diet. For example, although peanut butter is a relatively cheap source of protein, community members found it expensive and could thus only afford to buy it once a month (CM3). The students need to be more mindful of the poor economic circumstances of the community and take this into consideration when making dietary recommendations.

An outlier finding is that the interaction with others at the LG sessions was not only beneficial for improving physical health outcomes, but also had implications for mental and social wellbeing. Several of the community members voiced that they missed the companionship that the groups provided before they were stopped due to lockdown restrictions:

> I am glad about the students. I enjoy their company. I enjoy working with them. (CM3)

> And the week that they [students] come, we come to get company. (CM1)

This finding was also validated by the students ("For them it's much more different, they really not only want the pills that they need but they also want that emotional support as well" – S6).

Table 10.1 gives a broad summary of the findings regarding the differences in knowledge cultures of each party in the community-university relationship.

9   Implications of Findings for Bridging Knowledge Cultures to Create a More Equitable Community-University Relationship

We now discuss the implications of these findings in terms of creating more equitable power relations within the project and bridging the gaps in knowledge cultures. We also make some suggestions for action that can help to democratise the way knowledge is created, validated and disseminated to bridge knowledge gaps.

The first thing to mention is that this project was not originally conceived as a community-university *research* partnership. The main reason for the initiation of the project was to include CE within the health science curricula, both to satisfy university requirements to integrate CE and to better equip students to work in an interprofessional manner within diverse communities. The focus was therefore more on student development through service delivery to meet student outcomes, rather than on forming equitable research partnerships. Since the inception of the project, the programme developers have evaluated it from various perspectives (e.g., Joubert et al., 2019; Preece, 2017) and are keen to develop it to be more in line with accepted community-based research principles that promote democratic knowledge cultures (Costigan, 2020). Therefore, our discussions and suggestions are made with this understanding. We focus on the various inter-related and overlapping aspects of power relations such as decision-making and leadership, funding, the evaluation, and influence and impact of research outcomes. These should be interpreted within the socio-political knowledge environment (history of social oppression in South Africa and domination of Western, scientific knowledge); the institutional

TABLE 10.1   Comparison of academic versus community knowledge cultures

	Academic knowledge culture	Community knowledge culture
What is knowledge?	Biopsychosocial knowledge, knowledge of specific pedagogy and community engagement, knowledge of research, ethical processes, how to access funding.	The community is knowledgeable about their living conditions and how these impact on their ability to live healthy lives and implement the knowledge provided by the university. They are also aware of some indigenous substitutes for patented medication/food supplements.
How is knowledge generated?	Traditional/positivistic science (extractive research). At this stage, it is mostly Mode 1 form of knowledge generation as the community is not involved in research or determining the services provided. The partnership is focused on the education of students and education of community and provision of health services. Student learning is a key focus of partnership and is mediated and assessed according to a pre-determined curriculum. Funders dictate to a certain extent what services are provided and thus what knowledge should be generated.	Knowledge is mostly received from university. The community do generate their own understandings of how to apply it to their lives through self-reflection and discussion with peers. Some examples where community is a source of knowledge.
How is knowledge validated/ evaluated?	Peer review process: presentation of knowledge products at conferences that leads to submission of knowledge products for publications in journal or books. Publication depends on the approval of experts in the field and indicates that the produced knowledge and the way it is produced have been accepted by the scientific community. Student knowledge assessed according to pre-determined outcomes.	The community does not really consider the knowledge it holds to be as important as that of the health professionals from the university. However, they feel that their knowledge is validated though generational successive use. They evaluate the knowledge received by testing its useful-ness in improving their health.

(cont.)

TABLE 10.1   Comparison of academic versus community knowledge cultures (*cont.*)

	Academic knowledge culture	Community knowledge culture
How is knowledge diffused/ disseminated?	Knowledge is shared through a wide range of outlets (e.g., peer-reviewed scholarly journals and books; public media). Students acquire knowledge through a pre-determined curriculum constructed by university personnel according to requirements of statutory health bodies. Knowledge is transmitted (in most instances) by students to community by means of discussion and information pamphlets.	The community members share their knowledge with students (some evidence found). Community members share knowledge from engagements with students with family and friends through discussion and, in some instances, the creation of booklets.
How is knowledge used?	Knowledge is used 'to fill gaps' in the field of health sciences through contribution to academic debates. Knowledge is used to develop qualified health practitioners and curricula for training them. Evaluation of programme feeds back into improved curriculum	Knowledge is used to improve individual and collective health outcomes in community. Knowledge must be translated into behavioural change to be of use.

knowledge environment (traditional university transitioning towards a more engaged institution); and the knowledge setting within which the project is managed (health sciences within a rural context).

9.1   *Who Makes the Decisions?*

The findings clearly indicate that the university has been the main decision-maker in terms of who takes part in the programme, what knowledge and services they provide, where they are provided and how they are mediated in terms of communication, uptake and adaptation. This made sense at the start of the project as nothing would have happened if the university had not initiated the project. However, the findings also indicate that this one-sided decision-making process is not ideal for the sustainability of the project. As shown during the Covid-19 lockdowns, the university was severely hampered in continuing the programme and the community were not well enough organised to continue on their own. Although the community are consulted about what aspects of health they would like to discuss in a specific week, this is more about topics presented, rather than a change in the prescribed project planning. Based on the data gathered in this project, we suggest changes could be made on several levels to make the relationship more resonant of an authentic partnership in terms of decision-making about how knowledge is created, used and shared. For example:

- A core group consisting of representatives from each category of stakeholders (e.g., university lecturers, student representatives, local health professionals, community organisations, users of the programme) could be formed to meet regularly to reflect on roles, responsibilities and ways of working to find ways to constantly improve the outcomes for mutual benefit. This group could decide on evaluation processes and involve more than just the academic members in ongoing research on the project.
- More intense use of participatory pedagogies such as storytelling, visual methods, etc. by students to convey health knowledge would also enable the LG members to learn how to use these methods to further disseminate the knowledge among the wider community. The latter could also share their indigenous methods of knowledge and skills transfer to improve the pedagogy adopted by students. Participatory pedagogies encourage engagement of community members in the creation of knowledge (Farenga, 2020).
- The research element of the Trompsburg project, including this current research, was directed by and decided on by the university partner and they benefitted in terms of several publications by using Trompsburg as a research site. However, the research done relates to teaching and learning, and influences future engagement with the community. Although community members may think that research is of no importance to them, a community-based approach would enable them to engage in finding ways to improve their lives and this practical action would be of benefit to them. For example, lack of access to nourishing food was one concern mentioned by community and a community-based research project could help them to find sustainable ways to access good food to improve health (e.g., setting up and running of community-based vegetable gardens or cooperatives to buy food in bulk).

Closely related to decision-making is the question of funding.

9.2   Who Holds the Purse Strings?

In any partnership, money tends to dictate who is seen to be 'in charge' and thus has the power to make decisions. In this case, all the funding was sourced from and by the university, and thus if this partner were to lose funding, the project sustainability becomes questionable. The question here is how to make the project more sustainable by enabling the community to source or generate their own funds. If a community-based research project was initiated to develop the facility as a social enterprise of some kind, then it could continue to function as a health resource even if the current funders pulled out. This is something worth exploring as it would also provide additional income for community members and thus have extended social impact (Lumpkin et al., 2018).

9.3   *What Knowledge Is Valued and How Is It Validated?*

The findings indicate that, although some academics are open to learning from the community, there are others who still see their role as being the primary providers of knowledge to the community. There is a gradual shift in higher education towards realising the value of local knowledge in solving complex social problems (Hall & Tandon, 2021). However, to date, community-based research is still not embraced by the majority, and therefore capacity development among academics and students in this regard is important if they are to initiate and sustain CURPs. This would require that all programmes begin to integrate the idea of engaged scholarship into the curriculum, and particularly in programmes such as these where students are directly working with community (Albertyn & Daniels, 2009).

The community did not seem to value their own knowledge very much and perhaps this is because they have never engaged in research with the university and therefore view themselves more as knowledge recipients and less as knowledge producers. Community-based research has educational and emancipatory outcomes (Wood, 2020); therefore participation as co-researchers in a project would help them realise the importance and value of their lived knowledge and experiences. This is essential if they are to become community educators and disseminate the knowledge in the wider community.

9.4   *What Difference Does the Knowledge Make?*

Although this study did not set out to measure the impact of the Trompsburg project on the health of the community, other projects have conducted research on health outcomes in this community during the duration of the project (see, for example, Jordaan et al., 2020; Pienaar et al., 2017; Walsh et al., 2002) and postgraduate studies have been conducted on how the students view the collaboration (e.g., Mona-Dinthe, 2020). The university has therefore benefitted from using Trompsburg as a research site, but the findings of this study also indicate that the LG members think they have benefitted from the services rendered in terms of physical and mental health. Students feel better prepared for their future professions and so it appears that the knowledge generated has been of some benefit to all. However, it can be postulated that if knowledge sharing was conducted using a community-based research approach as explained above, it could have a larger and more sustainable impact in the wider community.

Research which involves dialogical interaction can change the way universities interact with community. As Moreno-Cely et al. (2021) argue, this should start with dialogue about knowledge and power relations within the project. Similarly, a participatory action-learning and action-research process starts with relationship building through dialogues around ethical ways of working, the respective outcomes each party desires, how best to work together and with whom in a given context, and identifying and addressing any learning needs that parties might have (Wood, 2020). Establishing such relationships promotes mutual learning and knowledge co-creation between different knowledge systems and allows for the inclusion and valuing of local/indigenous knowledge, which in turn contributes to the decolonisation of knowledge (Moreno-Cely et al., 2021) and leads to the creation of "ethical, inclusive and sustainable frameworks" (Wood, 2021, p. 3) to guide the community-university engagement.

In terms of the case study in question, adopting a more community-based research approach to the engagement would help to bridge knowledge cultures through enabling each partner to contribute their specific expertise towards attaining the research goals. However, given the unequal starting points in terms of education and resources, this would entail supporting the community to acquire the skills and knowledge needed to be able to participate on a more equal basis. In addition, one of the biggest challenges of universities is to maintain cash-flow and predictable income, and since most universities in South Africa get approximately one-third of their income from government, a consistently dimishing contribution, and the other two-thirds must be generated from fees (which is also decreasing), the application of smart partnerships in the triple or quadruple helix seems to be the best way forward. Unfortunately, the reliance on industry to fund many of the developemental challenges is becoming unrealistic and contributes to socio-economic and political tensions in the country. Inequality needs to be addressed, and we have to start by empowering and growing our communities via education at all levels of society (Cooper & Orrell, 2016).

10   Conclusion

This research set out to explore how knowledge in a community-university engagement was created, validated and disseminated by the respective parties in the Trompsburg project, as well as to determine the usefulness of the knowledge for the different stakeholders. Findings indicate that in this case, the university is the main decision-maker and leader in determining what knowledge is generated and shared. The limited evidence of community generated and shared knowledge and the uptake thereof by students is influenced by the perception of its value from both community members and students. Both university and community benefit from the service provided by the students. The relationship at this stage cannot be described as an equal partnership, since the power relations are skewed in favour of the university. The findings also indicate the need to adopt a more community-based research approach that would then improve the sustainability of the project in the long term. By engaging in more collaborative research with community stakeholders, including existing service providers and local government, solutions could be found to address the issues that impact negatively on health outcomes, such as food insecurity, the need for social interaction and sporadic unavailability of the students due to Covid-19. Ongoing reflexive dialogue between university and community representatives is necessary to encourage research that is "a process of thinking through ideas", rather than only being about the systematic "collecting [of] data that is then subjected to analysis by the external observer to ultimately emerge as a final product" (Rappaport, 2020, p. 19). Such dialogue is the basis for bridging diverse knowledge cultures to reduce power inequalities and decide on actions to make the change process more ethical, inclusive and sustainable.

Notes

1 The term Afrikaans institution refers to those intended to serve the white Afrikaans-speaking population since it was the language of instruction. Even although Afrikaans is also the primary language spoken by many so-called "Coloureds" in South Africa, only White students (with a few exceptions) had access to them until the demise of apartheid in the 1990s.
2 https://en.wikipedia.org/wiki/Trompsburg, accessed on 3 April 2022.
3 The Department of Corporate Governance and Traditional Affairs provides a profile of the district. Unfortunately, recent information on Trompsburg itself was not available.

References

Albertyn, P. R., & Daniels, P. (2009). Research within the context of community engagement. In E. Bitzer (Ed.), *Higher education in South Africa: A scholarly look behind the scenes* (pp. 409–428). SUN MeDIA.

Beaulieu, M., Breton, M., & Brousselle, A. (2018). Conceptualizing 20 years of engaged scholarship: A scoping review. *PloS One, 13*(2), 1–17. https://doi.org/10.1371/journal.pone.0193201

Cetina, K. (2007). Culture in global knowledge societies: Knowledge cultures and epistemic cultures. *Interdisciplinary Science Reviews, 32*(4), 361–375. https://doi.org/10.1179/030801807X163571

Cooper, L., & Orrell, J. (2016). University and community engagement: Towards a partnership based on deliberate reciprocity. In F. Trede & C. McEwen (Eds.), *Educating the deliberate professional. Professional and practice-based learning* (Vol. 17). Springer. https://doi.org/10.1007/978-3-319-32958-1_8

Costigan, C. L. (2020). Adopting community-based research principles to enhance student learning. *Canadian Psychology/Psychologie Canadienne, 61*(2), 111–117. https://psycnet.apa.org/doi/10.1037/cap0000207

Council on Higher Education. (2018). *VitalStats Public Higher Education 2016.* Council on Higher Education.

Creswell, J. W., & Creswell, J. D. (2017). *Research design: Qualitative, quantitative, and mixed methods approaches.* Sage.

Delport, A. (2005). Looking to the future with the past in mind: Confessions of an Afrikaner. *Journal of Education, 37*(1), 203–224. https://journals.co.za/doi/pdf/10.10520/AJA0259479X_161

Department of Corporate Governance and Traditional Affairs. (2020). *Profile and analysis district development model.* https://www.cogta.gov.za/ddm/wp-content/uploads/2020/07/District_Profile_Xhariep-1.pdf

Department of Education, South Africa. (1997). *Education white paper 3: A programme for higher education transformation.* Government Printers. https://www.gov.za/sites/default/files/gcis_document/201409/18207gen1196o.pdf

de Sousa Santos, B. (2014). *Epistemologies of the South: Justice against epistemicide.* Paradigm Publishers.

de Sousa Santos, B. (2017). *Decolonising the university: The challenge of deep cognitive justice.* Cambridge Scholars Publishing.

Díaz, S., Pascual, U., Stenseke, M., Martin-Lopez, B., Watson, R.T., Molnar, Z., Hill, R., Chan, K., Baste, I. A., Brauman, K. A., Polasky, S., Church, A., Lonsdale, M., Larigauderie, A., Leadley, P. W., van Oudenhoven, A. P., van der Plaat, F., Schröter, M., Lavorel, S., Aumeeruddy-Thomas, Y., Bukvareva, E., Davies, K., Demissew, S., Erpul, G., Failler, P., Guerra, C. A., Hewitt, C. L., Keune, H., Lindley, S., & Shirayama, Y. (2018). An inclusive approach to assess nature's contribution to people. *Science, 359*(6373), 270–272. https://doi.org/10.1126/science.aap8826

Dubow, S. (1992). Afrikaner nationalism, apartheid and the conceptualization of "race." *The Journal of African History, 33*(2), 209–237. http://www.jstor.org/stable/182999

Farenga, S. (2020). Participatory pedagogy and artful inquiry: Partners in researching the student experience. In J. Huisman & M. Tight (Eds.), *Theory and method in higher education research* (Vol. 6, pp. 81–98). Emerald Publishing Limited. https://doi.org/10.1108/S2056-375220200000006006

Farner, K. (2019). Institutionalizing community engagement in higher education: A case study of processes toward engagement. *Journal of Higher Education Outreach and Engagement, 23*(2), 147–152. https://openjournals.libs.uga.edu/jheoe/article/view/1457/1449

Fiske, E. B., & Ladd, H. F. (2004). *Elusive equity: Education reform in postapartheid South Africa*. Brookings Institution Press.

Flick, U. (2018). *Social research methods: Qualitative and quantitative approaches* (7th ed.). Sage.

Francis, D., & Webster, E. (2019). Poverty and inequality in South Africa: Critical reflections. *Development Southern Africa, 36*(6), 788–802.

Hall, B., & Tandon, R. (2015). *Are we killing knowledge systems? Knowledge, democracy, and transformations*. http://www.politicsofevidence.ca/349/

Hall, B., & Tandon, R. (2021). Social responsibility and community based research in higher education institutions. In B. Hall & R. Tandon (Eds.), *Socially responsible higher education* (pp. 1–18). Brill Sense.

Hall, M. (2010). *Community engagement in South African higher education: Kagisano no 6*. Council on Higher Education. https://www.che.ac.za/file/6428/download?token=wAwJA2l2

Harper, S. (2012). *The psychological impacts of Apartheid on black South Africans*. https://www.grin.com/document/264561

Higher Education Quality Committee, South Africa. (2004). *Criteria for programme accreditation*. Council on Higher Education. http://nr-online.che.ac.za/html_documents/CHE_accreditation_criteria_Nov2004.pdf

Jordaan, E. M., Van den Berg, V. L., Van Rooyen, F. C., & Walsh, C. M. (2020). Obesity is associated with anaemia and iron deficiency indicators among women in the rural Free State, South Africa. *South African Journal of Clinical Nutrition, 33*(3), 72–78. https://doi.org/10.1080/16070658.2018.1553361

Joubert, A., Botha, R. W., Morgan, H., Wilmot, M., & Hagemeister, D. T. (2019). Health professions students' interprofessional experiences on a rural learning platform. *South African Journal of Higher Education, 33*(6), 153–171. https://doi.org/10.20853/33-6-2898

Kemmis, S. (2010). What is to be done? The place of action research. *Educational Action Research, 18*(4), 417–427. https://doi.org/10.1080/09650792.2010.524745

Kilburn, K., Ranganathan, M., Stoner, M. C., Hughes, J. P., MacPhail, C., Agyei, Y., Gómez-Olivé, F. X., Kahn, K., & Pettifor, A. (2018). Transactional sex and incident HIV infection in a cohort of young women from rural South Africa. *AIDS, 32*(12), 1669–1677. https://dx.doi.org/10.1097%2FQAD.0000000000001866

King, M. (2016). *King IV: An outcomes-based corporate governance code fit for a changing world.* https://www.pwc.co.za/en/publications/king4.html

Kressin, N. R., Elwy, A. R., Glickman, M., Orner, M. B., Fix, G. M., Borzecki, A. M., Katz, L. A., Cortes. D. E., Cohn, E. S., Barker, A., & Bokhour, B. G. (2019). Beyond medication adherence: The role of patients' beliefs and life context in blood pressure control. *Ethnicity & Disease, 29*(4), 567–576. https://www.jstor.org/stable/48717979

Lumpkin, G. T., Bacq, S., & Pidduck, R. J. (2018). Where change happens: Community-level phenomena in social entrepreneurship research. *Journal of Small Business Management, 56*(1), 24–50. https://doi.org/10.1111/jsbm.12379

Mandela, N. R. (1994). *Long walk to freedom.* Abacus.

Memmi, A. (2013). *The colonizer and the colonized.* Routledge.

Mona-Dinthe, N. L. (2020). *Health sciences students' perceptions of collaborative practice on a rural learning platform, Xhariep District* [Master's dissertation, University of the Free State, Free State, South Africa]. https://scholar.ufs.ac.za/bitstream/handle/11660/10998/MonaDintheNL.pdf?sequence=1&isAllowed=y

Moreno-Cely, A., Cuajera-Nahui, D., Escobar-Vasquez, C. G., Vanwing, T., & Tapia-Ponce, N. (2021). Breaking monologues in collaborative research: Bridging knowledge systems through a listening-based dialogue of wisdom approach. *Sustainability Science, 16*(3), 919–931. https://doi.org/10.1007/s11625-021-00937-8

Mtshali, N. G., & Gwele, N. S. (2016). Community-based nursing education in South Africa: A grounded-middle range theory. *Journal of Nursing Education and Practice, 6*(2), 55–67. http://dx.doi.org/10.5430/jnep.v6n2p55

Musesengwa, R., & Chimbari, M. J. (2017). Community engagement practices in Southern Africa: Review and thematic synthesis of studies done in Botswana, Zimbabwe and South Africa. *Acta Tropica, 175*(1), 20–30. https://doi.org/10.1016/j.actatropica.2016.03.021

Nassaji, H. (2020). Good qualitative research. *Language Teaching Research, 24*(4), 427–431. https://doi.org/10.1177%2F1362168820941288

Neuman, W. L. (2011). *Social Research Methods: Qualitative and quantitative approaches* (7th ed.). Pearson.

Next Generation. (2021). *Corporate social responsibility.* https://nextgeneration.co.za/what-we-do/key-concepts/corporate-social-responsibility

North-West University. (2021). *Community engagement policy.* https://www.nwu.ac.za/gov_man/policy/index.html

Patel, J., & Govindasamy, P. (2021). *South Africans see corruption as worsening during President Ramaphosa's tenure.* Afrobarometer dispatch no. 476. https://www.scribd.com/document/530714883/Ad476-South-Africans-See-Corruption-as-Worsening-Under-Ramaphosa-Afrobarometer-Dispatch-15sept21#download

Pienaar, M., van Rooyen, F. C., & Walsh, C. M. (2017). Household food security and HIV status in rural and urban communities in the Free State province, South Africa.

SAHARA-J: Journal of Social Aspects of HIV/AIDS, *14*(1), 118–131. https://doi.org/10.1080/17290376.2017.1379428

Preece, J. (2017). Two case examples of community engagement. In J. Preece (Ed.), *University community engagement and lifelong learning* (pp. 123–144). Palgrave Macmillan.

Rappaport, J. (2020). *Cowards don't make history: Orlando Fals Borda and the origins of participatory action research*. Duke University Press.

Segal, D. L., Coolidge, F. L., O'Riley, A., & Heinz, B. A. (2006). Structured and semistructured interviews. In M. Hersen (Ed.), *Clinician's handbook of adult behavioral assessment* (pp. 121–144). Elsevier Academic Press. https://psycnet.apa.org/doi/10.1016/B978-012343013-7/50007-0

Smith-Tolken, A., & Bitzer, E. (2017). Reciprocal and scholarly service learning: Emergent theoretical understandings of the university–community interface in South Africa. *Innovations in Education and Teaching International*, *54*(1), 20–32. https://doi.org/10.1080/14703297.2015.1008545

Travica, B. (2013). Conceptualizing knowledge culture. *Online Journal of Applied Knowledge Management (OJAKM)*, *1*(2), 85–104. http://www.iiakm.org/ojakm/articles/2013/volume1_2/OJAKM_Volume1_2pp85-104.pdf

Van Henyningen, C. (1980). Christian national education. *Africa South*, *4*(3), 51–56. https://disa.ukzn.ac.za/sites/default/files/pdf_files/asapr60.9.pdf

Walsh, C. M., Dannhauser, A., & Joubert, G. (2002). The impact of a nutrition education programme on the anthropometric nutritional status of low-income children in South Africa. *Public Health Nutrition*, *5*(1), 3–9. https://doi.org/10.1079/PHN2001204

Welch, M., & Plaxton-Moore, S. (2017). Faculty development for advancing community engagement in higher education: Current trends and future directions. *Journal of Higher Education Outreach and Engagement*, *21*(2), 131–166. https://files.eric.ed.gov/fulltext/EJ1144557.pdf

Wood, L. (2022). An ethical, inclusive and sustainable framework for community-based research in Higher Education. In L. Wood (Ed.), *Community-based research with vulnerable populations: Ethical, inclusive and sustainable frameworks for knowledge generation* (pp. 267–292). Palgrave Macmillan.

Wood, L. (2020). *Participatory action learning and action research: Theory, practice and process*. Routledge.

Wood, L., & Zuber-Skerritt, O. (2021). Community-based research in higher education: Research partnerships for the common good. In L. Wood (Ed.), *Community-based research with vulnerable populations: Ethical, inclusive and sustainable frameworks for knowledge generation*. Palgrave McMillan.

World Health Organization. (2020). *Behavioural considerations for acceptance and uptake of COVID-19 vaccines*. WHO technical advisory group on behavioural insights and sciences for health, meeting report.

CHAPTER 11

Bridging the Knowledge Culture Gap between Early Childhood Development Practitioners and Academic Researchers

Experiences from the DUT K4C Hub, Durban, South Africa

Darren Lortan and Savathrie Margie Maistry

Abstract

This case study focuses on the differences in knowledge cultures between academic researchers and early childhood development (ECD) practitioners in Durban, South Africa, providing a historical context of ECD and the role of ECD practitioners in South Africa. The authors unfurl the relationship between the academics and practitioners, and how those who participated in this BKC research were first brought together as part of a doctoral study on. The trust in the relationship between the participants was key to undertaking this research process. They conclude with how the gap between academic researchers and ECD practitioners can be bridged.

Keywords

early childhood development in South Africa – trust – knowledge and wisdom – co-creating knowledge – epistemic injustice – relationship building in CBPR

1 Introduction

Oliver and Reddy Kandadi (2006) identify the key definitional features of culture to include the group or the collectiveness; a way of life; and the learned behaviours, values, knowledge and perceptions of the people. They define knowledge culture as "an organizational lifestyle which empowers individuals and motivates them to create, share, and apply knowledge in order to reach consistent organizational success and benefits" (Oliver & Reddy Kandadi, 2006, p. 8). Walczck (2005) in Dilmaghani et al. (2015, p. 4) intimates that the creation of a knowledge culture has the potential to facilitate and promote knowledge creation, sharing, transmission, and effective application for making decisions, strategic planning and measurable development of economic assets.

This case study focuses on the differences in knowledge cultures between academic researchers and early childhood development (ECD) practitioners in Durban, South Africa, and how to bridge this gap in the field of ECD education. The participants comprise authors of this chapter, a doctoral student at the Durban University of Technology (DUT) supervised by the authors, and three ECD practitioners based in the township of Umbumbulu, 40 kilometres south of Durban. We acknowledge with gratitude the participation and knowledge of the three ECD facilitators: Zanele Mpisane, Nomusa Mtshali and Sindisiwa Msomi. Unfortunately, due to COVID-19, we were unable to co-write the case study. We are satisfied that we have captured their views. We hope they are too.

The research undertaken is part of a macro project developed by the UNESCO Chair in Community Based Research and Social Responsibility in Higher Education, the Bridging Knowledge Cultures (BKC) Project. It explores in the context of community-university research partnerships within the Knowledge for Change (K4C) Consortium created by the UNESCO Chair, how to address extant power inequalities between diverse knowledge cultures of collaborating partners to make these partnerships sustainable and secure over time. This study asked the following research questions:

– What are the different ways in which knowledge is understood, constructed, validated and disseminated in academic and non-academic (community) settings?
– What are the practical challenges/obstructions that differences create for working across knowledge cultures and how do we address these challenges?

In this chapter, we first set the scene for the inquiry by unfurling the relationship between the aforementioned academics and practitioners. The key role players in this case study were first brought together as part of a doctoral study on ECD in South Africa. In order to obtain a comprehensive picture of this case study in relation to the doctoral research and the collaborative relationship with the ECD practitioners, we first describe the relationship between the participants and thereafter provide a historical context of ECD and the role of ECD practitioners in South Africa. Details of the research process undertaken is presented to answer the research questions, followed by the findings and discussions.

2   Situating the Case Study

The Knowledge for Change (K4C) Hub at the DUT was the first hub to be established in South Africa in 2017. The Rhodes University Community Engagement (RUCE) division together with DUT was formerly incorporated into the K4C Southern Hub in 2021. In the same year, North West University (NWU), in partnership with the University of the Free State (UFS), established the K4C Northern Hub. The Southern Hub's current research focus is education across the continuum of levels, namely ECD, primary, secondary and tertiary. Initially, this case study's intention was to explore knowledge cultures at all four levels of education. The ethical approval procedures for this CBPR enquiry could not be obtained by RUCE within the timeframe of the BKC project. The disruptions of the Covid 19 pandemic, especially within the education sector, further exacerbated the challenges for RUCE, who made the difficult decision to withdraw from the project.

It has become imperative for academic researchers working in community-based participatory research (CBPR), to raise at their universities the limitations of the current ethics structures, which tend to cater exclusively for conventional forms of research. We as the DUT team (two academic researchers and a doctoral student) continued with the BKC research project focusing on the doctoral student's study on integral education at the ECD level. The three ECD practitioners who participated in this case study have an ongoing relationship with the doctoral student and academic researchers since 2018. The overall goal of the doctoral study is the development of a framework for a transformative ECD integral education programme with Ubuntu values for social responsibility and civic participation towards participatory democracy in South Africa. It was possible to collect data for this case study based on the existing ethics approval for the doctoral research.

As mentioned above, the three ECD practitioners are from the district of Umbumbulu, and its surrounding areas is home to about 600,000 people. It is under-serviced with virtually no economy and a place where much suffering has taken place as a result of sporadic political and faction-based violence in the past (Machen, 2011). Since the advent of democracy in 1994, more roads, schools and clinics, and electricity and water are gradually being delivered in Umbumbulu. However, the fundamental problems of poverty, unemployment, crime and political violence remain very much a part of the fabric of township community life (Brankovic, 2019; Machen, 2011). Learners living in townships require a good deal of protection and resilience to overcome the obstacles and adversities in their context of development (Mampane &

Bouwer, 2011). This is the lived reality to which the larger majority of South Africa's population is subjected, and it is within this context that the doctoral study viewed the urgency of education interventions, generally, and ECD interventions in particular, and invited the three ECD practitioners to participate in her study in 2019.

3   Contextualizing ECD in South Africa

The early childhood period is considered the most important developmental phase throughout an individual's lifespan. What happens to the child in the early years is critical for the child's trajectory and life course (Irwin et al., 2007), particularly in South Africa with its plethora of social ills and various manifestations of violence. These are the formative years in which behaviour, attitudes and values that children are exposed to will be learnt through imitation and role-modelling and which will determine much of their later behaviour (Burton, 2008). South Africa's National Integrated Early Childhood Development Policy of 2015 (NIECD) confirms this critical link between ECD and outcomes later in life when it highlights that ECD investments bring about higher levels of positive self-regulation which lead to significantly less crime and greater public safety, reduced public violence, and greater social cohesion and civic participation (Republic of South Africa, 2015; Department of Basic Education, 2015).

South Africa has a deep and long history of violence, at the core of which lies colonialism and grand apartheid underpinned by patriarchal relations. Atmore (2013) reminds us that children in South Africa have historically been neglected and abused by the political ideologies and structures of the apartheid government. Prior to 1994, the apartheid education system provided compulsory education for white children and voluntary education for black children, creating a two-tier system. Early learning opportunities based on western models of play and school readiness were available for white children in government-funded pre-primary centres that targeted three- to five-year-olds. There was limited provision for all other race groups, of which black African children were the most disadvantaged (Ebrahim et al., 2021).

From 1940, nursery schools became facilities for the privileged White middle-class, with trained teachers, separated from crèches where African working-class children were only given custodial care. These racial disparities extended to the training of pre-school teachers. From 1958, most training courses for African teachers were restricted, while those for Whites, albeit on a smaller scale, were allowed to continue. Lower-level teacher training courses set up by the provincial education departments, were phased out by the end of 1990 (Department of Social Development, 2001).

The void in preschool education for the vast majority of Black (African) children led several women from their communities to organise preschools called Educare centres in the rural homeland areas and townships (Stevens, 1997). In many instances, these women had no formal training in early childhood education (ECE), most had not completed secondary education, and few had any formal knowledge of child development. Yet, these community women were motivated to organise ECE centres and become Educare teachers because of their love for young children and their awareness that children needed assistance to lead healthy and safe lives and be prepared for formal primary schooling. In support of the community initiated Educare centres and the absence of support from South African government agencies, non-government organisations (NGOs) assumed responsibility for training Educare teachers (ibid.).

By the 1980s, the state finally began to acknowledge the importance of ECD, especially in the wake of the high drop-out and failure rates among African children in schools. State involvement in education, as with all other sectors, at the time was characterised as inadequate, segregated, fragmented, uncoordinated and lacking a comprehensive vision (Department of Social Development, 2001). Thus, parents, communities and the private sector bore the responsibility for ECD provisioning while state-owned pre-primary schools were few in number.

Post-1994, the National Integrated Early Childhood Development Policy (Republic of South Africa, 2015; Department of Basic Education, 2015) has had the ambitious aim of transforming ECD service delivery to address the gap in universally available equitable services. However, there is a mismatch between the funding strategies and infrastructure to support the aim of the NIECD (Ebrahim et al., 2021). In most cases, NGOs continue to deliver ECD programmes with limited funding. Provision of ECD services include the traditional centre-based ECD model of provision, playgroups and family outreach programmes. Community facilities are often based in private homes where an ECD practitioner converts a portion of her house to accommodate children, or classes can be provided at centre-based facilities where a community has a dedicated building for the children, known as community-based centres (Atmore, 2013). In the absence of adequate subsidies to community-based early learning sites, most rely on parent fees. While this is affordable for those in well-resourced households, it is problematic for families living in poverty. The mushrooming of private providers with business orientations and unregistered sites continues to be a feature (Ebrahim et al., 2021).

The authors point to some of the concerns with regards to human resources in the ECD sector. Because of the lack of status and the under-development of a robust system to professionalise the field, ECD fails to attract high quality personnel. Harrison (2020) argues that it is imperative that South Africa has a well-trained workforce of early childhood teachers who can meet the needs of children but claims that there are many challenges that constrain a positive outcome. A significant number of children under the age of six do not have access to essential ECD services such as clean running water, adequate nutrition and safe structures to learn in. As a result of the vast difference in context, a distinction must be made between young children in rural areas and those in urban settings. The rural environment is often characterised by a lack of access to clinics, schools and adequate nutrition, which can lead to stunted growth in children (Ebrahim et al., 2021).

From the brief presentation on the historical and current ECD context in South Africa, it is clear that the potential for research and action is immense and urgent. Within this scenario, the relationship between academic researchers and the various stakeholders in ECD, the culture of academics, and their openness to knowledge democracy, the co-creation of knowledge and CBPR in the ECD sector becomes critical to South Africa's post-apartheid developmental and transformation agenda, which higher education institutions (HEIs) are required to contribute to (Department of Education, 1997).

4   Purpose and Objectives of the Study

Knowledge cultures exist in various sites of knowledge creation and sharing such as families, communities and institutions/organisations. However, differences in knowledge cultures exist within and between these knowledge sites while power dynamics are also at play. As an example, in the case of HEIs, the privileging of knowledge production through standardised western academic forms of research is one way in which the unequal and hierarchical relationship between the academic as researcher and community members as objects of study is evident. The BKC project literature points to tensions caused by the often-unspoken differences in understandings between the knowledge cultures within community settings and the academy. The literature points to one of the biggest challenges being the establishment of truly respectful and equitable knowledge accumulation partnerships.

The purpose of this case study is to understand the different knowledge cultures of university and community partners in the context of ECD training, identify the gaps and explore how to bridge the gap, if any. The objectives of this qualitative case study were:

- To understand the different ways in which knowledge is understood, constructed, validated and disseminated in academic and non-academic (community) settings;
- To examine the practical challenges that differences create for working across knowledge cultures and how to address these challenges.

5 Methodology

5.1 The Case Study Method

The case study method supports the explorative and descriptive nature of this study. A case study is defined as "an empirical inquiry that investigates a contemporary phenomenon (the 'case') in depth and within its real-world context" (Yin, 2014, p. 16). In case studies, "in-depth description of a process, a programme, an event, or an activity is undertaken" (Miller & Salkind, 2002, p. 2). The phenomenon under investigation in this case study is the epistemological worldview in community-university research relationships. The focus is on the ways of knowing and learning that highlights the different knowledge cultures in community-university research relationships and its impact on the co-creation of knowledge. One of the procedures that is followed in a case study is asking questions about an issue under examination or about the details of a case that is of unusual interest. The case is then described in detail and an analysis of the issues or themes is presented and an interpretation of the meaning of the case analysis is made (ibid.). Purposive sampling was used in this case study in selecting the three ECD practitioners as the sample of this study.

5.2 Research Participants

This study comprises six participants – five females and a male. Three were ECD practitioners (Z, N & S), two were academic researchers (D, the only male participant and M), who are the authors of this chapter and co-supervisors of K, a doctoral student. D, M & K are representatives of the Durban K4C Hub. The ECD practitioners and the two authors were originally brought together during the exploratory phase of K's doctoral study titled, *Integral Education for Early Childhood Development: Building Values through Indigenous Knowledge* in 2019 (Padayachee, 2022).

The ECD practitioners work in three different community-based pre-schools established by NGOs. The practitioners each have an entry level ECD qualification, which is meant to provide ECD practitioners with the necessary skills to facilitate the holistic development of young children and to offer quality ECD services in a variety of settings. However, research has shown that qualification level was not always associated with higher-quality outcomes, such as quality of care and learning (Human Sciences Research Council, 2009 in Atmore, 2013).

With eighteen years of ECD combined experience, Z, N and S are rooted in the communities in which they practice. They were considered well qualified experientially to form the participating practitioner team responsible for co-creating with the doctoral student the ECD integral education programme that was the final objective of the doctoral study. Prior to the commencement of the doctoral study, K spent more than five years working on the co-development of community training programmes in the field of ECD. At the time, she worked for a civil society organisation (CSO), whose office was located on the DUT campus where we are currently based. Our paths inevitably crossed because of our work with communities.

During the five-year period alluded to, K developed a relationship with Z and upon commencement of the doctoral programme, she was introduced to N and S and the communities with which all four of them collectively worked. In a sense K anchored the relationship between the community and university partners, representing the interests of both from the commencement of her doctoral research. She was a boundary spanner as contemplated by Christopherson et al. (2021), namely, an individual who crosses the boundaries of a social group to enable knowledge exchange, translate language, and share values among various groups. Over the years, their relationships transcended the boundaries created by varying approaches to the recognition of knowledge generated outside of academia, which is further elaborated in the findings of this study.

The participants in the exploratory phase of the doctoral study comprised parents and grandparents of children in the sample pre-schools and interested community members and key informants. The sample group of the ECD community, directly concerned with the education of their children, was apt because of their lived experiences and close understanding of the relevant issues. The conclusion of the doctoral study and the commencement of this case study overlapped unintentionally. K remained in contact with Z, N and S and with the both of us as her supervisors. Our relative familiarity with each other and collective approach to CBPR, together with the mutual recognition of our lived experiences, knowledge and wisdom made it easy for us to make the collective decision to approach this case study in the manner that we have.

5.3   Data Collection

In order to achieve the above objectives, an interview schedule was used for data collection through a focus group meeting. Even though it was a challenge to organise the data collection, given the Covid-19 context, the face-to-face interview method was preferred in this project to achieve our objective of exploring differences in ECD knowledge cultures.

The pre-determined questions were obviously instruments of the academic culture and opportunities were afforded to participants to bear them in mind rather than be governed by them. The interview schedule contained the following questions that guided our conversation:

1. How do we understand knowledge?
2. How do we understand culture?
3. What is/are the source/s of knowledge?
4. How do we bridge knowledge cultures between university and community?
5. How do we approach a process of co-creation, validation and dissemination of knowledge?
6. How did the ECD practitioners experience the process in which knowledge was co-created in the integral education research project with the doctoral student?

The setting for the focus group meeting of the participants was K's home (the neutral home of the boundary spanner). We sat around a circular table. The table was located at the edge of a garden, near the kitchen door of the home and a garage formed a boundary to the space in which the table was set. The expanse of the garden was visible to most of us. As an icebreaker to the conversation and using the analogy below as a way of explaining the purpose of the case study, D asked each participant to describe our surroundings. As each participant described what they saw, D began asking what appeared to be random questions about the surroundings. For example, in response to some descriptions, the colour of a flower was sought, or the exact number of birds that were visible, or who could see the clouds.

The directed questions were intended to introduce the idea that our responses were different and influenced by our individual perspectives, enabled and/or limited by our positions at the table. Our positions and concomitant views were then used as a metaphor for the differences in our perspectives on what constitutes knowledge; how knowledge is described and shaped by these perspectives; and how these perspectives may be different from others. After a brief discussion about our surroundings, D introduced the research topic to the ECD practitioners explaining the establishment of the K4C Programme by Drs Tandon and Hall, co-holders of the UNESCO Chair in Community-Based Research.

Right from the outset of the interaction between the ECD practitioners and us as academic researchers, it was noted that data gathering became a process; that the prepared questions actually elicited more questions, as it should happen in a case study (Miller & Salkind, 2002). Asking pertinent questions is a clear indication of the critical disposition of the ECD practitioners and their questioning also influenced the research process. Consequently, the whole research process was more organic than structured, notwithstanding the predetermined questions. The focus group meeting was recorded with the prior permission of all participants.

5.4   Data Analysis

M first transcribed participants' responses verbatim to ensure that actual utterances informed our thinking (Braun and Clarke, 2006). Data was analysed thematically, with the pre-determined themes drawn from the interview questions above. M then identified initial codes and organised data into meaningful groups to elicit new themes that arose. The themes were discussed with the participants as the first draft of the research report. All participants involved in the study agreed with the themes and the findings of the study. The participants recognised that although they were all at this stage of the proceedings, accustomed to the knowledge cultural devices of the academe (data, interview schedules, codes, themes and findings), they lamented the lack of intentionality in our approach to capture it all in the knowledge culture of the community. This may be an additional outcome of this case study.

6   Findings of the Study

6.1   Understanding Knowledge

First, S asked for clarification on what knowledge we were talking about, general knowledge or knowledge specific to universities. We then proceeded to understanding knowledge generally and then specifically from a community-university relationship perspective.

Knowledge was understood by Z as "coming from experiences and out of these experiences, I choose what knowledge to use and how. Knowledge is the collection of information from the environment and the people I associate with". As an example, N said that for the doctoral research, they had to go to the community to collect information and she considered this as valuable knowledge. However, she observed, "university knowledge is seen as people who know more and is more valuable". According to S, "there is no right or wrong knowledge. We put it together – theory and practice to make it right". Z's response was that:

> the knowledge we have is suppressed because we do not have the necessary qualification(s) on paper. I can teach very well because of my experiences. I have practical knowledge and teaching is done out of love which is different from a university [where] focus is on theory and seen as experts lacking in practical experience, [and] no love to share with the children.

S supported Z's statements by saying "with qualified persons, the child is programmed, and the child does not learn much". She added that the management of knowledge happens according to one's circumstances. "My parents wrote knowledge on a slate. It was not permanent as it had to be erased ... the knowledge disappeared, so my parents had to remember the knowledge".

S added to the way knowledge was learnt and managed in the past, by using her grandfather as an example. "He would not use a calculator to do his maths but his hands and head – not modern technology".

6.2   Understanding Culture

Z and N described culture as "a set of practices people engage in to understand what we have in common and what differentiates us". Z mentioned that: "Western culture suppresses community knowledge. As an example, in child development, local, indigenous knowledge is devalued because of western culture".

D's response was

> Culture is the collective approach to our common livelihoods (knowledge). Although there are aspects to our approaches to our livelihoods (knowledge) that distinguishes us from others within the collective, it is what we share in common that becomes culture. Culture refers to livelihoods in general and knowledge culture to knowledge.

M described culture as

the values and beliefs of individuals, groups and organisations that guided or influenced the way in which they behaved. These values and beliefs permeated all aspects of their lives. Peoples understanding of certain concepts such as knowledge may be similar, same or different depending on the values and beliefs they hold and their experiences.

According to K, culture refers to the "practices, customs, ideas, habits, behaviours, beliefs of a society or groups of people". The discussion on knowledge and culture by the participants led to the following question: What is the difference between knowledge and wisdom?

6.3 *Understanding Knowledge and Wisdom*
Z said that there is a clear difference between knowledge and wisdom.

> Information/knowledge is collected from an external source and wisdom comes from within the person. It is innate. In ECD, love comes from within to teach a child, so it is part of wisdom.

She added that she taught herself on how to teach a child: "It was the wisdom from within that taught me how to teach a child".

Z and S stated that knowledge is what you know to teach a child. All three practitioners agreed that "wisdom must come from within and must have love". Implicit in this observation is that knowledge is transmitted and/or acquired through instrumental understanding (thought-based) while wisdom does so through relational understanding (emotion-based).

D added his views on knowledge and wisdom which differed slightly from the practitioners' views: "Knowledge can be learnt and taught. Wisdom is not always learnt. It comes from within and also from experience, depending on the exercise that is being accomplished". To a large extent the observations of the practitioners are aligned with the academics in that knowledge can be transmitted while wisdom is innate.

Z then asked another question: "How do children with disabilities, such as children with autism, slow learning and dyslexia cope with processing information into knowledge"? She used the example of a teacher telling a story and asking the children to repeat the story.

> If there are three children with disabilities in the class, then they would provide a different version of the story in accordance with how they internalised and processed the information. Therefore, the teacher will

have to accept each child's version of the story according to how they internalised and understood the story. Most often, the teacher expects all the children to understand the story in a specific way, according to what she had planned to be the aim of the story. Moreover, if the child does not understand it this way, then the teacher thinks that the child is wrong and tries to correct the child so that the story is understood according to the teacher's version.

All three ECD practitioners admitted that they were guilty of telling children who did not answer according to their version of the story that they were wrong. Now, they will respond differently through their understanding that children interpret the information differently and that they should listen to their version of the story rather than saying that they are wrong. This may illustrate the difference between the promotion of an instrumental versus a relational approach to understanding.

The ECD practitioners viewed knowledge (general) as existing in the environment, in people and practical experiences. In comparison, university knowledge was viewed as theoretical with academics seen as the experts. A clear distinction is made between general knowledge (practical) and university (theoretical) knowledge. Interestingly, the practitioners related their knowledge to love (an emotion) while that of the academics is programmed. Even the way in which knowledge is learnt and managed in a community is different from the university. Community members manage their knowledge, for example, in traditional ways, such as through the telling of stories and not through modern technology. Importantly, they believe that the knowledge of those without the 'necessary qualification' is not valued. Practical knowledge is valued less than theoretical knowledge. The responses indicate, as do some literature, that there is no single conceptualization of knowledge (Oeberst et al., 2016) that there is no single definition of knowledge. The authors distinguish between individual and social notions of knowledge and point out that different disciplines conceptualise knowledge differently. They conclude that knowledge is not something that can be universally defined, but instead it is what a specific knowledge-related system accepts. The acceptance of what constitutes knowledge is influenced by the culture (values and beliefs) of the specific system. Knowledge is a social and cultural product (Hauke, 2019).

It was agreed by all participants that there is a difference between knowledge and wisdom, especially the source. The source of knowledge is external, and the source of wisdom is from within, and it must include love. D was of the view that wisdom is from within but also derived from external experience.

Yang (2017, p. 228) presents a view of wisdom as "a process which emerges in a specific context within a specific period of time through the interaction between an individual and a real-life situation that he or she faces. Accordingly, learning acquired from important life experiences can foster wisdom". "Wisdom is inherently concerned with ethical and moral conduct and the pursuit of social justice for all" (Ardelt, 2010 in Yang, 2017, p. 228), and "wisdom is not merely a result of inquiring and reflecting on the relationship between self and society, but it is also the embodiment of action taken to transform self and society towards a better whole" (Bierly et al., 2000 in Yang, 2017, p. 228). However, Jakubik and Muursepp (2021) point out that there is no commonly agreed upon definition of wisdom. It is not an entity that can have a strict definition or even an explanation. It is a process, an unending quest and, as mentioned by the participants, derived from both external and internal sources.

From the above discussion, we may conclude that the transmission of knowledge is an easier process than that of wisdom. The question then arises, can wisdom be transmitted from one individual to another, or does it require a high degree of self-awareness, reflection and introspection? These qualities may be taught as an enabler towards accessing one's wisdom but wisdom itself cannot be transmitted if we accept that it is innate, coming from within the individual.

An alternative would be to describe the process of transmitting something which is innate as promoting relational understanding, where the outcome is not an artefact, but a connection.

Z's question on differentiated learning and processing of information in relation to children with disabilities resonated with the earlier comment that knowledge is not wrong or right. The processing of knowledge and interpretation is largely influenced by our individual worldview and perspectives. Hauke (2019, p. 380) confirms the fluidity in the conceptualisation of knowledge when she states that

> knowledge may be thought of as the result of a personal relationship between ideas, sources of evidence (and resulting 'truths') and the individual. This is a dynamic relationship that shifts over time, is uncertain and contestable, but provides a working certainty that allows us to further develop that knowledge.

The example that Z provided on the teacher's response to the three children with disabilities caused all participants to reflect on how we tend to enforce our view as being the right one on those whom we consider to be less knowledgeable than we are. In this example, it is the teacher and the child; this relationship can be translated to university and community in which academics are guilty of seeing communities as less knowledgeable.

6.4   *The Co-Creation of Knowledge*

Z perceived the co-creation of knowledge as a combination of theory and practical knowledge. All three practitioners mentioned fear as the main obstacle to the co-creation of knowledge.

> Fear is the major obstacle for communities: they hold back their knowledge because they are scared that they do not know much. Fear of academics as experts.

When asked how we change this, they cited their own experience in the research project with K. N said that

> initially there was fear, but it did not remain. It disappeared because K brought it to the practical level. She asked them to talk about their experiences and declared that she did not know much about ECD. She mentioned that there were no right and wrong answers, and they were asked to speak from their own perspective. She did not refer to any study or theory as being the right answer.

Therefore, all three practitioners felt at ease and free to talk. They were surprised that they could participate in the co-creation of the ECD Integral Education programme. It "took them by surprise when they saw the knowledge they have" and accepted the fact that universities do not have all the knowledge in a specific field. "Community has experience and practical knowledge". The consolidation of academic and community knowledge must be done in such a way that it is seen as having equal value as partners. This is one of the hallmarks of an effective boundary spanner in community-university partnerships.

N then asked the following question: "Why is it that only the knowledge of professors from university is considered to be right"? As an example, she said that "in the case of Covid-19, only the culture of scientific knowledge is deemed relevant and important, not the culture of traditional knowledge". She said that traditional knowledge was completely marginalised in the understanding of the Covid-19 pandemic.

She pointed out the challenge is that there is an existing norm that the university does not go to the other side (community) because universities think they are superior, but communities are happy to work with universities.

Universities present their knowledge for discussion, not for participation and listening. Their knowledge is presented as right knowledge; the Covid-19 vaccination is a good example of scientific versus traditional knowledge cultures. N observed:

> Traditional knowledge is considered barbaric. Universities force us to use what they have. Sometimes they take knowledge from the community, make small changes and present it back to the community as the universities' knowledge – as proven, tested knowledge. Like the mhlonyane herb taken from the community. The Afrikaners used to take the method from the community and present as theirs.

Z explained that mhlonyane is an indigenous medicinal plant that has been used by local communities to successfully treat flu symptoms. She added that it then becomes a battle between science, the economy, and the community. For example, "garlic becomes expensive because the communities use it as a medicine, then the economy raises the price of garlic. The price of the knowledge and the product is increased. Communities are locked within a cage because of cost".

6.5   *Epistemic Injustice and the Validation of Knowledge*

The findings reveal that the co-creation of knowledge will mainly require changes to be made on the part of the university. For too long community knowledge has been appropriated, devalued and voices suppressed. The response that "local indigenous knowledge is devalued because of western culture" highlights the power of one knowledge culture over another. It clearly raises the issue of epistemic injustice. This also applies to the dominance of the university knowledge culture over the knowledge of communities as highlighted in the case of Covid-19 by one of the participants.

The appropriation of traditional/community knowledge by universities may be termed as a difference of 'knowledge cultures' – the one which is considered 'superior' is known to be usurping the knowledge of the other which is considered 'inferior'. And university knowledge is presented as right knowledge. What must happen for co-creation of knowledge to work? How should knowledge be validated and disseminated?

The ECD practitioners were unanimous in their responses. Z noted that "the barriers, especially the mindset/thinking that one is superior, and the other is inferior, needs to be broken from both sides". S added that

> when people are told often enough that they do not know anything, they eventually believe it. It is not enough to require of those who think they

are superior to stop. Those who have started to believe in the inferiority need to undo the damage and not wait for the other side to act.

The response to these questions (What must happen for co-creation of knowledge to work? How should knowledge be validated and disseminated?) was once again an organic process, leading to further questions and possible answers. The practitioners were of the view that the responsibility is on the academics to realise that they are not the experts on knowledge with regards to communities. The behaviour and attitudes emanating from academics serve to perpetuate the notion that the majority community are inferior, a notion that was instilled during the apartheid system of inferior education for the majority black community. Hence, the comment by S that "when people are told often enough that they do not know anything, they eventually believe it".

This was followed by a question of remediation: Where then do we meet with an idea? The response was through co-creation of knowledge but with the proviso that after co-creation everything must be 'tested'. When asked where? The unanimous response was "in the community where the knowledge was created".

The practitioners did not know how knowledge should be validated but were of the view that:

> together both parties have to reach an agreement on the way to validate the knowledge. When we reach a stage where we can value each other, respect each other, then we can come up with a way to validate the knowledge. Collaboration and partnership must happen all the way. The dissemination of knowledge can take place through media, especially the radio, community workshops and newspapers. There must be follow up because the dissemination of knowledge is not a one-off event.

Godinho et al. (2021) highlight that the use of participatory knowledge co-creation provides a means to address pertinent societal crises. However, they point to one way of ensuring its sustainability through institutionalisation of knowledge co-creation within existing and novel structures. Oeberst et al. (2016) suggest a systemic perspective to knowledge creation where the different systems become epistemic agents and collaboratively construct knowledge. If people participate in different knowledge-related communities, their activities would be expected to differ as a function of the different social systems. Their approach stresses that for successfully achieving the goal of collaborative knowledge creation, reflection about the conditions imposed by a system is an imperative. Higher education institutions need to reflect on and promote CBPR for collaborative knowledge creation between community and university.

6.6   *How Did Practitioners Experience Their Involvement in the Doctoral Study?*

The final question of how the practitioners experienced their involvement in the doctoral study provided the academic researchers with a comprehensive understanding of the effect of academic researcher attitude towards community partners in the research process. The practitioners mentioned they were impressed with the way in which the doctoral student approached them and explained the study and the importance of their participation in the study. Most importantly, she stated upfront that she was not the expert on the subject of ECD and was looking forward to learning from them, which put them at ease and mitigated their intimidation of someone from a university. Subsequent meetings with the DUT team further progressed the non-intimidating relationship in this community-university partnership. The group meeting for the case study readily revealed the mutually respectful relationship between the ECD practitioners and DUT personnel that was progressively established over the years. While we are confident that the description of the relationship as 'non-intimidating' was sincere, it would be remiss not to declare that we may not fully know how much was withheld due to politeness, respect and other cultural nuances and expressions that inadvertently impede authenticity.

7   Consolidation of Findings and Discussion

The findings reveal that there is no single definition of knowledge, and that our values and beliefs influence our notion of what knowledge is. We agree with Oeberst et al. (2016) who propose a systemic perspective to knowledge creation through which the difference in knowledge cultures between community and university can be bridged. In addition, more consideration should be given to the building of trusting relationships with community partners, the nurturing of boundary spanners, promoting epistemic justice through prevention of the appropriation and exploitation of community (indigenous) knowledge, the co-construction of knowledge and building knowledge democracy. Currently, institutional structures and procedures (policy) for ethics approval for CBPR at universities in South Africa is a huge challenge. This too requires transformation.

7.1   *Relationship Building in CBPR*

Establishing a trusting relationship between community and university is one, if not the most, important component of CBPR. Bivens et al. (2015, p. 6) affirmed the importance of building partnerships with the community for CBPR to co-create "knowledge which draws dynamically on multiple epistemologies and life worlds". According to Ray (2016), partnership within the context of civic and community engagement is fundamentally relational, and a relationship is always a work in progress. Much like deep friendships, partnerships need ongoing cultivation and care. They require sustained attention, stubborn commitment, flexibility, empathy, humility, patience, imagination, and a generous sense of humour. The practice of building community-university partnership relationships is not an easy task in the South African context in which structural racism demarcates the spatial divide between the 'privileged' and the 'marginalised Black' population. Invariably, the mistrust that accompanies the racial divide permeates interaction within the university, and within and between communities, students and academics (Hornby & Maistry, 2022). It is important to note that the interaction between the participants in this case study was cordial and may be attributed to the considerable work undertaken by participants with each other as part of the doctoral investigation. The time and effort invested into the relationship between the practitioners and doctoral student during this period served to set the scene for the research written about in this chapter. In a sense, the work undertaken during the doctoral investigation may be viewed as preliminary work in relationship building for this case study. Additionally, the role of academics as supervisors in the preparation of post-graduate students in CBPR is critical to the relationship development process. Academics need to understand that building relationships between student and community partners is time consuming and labour intensive. Given the diversity of South African communities and the complexities of a post-apartheid society, we have come to realise that academics also require a wide range of practical relational experience derived from working with communities to effectively implement and/or guide post-graduate students in CBPR. In practice, the development of strong, healthy community-university partnerships can be achieved through the core function of university community engagement.

7.2   *Doctoral Student as Boundary Spanner*

The doctoral student continued to play the role of boundary spanner in this case study. One possible way for boundary spanning to bridge recognised gaps in knowledge cultures, is for at least one person from each 'side' of the boundary to intentionally engage with a person from the other side. Such a relationship, committed to addressing recognised hierarchies at play in, and ameliorating their impact on, the community-university partnerships represents the beginning of the process of bridging the gap. By the time the six participants in this case study met to complete the task set before us, we were relatively familiar with each other and the trust that had developed during the doctoral study was evident in the ease of the research process in this case study. As mentioned earlier, time invested in relationship building early in the CBPR process is important.

7.3 Knowledge Democracy/Co-Construction of Knowledge

Hall and Tandon (2017) highlight three phenomena that intersect in knowledge democracy: (1) acceptance of multiple epistemologies, (2) affirmation that knowledge is created and represented in multiple forms (for example, text, image, numbers, story, music, drama, poetry, ceremony, etc.), and (3) understanding that knowledge is a tool for taking action to create a more socially just and healthy world and for deepening democracy. D reminded participants of the concept of 'knowledge democracy' by drawing an analogy with the equality of each vote in an election. The value of the single ballot cast by a billionaire is equal in impact to that of an hourly paid labourer. This principle was intended to demonstrate that in a knowledge democracy, the knowledge of the representatives of a university and the knowledge of the representatives of the community have the same value (multiple epistemologies). If this is not the case in practice, then the term knowledge democracy should not be used to describe the community-based research that is undertaken in community-university partnerships. Knowledge extraction may be a more fitting alternative to describe these scenarios.

The practitioners' reflections of their personal experience with the doctoral research project shows that the first step to knowledge democracy is investing in a relationship with community partners (discussed earlier) to allay their fears and mistrust of university academics. Importantly, academics have to be aware of and acknowledge the extant power imbalances inherent in the historical and prevailing context of higher education in South Africa. The consolidation of academic and community knowledge must be done in such a way that it is seen as having equal value as partners. This process is best facilitated through boundary spanning. We posit that such relationship building is an inherent and necessary enabler of the bridging of knowledge cultures, especially when both sides of the divide have boundary spanners bridging the divide.

Collaboration, partnership, respect, valuing each other were considered important factors to bridge the gap, essentially between the 'practical knowledge culture of community' with the 'theoretical knowledge culture of university/academics'. While it did not escape us (the academic researchers) that we were 'leading the discussion', the ECD facilitators played a key role in setting the scene and supporting the boundary spanner role. In retrospect, it may be claimed that indeed the first practitioner, Z, also had a boundary spanning role. Similar to a community of practice (CoP) which Adelle (2019, p. 2), describes as "a group of people who share a common interest or concern and who deepen their knowledge and expertise in this area by interacting on an ongoing basis", boundary spanners can fulfil a variety of related functions: they can connect people who might not otherwise have the opportunity to interact; provide an opportunity to share information; help people organise around purposeful action; stimulate learning through the transfer of knowledge from one member to another; and generate new shared knowledge that helps people transform practice.

In the context of the case study, the facilitators used the introductory remarks and questions to engender an organic 'easy flow of critical conversation'. Notwithstanding the inherent power dynamic at play, the conversational approach was an attempt to mitigate the implicit power asymmetry. In particular, the introductory remarks and explications were (to the extent possible) carefully stripped of the language of the academe, and nuanced in what was common to all of us. Once the hurdle of the introductory remarks was surmounted, it became easier for the six of us collectively to position the conversation as 'ours'. Even the questions that followed and guided the remainder of the conversation could be deemed 'ours'. The conversation led us naturally to where we needed to be – a place of contemplation and reflection about us; and the work we have accomplished.

7.4 Ethic Structures for CBPR in South African HEIs

As mentioned in the introduction, the initial sample for the case study anticipated participation from four different projects across Rhodes University and DUT. RUCE could not receive ethics approval for its case study in alignment with the time constraints of the BKC project. The DUT research team took advantage of the fact that although the doctoral study was nearing its completion, the interview schedule for this case study could be included as an extension of the data collection process, especially since the key informants has already been identified and 'briefed'.

Procedures for ethics approval for CBPR by the relevant ethics committees of HEIs is a challenge that requires urgent consideration by all HEIs in South Africa. Currently, such procedures are an impediment to effective implementation of CBPR (especially with respect to the co-design and co-construction of the inquiry). A number of HEIs have adopted processes that mitigate these impediments (Connected Communities, 2011; Flicker et al., 2007; Pienaar,

2014), but we have a long way to go before participatory research processes are enabled by participatory ethical clearance practices.

8   Conclusion

The South African oppressive apartheid history lends its own particular characteristic to understanding the notion of knowledge, knowledge cultures and bridging the gap between knowledge cultures. A critical lesson learnt from this case study is that relationship building is at the centre of community-university partnerships and CBPR, specifically for the South African context. The DUT researchers are appreciably aware that if the doctoral research had not laid the path of relationship building over a number of years prior to the case study, we would not have been able to collaboratively generate the knowledge to the extent that we have been able to do so in this chapter. To the extent possible, the power dynamics that may have been at play in this study have been mitigated. The DUT personnel are and have been aware of the unequal relationship between universities and communities from their own involvement in community engagement and development and have been keen to learn from the different knowledge cultures prevailing in the diversity of South African communities, prior to the commencement of the BKC project. But we are also aware from our involvement with structures of university community engagement that while there is some movement towards a better understanding of community-based research and egalitarian community-university partnerships, the process is a slow one and it will take time for the majority of academics to put this into practice.

References

Adelle, C. (2019). Creating knowledge democracy in South Africa: The role of communities of practice. *South African Journal of Science, 115*(7/8), 1–3.

Atmore, E. (2013). Early childhood development in South Africa: Progress since the end of apartheid. *International Journal of Early Years Education, 21*(2–3), 152–162. https://doi.org/10.1080/09669760.2013.832941

Bivens, F., Haffenden, J., & Hall, B. L. (2015). Knowledge, higher education and the institutionalization of community-university research partnerships. In B. Hall, R. Tandon, & C. Tremblay (Eds.), *Strengthening community university research partnerships: Global perspectives* (pp. 5–30). University of Victoria and Participatory Research in Asia (PRIA). http://hdl.handle.net/1828/6509

Brankovic, J. (2019). *What drives violence in South Africa?* Research Brief, Centre for the Study of Violence and Reconciliation.

Braun, V., & Clarke, V. (2006). Using thematic analysis in psychology. *Qualitative Research in Psychology, 3*(2), 77–101.

Burton, P. (2008). Dealing with school violence in South Africa. *Centre for Justice and Crime Prevention (CJCP) Issue Paper, 4*(1), 1–16.

Christopherson, E. G., Howell, E. L., Scheufele, D. A., Viswanath, K., & West, N. P. (2021). How science philanthropy can build equity. *Stanford Social Innovation Review, 19*(4), 48–55.

Connected Communities. (2011). *Community-based participatory research: Ethical challenges*. Durham Community Research Team, Centre for Social Justice and Community Action, Durham University.

Department of Basic Education. (2015). *The South African National Curriculum Framework for Children from Birth to Four*. Department of Basic Education. https://www.education.gov.za/Portals/0/Documents/curriculum%20docs/NCF%202018/NCF%20English%202018%20web.pdf?ver=2018-05-14-124718-317

Department of Education. (1997). *Education White Paper 3: A programme for higher education transformation*. Government Gazette number 18207.

Department of Social Development. (2001). *The Nationwide Audit of ECD provisioning in South Africa*. Department of Social Development. https://www.researchgate.net/publication/228799598_The_nationwide_audit_of_ECD_provisioning_in_South_Africa

Dilmaghani, M., Fahimnia, F., Abouei Ardakan, M., & Naghshineh, N. (2015). Function of knowledge culture in the effectiveness of knowledge management procedures: A case study of a knowledge-based organization. *Webology, 12*(1), a134.

Ebrahim, H. B., Martin, C., & Excell, L. (2021). Early childhood teachers' and managers' lived experiences of the COVID-19 pandemic in South Africa. *Journal of Education, 84*, 204–221.

Flicker, S., Travers, R., Guta, A., McDonald, S., & Meagher, A. (2007). Ethical dilemmas in community-based participatory research: Recommendations for institutional review boards. *Journal of Urban Health, 84*(4), 478–493. https://doi.org/10.1007/s11524-007-9165-7

Godinho, M. A., Borda, A., Kariotis, T., Molnar, A., Kostkova, P., & Liaw, S.-T. (2021). Knowledge co-creation in participatory policy and practice: Building community through data-driven direct democracy. *Big Data & Society, 8*(1). https://doi.org/10.1177/20539517211019430

Hall, B. L., & Tandon, R. (2017). Decolonization of knowledge, epistemicide, participatory research and higher education. *Research for All, 1*(1), 6–19.

Harrison, G. D. (2020). A snapshot of early childhood care and education in South Africa: Institutional offerings, challenges and recommendations. *South African Journal of Childhood Education, 10*(1), 1–10.

Hauke, E. (2019). Understanding the world today: The roles of knowledge and knowing in higher education. *Teaching in Higher Education, 24*(3), 378–393. https://doi.org/10.1080/13562517.2018.1544122

Hornby, D., & Maistry, S. (2022). Developing relationships for community-based research at Rhodes University: Values, principles and challenges. In L. Wood (Ed.), *Community-based research with vulnerable populations: Ethical, inclusive and sustainable frameworks for knowledge generation*. Palgrave Macmillan.

Irwin, L. G., Siddiqi, A., & Hertzman, C. (2007). *Early childhood development: A powerful equalizer*. Final report. WHO. https://factsforlife.org/pdf/a91213.pdf

Jakubik, M., & Muursepp, P. (2021). From knowledge to wisdom: Will wisdom management replace knowledge management? *European Journal of Management and Business Economics, 31*(3), 367–389.

Machen, P. (2011). *Durban's history, our communities: Umbumbulu*. Ethekwini Municipality Website. https://www.durban.gov.za/

Mampane, R., & Bouwer, C. (2011). The influence of township schools on the resilience of their learners. *South African Journal of Education, 31*, 114–126.

Miller, D. C., & Salkind, N. J. (2002). *Handbook of research design & social measurement*. Sage.

Oeberst, A., Kimmerle, J., & Cress, U. (2016). What is knowledge? Who creates it? Who possesses it? The need for novel answers to old questions. In U. Cress, J. Moskaliuk, & H. Jeong (Eds.), *Mass collaboration and education* (Vol. 16). Computer-supported collaborative learning series. Springer. https://doi.org/10.1007/978-3-319-13536-6_6

Oliver, S., & Reddy Kandadi, K. (2006). How to develop knowledge culture in organizations? A multiple case study of large, distributed organizations. *Journal of Knowledge Management, 10*(4), 6–24.

Padayachee, K. (2022). *Integral education for early childhood development: Building values through indigenous knowledge* [Unpublished doctoral thesis, Durban University of Technology].

Pienaar, S. (2014). Considering ethics: Enabling participatory knowledge sharing. In M. Erasmus & R. Albertyn (Eds.), *Knowledge as enablement*. Sun Press.

Ray, D. (2016). Campus–community partnership: A stubborn commitment to reciprocal relationships. *Diversity and Democracy, 19*(2), 8–11. https://dgmg81phhvh63.cloudfront.net/content/user-photos/Publications/Archives/Diversity-Democracy/DD_19-2_SP16.pdf

Republic of South Africa. (2015). *National Integrated Early Childhood Development Policy*. Government Printers. https://www.gov.za/sites/default/files/gcis_document/201610/national-integrated-ecd-policy-web-version-final-01-08-2016a.pdf

Stevens, F. I. (1997). Preschool education for Black South African children: A descriptive study of 32 Educare Centers. *The Journal of Negro Education, 66*(4), 396–408.

Yang, S. (2017). The complex relations between wisdom and significant life learning. *Journal of Adult Development, 24,* 227–238. https://doi.org/10.1007/s10804-017-9261-1

Yin, R. K. (2014). *Case study research design and methods.* Sage.

CHAPTER 12

Towards Transdisciplinarity in the Co-Construction of Knowledge

The Peace and Region Program at the University of Ibagué K4C Hub, Colombia

Irma Flores, Luisa Fernanda González, Andrés Astaiza and Daniel Lopera

Abstract

This case study presents the qualitative case study of a community-university partnership between the Peace and Region Semester (PRS), a service-learning curricular strategy of the University of Ibagué, and the Community Aqueduct Acuamiramar (CAA). It shares the approach of the PRS strategy, analysing the imbalance in power between the university and the community, and the tensions that arise between the framing of the knowledge culture in the university's policies, its practice through the PRS program, and the relations with CAA. The results showcase the learnings of trying to undertaken an inter-disciplinary training program for students and the challenges in working across knowledge cultures.

Keywords

power – university social responsibility – service learning – inter-disciplinary programs – dialogues of knowledge – tensions in research process

1   Introduction

Over the past forty years, around the globe the notion of knowledge has increasingly shaped discourses on development and progress. Discussions around 'knowledge society' and 'knowledge for development' have highlighted different types of knowledge as crucial drivers for economic and social development (Assche, 2013; Hornidge, 2012). However, until a few decades ago, the idea of knowledge-related cultures had little diffusion. Knowledge creation was assumed to be a matter of rational, objective and technical procedures undertaken by scientists. If there was only one scientific method and one type of knowledge, the notion of culture could not be applied to science (Knorr-Cetina, 2007).

Studies on knowledge cultures gained importance in the 1970s, with the trend of the new sociology of science. Fieldwork began to be conducted in scientific laboratories to investigate the processes of knowledge construction and to promote the understanding of knowledge cultures as a structural feature of contemporary societies (Knorr-Cetina, 2007). In the 1960s and 1970s, Latin America, Africa and the Caribbean were the scene of a profound questioning of social research. Positivism, an approach based on the objective measurement of sociological, political and cultural phenomena, was confronted with the concerns of independence movements in Africa, Asia and the Caribbean, as well as with democratic struggles in Latin America, Europe and North America. In these diverse contexts, a revolution about the transformative role of science and research was taking place that would redefine the links between research, action and learning. Today, many names are associated with the various developments of this emerging paradigm, some of the best known being participatory action research, southern epistemologies, or critical pedagogy (Hall, 2021).

This movement has significantly influenced the work of higher education institutions. Despite the trends of internationalisation and commercialisation that characterise the educational and research landscape today, proposals based on Community-University Engagement (CUE) and Community-Based Research (CBR) have been implemented by an increasing number of universities worldwide, constituting a fundamental component of the emerging knowledge democracy movement that brings together social activists, university researchers and students in community-based action research projects (Hall et al., 2015; Koekkoek et al., 2021).

Our chapter presents the qualitative case study of a community-university partnership between the Peace and Region Semester (PRS), a service-learning curricular strategy of the University of Ibagué[1], and the Community Aqueduct Acuamiramar (CAA).[2] This research was conducted by the IAPaz Colombia K4C Hub, which is a partnership between the University of los Andes, University of Ibague, and CINDE Foundation (International Center for Education and Human Development). The chapter shares the approach of the PRS strategy. The case analyses the imbalance in power between the university and the community, and the tensions that arise between the framing of the knowledge culture in the university's policies, its practice through the PRS program, and the relations with CAA. To conduct the research we used documentary analysis, focus groups and semi-structured interviews as instruments for data collection. Data collection and analysis were carried out simultaneously, based on open, axial, selective and theoretical contrast coding, supported by the use of Nvivo 11 software (Charmaz, 2006). The results showcase the learnings of trying to undertaken an inter-disciplinary training program for students and the challenges in working across knowledge cultures between CAA and the PRS.

2   Context

2.1   *Peace and Region Semester*

The PRS is a curricular strategy, created in 2011, for integral education offered by the University of Ibagué to all undergraduate academic programs, within the internal policy of University Social Responsibility (USR). Its mission and its commitment to integral education and regional development comprises two main components – (1) to promote the training of students through an experiential setting, and (2) strengthening public and private organisations and actors that work for the sustainable development of the region and the construction of peace. The program seeks to promote the educational and institutional identity of the university as a regional higher education institution (University of Ibagué, 2021a).

The importance of the PRS lies in its commitment to peace building in Colombia. This is a response to the 60 years of civil violence and armed conflict in Colombia, as well as an opportunity that arises from the peace agreements that the country has experienced. PRS articulates teaching, research and social projection through the participation of students in interdisciplinary projects of long-term local development. It places the university's students in local areas and trains them to understand the context of development in the state of Tolima and to learn the components of participation in development projects.

The program's goal is to develop critical thinking and citizen skills in the students. Among its strategies, it includes the formation and installation of interdisciplinary teams of students in different municipalities, so that during an academic semester they participate in long-term local development projects. The students are placed after making arrangements with local actors involved in the development process, and are accompanied by a regional advisor to support the pedagogical process. Interlocutors are the main contact with the organisations and municipalities, and help in developing the projects undertaken by the students to tackle specific problems (University of Ibagué, 2021a).

PRS seeks to transcend the limits of discipline training and promote scenarios of citizen education and ethical learning through experiencing the political, cultural and social life in a municipality and getting involved in local development projects. Likewise, it allows the university to make its processes of social projection, training, and research more pertinent (University of Ibagué, 2021a).

As a training strategy, PRS favours collaborative work among different actors – students, technical professors, regional advisors, directors, local entities and members of the community. The pedagogical model is oriented towards an integrated education with the development of the human being beyond its cognitive dimension (University of Ibagué, 2014, p. 16). It is based on service-learning, a methodology oriented towards citizenship education based on active pedagogies, experience and service to the community (Batlle, 2007). The main features of the PRS approach are critical understanding of the social context, critical and reflective thinking, interest in producing social change, development of participatory citizen practices, interpersonal development, and skills for teamwork situated in diverse cultural contexts (University of Ibagué, 2021a).

The engagement between academia and the community is led by the regional advisors who facilitate the definition of common objectives and the collaborative work of students, regional and university actors, which has both social and pedagogical value. The program takes place over 16 weeks, coordinated with local organisations. The involvement of the regional advisors with the actors and organisations in the territory is permanent, which favours continuity of processes and the linking of new student teams (University of Ibagué, 2014).

2.2 Acuamiramar Community Aqueduct

In Colombia, there are more than 12,000 community aqueducts, some of which are 20, 30 and even 70 years old. These organizations represent the ancestral heritage and cultural construction of one of the richest expressions of participatory environmental management in the country: Community aqueducts are defenders of water in their rural and urban territories (Giraldo, 2009; RETACO, 2017).

The city of Ibagué has 32 community aqueducts that supply water to 20 per cent of the city's inhabitants. These organizations are self-managed by communities in low-income neighborhoods. In the absence of water and sewage services, these communities have been forced to organize themselves to access basic services. In addition, urban planning in the face of the city's expansion and scarce technical assistance does not respond assertively to the water requirements of everyone residing in the city. The city faces the challenge of expanding its water and sewerage coverage, a challenge that poses risks because the old structures were not designed for the exponential growth of the city. This risk increases in communities that are supplied by community aqueducts (Garzon Quiroga, 2020; Correa, 2020).

Acuamiramar is a community enterprise[3] that manages one of the 32 community aqueducts, providing residential public aqueduct and complementary services in the Miramar neighbourhood of the Municipality of Ibagué. It is endowed with legal status, administrative and financial autonomy, and has its own and independent assets and common funds.

Acuamiramar aims to supply water in the Miramar neighborhood by providing residential public aqueduct services. The organization is committed to the integral management of water as an element of community life and well-being, continuously seeking improvement, efficiency and coverage, while respecting the commitment to sustainable development as a community organization (Garzon Quiroga, 2020). The Acuamiramar aqueduct is in a process of strengthening water governance through institutionalization, commitment, culture, citizen oversight and participation. Convergence with PRS is to help strengthen Acuamiramar's capacities for organising, designing, and self-managing in its territory, and preserving the common purpose of safeguarding water resources through adequate provisioning of water.

In 1991, community aqueducts began to be recognized by Colombian law and by private entities, as possible guarantors of water supply in Colombia. However, community aqueducts are treated by municipal and national entities as public service companies, without any type of restriction regarding their origin, function and the spirit with which these community organisations were created (Correa, 2020).

Water as an element of community power allows social mobilization projects necessary to defend the dignity and life of the most vulnerable communities in the country. Water has an openly political connotation, which supports social organization around popular struggles for access to water. However, large sections of the community in question do not identify with the struggles raised by some community leaders and academics who try to build the conditions for civil and community resistance (Cataño, 2014). In this sense, our research is relevant because it is a case where the academic culture comes into contact with a community aqueduct, showing if this confluence favours the construction of spaces of social resistance around water care, or if, on the contrary, it helps to reinforce a business vision about water management (Correa, 2020). In the Acuamiramar case, knowledge about water management and preservation is getting privatized and the academy may be reinforcing this dynamic by not considering the community knowledge that gave life to Acuamiramar.

3   Methodology

The research undertaken by the Colombia Hub was designed and implemented as a case study. According to Stake (2006), this methodology allows for the construction of a toolbox and resources to collect information from multiple sources of evidence in an organized and coherent manner, useful for analysis and the participatory construction of knowledge. Several authors (Stake, 2006; Yin, 2000; Lincoln & Gubba, 1981) define this method as the way to holistically study the interrelationships and natural contexts of the problem. In addition to the collection of information obtained through different sources, research designed as case studies is privileged when these sources are triangulated to give greater validity and reliability (Mertens, 2005; Stake, 2006).

The design for this case study began with mapping the different stakeholders (Figure 12.1) involved in the processes of the Acuamiramar project. This mapping was carried out in collaboration with the PRS pedagogical and administrative management team. Together, we first identified the key actors who carry out the actions in the territory and defined how they would participate in the construction of the case. At the same time, we identified and consulted secondary sources containing the guidelines that underlie the actions to understand the methodological proposal through which PRS acts in the field.

In defining the primary and secondary sources of information, we developed instruments that allowed us to collect the necessary data to understand how the Acuamiramar project operates and how it does or does not enable the building of bridges between academic and community knowledge cultures.

To analyse the secondary sources, a matrix was constructed that allowed the analysis of the documents through pre-established categories. In the case of primary sources, individual interview guides were designed by PRS managers, professors, regional advisors and interlocutors. Guiding questions for the focus groups were developed by the PRS management team and the community. Information was collected from students' reports who participated in the Acuamiramar project.

The information was transcribed and analysed using the analysis methodology proposed by the Grounded Theory (Charmaz, 2006), using the Nvivo 11 software. The information collected with the different instruments was triangulated and grouped by categories, both pre-established and emerging.

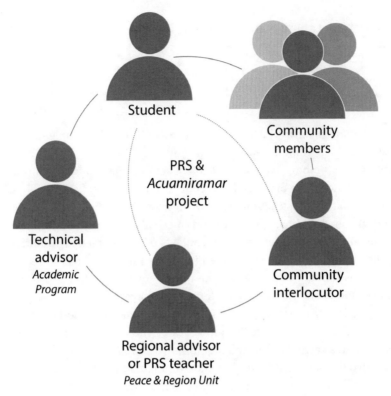

FIGURE 12.1   Stakeholder map of the case study

4   Results

Data analysis generated three emerging categories that helps us comprehend the knowledge cultures between Acuamiramar and PRS, focusing on power relations, the diverse ways in which knowledge is understood, constructed and validated, and the challenges found in working across knowledge cultures. These categories are:

1. Between disciplinary, interdisciplinary, and dialogue of knowledge
2. PRS as a process that involves actors from the university and the community
3. Two knowledge cultures between PRS and Acuamiramar.

The results also showcase the experience of engaging in a transdisciplinary knowledge culture-oriented study, where technical and professional support from the university to the community interacts with processes aimed at building interdisciplinary knowledge.

4.1 Between Disciplinary, Interdisciplinary, and Dialogue of Knowledge

The University of Ibagué acknowledges that its campus is not the only place to build knowledge. For this reason, the institutional curriculum explores alternatives to contribute to the education of citizens and professionals committed to the territory of Tolima and its development. One of the ways to operationalise this is through the PRS as a dynamic learning experience in which students develop competencies and skills, both disciplinary and civic, by interacting with communities. Through participation in projects, students, in interdisciplinary teams, are expected to develop an action plan consistent with the needs of the municipalities and local development agendas (University of Ibagué, 2020, p. 23). In that regard, the students are not engaging from a purely disciplinary perspective but from the perspective of development, through dialogue with the various communities and the knowledge communities possess.

> We stand from a perspective where the student, although, it is not a disciplinary experience and we must be clear that as far as possible, what interests us is the development of projects to solve certain problems and that this contributes to improving the quality of life of communities ... we make a significant effort because, for the whole experience to be more motivating for the student, we anchor it to certain disciplinary topics. (Focus group discussion, PRS)

This framework of knowledge could hinder the relationship with other knowledge in co-construction, and this strategy operates differently in certain projects, as stated by regional advisors:

> Because, as I was saying, the projects that PRS take up in some cases are purely disciplinary, where they will have to apply the knowledge of their discipline ... in others that are interdisciplinary projects, they must apply a series of skills and knowledge that do not belong to their academic training, but that does carry it through their academic training. (Interview, regional advisor)

Some of the projects are already structured from the beginning, so they do not necessarily represent a co-construction bridge between the academy and the communities. In other cases, a transdisciplinary team can emerge when interests converge between different actors. The structure in which PRS operates migrates between disciplinary and transdisciplinary forms. In some cases, knowledge from the disciplinary vision is validated and, in others, discoveries emerge about the importance of working from the knowledge that resides in the communities themselves.

The primary aim Is that the projects that are worked on in the territory are motivating and meaningful for students. When the projects are anchored in disciplinary topics, students are interested and apply the knowledge learned throughout their careers. When they are living in the territory, sometimes significant learning is built by understanding different scenarios learnt through dialogue and the exchange of knowledge with community members. However, these variations are significant in terms of how the PRS is operating with different practices and ways of constructing knowledge.

In the case of Acuamiramar, there is both a disciplinary and interdisciplinary approach, as described by the regional advisor:

> We articulated the Civil Engineering program with Professor LEP... who helped us to say, no, look, you can do this kind of thing and you can give it an interdisciplinary approach if we also do some campaigns for water. (Interview, regional advisor)

There was a discovery for a broader, transdisciplinary vision, as described by the technical professor:

> trying to guide the work of a student in a community, one finds that the community has ways to address their problem that is not stated in the disciplinary knowledge but are innovative and work. So, what we have to do is to document them... But there are also other ways of doing things ... we are going to build knowledge, together, the community and us. I think you call that methodology Participatory Action Research. (Interview, technical professor)

An example where the processes described can be evidenced, is the formulation of the action plan in the projects. To accomplish the purposes of the PRS, regional advisors, interlocutors and students formulate an action plan, which incorporates the understanding of the social context of Acuamiramar, the organization:

> The projects in which students participate have a clearly defined beginning, middle, and end. Before the students are linked to the organization, part of the proposal is arranged and structured between the regional advisor and the interlocutor of the organisation ... later, the student enriches the components of the project and proposes routes

of action in the semester plan, which is validated during the installation meeting and transformed as the semester progresses. (University of Ibagué, 2021a, p. 13)

The development of the action plan requires a series of activities and processes aimed at achieving a final product that is socially relevant and contextualized. Regional advisors, students and interlocutors make contributions to the construction of the semester plan, which allows different perspectives to be integrated and a flexible and participatory framework to be configured. It should be noted that, as a requirement to start the PRS, students must take a course on human and sustainable development and methodologies for approaching the specific problems of communities. However, the process is framed in a knowledge culture where the distinctions between popular knowledge and academic knowledge come into contact but do not enter a transcultural dialogue. This is visible in the tendency to choose the organisation according to the professional profile of the student:

> We agreed with the University of Ibagué, and they provided us with two students, two engineers, to do the topographic survey of the cadaster for the aqueduct. (Focus group discussion, community members of Acuamiramar)

Likewise, knowledge products generated by the students end up confined to their disciplines of origin, because the interaction between PRS and Acuamiramar occurred in an institutional framework which sought the integral education of students. The linking of the organizations with PRS is based on the practical needs perceived by the actors in the communities.

In that sense, using the analytical framework for the study of knowledge cultures in the BKC project, the knowledge setting is characterized by knowledge practices where the roles of each actor are well defined within the framework of a pedagogical process that is formally oriented towards interdisciplinary learning, but which ends up developing within the confines of a discipline according to the needs of the organization. Due to this, it seems that the pedagogical process that takes place in PRS does not manage to consolidate some of its purposes of interdisciplinarity.

On the other hand, the PRS has a learning strategy called *Understanding of the Territory*, where the students interact with peers from other academic programs and put disciplinary knowledge in conversation with other types of knowledge to solve contextual problems:

> They have an activity called Understanding of the Territory. That is, within the project that they do, another one, and that another project is entirely social or environmental. (Interview, technical professor)

However, it is a complementary activity of the project and not something that is fully integrated into the process to promote an interdisciplinary learning experience. In addition to this, it should be noted that knowledge dissemination does not involve members of the community or those of the university. Socialization processes only occur between the student, the regional advisor and the interlocutor. The knowledge products are documents on how the project was formulated, the presentation of a final report of the experience by the student, and some products for the organization, such as designs or legal orientation guides.

> The student submits a document called the Experience Report. In this document, the student describes the development of the project. Let us say this document could give some information about the project development and this information could be useful for a systematization process. (Interview, regional advisor)

Taking this into account, the knowledge that emerges from this co-construction has a pending debt, which is its dissemination. PRS uses some strategies to socialize knowledge, like the institutional repository that organizes and preserves the documents produced at the university. Nevertheless, there is a need to generate spaces for reflective dialogue on these experiences where different actors participate and share knowledge.

4.2 The PRS as a Process That Involves Actors from the University and the Community

For the University of Ibagué, it is not enough to generate knowledge only for one discipline when there is the possibility and opportunity to strengthen the training process through practice and research to respond to the needs of the communities in the territory. Thus, in the search to generate participatory spaces for the construction of knowledge that contributes to regional development, the University of Ibagué conceives teaching and learning as a participatory process mediated by research in the territory, in which the student participates accompanied by the regional advisor. As a product of this experience, students build knowledge to solve problems of the territory, which strengthen the work of regional advisors and ensures that students learn skills, competencies, values, critical thinking, and comprehensive understanding of the territory.

> Learning is based on an educational triad. The student's engagement demands a role different from the usual from regional advisors and different actors in the territories. Regional advisors and interlocutors from the organization's become facilitators or mediators of the process and direct their efforts to encourage participation and the exchange of knowledge. (University of Ibagué, 2021a, p. 33)

During the PRS, students develop different activities within the framework of the implementation of the action plan. To achieve these activities, students create a semester plan, a schedule that defines the field activities for the collection and analysis of information, as well as learning meetings, workshops and processes for formal evaluation. Under these training expectations, it is possible to find some spaces in which students of different disciplines, such as mechanical engineering, lawyers, the interlocutor, or members of the community, engage in a dialogic effort to understand problems and solutions, in which the language of the territory is appropriated.

> During the development of the experience, the regional advisors and technical professors who accompany students through a pedagogical dialogue, become referents for critical and ethical reflection on the action, as well as agents of transformation from a triple link with local governments, communities in the region, and students. (University of Ibague, 2021a, p. 29)

The PRS methodological guidelines state the importance of regional advisors and students working directly with the community, but despite this, in the analysis of the data, we found that these actors maintain a closer relationship with the interlocutor and a less direct relationship with the community. This may be due to the leadership role given to the interlocutor in the PRS guidelines, but it may also be associated with their negotiation role with university stakeholders.

> Approximately every three weeks a follow-up meeting is held between the interlocutor, the regional advisor and the student. This meeting serves to review the progress of the project in the implementation process. There is also a network that holds several meetings, weekly, including phone calls or WhatsApp chats. (Focus group discussion, PRS)

In the case of the Acuamiramar project, the interlocutor has a close relationship with the students and constantly accompanies them. As expressed by one of the regional advisors, this is justified by the understanding that it is the interlocutor who remains in the territory, which generates greater communication and closeness with the community:

> When we do the visit, we review what they did, and also take some time to meet with the interlocutor. Yes, we always like the organization to delegate a person who has the most direct contact with the student and the community. (Interview, regional advisor)

As a result, the principle of participation, as stated in the PRS guidelines, vanishes in practice since not all the actors involved in the project (regional advisors, interlocutors, students, and community) participate equally in the different phases of the process. The relevance of the interlocutor is undeniable since it is fundamental to operationalise the project in all its phases. By shadowing the students closely throughout whole process, the interlocutor generates the conditions through which the link between the students and the community is established.

The community recognizes the interlocutor as a stakeholder who maintains a constant link with the student's processes and the university-community agreement. On the other hand, in their reports, the students recognize the interlocutor as the person in the community with whom they interact daily and with whom they define the actions to be taken within the project:

> The development of this project includes the active participation of the board of the AAC, particularly the interlocutor who will be the bridge between me and the entity. He is the one who approves and monitors the different changes that I make during the development of the project. (Student report)

One aspect to highlight is community feedback on the student's work at the end of the experience in the Acuamiramar project. In the focus group with the community, we observed that the interlocutor is the one who has more knowledge than the rest of the community about the student's performance and the results of the work. Considering the important role that the interlocutor has in the agreement between the university and the community, several questions arise: How could a training program for interlocutors be designed to make their role more effective? What are the topics on which the university could train them?

One of the changes expected among those who take part in the PRS training is a critical reflection of the experience in the territory and the pedagogical strategies implemented, focusing on competencies, critical thinking and regional development. However, from the analysis of the data, we perceive that the reflection and transformation are focused on the PRS training model and is not explicitly oriented to modify community participation strategies. It is evident that in the meeting between students and regional advisors, the learning from the PRS is evaluated; participation of the students throughout the semester is reflected on from an operational perspective. Also, fulfillment of the objectives was reviewed; there was little critical reflection on participation.

> In this space, we [make] a global analysis of the experience, and that is what we call this learning meeting, lessons learned at the end of the process. (Interview, regional advisor)

The management network of the program is complex, because it implies spatial arrangements, defining a clear organi, zational structure and defined procedures, as well as respecting the different cultural forms. This is not easy, especially when there is a tripartite relationship – students, regional advisors and local stakeholders – that requires constant care and attention. It also means that the regional advisor must travel frequently throughout the department (territory) or other neighboring departments of the country during the semester. It is observed that the high demand for work plus the need for a deep monitoring process are aspects that require time, and this tends to make the processes more complex. Faced with the reality of the territories and contexts, these aspects privilege an operational-type training, which is neither expected to nor designed to promote participation. This is consistent with the institutional policy and the pedagogical model of the PRS.

4.3   Two Knowledge Cultures

In the relationship between Acuamiramar and PRS we can see two different knowledge cultures. Acuamiramar is a culture of knowledge that arises from the community's relationship with water, ancestral knowledge, and common sense. By contrast, the knowledge culture of the academy focuses on technical aspects.

In reviewing different documents about community participation in the construction, organization and care of community aqueducts in the state of Tolima, we found that for several decades, rural and marginalized urban communities have had to self-manage ways of supplying water to their communities.

The public administration in Colombia has not provided an effective response to the supply and organization of water for them.

> Human communities have always defined their spatial location concerning water, to water sources. For this reason, to go to the origin of community water management is to investigate the primordial memory of the relationship of people, families, and communities with water.
>
> Over time they appropriated technologies and built access to water sources in a family and community way based on self-management and trust, and thus supplied that need of any population when it arrives at a territory: a roof, water, and food.
>
> The population that benefits from the community aqueducts are essentially peasant population that develops agricultural practices, some activities with animals, or the cultivation of vegetables used for consumption.
> (RETACO, 2017, pp. 12, 23)

In the case of the Acuamiramar aqueduct, communities, settled near water sources, needed to find a way to supply water to their fields and for their families. They organized themselves with two other neighboring communities and presented a proposal to the municipal government for "the purchase of land where the Boquerón, Miramar, and Ricaurte aqueducts were supplying an area of 2.5 hectares, for the reforestation of its watershed" (Cataño, 2014, p. 42).

At that time, the Miramar community was a rural area located near a stream or micro-watershed. The villagers organised themselves to build wells and channeled the water resource.

The aqueducts show a culture of knowledge associated with daily experience, common sense, and learning through collaboration between families and the community. Furthermore, they share ancestral knowledge for the construction of wells, using natural resources such as guadua[4] to channel water from the streams and supply the community.

Currently, despite being in a conurbation area with the city of Ibagué, the community continues to have activities associated with rurality, and water is a fundamental resource to maintain these rural activities.

Regarding community participation in water management, there is currently an organisation in which some members of the community are part of a Community Board of Directors which manages the aqueduct. The aqueduct constituted as a public service company displaced community participation in the administration and maintenance of the aqueduct.

> We organised ourselves as a solidarity service company and created a CBD made up of some members of the community to manage and maintain the aqueduct and incorporate all the products that a public service company requires. We began contracts, reports, accounting, and everything related to managing it properly. (Aqueduct administrator interview)

Unfortunately, throughout the history of community aqueducts, there has been a lack of support from the national and local governments for their proper functioning, which has meant that they do not comply with sanitation and management standards, thus justifying their privatisation. As a result, a business culture has displaced the community knowledge culture, and it is the business culture that interacts with the academic culture.

As for the academic culture, we found that it related to the community culture from a technical perspective. The type of consultancy offered is related to the maintenance of the network cadastre, the administration of the service, and the attention to users. In this sense, the academic knowledge culture of the university approaches community problems from a positivist-oriented episteme.

> I saw some new guys in the neighbourhood who were measuring. Not knowing what they were doing, I asked the aqueduct administrator, "What are those guys doing?" He answered: "The aqueduct made an agreement with the University of Ibagué and they provided us with two guys, two engineers, to do the topographic survey of the cadaster". (Focus group discussion with community members)

This shows the encounter between two cultures of knowledge that are far from achieving convergence to mutually strengthen each other. On the contrary, it seems that the actions of the academic culture are strengthening positivist episteme dynamics, rather than orienting itself to engagement with the community to promote self-management and community participation in decisions regarding the aqueduct.

5   Analysis

From what has been described above, it is possible to highlight some central knowledge frameworks that interact in the PRS experience, their characteristics, and possible tensions.

In the first instance, a distinction must be made between the frames of meaning that reside in the institutionally declared knowledge and those that end up being practiced. PRS theoretically declares itself to be a transdisciplinary experience (knowledge beyond disciplinary frameworks), where the co-construction of knowledge is a fundamental issue in the exercise of social transformation. However, in practice, some processes are seen to be operating under a framework tending to validate disciplinary knowledge for the selection of students to be placed with the organizations. In the Acuamiramar case, the disciplinary frame operated with the interlocutor from the organization to send students of a certain discipline (engineers).

A similar tension between disciplinary frameworks and transdisciplinary experience operates in the construction of the action plans that students develop. The actions developed during the experience of the Acuamiramar project were structured to maintain a disciplinary form that, at times, already conditions the type of response to be obtained from the practice of those actions. Of course, this implies the reproduction of the idea of valid and invalid knowledge, as well as the construction of conversational forms that ratify the figure of the expert, in contrast with others that observe the experience from the point of view of engagement and co-construction. The tension operates from structural forms that maintain a separation between disciplinary programs and training designed with a more transdisciplinary approach. This is a challenge already observed by regional advisors, which will require constant reorientation of PRS, both internally (university) and externally (regional).

Another framework of meaning is the focus given to the result in comparison to valuing the process of learning. The experience itself and its orientation as a regional consultancy assumes, on part of the student, a knowledge related to meaningful participation and integration with the community. Structural and procedural characteristics, framed mainly due to financial reasons, imply a constant challenge away from such orientation. Navigating these challenges, and the power dynamics that emerge from the recurring relationships between regional advisors, interlocutors and students, has been an important task for PRS to constantly observe and map. For example, one tension lies in the fact that the high number of processes that a regional advisor may have to carry out diminishes his or her capacity to unpack a life experience from multiple dimensions for the students. The administrative functions are key, since the disciplinary requirements of each experience can affect the quality of the advisor's role. This does not imply that agreements should be organised to only connect the component of understanding the territory in the specific project being developed. It is possible to connect understanding of the territory with the specific actions that are agreed upon through relational reading during the formative processes undertaken with the students at the beginning of the program. Building this however requires time and deep involvement by the regional adviser, which is not always possible.

It is also possible to glimpse tensions between a certain instrumental knowledge to deliver concrete products from each semester experience vis-a-vis highlighting the process that is carried out and the progress even if 'early victories' have not been obtained, because it is not always possible to achieve milestones in the short term of a PRS experience over the semester. The operational action plans created to guide the PRS experience of each student is based on the needs of the organization or the assigned project. These are artifacts of knowledge that detail a procedure. We name it as an artifact because from them it is possible to glimpse an operating epistemological perspective and a certain way of conversing and constructing the knowledge that will be given during the semester. The plans highlight the general objectives or purposes to be fulfilled as well as concrete actions to be developed; these may operate more from a framework of relational sense with the purpose of the organization in the particular territory in which it operates, or as precise indicators of specific development where the support of the technical advisor is fundamental. It depends, to a great extent, on the way the action plan is built and the forms of knowledge that are highlighted, as well as the agreements reached with the interlocutors. Are these agreements based mainly on concrete products or are they agreements that interact relationally with transdisciplinary as the central purpose? Cultural forms indicate a greater tendency towards the concrete and the factual, as well as the disciplinary. This challenge is latent and recognised by members of PRS in the exercise of agreements between the different actors, especially between the institutional actor (university) and the organization. The agreements are mediated by financial and operational needs, which orients the requirements from the program. It is important to clarify that by using the word 'disciplinary' we are not assigning a negative or fragmented connotation, but are rather demarcating a tension existing between a formative process oriented towards the disciplinary and one oriented towards the transdisciplinary.

In terms of knowledge dissemination, there is more emphasis on presentation and understanding of what has been done among advisors, students and interlocutors. Knowledge artifacts can be identified here, such as final reports or concrete products which may tend to be more attractive as evidence of contribution. These reports and products are delivered in what are called 'closing meetings' and the experience can be reflected upon in 'learning encounter days'. However, doubts arise about the dissemination of this knowledge to the community in general or other members of the organization. It seems that a structural characteristic of workload will also operate here, which makes it difficult to accompany or review broader perceptions of the organizational

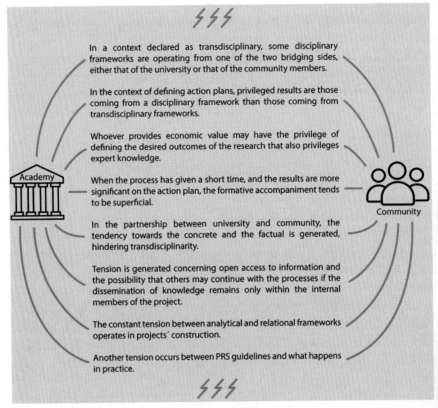

FIGURE 12.2   Principal tensions observed in the generation of bridges for the co-construction
of knowledge between academia and communities

actor. In the processes known to PRS, this is clear and various strategies are observed that allow them not only to publish the reports made by the students in a repository but also generate articles and dissemination events. However, the formation of interlocutors who act as amplifiers of the experience and its partial results in the territory becomes essential for the dissemination of knowledge.

Some principal tensions we observed when trying to bridge knowledge cultures and co-construct knowledge between academia and communities is given in Figure 12.2.

In summary, PRS is a highly ambitious proposal of engagement which respects the process and emphasizes the transdisciplinary and collective construction of knowledge for the development of the state of Tolima. However, tensions persist at the level of the frameworks of meaning in which the different actors involved in PRS operate, as well as the conflict and difficulty in operating within what is formally described and what is possible in practice

The tensions in constructing an experience from analytical frameworks of meaning – that reduce and fragment the project or the functions, losing their relationship with the whole – in contrast with highly relational exercises that detail the parts and work on them without losing their connection with the whole, stand out. This depends entirely on how engagement with each organization and in the specific territory is structured, and is mainly based on the frameworks of perception the regional advisors, the interlocutors and even the students themselves hold. Central issues, such as broad reflection about the territory, development and the construction of a dignified life, necessary to obtain early victories and to achieve clarity in the processes, hinder progress in terms of more substantial objectives and processes. The epistemological perspectives of the actors are much more oriented to the constructivist, where a type of knowledge is centered on the realization of something concrete and on applying previously defined theories, rather than on participatory processes. This is without detracting from the fact that instrumental concreteness is also fundamental for the advancement of actions.

Finally, there are the constant challenges to make the experience work from a disciplinary perspective against the transdisciplinary; the student's assumptions about the experience before living it; the highly diverse territorial dynamics with government agencies, social and productive organizations and collectives; the expectations regarding the action plan; the demands in terms of the time required for adequate support for particular interests against the need for a comprehensive training in PRS. These are not easy challenges to deal with to establish, maintain and improve the training bridges between the university and the organisations in the territory.

6   Conclusion

This case study of Acuamiramar, within the framework of the PRS, allows us to not only identify a series of challenges or tensions between the university-community relationship but also to explore possible recommendations to favor the generation of knowledge cultures from a transdisciplinary point of view. In these confluences of ways of thinking and building knowledge, we can observe that when the knowledge frameworks are not clear to all, or when there is no parallel training for all the actors involved to recognize and explore them, these tensions will occur. Perhaps it is because the academy maintains a position of power that privileges expert knowledge over everyday knowledge. One possible route to break this inequity is for the academy to recognise the value of other epistemologies and their paths. This can be achieved through concrete actions that transform how the academy has conventionally operated.

Likewise, the need for integration as outlined in the university's policies implies a constant, critical and transforming connection with the context of the territory. The problems that are manifested in a particular regional context cannot be easily defined within disciplinary boundaries, so there is the need to look towards transdisciplinary. In this sense, the formative work, not only for students but for all the actors involved, implies learning to approach projects or challenges that are not structured under the domain of a particular discipline. This is vital for the coherence of the PRS and its relationship with the various organisations in the territory and is highly consistent with the formal statement of the University of Ibagué regarding the construction of knowledge (University of Ibagué, 2021b, 2022). The ways to operationalize this could imply not emphasizing students be anchored to a particular discipline but seeing them as people learning skills who, according to their profile and interest, are linked to a project at a level beyond disciplines. In this sense, disciplines do not come to PRS, as in the case study observed, but students come from a variety of interests to live a participatory experience.

Implementing this requires a substantial change in the cultures of knowledge commonly operating in academic environments and the need to establish new ways to expand the frameworks, perspectives, recognition and respect for the transdisciplinary approach. A clear difference between professional practice and a PRS experience, for example, would be that the professional practical experience already has disciplinary or interdisciplinary structured challenges build in, which is why the organization requests a practitioner from a particular discipline, unlike PRS that operates under a transdisciplinary framework because the challenges or projects that the student addresses are not already structured. The way in which the objectives, actions or functions are structured in PRS is key for interaction with communities in the development of the project.

The transdisciplinary approach lays the foundations for a more participatory exercise to deal with the diverse ways in which the actors involved perceive the problem and reach agreements for action. In this case, the figure of the interlocutor is extended to all the relevant actors in the situation, and not just the person who is identified in the legal agreement between the university and the organization. The question is: what forms the role of the interlocutor? Surely, 'taking part in a dialogue', as mentioned in the standard definition of the role, is not unique to a single person, as this framing is inconsistent with the participatory and transdisciplinary approach. It is proposed to address this using a concept present in organizational cybernetics known as 'amplification of variety' (Díaz, n.d.). It implies that all of us, teachers of academic programs, students, and the organizations we partner with, amplify the capacity of PRS, that is, amplify the framework of knowledge that allows us to address complex situations (not structured in a disciplinary way) as a collective and in a participatory manner. Therefore, every teacher at a regional university such as the University of Ibagué is an amplifier of peace and of a transdisciplinary epistemology, regardless of whether he/she works in other functions for a particular project from his/her disciplinary framework or not. What is important is that he/she can learn to migrate beyond the discipline to other cognitive structures. Specifically, for PRS, its curriculum would allow training in knowledge cultures that are not only disciplinary but also transdisciplinary.

In a highly relational way, 'variety reduction' could operate in proposing a series of articulated projects or challenges with regional missions that reduce the apparent variety of process options in each organization and articulate common challenges. Thus, the regional advisors address a reduced set of articulated challenges, linking a wide variety of students. These adjustments would favor constant dissemination of the experiences and partial results that are generated involving all the actors.

If we want to create conditions for the confluence of knowledge cultures between the university and community, we must develop learning and training that is oriented towards transdisciplinarity (Díaz, n.d.). This implies the recognition of knowledge frameworks operating in any relationship and the need to train both teachers and students internally, and organizations and communities externally, about the importance of bridging the knowledges each brings, to learn to *observe how we are observing* the phenomena, and converge our different views and feelings. Transdisciplinary practice goes much beyond the unidirectional relationship in which the university goes to the territory, or a bi-directional one in which the university also receives from the territory; it is oriented to be a recursive process in which one cannot operate without the other because they are mutually constituted.

Notes

1 The University of Ibagué is a small private regional higher education institution that is located in the city of Ibagué, in the state of Tolima, approximately 211 km from the capital of Colombia, Bogotá.

2 Community-run aqueducts in Colombia are non-profit and community-driven, organized civil society groups that provide water to households in rural and semi-urban areas.

3   A type of social enterprise with a director, management, and employees co-created as a
    structured organization with all assets controlled, managed and directed by the community.
    In the early days of the aqueducts, only the community participated in them; years later,
    many have become companies with private, public, and community partners.
4   A plant from the bamboo family that is used as a tube to canalize water.

References

Assche, K. (2013). *Epistemic cultures, knowledge cultures and the transition of agricultural expertise: Rural development in Tajikistan, Uzbekistan, and Georgia.* Zef Working Papers Bonn University.

Batlle, R. (2007). *Juventud, ciudadanía y Aprendizaje-Servicio. ¿Qué jóvenes y cuál ciudadanía?* [in Spanish]. http://roserbatlle.net/wp-content/uploads/2009/03/juventud-ciudadania-y-aprendizaje-servicio.pdf

Cataño, W. (2014). *El agua como elemento de poder comunitario: el caso de los Acueductos Comunitarios de la Comuna 13 de Ibagué.* Trabajo de grado como prerrequisito para optar el título de Magíster en Territorio, Conflicto y Cultura. Universidad del Tolima Facultad de Ciencias Humanas y Artes Maestría en Territorio, Conflicto y Cultura. [in Spanish].

Charmaz, K. (2006). *Constructing grounded theory: A practical guide through qualitative analysis.* Sage.

Correa Zuluaga, S. (2020). *La gestion comunitária del agua en Colombia en tiempos de pandemia covid-19* [in Spanish]. http://biblioteca.clacso.edu.ar/clacso/gt/20210520115142/GESTIONCOMUNITARIADELAGUA2021.pdf

Denzin, N., & Lincoln, Y. (2000). *Manual de Investigación cualitativa* [*in Spanish*]. Gedisa.

Díaz, C. (n.d.). *Cibernética Organizacional y Sistema Viable.* https://www.agr.una.py/descargas/biblioteca_digital_gestion_riesgos/C/CIBERNETICA_ORGANIZACIONAL.pdf

Garzon Quiroga, A. C. (2020). *Propuesta de Diseño Para el Mejoramiento de la Calidad de Agua Para Consumo Humano del Acueducto Comunitario Acuamiramar de la Ciudad de Ibagué.* Universidad Nacional Abierta y a Distancia (UNAD). https://repository.unad.edu.co/bitstream/handle/10596/36736/acgarzonq.pdf?sequence=3&isAllowed=y

Giraldo, N. C. (2009). Acueductos comunitarios: Patrimonio social y ambiental del Valle de Aburrá. *Avances en recursos hidráulicos* [in Spanish], 20. https://repositorio.unal.edu.co/bitstream/handle/unal/28458/14332-42668-1-PB.pdf?sequence=1&isAllowed=y)

Hall, B. L. (2021, April 8–10). To change the world: Latin American contributions to the development of participatory research Jornada Internacional de Investigación con participación comunitaria CEADES Bolivia, Webinar.

Hall, B., Tandon, R., & Tremblay, C. (Eds.). (2015). *Strengthening community university research partnerships: Global perspectives, University of Victoria and UNESCO chair in community based research*. Victoria and New Delhi.

Hornidge, A.-K. (2012). Knowledge in development discourse: A critical review. In Hornidge, A. K. & C. Antweiler (Eds.), *Environmental uncertainty and local knowledge Southeast Asia as a laboratory of global ecological change* (pp. 21–54). Transcript.

Koekkoek, A., Van Ham, M., & Kleinhans, R. (2021). Unraveling university-community engagement: A literature review. *The Journal of Higher Education, 25*, 3–24.

Knorr-Cetina, K. D. (2007). Culture in global knowledge societies: Knowledge cultures and epistemic cultures. *Interdisciplinary Science Reviews, 32*(4), 361–375.

Mertens, D. (2005). *Research and evaluation in education and psychology: Integrating diversity with quantitative, qualitative, and mixed methods*. Sage.

RETACO (Red Nacional de Acueductos Comunitarios de Colombia). (2017). *El derecho a la augestion comunitaria del agia*. https://www.ohchr.org/sites/default/files/Documents/Issues/Water/Accountability/RedNacionalAcueductosComunitarios Colombia.pdf

Stake, R. (1998). *Case study research*. Ediciones Morata.

Stake, R. E. (2006). *Multiple case study analysis*. The Guilford Press.

University of Ibagué. (2014). *Institutional educational project*.

University of Ibagué. (2020). *Peace and region program. General information. Semester A 2020.*

University of Ibagué. (2021a). *Master document of the formative model of the peace and region semester.*

University of Ibagué. (2021b). *The necessary university. A proposal for the re-signification of the University of Ibagué.*

CHAPTER 13

Decolonising Knowledge for Social Change

Experiences of the Salish Sea K4C Hub, Canada

Suriani Dzulkifli, Crystal Tremblay, Walter Lepore, Tanya Clarmont, Carol Hall and Sebastian Silva

Abstract

The history and impacts of colonisation in Canada are important for the efforts of the Salish Sea K4C Hub in decolonising knowledge. In this case study, a brief understanding of this history is presented to contextualise the ongoing movements towards Indigenous self-determination across all aspects of life and for the building of capacity for research and training in support of these rights. Delving into the principles and vision of the hub and a brief background of the university credited CBPR course offered by the hub helps discern the key impacts of the course, and offers some reflections and recommendations in bridging different knowledge cultures between universities and communities.

Keywords

colonisation of knowledge – decolonising knowledge – Indigenous self-determination – CBPR course impacts

1 Introduction

The Salish Sea is the network of coastal waterways surrounding the traditional territories of the Coast Salish and Straits Salish Territories of the lǝk̓ʷǝŋǝn and W̱SÁNEĆ Peoples and the southwestern portion of mainland British Columbia (BC), Canada.[1] The term Salish Sea was selected as the name of the Hub to reflect the desire to focus its work in this area of Canada, to value the knowledges and life experience of local Indigenous people, and to describe the intricate ways we hope the hub will extend into local communities.[2]

Established in 2018 as part of the Knowledge for Change (K4C) Global Consortium, the Salish Sea Hub (SSH) is a partnership between the University of Victoria (UVic), the Victoria Native Friendship Centre (VNFC) and the Victoria Foundation (VF). The overall purpose of this hub is to decolonise knowledge production and promote the co-creation of knowledge through community-based and Indigenous-led research training and mentorship.

The SSH consists of a group of six certified mentors of multidisciplinary, multilingual, and multicultural backgrounds (see UNESCO Chair CBR-SR, 2022). Together we have co-developed an upper-level undergraduate course offered through the Department of Geography at the University of Victoria, which introduces students to the theory and practice of community-based participatory research (CBPR) and Indigenous ways of knowing, and exposes them to experiential learning opportunities with local community partners. With a special focus on addressing community-identified research needs linked to the UN Sustainable Development Goals (SDGs), the overarching objective of the course is to advance community-engaged research and learning within and outside academia, and contribute to the decolonisation and Indigenisation of higher education in Western Canada. In this chapter, we discuss some of the challenges and learnings we came across as we incorporated Western and local Indigenous knowledge systems into the design and delivery of this course, taking into consideration colonial, hierarchical, patriarchal power structures that still influence the work of community-university partnerships in Canada. As part of the BKC project, we were also interested in exploring the impacts of the hub's undergraduate course in working across knowledge systems outside and within the academia.

We begin this chapter by briefly describing the history and impacts of colonisation in Canada and the ongoing movements towards Indigenous self-determination across all aspects of life (i.e., general knowledge environment). Situating this history is important within the context of the efforts and priorities of the hub's institutional members to build capacity for research and training in support of the rights and well-being of Indigenous peoples and other social groups that have been historically marginalised (i.e., institutional knowledge environment). We then describe the local knowledge setting and practice by delving into the principles and vision of the hub and a brief background of the course. To discern the key impacts of the course, we present the findings of a case study of the hub that was carried out with the collaboration of its mentors, partners and students. Lastly, we offer some reflections and recommendations in bridging different knowledge cultures between universities and communities.

2   General Knowledge Environment: Impacts of Colonialism
       in Canada

In Canada, there is an on-going history of racism, oppression and discrimination towards Indigenous peoples and their knowledge systems, which has led to the annihilation of Indigenous ways of being and knowing. This epistemicide (de Sousa Santos, 2016) has forced the disconnection and displacement of Indigenous peoples from their land, culture, language, and community, stretching back to hundreds of years when European settlers seized unceded Indigenous lands for resource extraction and conquering of new settlements. In furthering their colonialist and imperialist agenda, the European colonisers intentionally implemented displacement and assimilation policies with the aim of removing and severing Indigenous peoples from their lands and culture.

One of these policies was the Indian Act, passed in 1876 by the Canadian government, which still operates today undermining Indigenous peoples' identity, sovereignty and nationhood (Bartlett, 1988; Dickason & Newbigging, 2015; MacDonald & Steenbeek, 2015; Ray, 2016). The Indian Act controls many aspects of the daily lives and wellbeing of the Indigenous peoples in Canada, and it has had a profound adverse impact on the translation and transmission of knowledge in Indigenous communities. With the aim of assimilating the Indigenous population and bringing them under one form of law and one way of life, the Indian Act abolished traditional forms of governance, including the restriction of women in decision-making and replacing their leadership roles with a patriarchal, male-only elective system that are contrary to the often matrilianal leadership roles of Indigenous women in political, economic and social life in their communities (Sayers, 2001).

Until 1951, the Indian Act also prohibited *potlatches*, an Indigenous cultural ceremony that involves gift giving and feasting on important occasions such as naming ceremonies, change of leadership, births and deaths. Potlatches were considered a major barrier to assimilation as it maintains legal traditions of the Coast Salish people with the redistribution of wealth, refinement of oral histories, and affirmation of territorial boundaries (Cole & Chaikin, 1990). The prohibition of these cultural ceremonies has resulted in a major breakdown in the ability of older generations to preserve their own culture and to share important stories about laws and traditions with younger generations (Kan, 2015).

Further genocide and oppression of Indigenous knowledge systems occurred during the implementation of the Indian Residential Schools (IRS) system – operated by the Anglican, Roman Catholic, Methodist, Presbyterian United churches, among others, and funded by the Canadian government – in which Indigenous children were abducted from their homes in attempts to 'kill the Indian in the child' and assimilate them into the Western culture (Charles & Lowry, 2017). Canada's last residential school closed in 1996, and over the course of 125 years, more than 150,000 children were forcibly removed from their communities and placed into IRS; many of them never returned home (Royal Commission on Aboriginal Peoples, 1996; Truth and Reconciliation Commission of Canada, 2015). The majority of children were held captive and isolated from their families and all their kinship ties for the entire time they attended IRS.

In this regard, it is important to note that, within Indigenous communities, the extended kinship system plays an integral role in the function of children learning and inter-generational transfer of knowledge (Poonwassie & Charter, 2001). The education system of residential schools replaced a reciprocal and holistic learning and teaching cycle strongly founded in relationships and cultural pedagogies of discovery and interdependency, with a pedagogy based on authority, control, force, individualism and competition. The IRS education system introduced a new way of learning to Indigenous peoples as a mechanism to Christianise, colonise and assimilate Indigenous children (by teaching them foreign values and customs), and to destroy their cultures, beliefs, languages and sense of pride (by shaming them into rejecting their own culture, traditions, spirituality and language) (Haig-Brown, 1988). Indigenous children who were forced to attend IRS suffered from physical, psychological and emotional abuse which affected the generations that followed, causing intergenerational trauma (Charles & Lowry, 2017; Methot, 2019). These traumas are still felt today and have left a legacy of poverty, economic marginalization, unemployment, addiction, homelessness, and ongoing racism and stigmatization in systems such as health care and education (Methot, 2019).

3   Decolonizing Knowledge Production and Dissemination

In recent years, conscious efforts have been made in decolonising knowledge and institutions, including recognising Indigenous ways of knowing, to address the harmful impacts colonialism and imperialism have brought onto Indigenous communities (Smith, 1999; Wilson, 2008). Within a broader movement across Canada and globally, a number of initiatives have taken shape in support of meaningful community engagement and Indigenous-led research, as a response to the United Nations Declaration on the Rights of Indigenous Peoples (UNDRIP) in 2007, the Declaration on the Rights of Indigenous Peoples Act (DRIPA) created in 2022, and the Truth and Reconciliation Commission's (TRC) Calls to Action in 2015, among several others.[3]

The Canada Research Coordinating Committee (CRCC), for instance, was created in 2017 to help advance federal research priorities and the coordination of policies and programmes of Canada's research funding agencies. One of its key priorities is to support and enhance the capacity of First Nations, Métis and Inuit communities to lead their own research and partner with the broader research community.[4] The CRCC, with extensive engagement across the country, launched a national Indigenous research framework to strengthen Indigenous-led research in November 2019. Alongside these national shifts, several First Nations and Indigenous organisations have developed their own research protocols and strategies should they choose to partner with external institutions and organisations (e.g., the National Inuit Strategy on Research). Indigenous communities have also been at the forefront in creating research principles and ethics to assert control over data gathering processes and governance (e.g., the Ownership, Control, Access and Possession [OCAP] principles[5]) and have advanced Indigenous research approaches, most of which are community-based. In 2018, the Tri-Council Policy Statement set the ethical standard for research that involves the First Nations, Inuit and Métis Peoples of Canada.[6]

In line with this decolonising and Indigenising movement, mainstream universities –the University of Victoria included– have been developing spaces for recruiting and retaining Indigenous students and faculty members (e.g., through equity, diversity and inclusion policies and programmes, and preferential or target hirings), and offer programmes that incorporate Indigenous content. According to the 2016 Canadian Census, Indigenous peoples constitute 5% of the population and, although in the last two decades there has been a steady increase of Indigenous students in the postsecondary sector (now reaching also 5%), there has been a consistent 14% gap in the completion rates between Indigenous and non-Indigenous undergraduate students since the 1990s (Smith and Bray, 2019). Also, Indigenous PhD students are still highly under-represented in Canadian universities (i.e., 1%), in the same way that Indigenous peoples comprise of only 3% of college instructors and 1.4% of university professors, and there is between 15% to 20% wage gap between Indigenous and non-Indigenous professors (ibid.).

4   Institutional Knowledge Environment: The Salish Sea Hub Partners

The SSH works to contribute to the decolonising of knowledge production and dissemination within and outside acedemia. The hub supports its partners to come together and co-lead research that has been identified by the communities in which we serve. Each partner organisation of the SSH has a strong mandate to improve the lives of the people and communities in which they operate and is committed to doing so. They are each recognised in the region as being leaders for their commitment to community engagement and decolonisation. These commitments are woven through the strategic visions and mandates of the organisations that have various mechanisms and programmes that support this work.

4.1   *Victoria Native Friendship Centre*

The Victoria Native Friendship Centre (VNFC) is an urban Indigenous organisation grounded in Indigenous worldviews and cultures, which serves the diverse Indigenous communities living in the Capital Regional District of Victoria, BC. The VNFC is one of 118 centres across Canada that are part of the Friendship Centre Movement that helps connect people to the local community, provide cultural support, and aims to bridge some of the gaps between Indigenous and non-Indigenous people in urban settings. The VNFC's mandate is to encourage and promote the well-being of urban Indigenous people, by strengthening individuals, family and community. Community engagement is central to achieving VNFC's mandate, and CBPR methods have been at the core of that engagement since opening in 1969.

All programming offered at VNFC is culturally enhanced and developed specifically to respond to the needs of the surrounding urban Indigenous community. Urban life for Indigenous peoples is considerably different from that of reserves and other rural areas given a number of distinctive characteristics they face, such as: (a) economic marginalisation – urban Indigenous residents tend to be poorer than their non-Indigenous neighbours (Obonsawin & Howard-Bobiwash, 1997) and are also likely to experience higher rates of unemployment, single parenthood, homelessness, and domestic violence (Janovicek, 2007); (b) cultural diversity – urban Indigenous population is made up of individuals and families that arrive to urban centres from many different Indigenous communities, whether from reserves, smaller towns or other cities (FitzMaurice & McCaskill, 2011);[7] and (c) legal diversity – urban Indigenous residents represent a complex mix of legal classifications across conflicting responsibilities of the federal government and other levels of jurisdiction (FitzMaurice & McCaskill, 2001; Palmater, 2011).[8] These characteristics create real challenges in terms of providing programmes, services and funding to urban Indigenous people.

VNFC has developed a strong leadership team who works with community to undertake research for the purpose of enhancing programming, securing funding, and creating programmes that aptly respond to community needs in a culturally safe and timely way. The VNFC services are available to the 17,000 Indigenous people living in the Capital Regional District, including the 2,500 residents from the First Nations communities in the southern Vancouver Island region. The VNFC, as other Friendship Centres, can be considered a hub of Indigenous culture (Howard, 2011). It works with and shares several Indigenous knowledge systems reflective of the diversity of Indigenous peoples that are part of their community and benefit from their services. Protocols for sharing and disseminating these knowldeges is often guided by the Elders and Advisory councils who ensure that the appropriate measures are followed. This might include specific ceremonies, gifting protocols, witnessing, and ways of working together that are unique to the customs and traditions of local Indigenous peoples and their communities.

4.2   Victoria Foundation

The Victoria Foundation (VF) is a philantropic organisation that has a vision to create a vibrant, caring local community. The Foundation grounds its work in community knowledge, and it supports hundreds of initiatives, both large and small across southern Vancouver Island and beyond. In doing so, it enables non-profit organisations to respond to the most pressing concerns and needs in this community such as housing, food equity, gender equality and inclusion, to name but a few. The Foundation also works closely with the local community to conduct the annual Victoria's *Vital Signs* community report, which measures the vitality of the region, identifies concerns, and supports actions on issues that are relevant and critical to improving quality of life. VF has been a strong proponent and leader of advancing the UN SDGs in the local community and has introduced the SDGs as a framework into the Vital Signs initiative as well as its other leadership initiatives.

The Foundation was one of the initial signatories to the Philanthropic Community's Declaration of Action as a pledge to maintain an active commitment to reconciliation based on the Truth and Reconciliation Commission's Calls to Action. The VF Reconciliation Task Group provides input and recommendations to the Board of Directors and staff to continue its work to engage in reconciliation.

4.3   University of Victoria

The University of Victoria (UVic) is a mid-size, public research university highly engaged with its local, regional and national communities, respectfully acknowledging its unique place situated on the traditional territories of the ləkʷəŋən Peoples and W̱SÁNEĆ First Nations. Guided by the values and wisdom of the Coast Salish First Peoples, the University's first Indigenous Plan

(2017–2022) provides an important path for reconciliation that is informed and woven throughout the university's research, teaching and service initiatives. A focus on and appreciation for the unique cultural, physical and social environment on which the campus sits is part of the university's identity. UVic is ranked strongly for promoting Indigenous visibility, and first nationally for Open Access publications, commitment to Truth and Reconciliation Commission (TRC) Calls to Action, and open curriculum (University of Victoria, 2022).

4.4 Principles, Visions and Institutional Challenges of the Salish Sea Hub

The work of the hub is oriented to address and create community interventions and innovations addressing the UN SDG with a particular focus on good health and well-being (SDG3), quality education (SDG4), gender justice (SDG5), reduced inequality (SDG10), and climate action (SDG13). The SSH is committed to promoting the full and effective participation in all matters that concern Indigenous peoples and their right to remain distinct and pursue their own visions of economic and social development. As such, the hub is specifically grounded in Indigenous ways of viewing and knowing the world to bridge knowledge and research out of academia and into communities. A focus of the hub is to centralize the voices, stories and experiences of underrepresented communities through CBPR, including youth, Elders/seniors, 2SLGBTQ+ peoples, new Canadians and refugees, and the unhoused community, to name a few.

While the SSH demonstrates a respectful working relationship between all of its partner organisations, it has to be acknowledged that relationship-building has not been spontaneous or without challenges. Interviews conducted as part of this research for the BKC project reveal that, from the university's perspective, building trust with community partners is often seen as 'invisible work', usually not recognised in the academia, while community organisations find it difficult to navigate relationships with the university, not knowing 'how it works or which support to connect with'.

Although the collaborative work of the hub is institutionally established by a non-binding MoU signed by the three partner organisations, personal relationships play a crucial role in breaking down barriers between community organisations and the university. For instance, at present, the SSH mentors affiliated to the VNFC depend on their personal contacts with the UVic representatives of the SSH to help them connect with the right person or department at the university. VNFC and VF have the insight and familiarity of working with each other and other community organisations due to the similarity of their mandates and works cultures, compared to working with UVic. The lack of cultural awareness, community knowledge and familiarity at the university does not contribute to the advancement of community-university engagement and knowledge co-creation outside the boundaries of academia.

5   Knowledge Setting: Training the Next Generations in CBPR

In working towards the hub's goals of decolonising knowledge production and dissemination, while featuring diverse voices and centring Indigenous ways of knowing, we have co-developed a university credited CBPR course. The course was developed in consultation with Elder Advisors, and is offered as a 400-level Geography course in the Department of Geography, where Tremblay, the academic lead of the SSH, is a faculty member. The course is grounded in decolonisation, knowledge democracy, anti-oppressive, arts-based, and Indigenous methodologies through study of the literature, case studies, presentations by community-academic partners, practicum term projects in community and self-reflection activities.

The CBPR course has been offered during four academic terms between 2020 and 2022 for a duration of three months each, and a total of 61 students have completed the course successfully. While this course is offered to upper-level undergraduate students, several graduate level students have also enrolled in it due to its unique design and content. There have been eleven community organisation partners to date, many of whom have ongoing projects spanning throughout the terms, with students handing off projects to the new cohort. Since the course launched in 2020 during the COVID-19 pandemic, it has been delivered virtually, including all community-led projects with the students for the first two terms with the support of Zoom and Brightspace, a learning management system that the university uses. The third term was the first time that the course was conducted in person; however, as COVID-19 policies at the university and some community organisations differ, a few community-led projects were conducted online.

Indigenous Elder Advisors in partnership with the VNFC play an active role in the course to provide guidance and training to students and hub mentors. Despite this important collaboration from the community partners, the UVic faculty member is the only one responsible for sourcing, finding and designing community-based projects, and the timing of the course, reflecting the continued power imbalance in favour of the university in terms of decision-making and governance of the course. Similarly, other SSH mentors who are not UVic professors are not formally recognised or funded by the university and funds to support their participation needs to be obtained each term the course is offered, inhibiting the achievement of our goals as a hub and keeping the course offering precarious.

6 Case Study: Knowledge Co-Creation at the Salish Sea Hub

The case study research for the BKC project started in August 2021 and ended in November 2021. The hub's mentors co-designed the study; however, not all mentors were able to be active participants of the project due to the lack of capacity and resources (i.e., time, funding), which has been an ongoing challenge of the hub. For the duration of the research, we frequently met via Zoom to design the research, choose appropriate conceptual frameworks, research questions, timeline, participants, and methods, which are discussed in the following sections.

We identified several groups to recruit for the research – previous students who had completed the CBPR course, representatives from VNFC and VF as community partners of the hub, and representatives of UVic from the Office of the Vice President Research as an academic partner of the hub. We contacted former students via email regarding the project and six agreed to participate. The student participants received a gift card of $25 as a gesture of appreciation for volunteering their time. Further, each mentor of the hub identified and communicated with their colleagues and were invited to participate in an interview.

6.1 Methods: Focus Group, Interviews and Arts-Based Activity

Due to ongoing COVID-19 restrictions we conducted one focus group and several interviews with our participants as these were the safest and most feasible methods to carry out the research under the given circumstances. To engage the students, we facilitated a 90-minute focus group via Zoom at the end of the first week of September 2021. Two SSH mentors from UVic facilitated the focus group with the six students. The students were invited to reflect on their understanding of multiple knowledge systems (i.e., Indigenous, community-based, arts-based) introduced in the course, their experience of being involved directly in community-led projects, and the impacts the course had on their learning and their personal and professional lives.

In addition to asking the students discussion questions, we also incorporated an arts-based component where we requested them to draw or share a photo of what 'knowledge' means to them. Towards the end of the focus groups, the students were given 10 minutes to do this arts-based activity. By using an arts-based method, the students were able to conceptualise their understanding of knowledge critically without the limitations of words. Using the arts in learning and teaching can "foster deeper awareness of self, one another and the world, richer engagement with study, greater confidence and resilience" (McIntosh, 2013, p. 4), which can complement our understanding of the course's impacts on the students learning.

The interviews with hub partners (UVic, VNFC and VF) were conducted between September and October of 2021. We separately interviewed a total of six participants (two representatives from each institution/organisation). Responses from the focus group and interviews were analysed and thematically coded by two SSH mentors using the inductive approach, allowing the data collected to determine the themes. Upon analysing the content of focus group discussion and interviews, the two mentors identified the themes from the data separately. They then met up to discuss the themes that they had each identified. Both mentors identified similar themes without major discrepancies.

7   Findings

The common themes that emerged in all of the interviews and focus groups, and the findings of the project are shared below.

7.1   Theme 1: Re-defining 'Knowledge'

For centuries, 'knowledge' had been understood through Western Eurocentric lenses. For Linda Tuhiwai Smith (1999), a world-renowned professor of Indigenous education,

> the arguments of different Indigenous peoples based on spiritual relationships to the universe, to the landscape and to stones, rocks, insects and other things, seen and unseen, have been difficult arguments for Western systems of knowledge to deal with or accept. (p. 84)

Yet, it is crucial to challenge the Western points of views in order to bridge the different knowledge cultures. We must first understand what we know and consider as knowledge. One clear theme that emerged was the expanded understanding of what 'knowledge' is. Different knowledge cultures may view, consider, and accept different elements as knowledge.

In the perspectives of civil society organisations, both SSH community partners – i.e., the VNFC and VF – perceive knowledge as place-based and community-centred. Community knowledge is what informs their programmes, services and other projects for their organisations as they are designed and built based on a needs-based approach in their local communities. In the case of VF, their work has shifted from donor-focused to community focused, as one of their representatives mentioned that they were "taking action based on what is coming from [the] community", recognising that knowledge comes in different forms. They acknowledge that as an organisation they work as an intermediary between donors and community members, and have the obligation to learn from the community as "without them, we do not know much" about what is really needed. Using this community-centred approach, the VF releases a yearly report called *Vital Signs*, and creates programmes to help address community issues highlighted in the report, ensuring that all voices are heard.

Similarly, the VNFC is community-responsive by gathering community knowledge from its members to provide them with services and programmes that are Indigenous-led and created based on their needs. Hence, all of their services and programmes are unique to their own site. They describe knowledge as "the accumulation of information ... things that have been tried, that worked, that failed, learning from those processes brings us knowledge". Knowledge also needs to be easily shareable and accessible. In the 52 years of providing services to urban Indigenous communities, they share the knowledge and best practices collectively among other Friendship Centres across the province on services of shared priority. This could be, for example, information about "financial literacy, nutrition, counselling, folded into training processes", highlighting that the oral transmission of knowledge remains very important to their organisation.

On the other hand, UVic views knowledge in the form of research, scholarship and experiential knowledge, which they describe as "evidence-based and sustained experience knowledge" and bringing these different kinds of knowledge together at the university. They elaborated on experiential knowledge as "transmission of extended experience", for example, from working with Indigenous communities such as the Elders. The knowledge is then produced typically in the forms of publications and conference presentations that are often aimed to measure impact factor. Notably, UVic is in the midst of creating a committee to reevaluate and measure knowledge production as a way of not excluding knowledges cultures and navigating a new way of translating the impact measurement of these knowledges.

Therefore, knowledge is not limited to just academic knowledge. We acknowledge and accept that knowledge expands beyond the restricted academic/scientific knowledge including but not limited to Indigenous, local and other types of knowledge systems that derive from the community. The students from our CBPR course also noted how the course impacted their new understanding of 'knowledge', which is discussed as a subtheme below.

7.1.1   Subtheme: New Understanding of 'Knowledge'

By using the arts in our CBPR course with community partners, we invited the students to reflect on the expanded definition and meaning of 'knowledge' as a way to connect the different types and sources of knowledge. To demonstrate this, the focus group participants, who were former students of the hub's CBPR course, were asked to draw or share an image that expressed their understanding of 'knowledge' since completing the course. Through visual representations, they shared their outlook that knowledge was represented in different forms. Using the images they had drawn or selected, they highlighted the importance of recognising knowledges that were outside of the university, and that the process of knowledge creation had to be collaborative. Speaking specifically to the relationship with local Indigenous communities, the participants mentioned that this collaborative process was pertinent to reconciliation as the process was sometimes more important than the outcome. We share below some of the participant's visual representations and interpretations of 'knowledge' in their own words. All names used are pseudonyms.

One former student, Molly, drew this image (Figure 13.1) in describing her expanded understanding about 'knowledge' upon taking the CBPR course:

She shared,

> When asked to picture our thoughts about knowledge, I imagined something very vibrant, fluid and collaborative, much like a garden can be. In the image, you can see components both above and below the soil, demonstrating that knowledge may not always be where we expect and that it can appear in many forms. In the photo, there are many contributors, such as pollinators and the sun and a lot of diversity, much like my experience in the class. What is not pictured here, though could be demonstrated further with this concept, are spaces where there is only one entity creating knowledge, which might result in a mono-crop, or areas where knowledge extraction is harmful, perhaps resulting in a garden with poor health. For the most part, however, I wanted to represent the knowledge that we encompassed in class, one that prioritises not only the product, but the process as well.

Another former student, Samantha, drew this image (Figure 13.2) of what she understood of knowledge from taking the CBPR course:

FIGURE 13.1   Molly's drawing of her representation of knowledge as a garden with many
different contributors

She explained,

> This image is a conceptualisation of human made knowledge through
> comparison of thoughts and knowledge. Thoughts are resembled by the
> curvy lines and knowledge is resembled through the curvy lines that lead
> to a bubble. People are resembled by diverse stick figures. I view human
> made knowledge as something that stems from thoughts and experi-
> ences that can stem from an individual and/or a collective.

Instead of drawing, Sierra shared this picture (Figure 13.3) to describe her
new understanding of 'knowledge' from her involvement in the CBPR course.
According to her,

> The photo is what I think of when I hear the word knowledge after taking
> the CBPR course. I learned how incorporating Indigenous (non-Western)
> epistemologies and ways of knowing is integral on the road to reconcilia-
> tion. It inspired me to become a more confident student by validating my
> learned experiences and my natural ability to relate to the environment
> around me. There is no knowledge without the earth and all those who

FIGURE 13.2   Samantha's drawing of knowledge as exchanges of thoughts and experiences

FIGURE 13.3   The image Sierra chose to represent her understanding of knowledge
SOURCE: DREAMSTIME.COM, AN ONLINE ROYALTY FREE STOCK
PHOTO COMMUNITY

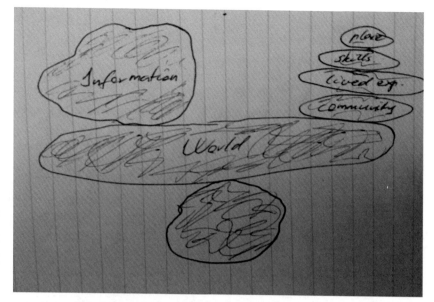

FIGURE 13.4   Kisborkai drew his representation of knowledge as having to be in balance

inhabit it, and CBPR encourages a respectful sharing of that knowledge in hopes of creating a more inclusive world.

Kisborkai drew this image (Figure 13.4) as a representation of what knowledge is to him, following his participation in the CBPR course. He described,

> This image of balancing stones represents the information that we have in society has to be in balance with the lived experiences including all of the little components of the world around us. In the same context, I am really fascinated by the First Nations culture because they are willing to understand everything around them. So, their knowledge comes from their environment as well. And I think that the university's knowledge has to come from the outside in the same way, and when they develop their knowledge, it has to be disseminated back into the community because that is the only way to keep it balanced. We can't have all knowledge in isolation to maintain the balance. To me that is knowledge, to accept everything around us and it is a necessary part of it.

These images that were either drawn or chosen by the students and their interpretations of them, suggest that they now have a new, deeper and richer understanding of what knowledge is. All of them recognised and accepted that there is knowledge outside of the classroom, outside of the preferential system, and within oneself, that is, each person's experiences. The CBPR course has helped them realise the power over knowledge, on whose knowledge is accepted as 'valid'. It has made them aware of the extractive nature of the relationship between institutions and Indigenous communities, and how important it is for university and Indigenous communities to work together, collaboratively, with reciprocity and respect.

7.2   Theme 2: Relationship as a Fundamental Aspect of Knowledge Creation and Working Collaboratively

Scholars highlight that relationships are at the heart of CBPR practice, especially since the approach involves the active participation of co-creating knowledge with groups of people (MacKinnon, 2018; Rappaport, 2020). Unsurprisingly, when it comes to working in partnerships with communities, relationships as the core of CBPR and knowledge co-creation was an overwhelming theme that emerged from analysis of the participants' interviews and focus group responses. All of the hub partners as well as the former students of the CBPR course stated that having a strong foundation in relationships with communities eases the processes of working together collaboratively. It would also set precedents and increase the possibility for future collaborations.

In this regard, a challenge highlighted by the VNFC representatives was the excessive expectation from others when working with an Indigenous organisation as "there is a lot of pressure to help others participate in reconciliation. The responsibility to inform and educate people to help them participate in Indigenous spaces". Separately, this challenge was also acknowledged by the UVic representatives, that as a university, they sometimes "overuse community partners but no one is tracking how much is being asked". Better coordination and organising at the institutional level are needed to avoid overuse issues. In preventing this from further happening, the university is starting to create a community portal to track their requests of community partners.

In managing expectations while working in collaboration with others, one VF representative highlighted that

> it's important to think about what is the best for both sides of the table; decide early on how to work with each other and being clear about expectations at the beginning, discussing deliverables at the start, and not making it up as you go. Knowing when to step away is important too.

An initiative like the SSH allows for a continuous space to establish the work and values that are needed in relationship building, and to practice the importance of nurturing these relationships bringing the values of trust, respect and reciprocity forward.

As one of the highlights of this CBPR course, the former students mentioned that the course provided them with the opportunity to build relationships with the community partners as well as with others in the course (e.g., other students, professors, mentors) more closely than they normally would have. They recognised that the relationships developed also gave them the opportunity for networking that was lacking in the other courses they were enrolled in. However, while the students enjoyed building these relationships with community partners, they found that their involvement in community-led projects ended abruptly after three months following the university's schedule of the end of a term. Some students shared that the timeframe for the course to complete the project was too short. Further, there had been no clear expectations for both the students and community partners when the course was over. Nevertheless, there are several efforts to continue the student-community partnerships following the course, such as through directed studies, honours projects, work study, or other funding sources that enable the students to continue working on projects after the course ends. This has its own challenge in capacity as trying to maintain so many projects and students (without funding) is problematic.

7.3 Theme 3: Learning through Active Listening

Bishop (1994) reminds us that listening is an essential element in building alliances and working collaboratively. In this study, both the hub's community partners and former students identified active listening as one of the important skills required to build relationships with local communities. When working with communities of different cultural backgrounds and ways of knowing, such as the Indigenous communities, active listening is one of the useful skills to understand the community partners' needs as well as to learn from them with humility and empathy. The representatives at the VF highlighted that as humans, "we have innate assumptions about others", and so it is important that "we unlearn and debunk these assumptions by learning about other people through collaborations" with different organisations and populations, and practising active listening. In this regard, it is important that "we make sure all voices are heard, [thus] our work must be driven by real curiosity to learn". Requesting for and receiving feedback from others are also continuous processes of learning when using active listening and reflection.

Likewise, the VNFC practices active listening with its community members, especially when the programmes and services are catered specifically to the members' needs. This makes the practice of active listening vital to their work.

Interestingly, the VNFC representatives highlighted that from their many experiences of working with universities, people in academia have the tendency of overthinking, and so they often over-speak as well. This shows there is a lack of practice in active listening that academics need to start adopting into their work, particularly when it involves working with communities to address problems and needs they have identified.

It is particularly interesting that there was no mention of active listening by the university as a key element in bringing together knowledge with communities. This is especially important given their observations of asking too much, and not compensating enough when asking Indigenous peoples to participate in university activities and research. Thus, it appears that there is more of a need to emphasise and include active listening in university practice when it collaborates with communities, something that CBPR requires researchers to do as a way to foster reciprocal collaborations with humility and respect. Through active listening, academics will be able to learn, appreciate and respect the value of other experts' knowledge that is all around them. Active listening is one way of fostering openness and humility in learning that the university must normalise. Active listening in CBPR is not just an asset or recommendation, it is a need.

7.4   Theme 4: Reflection as an Important Practice in CBPR

According to H. S. Kim, an expert in nursing practice, reflection is "a process of consciously examining what has occurred in terms of thoughts, feelings, and actions against underlying beliefs, assumptions and knowledge as well as against the backdrop in which specific practice has occurred" (1999, p. 1207). Building on this definition, Cameron et al. (2000) explain that by applying reflective practice we gain "new understandings [which] can lead to a transformation in perspective and an eventual change in practice" (p. 218). Indeed, the importance of reflection is the next theme that emerged. Although addressed separately, it is closely connected to active listening.

The representatives from one of the hub's community partners and the former students of the course mentioned how they found reflection as an important component of CBPR. According to the representatives at the VF, they discovered that reflective practice helped them improve the effectiveness of their work and programme with the community. They mentioned that the VF as an organisation has always worked in partnerships with different communities that came with their own sets of knowledge, experiences, concerns, ideas and suggestions. Reflection helped them make informed decisions and take local actions.

Reflection requires the skill of active listening in order to truly understand a situation. Practicing reflection can also lead to reflexivity when we are aware of our judgements, assumptions and biases before making a decision or committing to an action. The students enrolled in the CBPR course also found this to be true. They mentioned that participating in the course had allowed them the opportunity to reflect on a regular basis through discussions, assignments, as well as their interactions with community partners, mentors and other students. Being involved in the course offers them the possibility to learn, unlearn and re-learn the nature of relationships between colonial institutions (e.g., universities) and Indigenous communities, making them aware of the impacts of historical and ongoing colonisation, privilege and power imbalance between the two entities. Learning this had allowed the students to be both reflective and reflexive of their own positionality in society, their biases, judgements and assumptions. One student shared that being involved in this course had challenged him to be accountable of his white privilege and encouraged him to practise decolonisation in his daily life.

8   Reflections and Recommendations to Bridge Knowledge between Academia and Community

First, there has been a discrepancy in perception of what knowledge is, and the value it holds. Indigenous knowledge and knowledge from local communities, for example, are often viewed as 'inferior' and at times deemed 'invalid' by universities for the fact that they are not knowledge produced or validated by the institution. As a consequence of this colonial hegemony held by universities, it contributes to the epistemicide of other knowledge systems and the perpetuation of colonisation in our systems and everyday lives. As a way of preventing this from further happening, universities need to decolonise research and teaching practices by recognising and accepting knowledge in all forms, including those that are community based and outside of academia. By integrating different knowledge systems into the design and delivery of our course, we have helped students, who are the next generation of researchers, to expand their perspectives and create a new understanding of what is considered as 'knowledge', which we hope will have broader impacts in their lives and communities going forward.

Second, we learned that there are challenges for local communities to navigate relationships with universities given the specific mandate and complex organisational structure of the institution. The shifting structures of the university in regards to community engagement has been a challenge and remains as one of the barriers for community-university partnerships and engagement. Local communities currently depend on personal contacts at universities, and at times, universities tend to overextend community partners, especially non-profit and Indigenous community organisations. In bridging this gap, better coordination and planning at the institutional level of universities is needed. Universities should consider to prioritize relationship building with local communities by investing time and resources to get to know them and their (working) culture. Universities also need to dedicate a unit or structure to community-university engagements that allows for easier navigation to foster collaborations. This unit could assist with enhancing and facilitating cultural awareness among university researchers when it comes to working with communities.

Third, there has often been a lack of practice in listening to communities by universities when working with communities. University researchers have the tendency to over-speak and assert their ideas without, first, listening to the communities and, second, taking their needs into consideration. Due to this lack of active listening, universities struggle to view local communities as 'experts', or compensate them fairly for their contributions, when in fact Indigenous communities have their own highly evolved knowledge systems and ways of being that include vast knowledge of the territories they call home. Active listening helps to promote and bridge the understanding of these different knowledge cultures. As uninvited guests to the Indigenous territories, universities must start listening actively to Indigenous communities, and honour, respect and learn from, with humility and openness, the knowledge these communities have and share. Academics are urged to embrace and incorporate active listening in their work when they collaborate with communities, as it helps to understand their needs and allows for an open and respectful learning environment. The CBPR course has highlighted the usefulness of active listening when working with communities. Particularly, the course provided a space for students to practice and apply this skill. While active listening is one of the core aspects of CBPR, it requires practice.

Fourth, there is a need for reflection when working with local communities. We learned that reflection contributes to the effectiveness and improvement of community programmes and collaborations. Reflection helps to bridge different knowledge cultures as it provides us with the space to learn, re-learn and unlearn our assumptions and biases, which can ultimately lead to changes in beliefs and behaviours. Being both reflective and reflexive is important when we collaborate with communities as they enable us to make more informed decisions and take more purposeful actions. It is important to note that active

listening and reflection go hand in hand as one needs to be able to listen atten-
tively before reflecting. The CBPR course has allowed for a space that promotes
reflection on a regular basis among students through the different activities
facilitated in the course. This has challenged the students and instructors to
reflect on their positionality, biases, assumptions and privileges when working
with the local communities.

9 Conclusions

This case study shows a series of challenges and lessons we have encountered
from the inception of the SSH to the on-going delivery of a pedagogical product that contributes to bridging the different knowledge cultures of the partner
organisations that make up the hub. We hope that by sharing our learned experiences and best practices we will inspire more universities to foster ethical,
reciprocal and respectful partnerships with communities.

The collaborative course design and delivery by the civil society organisations and higher education members of the hub, along with the support of
local community partners, have been proved effective in developing soft skills
in community engagement that are useful not only for students' academic
work, but also for their professional and daily lives. The SSH's CBPR course has
been able to provide the space to train students to be more attentive listeners
and learners. Former students of the course shared that they were able to learn
and sharpen their skill in active listening through their hands-on learning with
the community partners in the community-led projects. Being able to apply
that skill and knowledge on the ground was very important to them as it added
meaning to their experience in community engagement. One of the students
found the skill of active listening she had learned in the CBPR course so useful
that she started to practise it in other parts of her life, such as in her work-
place. Through this course, the SSH also managed to introduce the students
to the benefits of critical reflection and provided them with the environment
to apply this practice, heightening their awareness of the importance of co-
conducting ethical research with community partners.

The way we have worked as a hub has also contributed to strengthening
existing institutional relationships among the partner organisations. We have
consciously prioritised building and nurturing relationships of trust and
respect among the members of the hub and with our local partners. This has
helped to strengthen and ease the collaborative work and projects we undertake together, despite significant epistemic differences. Recognising that relationships are at the core of community-university engagement, we aim to

enhance and better support this practice in academia by promoting respectful and mutual collaborations with community. Students also had the opportunity to build relationships organically with the community partners, instructors, mentors and other students – an opportunity they typically do not have in other courses.

Without minimising these important achievements at the level of knowledge setting/practice and institutional knowledge environment, the hub has also faced critical challenges at the institutional and policy level to meet its objectives. Our pedagogical practice had to adjust to a more traditional teaching approach that does not fully allow for the application of pedagogical principles that underpin the teaching of CBPR and promote equitable and responsible partnerships between universities and communities (see Tandon et al., 2016). The impossibility to extend the students-community relationships beyond the formal duration of a university course (13 weeks) and the lack of formal recognition of non-university instructors have been some of the challenges hindering student learning. Regarding the former, while students were required to adhere to the timeline and expectations of an undergraduate course, the end of the course represents, for the most part, the interruption of the student-community partner relationship, which contradicts CBPR practice that encourages flexibility and continued fostering of relationships. Although we as a hub tried to incorporate CBPR values as much as possible –while complying with university requirements– working within these boundaries has proven challenging for the course participants. Regarding the latter, it is important to acknowledge and work to reduce the differences in material conditions of partners involved in participatory research and teaching. That is, when community groups engage in a participatory academic project, their committed time is usually unpaid and is in addition to their day-to-day responsibilities; however, academics are often paid for the time they devote to research and teaching, and even students ultimately receive credentials and higher status because of their work in/with communities. As one of our community partners expressed, "there seems to still be a real commitment to status through what letters follow your name and if you don't have [any] letters after your name then you are treated different[ly], especially when Indigenous knowledge [keepers] get paid in coffee mugs and parking passes, and not as experts in their field".

Overall, it is important to recognise that while significant progress has been made in terms of inclusion of Indigenous content and epistemologies in curricula, engaged research and community engagement at many universities in Canada, UVic included, much remains to be done to deliver community-based pedagogy. The way teaching is generally delivered in Canadian higher education institutions remains culturally biased and inadequate to preserve, protect and promote Indigenous languages and knowledge, as well as to acknowledge cultural sensitivities surrounding the integration of Indigenous and traditional worldviews into Western educational systems.

10   First Author's Note

As a Malaysian, I do not have a family name. To cite this chapter, please use my full name: Suriani Dzulkifli. This is another way to create visibility for non-White women like myself.

Notes

1   The term 'Salish' refers to a linguistic grouping of North American Indigenous tribes located in what are now the province of BC, and the northwestern U.S.

2   In Canada, the word Indigenous is capitalized because it is used as a proper name to refer to a group of ancestral political and historical communities and societies – and any aspect of their cultures – that existed in particular territories prior to contact with Europeans (Weeber, 2020; IJIH, n.d.). The term is also capitalized as a sign of respect in recognising it as an identity, and not just an adjective.

3   The Truth and Reconciliation Commission of Canada (TRC) was active from 2008 to 2015. It was organized by the parties of the Indian Residential Schools Settlement Agreement, which included Residential Schools Survivors, the Assembly of First Nations, Inuit representatives, the federal government and the church bodies (NCTR, 2002). To inform about what happened in residential schools, the TRC documented the truth of Survivors, their families, communities and anyone personally affected by the residential school experience. Its final report outlined 94 calls to action for reconciliation between settler Canadians and the Indigenous People in Canada. The report be found in full here https://nctr.ca/records/reports/

4   The Canadian Constitution recognizes 3 groups of Aboriginal peoples: First Nations, Inuit and Métis. These are 3 distinct peoples with unique histories, languages, cultural practices and spiritual beliefs (Government of Canada, 2022). The First Nations are Indigenous peoples who are not ethnically Inuit or Métis. The Inuit are the Indigenous communities who live primarily in Northwest Territories, Nunavut, northern parts of Quebec and coastal Labrador, while the Métis refer to Indigenous peoples who are mixed First Nations and European ancestry (see The Canadian Encyclopedia, 2022; IJIH, n.d.).

5   The OCAP principles assert that First Nations have control over data collection processes, and that they own and control how this information can be used. These principles support strong information governance on the path to First Nations data sovereignty by ensuring that the data are collected, protected, used and shared ethically, respectfully and responsibly. See more information on the OCAP principles: https://fnigc.ca/ocap-training/

6   Tri-Council Policy Statement is a a joint policy of Canada's three federal research agencies – i.e., the Canadian Institutes of Health Research, the Natural Sciences and Engineering Research Council of Canada, and the Social Sciences and Humanities Research Council of Canada – that provides ethics guidance that applies to all research involving human participants. See: https://ethics.gc.ca/eng/tcps2-eptc2_2018_chapter9-chapitre9.html

7 A study completed by the VNFC in 2022 found that there are over 70 distinct First Nations represented by the Elders and Seniors group that participate in the VNFC programming.

8 Different categories apply to Aboriginal peoples in Canada (status Indians, non-status Indians, treaty Indians, non-treaty Indians), in addition to the distinction between First Nations, Métis, Inuit. The term 'Indian' is still commonly used in legal documents, although it has fallen into disuse in Canada, and most people consider it to be pejorative.

References

Bartlett, R. H. (1988). *The Indian Act of Canada*. University of Saskatchewan, Native Law Centre.

Bishop, A. (1994). *Becoming an ally: Breaking the cycle of oppression*. Fernwood.

Cameron, G., Hayes, V. E., & Wren, A. M. (2000). Using reflective process in community-based participatory action research. *Reflective Practice, 1*(2), 215–230. https://doi.org/10.1080/713693147

Charles, G., & Lowry, G. (2017). Toward a creative-critical approach to narratives of student-to-student abuse in Canada's Indian Residential School System. *Cogent Arts & Humanities, 4*(1). https://doi.org/10.1080/23311983.2017.1410081

Cole, D., & Chaikin, I. (1990). *An iron hand upon the people: The law against the Potlatch on the Northwest Coast*. Douglas & McIntyre.

de Sousa Santos, B. (2016). *Epistemologies of the South: Justice against Epistemicide*. Routledge.

Dickason, O. P., & Newbigging, W. (2015). *A concise history of Canada's first Nations* (3rd ed.). Oxford University Press.

FitzMaurice, K., & McCaskill, D. (2011). Urban Aboriginal people in Canada: Community trends and issues of governance. In D. Long & O. P. Dickason (Eds.), *Visions of the heart: Canadian Aboriginal issues* (3rd ed.). Oxford University Press.

Government of Canada. (2022). *Indigenous peoples and communities*. https://www.rcaanc-cirnac.gc.ca/eng/1100100013785/1529102490303

Haig-Brown, C. (1988). *Resistance and renewal: Surviving the Indian Residential School* Arsenal Pulp Press.

Howard, H. (2011). The friendship centre: Native people and the organisation of community in cities. In H. Howard & C. Proux (Eds.), *Aboriginal peoples in cities: Transformations and continuities* (pp. 87–108). Wilfred Laurier Press.

International Journal of Indigenous Health (IJIH). (n.d.). *Defining aboriginal peoples within Canada*. https://journals.uvic.ca/journalinfo/ijih/IJIHDefiningIndigenous PeoplesWithinCanada.pdf

Janovicek, N. (2007). *No place to go: Local histories of the battered women's shelter movement*. UBC Press.

Kan, S. (2015). *Symbolic immortality: The Tlingit Potlatch of the Nineteenth Century* (2nd ed.). University of Washington Press.

Kim, H. S. (1999). Critical reflective inquiry for knowledge development in nursing practice. *Journal of Advanced Nursing, 29*(5), 1205–1212.

MacDonald, C., & Steenbeek, A. (2015). The impact of colonization and Western Assimilation on Health and Wellbeing of Canadian Aboriginal People. *International Journal of Regional and Local History, 10*(1), 32–46.

MacKinnon, S. (2018). *Practising community-based participatory research: Stories of engagement, empowerment, and mobilization* (MacKinnon, Ed.). Purich Books.

McIntosh, P. (2013). The current educational climate: Why the creative arts and humanities and so important to creativity and learning in classroom. In P. McIntosh & D. Warren (Eds.), *Creativity in the classroom: Case studies in using the arts in teaching and learning in higher education* (pp. 1–8). Intellect Books Ltd.

Methot, S. (2019). *Legacy: Trauma, story and Indigenous healing.* ECW Press.

Obonsawin, R., & Howard-Bobiwash, H. (1997). The Native Canadian Centre of Toronto: The meeting place for Aboriginal people for 35 years. In F. Sanderson & H. Howard-Bobiwash (Eds.), *The meeting place: Aboriginal life in Toronto* (pp. 25–59). Native Canadian Centre of Toronto.

Palmater, P. D. (2011). *Beyond blood: Rethinking Indigenous identity.* Purich Publishing Ltd.

Poonwassie, A., & Charter, A. (2001). Counselling Aboriginal students: Bridging of conflicting worldviews. In K. P. Binda & S. Callious (Eds.), *Aboriginal education in Canada: A study in decolonization* (pp. 121–136). Canadian Educators' Press.

Rappaport, J. (2020). *Cowards don't make history: Orlando Fals Borda and the origins of participatory action research.* Duke University Press.

Ray, A. J. (2016). *An illustrated history of Canada's native people: I have lived here since the world began* (4th ed.). McGill-Queen's Press.

Royal Commission on Aboriginal Peoples. (1996). *Report of the royal commission on Aboriginal peoples.* Minister of Supply and Services Canada.

Sayers, J. F. (Ed.). (2001). *First Nations Women, Governance and the Indian Act: A collection of policy research reports.* Status of Women Canada.

Smith, L. T. (1999). *Decolonizing methodologies: Research and Indigenous peoples.* University of Otago Press.

Smith, M. S., & Bray, N. (2019). The Indigenous diversity gap. Where are the Indigenous Peoples in Canadian universities? *Academic Matters.* https://academicmatters.ca/the-indigenous-diversity-gap/

Tandon, R., Hall, B., Lepore, W., & Singh, W. (Eds.). (2016). *Knowledge & engagement: Building capacity for the next generation of community based researchers.* Participatory Research in Asia (PRIA).

The Canadian Encyclopedia. (2022). *First Nations in Canada.* https://www.thecanadianencyclopedia.ca/en/article/first-nations

Truth and Reconciliation Commission of Canada. (2015). *Honouring the truth, reconciling for the future: Summary of the final report of the Truth and Reconciliation Commission of Canada.* http://www.trc.ca/websites/trcinstitution/File/2015/ Honouring_the_Truth_Reconciling_for_the_Future_July_23_2015.pdf

UNESCO Chair CBR-SR. (2022). *Canada K4C Hub (Salish Sea).* https://www.unescochair-cbrsr.org/canada-k4c-hub/

University of Victoria. (2022). *Rankings & reputation.* https://www.uvic.ca/about-uvic/ rankings-reputation/index.php

Weeber, C. (2020, May 19). Why capitalize "Indigenous"? *Sapiens.* https://www.sapiens.org/language/capitalize-indigenous/

Wilson, S. (2008). *Research is ceremony: Indigenous research methods.* Fernwood Publishing.

PART 3

Learning to Bridge Knowledge Cultures

∵

CHAPTER 14

The Art of Bridging

Rajesh Tandon, Andrea Vargiu and Budd L. Hall

Abstract

Recognising that differences in knowledge cultures and power in the co-construction of knowledge exist, means that work is required to create mechanisms for bridging. Drawing on the experiences of how such bridging was attempted in the ten case studies, this chapter shares insights into what are the keys to the art of bridging. In doing so, it also makes evident several layers of institutional and policy challenges that may need to be addressed for the practice of bridging to be effective.

Keywords

bridging – power – acceptance – community knowledge – boundary-spanner – research partnership

∴

The purpose of this global study has been to provide evidence on the differences between how knowledge is created, validated, shared and acted upon in academic and community settings. We refer to these as knowledge cultures. They could be described as differing modes of knowledge production, but knowledge cultures is a broader concept incorporating production, validation, sharing and acting. As stated in the Introduction, the ability to create respectful and egalitarian knowledge partnerships depends on recognition that what we refer to in English as knowledge, is understood in quite different and diverse ways outside of the academy. When academics write about the creation or co-creation of knowledge, there is often an assumption that the concept of knowledge is universally understood as the same in all structures of society. However, the chapter on Community Knowledge Cultures explains what the case studies revealed in detail about the nature, scale and diversity of elements that make up community knowledge cultures in different contexts. The failure to recognise the differences in knowledge cultures has meant that even within the world of knowledge co-construction, power imbalances persist; therefore, creating mechanisms that bridge the different knowledge cultures remain somewhat fragile and mono dimensional. Each of the ten case studies provide some insights into how the bridging was attempted to try and connect what have been separate archipelagos of knowledge. This chapter shares insights into what are the keys to the *art of bridging*.

1   Acceptance and Acknowledgement of Community Knowledge as Legitimate

The foundation of the bridge is laid upon the acceptance and acknowledgement by academics of community knowledge as different and legitimate. The Sangwari case study in Raipur, India is in a region with a high percentage of Indigenous (tribal) peoples. They share their findings that in rural tribal areas where they work, they learned that there were at least three distinct knowledge systems in operation. Traditional birthing practices and maternal care co-exist with Ayurveda health knowledge and Western maternal and childcare practices promoted by others, among them UNICEF. In the Acholi region of Uganda, the K4C hub at Gulu University describe the *epistemic privilege* of African Indigenous Knowledge Systems (AIKS) which have a relational ontology. Knowledge is represented through dance, ceremony and rituals which are inseparable from land, culture, language and spirituality. The team based at the Islamic Science University of Malaysia, the Mizan K4C hub, noted that while the Orang Asli (Indigenous peoples) of Malaysia have a distinctly different way of understanding the world, little progress has been made over the last 30 years in terms of broad academic acceptance of these knowledge forms or indeed of their land and human rights.

In East Africa, the Nyerere K4C hub based at the Nelson Mandela African Institute of Science and Technology describes itself as a colonised, western-knowledge dominated university. Located on land shared for thousands of years with the Maasai peoples, Maasai knowledge has been disregarded and disrespected. Their study of water resource practices through the creation of traditional water canals provides evidence of sophisticated understanding of how to bring water to their cattle as well as crops. The fact that the care of water irrigation canals is at the centre of village life was seen as eye-opening for the academics. The Nyerere hub authors note,

> Community knowledge, handed down over generations, is not antagonistic to expert knowledge. The production, use, validation and dissemination of community knowledge may revitalise university-community linkages by promoting local participation in higher education initiatives

to counter the power asymmetries that usually hinder engagement with communities (Fernández-Llamazares & Cabeza, 2018). Social responsibility in higher learning requires academic and research institutions to open up to society's real problems, narrowing the expert-community power inequalities that exist (Bodorkós & Pataki, 2009). By borrowing experiences from local communities on how knowledge is generated and handed down from generation to generation, hub members gained insights on how to practice a locally relevant pedagogy. Our hub is currently not practicing this.

The case study from Durban argues that practitioners of early childhood development (ECD) found knowledge of the people practical, and that of the academics largely theoretical. Academics tend to 'devalue' such practical knowledge as it is not recorded and codified in the manner of formal knowledge representation by experts. While researchers seemed to have understood that the community knowledge on ECD available with the community is useful, acceptance of the same as 'equally valid' was contested as no formal qualifications were associated with the production of such knowledge. Their case study claims,

> Traditional knowledge is considered barbaric. Universities force us to use what they have. Sometimes they take knowledge from the community, make small changes and present it back to the community as the universities' knowledge – as proven, tested knowledge. Like the mhlonyane herb taken from the community. The Afrikaners used to take the method from the community and present as theirs.

The study of the knowledge of the fisherfolk in East Java, Indonesia was undertaken by the Sunan Ampel Islamic University K4C hub. They opened conversations about the understanding of knowledge with the Kenjeran community who live from fishing and have done so for thousands of years. The very concept of knowledge they report in the various Indigenous cultures of the region is far more complex than the Western European versions. Importantly, they note that the traditional knowledge of the fisherfolk is not static. Unlike how traditional knowledge is often portrayed, Kenjeran fishing knowledge has adapted to many changes over the years. The ability of the fisherfolk to find locations in the open sea without GPS, depending on mythological stories and observations of currents, is just one of the remarkable range of knowledge of the sea used by them, but not available to academics.

The authors of the case study from Ibague region of Colombia describe the tensions that arise when well-intentioned faculty/student-community interactions in Tolima region attempt to co-create knowledge for finding solutions to practical needs of local communities. The academics continue to maintain a blind spot about differences in knowledge cultures since they have not yet learnt the meanings of community knowledge in everyday life. Similar dynamics are analysed in the case study from North-West University (South Africa) where intellectual acceptance of the need for community knowledge to address the SDG agenda is reported from some academics but normative meaning of 'scientific' knowledge remains attached to the experts (Wood, 2020).

Reporting such a dynamic from the Jaipur hub,

> It was very clear from the discussions that those who have been managing waste locally through traditional practices are happy and proud of it. However, with launch of SBM, a system of waste segregation at source was introduced without any consultation with the local community. A new system was imposed on them – that of giving their segregated waste to the garbage collection van. They are hesitant to accept it as an alternate practice to their traditional practice of waste management and replace their knowledge that has been validated in their community over a long period of time.

In the absence of understanding and acceptance of community knowledge cultures, the case studies reaffirm the challenge that academia faces in co-creation. The professional training of researchers exclusively focuses on the 'scientific' method (related to each discipline). When they are expected to 'co-create' knowledge, they naturally tend to assume that there is a single knowledge culture, method and practice, which they have been 'schooled' in. Without emotionally appreciating and cognitively accepting the diversity of knowledge cultures, attempts to bridge remain superficial. Orienting academic researchers to such a diverse reality of knowledges tends to prepare them professionally to practice 'co-creation' respectfully. When academically trained researchers acknowledge, in their hearts and minds, the historical existence and continued practices of community knowledges as legitimate forms of knowing, the common ground for connections emerges.

2   Relationships of Trust Are the 'Cement' of Equitable Research Partnerships

Once experiential knowledge of people living in communities, ancient land-based knowledge of Indigenous peoples and the epistemic privilege of those experiencing lives of poverty, different abilities, homelessness, and more are recognised as legitimate, the challenge is to move beyond the traditional walls of academia to establish relations of mutual respect. Establishing a trusting relationship between community and university is one, if not the most, important component of co-creation. Bivens et al. (2015) affirmed the importance of building partnerships with the community for CURP to co-create "knowledge which draws dynamically on multiple epistemologies and life worlds" (p. 6).

This may be the biggest challenge of all because the eyes and ears of many of us as academics have been made blind and deaf by having been steeped in the assumptions of Western science. But even if we have found respect for the knowledge created in other ways, the history of academic research has created its own path of limitations. Much of academic research has been used to extract information from communities for analysis and publications. Research remains an *ugly* practice in the eyes of Indigenous communities around the world as an instrument of subjugation. And even when scholars are well intentioned, the academic knowledge culture is constructed within short-term 'projects' of three to five years. Moving from one project to another is the name of the game. The establishment and maintenance of authentic, on-going relationships where people know each other as people and not as subjects, experts or helpers may need a much deeper shift than currently adequately examined by even those in the field of engaged scholarship. Relationships across different cultures, classes and status require proactive efforts by academics, whose own training is often one of detachment, objectivity, distance from the community and unemotional non-engagement.

Each of the case studies is the result of the building of relationships of trust. The K4C hub in Durban, South Africa is an engagement between scholars at the Durban University of Technology and a long-time group of early childhood practitioners. One sees in the description of how they worked together that they are friends. They know each other. They meet in each other's homes and work from a position of mutual respect. In Durban they say that knowledge is love.

> According to Ray (2016), partnership within the context of civic and community engagement is fundamentally relational, and a relationship is always a work in progress. Much like deep friendships, partnerships need ongoing cultivation and care. They require sustained attention, stubborn commitment, flexibility, empathy, humility, patience, imagination, and a generous sense of humour.

In Gulu, the hub itself has been driven more from the community side than from the university side. Youth in the community, women in design start-ups, Elders from Acholi land and Busoga all have taken a lead in the conversations about knowledge. As one of the community researchers noted, "When I enter in the home to have a conversation, I am entering into a relationship". So, while from an historical perspective Indigenous knowledge has not been valued by the university, the K4C hub is going about things in a different way. Similarly, the team from the Nyerere hub in Arusha acknowledging their university as a colonial construct, has set out to break with Western knowledge traditions to establish on-going relations of knowledge exchange on a mutually respectful basis with the Maasai who live in the region.

In the Tolima region of Colombia, the University of Ibague's Peace and Region programme of student engaged research is predicated on the reality that knowledge is locally contextualised, and that co-construction depends on the creation of structures for permanent sets of students and their teachers to live in communities for months at a time. In the Jaipur case, reluctance of the community to partner with academia around waste management was largely due to sporadic and project-based community engagement. Such occasional and temporary orientation to engagement with community does not build trust between parties.

Co-creation of knowledge relies on two precious resources: trust and time. Positive and durable societal change in the community can take place only if relationships are built on mutual trust. Therefore, engaged scholars need to put a special effort in building and keeping trustworthy relationships with and among community members. This was the case in Sassari, Italy, where a K4C hub is located. The case of Sassari hub is not presented in this book, but the hub actively collaborated on the BKC project. Structured reflexive analysis of their experience provides evidence to show that trust was built in many initiatives carried out under diverse situations. This is also a recurring issue in literature (Lucero et al., 2018).

Building and maintaining trustworthy relationships with and within the community requires community-based researchers to engage in often long and delicate negotiation processes, and therefore entails peculiar relational abilities and time.

The logic of time-bound projects which depend on external funding may easily lead to frustration when all efforts and time dedicated to setting up a trustworthy environment collapse. This happened in Sassari in a specific occasion, when the promise of further funding that would cement a well-in-place community-university dialogue progressively faded away. The disappointment was two-fold: vis-à-vis the researchers' own expectations, but also those of the community. Researchers did comply with the funder's mandate, but the results were not in line with what they came to expect, nor with the hopes that their work raised in the community. An ordinary research project typically requires researchers to be mainly, if not exclusively, accountable to their academic community and their funders, whereas engaging with a community implies more articulated forms of social accountability (Vargiu, 2014). Building and nurturing relationships of trust with local communities is the key to effective and mutually beneficial bridging of different knowledge cultures.

3   Learning to Listen: The Power of Story

When academics learn to listen (and resist from talking), to not just words but the emotions behind them, relationships begin to develop. When academically trained researchers practice rebalancing feelings and thinking, the process begins to support relationship building. This process entails time, requires patience, and happens gradually. When academics unlearn self-indulgence, mutuality occurs. Their capacity to cope with stress and anxiety caused by such unlearning helps build next steps in building the bridge. The capacity of academics to accept oral storage and transmission of community knowledge, and openness to non-written documentation and records as legitimate sources of knowledge helps to support the 'arch of scaffolding' of the bridge. Capacity to understand stories and anecdotes as data helps bridge-building.

The K4C hub based at North West University stressed the importance of using participatory techniques in the co-creation of knowledge. These techniques recognise that community knowledge cultures are based on everyday practices of knowledge sharing which go beyond the traditional academic norms. They reported that

> Community members also conveyed their knowledge through storytelling, which is a form of knowledge sharing embedded in traditional African culture. (A grandma teaches you with stories, she sits with you, teaches you, tells you that story to allow you to understand.)

But our colleagues from Manipal University in Jaipur say that based on their experience, academics "lack direction and experience in community-based participatory research approaches". They go on to tell of conflicts over the sharing of knowledge of waste management practices between the communities and the local government. The local government has not listened to the communities in this case. The communities that the Jaipur team worked with were sceptical about the value of academic inputs on the issues of waste management. Universities have in the past never been involved in such practical matters as waste management. What can they do?

Describing the process of listening as transformative, we return to the case study from Durban: "Fear is the major obstacle for communities: they hold back their knowledge because they are scared that they do not know much. Fear of academics as experts". When asked how we change this, they cited their own experience in the research project with K. N said that

> initially there was fear, but it did not remain. It disappeared because K brought it to the practical level. She asked them to talk about their experiences and declared that she did not know much about ECD. She mentioned that there were no right and wrong answers, and they were asked to speak from their own perspective.

The Gulu K4C team has found the use of traditional forms of meetings to be key to learning to listen. The Wang OO practice of meeting and sharing around a bonfire was an effective way of tapping into the knowledge of Elders. The bonfire has the power to bring people together. It creates a space for speaking from the heart and for listening to each other. The Gulu hub has found that dance, poetry, music and theatre is an excellent way for youth in the community to share knowledge. The Gulu case demonstrates how centering relationships becomes key when listening to stories happens. As narrated by an academic:

> As a researcher, as soon as I entered her house, I entered a relationship. She was not interested in my research questions; she was interested in sharing her story. She invited me into her life by sharing her story. She served me food; I met her family and neighbours. I am not a stranger; I am a trusted friend worthy of sharing food and discussing a common issue. That conversation provided far more insight than if we had met as strangers. But she is now part of this research, and I am bound ethically to continue to work on this issue and other issues that come up in that community – not just on my terms. I am no longer other, and that comes with responsibility. Research is about people's lives – real people – not objects. It is serious.

A Gulu community partner reflected on a research project they were in, where they felt objectified and excluded:

the decisions were made by researchers or the lead team. Once you have made up your mind, you don't want to listen to anyone, no one wants to listen, she needs to say yes, I've got it, it's me, it's me who has this, it's me who got the money, we will have this. So, you don't listen to anybody else. So, we lose out a lot on that.

The Gulu case illustrates the power of stories, music and dance, and capacity for deep listening. When all five senses – hearing, seeing, touching, tasting and smelling – are activated, such listening becomes possible. Being in the relationship, not just quickly conceptualising, becomes modus operandi for such listening to occur.

The Mizan hub in Malaysia working with Orang Asli communities set up separate focus groups for women, Elders and youth to make sure that all members of the community were heard. The community setting for storytelling encouraged many youth to pay attention to the experiences of Elders. In the Arusha case, listening to Maasai stories about water management, helped academic researchers develop a sense of appreciation and respect of community knowledge. Being with Maasai, in their village, on their territory, in their culture, enabled such *listening* to occur.

The Sassari hub experience around learning to listen brings in the added complexity of languages. Hub members note:

> Members of a linguistic community typically maintain a very pragmatic relationship with their spoken language. The language spoken in Logudoro, for instance (an area of Sardinia where one of the variants of the Sardinian language is currently spoken nowadays), provides for different terms to designate what in English is simply 'a lamb'. The term *anzone* is generally used, but kids can also use the expression *memmè*. A lamb who is still sucking milk is a *coddettàriu*, while a one-year-old lamb is a *saccàggiu*, or *saccàju*. And many are the adjectives that this language (like other variants of the Sardinian language) provides to designate peculiar conditions or states of lambs. For instance, an *anzone muroninu* is a plump lamb, while an *anzone ràsinu* is a shoddy lamb born between winter and spring. And so forth. This variety of terms mirrors the amplitude and richness of the knowledge culture that generated it.

Training of academic researchers rarely focuses on 'learning to listen', both to words and the emotions underlying those words. Community knowledge is narrated and learnt through stories, shared on festive occasions and ceremonies. When required to listen, listen again and be deep in emotions, the academic researcher gets stressed since they have been socialised into treating emotions as 'polluting' the research process.

4   Moving beyond Communities' Sense That They Do Not Know

Overcoming initial hesitancy and sense of 'we don't know much' by the community requires practical support from academics to encourage, listen and value community knowledges. As academic research work began to be associated with expertise, as community knowledges was labeled as 'unscientific' by outsiders, as European languages became dominant means of knowledge production and dissemination, it undermined communities' confidence in their own knowledge. The power associated with 'expert' knowledge of universities has resulted not only in society believing in the truth claims of experts but has undermined the confidence of those outside the academy. Overcoming feelings of distrust, scepticism and self-doubt is key to building bridges of respectful sharing of a community's different knowledges.

As a matter of fact, the typical top-down approach of scientific research to addressing societal challenges is usually internalised by community members along with its patronizing aspects. This can be rather reassuring for most actors involved who enter the relationship with a clear and relatively stable set of roles and storyline. A co-creation process implies a rupture of the typical role-set of the inquiry situation. This might be disturbing for some, as it questions the main ordering codes and principles, and requires a rearrangement of power relations within the community itself. And this therefore implies rearticulating the existing asymmetries among different kinds of knowledges.

The Durban hub notes that when speaking of early childhood practices communities are afraid of experts from universities. The process of building trust, of building relationships takes time. The early childhood practitioners that the university researchers worked with have become permanent colleagues, not just sources of data for a quick research project. This patience and attention to meeting where community members feel comfortable has been key to overcoming the reluctance of community members to speak.

In working with the Orang Asli in Malaysia, the Mizan hub found that the youth in the communities were keen to speak up as they were very interested in finding ways to retain their language, culture and identity. But it took some effort to facilitate 'speaking up' in the presence of university researchers. Urban poor communities in Jaipur initially denied having any knowledge of waste disposal and looked at government officials and researchers from the Manipal hub as experts. This self-denial is common to many communities when faced with 'experts' and takes some time to overcome.

Describing this process of overcoming self-doubt, the case study from North-West South Africa explains:

> The community did not seem to value their own knowledge very much and perhaps this is because they have never engaged in research with the university and therefore view themselves more as knowledge recipients and less as knowledge producers. Community-based research has educational and emancipatory outcomes (Wood, 2020); therefore, participation as co-researchers in a project would help them realise the importance and value of their lived knowledge and experiences. This is essential if they are to become community educators and disseminate the knowledge in the wider community.

Even the very confident fisherfolk community in Surabaya have been hesitant to approach the university for collaboration in research, despite having long-standing relationships; it is assumed that the research process begins in the university!

In many situations, academic researchers take on face value self-doubt and initial reluctance of local communities to speak about their own knowledge. Facilitation to enable voicing of community experiences, and basis of their everyday actions, can promote a slow shift towards articulation of their knowledges.

5   A Role for Boundary-Spanners and Interlocutors

Given the cultural, linguistic and status differentials between academics and community, effective mediation processes help to kick-off 'bridging'. There is a critical role for interlocutors, boundary-spanners and intermediaries, who may well come from either or both the community or academic side. Such functions need to be performed creatively and contextually. Given the major disconnect between academic and community knowledges, some persons, agencies, or actors play the role of connectors or boundary spanners. But, connectors need to remain accountable to both parties; mechanisms to hold mediators accountable to both community and academic knowledge cultures and perspectives have to be operationalised and demonstrated.

The Sassari hub took this statement seriously and tried to compose their tradition of collective reflexivity practice with what Michel de Certeau (1990) defines as "the subtle art of tenants", i.e., the ability to creatively inhabit spaces that are rigidly encased by oppressive social structures. To do so, the hub set up what they call 'community inquiry groups'. This expression was borrowed with a slight modification from Duijn et al. (2010) who rather speak of "communities of inquiry" to refer to people who meet to "co-produce knowledge to cope with practical challenges:" groups that are located "in the middle between science and practice", and thus allow for incorporation of multiple epistemologies to address composite issues.

All of the K4C hubs have found identification of persons who are able to play connector roles because of their personal histories as key to building knowledge culture bridges. In Durban, the early childhood education practitioners who lived and worked in the community played this role. In Gulu, recent graduates of Gulu University, local NGO and business leaders have played a key role in bridging youth culture and the university researchers. Meeting in community settings has been a key to creating spaces for epistemic equity. In Malaysia, the Orang Asli teachers played key roles as intermediaries. The students at the teacher training college, who belonged to the community, acted as intermediaries for communication and conversation between the academics and local Orang society. In Ibague, the local organisers in each of the communities which were part of the Peace and Region project have played an essential role in bringing the students and community together. In east Java, in the case study of the fisherfolk's knowledge of the sea, several members of the university have worked to support fisherfolk from these communities for many years. They have gotten to know the most knowledgeable fishers and together these people from the village side and the university side have become boundary-spanners. In the Jaipur case, MHT, the hub partner, facilitated the formation of a community action group (CAG). CAG members were trained on various aspects such as the importance of collective leadership and understanding the various schemes of the government for slum-dwellers. They were able to provide the connection between the academics and the community when issues of waste management were being discussed.

A key principle for connecting the local with the global at the Sassari hub relies on respect and valorisation of cultural diversity and linguistic variety. During several years, the FOIST Laboratory (the hub's academic partner), along with others from Germany, Spain, Portugal, Romania and Sweden, was a partner in an Erasmus programme named 'Euromir – Migrations and Minorities in Europe'. This was a thematic network on peace and intercultural relations which allowed for mobility of university staff and students, but also for the organisation of residential seminars which were in turn hosted on the partners' premises. No single working language was pre-defined, as participants were invited to express themselves by choosing their preferred language. This rule would eventually imply that the same person could use different languages or opt for multiple means of expression so as to make oneself understood by others.

This choice reflected the conviction that power relations and inequities are deeply rooted in the foundations of academic systems. The struggle over the legitimate monopoly of symbolic power is also a struggle over language and the capacity to impose meanings through a system of symbolic violence (Bourdieu, 1977, 1991, 2001). The pervasiveness of the English language within academia hinders the possibility for multiple epistemologies to unfold to their full potential. In this perspective, epistemic justice and knowledge equity (Santos, 2006) are a matter of respect for less diffused languages and cultures, and also the very pre-conditions for ensuring that the scientific authentic quest for knowledge can continue to flourish. Multi-lingual connectors play a crucial role in facilitating bridging between the community and academia.

The cultural, linguistic and perceptual gaps between the world of academe and the everyday world of most local, under-privileged, excluded communities is rather large in most countries. There are no 'normal' social connectors on either side, or 'normal' social occasions to 'meet and greet'. Therefore, the connections between the two sides need to be facilitated. Typically, local civil society, artists, journalists, students and/or retired teachers and government officials tend to become such connectors, by virtue of knowing the two worlds, and having had some experience of interacting with such diverse parties. Such intermediation is an important competence, not widely available in all settings.

6 Structures for Shared Leadership and Decision-Making

Results from a previous global study of community-university research partnerships indicated that the creation of visible structures within the university was key to supporting the transition from disciplinary academic-led knowledge creation to interdisciplinary co-construction of knowledge with community. Administrative structures within universities provide spaces for the recognition of on-going co-structured research projects, for sharing tools and strategies for doing community-based research work, and for tracking the impacts. So too, spaces for shared leadership, analysis of findings and planning of action within research projects needs to be attended to intentionally.

The Salish Sea Hub in Victoria, Canada is a partnership between the University of Victoria, the Victoria Native Friendship Centre and the Victoria Foundation. These three groups share decisions about the direction of the hub. On a project level, the team at North-West University in South Africa created a joint community-university research structure to manage the research from the beginning to the end. Reflecting on that experience, the case recommends:

> A core group consisting of representatives from each category of stakeholders (e.g., university lecturers, student representatives, local health professionals, community organisations, users of the programme) could be formed to meet regularly to reflect on roles, responsibilities and ways of working to find ways to constantly improve the outcomes for mutual benefit. This group could decide on evaluation processes and involve more than just the academic members in the ongoing research under the project.

The Gulu hub is essentially a joint community-university space which facilitates interpersonal and inter-community communications. At Ibague, the Peace and Region programme structure is a permanent bridge-builder between the community and university. In East Java, at the project level, they have created a Pokja Kelopok Kenja working group to share leadership over the course of the project.

The experiences of Gulu with Acholi Indigenous community confirm the need for such spaces for leadership, if co-creation is to be based on bridging the different knowledge cultures:

> From a broader social perspective, we draw on the warning of Achebe to caution against relying too much on the university as an institution and structure of knowledge plurality and a universality of knowledge cultures. Rather, as we seek out spaces for survival, flourishing and living together, we need to perhaps recognise and validate a plurality of spaces where this can happen differently, with tolerance, respect and dignity.

The Surabaya case reaffirms the need for creating local structures that can continue the relationship between academia and community even after a specific research project is completed. Continuity of conversations are critical to identify new research questions arising from the lived experiences of the community.

From the experiences of the Jaipur case, the authors pose critical reflections.

There is need to strengthen academics' capacity to encourage, promote, regulate and sustain research partnerships with the community. Given the static culture of universities and the longstanding tradition of independent scholarship, it is essential to ask whether universities are genuinely ready to contribute appropriately to initiatives that move away from a short-term charity model of community service to fulfil the potential of long-term social justice initiatives through community research collaborations. (Marullo & Edwards, 2000; Ostrander, 2004)

While most academic and research institutions do encourage their students and academics to 'go to community', very few have mechanisms, or even motivation, to 'invite' the community inside the academy. While outreach is encouraged, 'inreach' is ignored. Even in the absence of formal structures within academia, project level joint decision-making research structures can be very productive in bridging the two knowledge cultures. Investment of time, effort and resources towards such a shared, co-governing mechanism helps to create spaces for mutual engagement on a concrete research project.

...

The lessons from the comparative analysis of the ten case studies presented in this chapter are lessons of hope and frustration. The cases relate to the practice of co-creation of knowledge that each K4C hub has been engaged in for the past four to five years. The leaders of the hub are trained mentors in community-based participatory research. Each hub is already building capacity of students and community practitioners in this methodology of co-creating actionable knowledge. Each hub focuses on locally contextualised SDGs that is prioritised in partnership with the community and other stakeholders. In the very design of each hub is a formal partnership with some local organisations – civil society, local government, community association, etc. Hence, building bridges is inherent in the very DNA of each K4C hub.

Each hub is attempting to create a safe space for conversations about different knowledge cultures, and how to bridge them. Each hub is building capacity of next generation of researchers while producing locally actionable knowledge in partnership. Yet, it is difficult. It is difficult because the understanding of community knowledge cultures is weak, and hitherto unexplored.

Despite structures and mechanisms of partnership, and despite extensive mentorship training of hub leaders, it has been a challenge to sustain mutually respectful partnerships. This study of 'bridging' manifests the same, creating a space and an opportunity to explore the question. In the process, the comparative analysis of the case studies indicates more about what is required than about what bridging efforts are taking place:

- Acceptance, acknowledgement and valuing of community knowledge
- Importance of building and nurturing trusting relationships
- Practicing capacity to listen to stories, as data, in oral forms
- Support to overcome fears, hesitations, self-doubt of community partners
- Energies of boundary spanners, connectors and intermediaries
- Structures of shared leadership and decision-making

The above key findings are critical, yet not astonishing. These are neither new, nor impractical. The realities of the practice of co-creation of knowledge around the world, in sites designated with that purpose, do suggest the difficulties and challenges. At best, K4C hubs have become transitional spaces to learn and unlearn knowledge cultures, research practices and partnerships. But certain rituals and norms narrated in the case studies, as analysed in this chapter, are important to deepen the practice of co-creation of knowledge. Bridging efforts need to be founded on contextual appreciation of 'what is being bridged'?

The comparative analysis in this chapter has also thrown up several layers of institutional and policy challenges that may need to be addressed for the practice of bridging to be effective. These are elaborated and explored in the next chapter to further 'bridging knowledge cultures'.

References

Bivens, F., Haffenden, J., & Hall, B. L. (2015). Knowledge, higher education and the institutionalization of community-university research partnerships. In B. Hall, R. Tandon, & C. Tremblay (Eds.), *Strengthening community university research partnerships: Global perspectives* (pp. 5–30). University of Victoria and Participatory Research in Asia (PRIA). http://hdl.handle.net/1828/6509

Bodorkós, B., & Pataki, G. (2009). Linking academic and local knowledge: Community-based research and service learning for sustainable rural development in Hungary. *Journal of Cleaner Production, 17*(12), 1123–1131. https://doi.org/10.1016/j.jclepro.2009.02.023

Fernández-Llamazares, Á., & Cabeza, M. (2018). Rediscovering the potential of Indigenous storytelling for conservation practice. *Conservation Letters, 11*(3), e12398.

Marullo, S., & Edwards, B. (2000). From charity to justice: The potential of university-community collaboration for social change. *American Behavioral Scientist, 43*(5), 895–912.

Ostrander, S. A. (2004). Democracy, civic participation, and the university: A comparative study of civic engagement on five campuses. *Nonprofit and Voluntary Sector Quarterly, 33*(1), 74–93.

Ray, D. (2016). Campus–community partnership: A stubborn commitment to reciprocal relationships. *Diversity and Democracy, 19*(2), 8–11. https://dgmg81phhvh63.cloudfront.net/content/user-photos/Publications/Archives/Diversity-Democracy/DD_19-2_SP16.pdf

Wood, L. (2020). *Participatory action learning and action research: Theory, practice and process*. Routledge.

CHAPTER 15

Conclusion

Budd L. Hall

At the beginning of the Bridging Knowledge Cultures project, we had asked ourselves:

1. In what ways are trusting and respectful community-university research partnerships established?
2. How can different knowledge cultures be bridged such that perceived or actual power inequalities between collaborating partners are taken into consideration?
3. What capacities, methods, practices make building these bridges sustainable and secure over time, to be able to contribute to better lives, social justice, climate solutions and healthier communities?

The studies carried out by the Chair's K4C hubs, which are presented as ten case studies in this book, sought to seek the answers. The secondary available literature of the diverse contexts, actors and language of knowledge cultures, especially the manifestations and formations of community knowledge cultures, and an analytical framework has been presented in Chapters 2 and 3. The previous chapter has systematised learnings from the case studies. In this chapter, we attempt to explore the imperatives of bridging knowledge cultures for future research and practice.

The knowledge settings which we examined were the sites of practice in each K4C hub. The story of each hub showcases how the university and community partners understand the creation and use of knowledge and what the hub has done to help bridge the differences. What emerges are positive stories of co-creation, trust building and mutual respect between the hub members. Building and sustaining such relationships are not without challenges, which the hubs have faced in trying to work across trans-disciplinary and community-university boundaries.

In addition to the micro context of the concrete co-creation projects, the hubs have also reflected on institutional/organisational practices and systems (meso level) as well as the general national knowledge environment, policy and funding frameworks in their country (macro level).

The analysis of the hubs' experiences, and the framework for enquiry, throws light on three aspects of knowledge cultures.

1   Understanding of Knowledge Has Different Starting Points

For many academically trained and professionally certified researchers and knowledge workers, knowledge is created, used, stored and communicated only through 'scientific' means. In their worldview, knowledge is the domain of the academy. In the academy, meaning and practice of knowledge are axiomatic. Thus, knowledge culture is taken for granted, as a part of professional training, to imply what academically trained researchers and knowledge workers do.

Academic knowledge creation tends to emphasise value neutrality, distancing from everyday life, feelings and lived experiences, thereby relying exclusively on external standards and protocols of assessing validity of such knowledge. Academic knowledge production is often highly individualistic and competitive; its validation is determined by bureaucratic rules and procedures which are permanent and pre-determined, external to the very act of producing knowledge. Knowledge sharing is linked to individual incentives and careers, with publishing standards acting as gatekeepers. In much of the academic system of knowledge production and dissemination, elderly and tenured professors based in global elite research institutions are mandated to be the standard-bearers.

Community knowledge(s), on the other hand, is located within the 'main business of life'. Practices of community knowledge are linked to everyday life and the immediate context of the community is the site for producing knowledge – place-based, contextual, contemporary, practical – unlike academic knowledge which puts emphasis on generalisations and on the search for universal truths. Since it helps to solve challenges of everyday life, community knowledge is pragmatic. Contrary to popular imputations, community knowledge is not stagnant or ancient or traditional; it changes with and over time, and is a dynamic response to changes in the immediate and larger socio-ecological contexts. Given its close links to everyday life challenges and expressed as a part of their worldviews, community knowledge production and sharing is functional and need-based. As such functional requirements change over time, as the 'business of life' moves ahead, procedures and practices of knowledge also adapt to such shifts. Community knowledge has a normative frame defined by the values of the community and the surrounding eco-system. A community's everyday cultural symbols, languages and practices 'curate' and validate their knowledge. Community knowledge derives internal validation from their worldviews. Protocols for validation are rooted in community ethics and principles of cooperation and mutual aid. Understanding the inner meanings, feelings and norms practised in a community is essential to recognising, understanding and making sense of what is community knowledge.

Both knowledge cultures differ significantly since the underlying worldviews are so vastly different. Academic knowledge is linked to instrumental rationality to control 'nature' for progress; community knowledge is linked to 'lived-in' emotionality to understand and 'live with' nature.

Academic researchers often ignore the rituals, ceremonies and symbols in communities as if these are merely a community living life, without understanding its meanings. They tend to label community knowledge as 'subjective', irrational, dogmatic, etc. In the absence of an understanding about a community's knowledge culture, it is assumed that there are no regulators and standard-bearers of knowledge and its validity. Community elders are designated knowledge-keepers and behaviour regulators in most Indigenous communities; given the spiritual elements of such community knowledge, these Elders and community knowledge keepers also lead rituals of spirituality and ceremonies. These practices are then overlooked as sites and processes of knowledge production by those who do not recognise that knowledge systems can be diverse.

Thus, academic researchers often initiate processes of 'co-creation' of knowledge with limited comprehension of what is community knowledge(s), and the shared meanings and knowledge practices valued by a community. Academic partners engaging in CURP are often always surprised to learn about the distinctive culture of knowledge in communities. The ten K4C hubs in our study also made this 'discovery'.

Examining this critical distinction between the knowledge cultures in academia and community, and finding a working definition of knowledge culture, was a central focus of this research. As part of the theoretical framework (Chapter 2), we defined *knowledge culture* as:

> a set of local value-based practices, rules and beliefs, which, in a given organisation, community, area of professional expertise and/or discipline, create and reinforce shared meanings, expectations, identities and generalised rationales about knowledge production processes (creation, validation, dissemination and use). A knowledge culture as it relates to community-university research partnerships (CURP) is embedded in the traditions and history of both, its participating members and its partnership configuration, and thus includes its own intra- and inter-organisational structures, alongside roles, division of labour, norms, formal and informal arrangements and mechanisms, collective beliefs, (im)personal

interactions/relations and cultural forms – e.g., images, symbols, heroes, rituals and vocabulary/language. These cultural elements shape the way knowledge production is performed within and across organisations and/or communities in any given CURP setting

The most significant insight from this study is the distinctive and different knowledge practices for production and sharing in communities that remain invisible and out-of-sight to the academy. Recognition of diversity of knowledge sites – and associated practices, beliefs and systems – is fundamental to effective co-creation of knowledge. As academic discourses on multiple modes of knowledge production gain momentum, as conversations about 'decolonising' higher education multiply, it is imperative that the differences between the singular academic knowledge culture and the plural community ones are recognised and bridged.

2   A Bridge Is Built by Partners

In the process of co-creation of knowledge, academic researchers commonly start from their own singular, academic understanding of knowledge production – its methods and tools of data collection and analysis, and standards of validity. The very reason for co-creation is to add value to what academic researchers can do on their own; if there is no added value, then why bother to co-create? Hence, co-creation starts with recognising different knowledge systems do exist, knowledge is available in non-academic (community) settings, and needs to be valued.

Effective co-creation entails recognition of different understandings of knowledge, its tools of production and methods of dissemination by community partners. Therefore, *acceptance and acknowledgement* of knowledge available in community settings as different and legitimate is a critical first step in facilitating a bridge between community knowledge and academic knowledge. This acceptance and acknowledgement of different yet legitimate knowledge in non-academic partners must become a foundational principle of any efforts at co-creation and building bridges.

Given past histories of apathy towards academic and community actors, as well as a dismissive attitude of academic researchers towards knowledge and experience of community actors, co-creation requires establishing relations of mutual trust. *Relationships of trust* are the cement for bridging knowledge cultures. Once experiential knowledge of people living in communities, ancient land-based knowledge of Indigenous peoples, and the epistemic privilege of those experiencing lives of poverty, different abilities, homelessness, and more, are recognised as legitimate, the challenge is to move beyond the walls – physical, intellectual and emotional – of the academy to establish mutually respectful connections. Building relationships of trust takes time and investment of resources (funds, human resources, organisational structures) and is essential for meaningful research partnerships that attempt to bridge different sets of knowledge and epistemologies. Recognising and valuing community partners needs to be conveyed in a manner that is respectful and dignified. A series of interactions need to be planned over time for bridging the differences in cultures, languages and ethics. This is easier said than done.

Training of academic researchers tends to buttress a sense of arrogance rooted in superior knowledge and scholarship. Trained to speak their own expertise incessantly, listening is not a hugely common practice amongst academic researchers. Blinded by beliefs of neutrality and objectivity, their capacity to listen to others' words and feelings is limited. When academics 'learn to listen', relationships begin to develop.

Balancing feelings with thinking supports relationship building. This process happens gradually, needs time, requires patience. When academics 'unlearn', mutuality occurs. *Empathic listening* entails 'unlearning', which creates some tension and anxiety in all persons. The capacity to cope with distress and anxiety caused by such 'unlearning' helps create the partnerships required to build bridges.

Academic knowledge creators rely heavily on the written word in the research process, from production to dissemination. In communities, however, knowledge production and sharing occurs through parables, stories, anecdotes, hymns, dance and/or songs. Oral traditions of knowledge production and dissemination are structurally different from written academic traditions. The capacity of academics to accept oral storage and transmission of knowledge, and their openness towards non-written forms of documentation and records as legitimate sources of knowledge, help to support the *arch of scaffolding* of the bridge to be built. Academic researchers demonstrating a capacity to understand stories and anecdotes as types of data further helps the process of bridge-building. Academic research in recent decades has got bogged down in statistics and numbers, as ever sophisticated tools of algorithms have become available. As a consequence, oral, artistic and physical manifestations of community knowledge are not even recognised, and are dismissed as 'unscientific'.

3   Rebalancing Power

The case studies have demonstrated, initiatives to co-create knowledge typically begin from academic researchers. Communities hesitate to initiate the partnership for knowledge co-creation. There are multiple reasons for this – communities themselves fail to acknowledge that they are sites and producers of valid knowledge; they view the academy and the researcher as 'holders of knowledge'; the knowledge economy makes them believe knowledge can only be gained and learnt in the academy; and they see themselves through the lens of the academy as illiterate, uneducated, invisible. Above all, communities lack the power to begin building the bridge.

The cultural, linguistic and status differentials between academic researchers and community actors are so large in many contexts that making connections to initiate dialogues becomes difficult. Hence, an effective *mediation process* helps to kick-off bridging and rebalance the power. Interlocutors, boundary spanners and intermediaries, who may well come from either or both the community and academic side, play an important role in facilitating the rebalancing of power. The case studies have illustrated the relevance of such intermediation, in whatever form it occurs, to start the bridging process. In some cases, local civil society organisations or school teachers or local government officials acted as the connector intermediary, performing the facilitator functions creatively and contextually.

There are several practical questions that need to be addressed in operationalising mediators between community and academia: Where should the mediators be located? How should they be funded? What decision-making capacity do they need? What skills are necessary? Should it be an individual or a team, with a formal or informal role? How should they demonstrate their accountability to both the community and academia?

A common finding from the BKC study and previous studies done by this UNESCO Chair is the need for a dedicated unit in academia for anchoring the co-creation and bridge building process. Academic institutions are large and divided into multiple units which typically act in silos. To build equitable partnerships with communities, a clear structure within the academy is required. The case studies demonstrate the value of such an administrative mechanism in order to enable and sustain partnerships beyond specific projects.

The creation of *visible structures within the academy* is key to supporting the transition from disciplinary, academic-led knowledge creation to inter-disciplinary co-construction of knowledge with community. Administrative structures within universities provide spaces for the recognition of on-going co-structured research, for sharing tools and strategies for doing community-based research work, and for tracking the impact. Likewise, spaces for shared leadership, analysis of findings and planning of action within the research process need to be attended to intentionally so that needs and priorities of community partners are respected and responded to, and power is tilted a little bit further towards the community.

4   Missing Glues and Hopeful Futures

Several missing glues have been flagged from the case studies, which need sustained future attention. Despite the important success stories of the field cases we have shared in this book, overall we continue to observe the same patterns as in our 2015 study: many community-university research partnerships work well despite – and not because of – existing policies that seem to discourage, rather than incentivise, equitable partnerships. In cases where institutional support for co-creation of knowledge was available in academic institutions, some encouragement and resources were made available to those academics who took the risk of trying to bridge knowledge cultures. But this support remains largely precarious and uncertain, mostly dependent on commitment of top leadership (which changes frequently).

The analysis of significant institutional/structural mechanisms at meso levels and policy support at macro level was not sufficiently carried out to lend any fine comparative conclusions. However, several national contexts in this study do suggest an emerging trend of supportive national policies and research funding arrangements. In addition to Canada, recent examples of such shift are visible in South Africa and India. The National Education Policy 2020 in India has explicitly acknowledged diversities of knowledge systems, valuing linguistic plurality and engaged teaching and co-creation of knowledge. In situations where national policy in higher education and research is explicitly supportive of co-creation, where policy recognises that community knowledge is important and that linguistic and cultural diversity will need to be taken into account for harnessing such community knowledge, academic leadership is more inclined to invest institutionally. Research funding agencies also look for policy signals to align their research priorities. These trends need to be welcomed and incentivised for future research funding.

Still more systematic research of bridging is called for as community knowledge cultures are studied in-depth. K4C hubs facilitated by the UNESCO Chair are becoming privileged and safe sites for bringing community and academic knowledge cultures closer. They provide a platform for sharing emerging learnings about the challenges in building partnerships and ways to deal with them. Therefore, K4C hubs can be seen as *transitional spaces to* learn and practice innovative methods of bridging knowledge cultures. Yet, even such K4C hub sites had difficulty in coming to grips with understanding what is a community knowledge culture; in fact, even the very meaning of knowledge culture escaped their recognition. The trajectory for unlearning and relearning to acknowledge a community knowledge culture exists even by those academics trained as mentors in this approach to research and value system demonstrates the long road ahead towards recognising and valuing diverse knowledge cultures.

During the three-year period when this international study was conducted, several global policy mandates have emerged to support the basic thesis of bridging knowledge cultures. A landmark report was released by UNESCO's International Commission on Futures of Education in 2021, *Reimagining our futures together: A new social contract for education.* Its main recommendation is to embed educational programs within the larger societal context of today, and the future. It notes that, "knowledge data and evidence must be inclusive of diverse sources and ways of knowing" (International Commission on the Futures of Education, 2021, p. 154). The report further notes that, "Decolonizing knowledge calls for greater recognition of the validity and applicability of diverse sources of knowledge to the exigencies of the present and future" (p. 126). The Chair of the International Commission, HE Sahle-Work Zewde eloquently captures the call to action as follows, "The future of our planet must be locally and democratically envisioned. It is only through collective and individual actions that harness our rich diversity of peoples and cultures that the futures we want can be realized" (International Commission on the Futures of Education, 2021, p. VII).

Following closely behind the release of the Futures of Education report was the universal adoption of UNESCO's Recommendations on Open Science in November 2021. Expanding the meaning of science to be open to not merely fellow scientists but also practitioners and citizens, Open Science recommendations also endorse the recognition of community knowledge. Its Open framework has a quadrant of public engagement of science (including citizen science), as well as openness to multiple epistemologies (hitherto excluded knowledge systems, Indigenous knowledge, etc.).

Open science should not only foster enhanced sharing of scientific knowledge solely among scientific communities but also promote inclusion and exchange of scholarly knowledge from traditionally underrepresented or excluded groups (such as women, minorities, Indigenous scholars, scholars from less-advantaged countries and low-resource languages). (UNESCO, 2021, p. 5)

The Recommendation further notes that open science "opens the processes of scientific knowledge creation, evaluation and communication to societal actors beyond the traditional scientific community". (UNESCO, 2021, p. 8)

The conversations and recommendations arising from UNESCO's Third World Higher Education Conference in Barcelona (May 2022) reinforced the perspective of co-creation of knowledge to address critical challenges of our times like growing inequality, post-pandemic health risks and rapid climate distress. Presented during the conference was a report by the UNESCO Expert Group, *Knowledge-driven actions: Transforming higher education for global sustainability*. The fundamental message from this ground-breaking report is, "the imperative of becoming open institutions, fostering epistemic dialogue and integrating diverse ways of knowing" (UNESCO, 2022, p. 101).

Most significantly, for the first time, the Third World Higher Education Conference had a special session on ways to synergise the teaching and research functions of higher education with Indigenous knowledge systems. The report on the session on Indigenous Perspectives on Higher Education notes that,

To favour the well-being of all people inclusively and the sustainability of societies overall, higher education systems must be deconstructed and co-created into new structures that respect and incorporate Indigenous knowledge and values. They should be redesigned to feel inclusive to Indigenous students and should explore what Indigenous wisdom and culture – developed over millennia – can offer humankind rather than expecting students to conform to existing norms. (Canadian Commission for UNESCO, 2021, p. 6)

All of the above global policy convergences create an enabling policy environment to promote and deepen bridging academic knowledge and community knowledge by recognising and valuing different knowledge cultures. Higher education institutions can use these enabling policies to move towards inter- and transdisciplinary modes of producing and circulating knowledge; to become open institutions, fostering epistemic dialogue, integrating, respecting and valuing diverse ways of knowing; place truth-seeking skills at the core of the curriculum to reignite imaginations and promote divergent thinking.

They can occupy a stronger presence in society through proactive engagement and partnering with other societal actors, and establish a new social contract for education.

We have no doubt that co-created learning and knowledge can repair injustices, and contribute to just and sustainable futures. We know that redesigning structures and cultures of historically rigid academic institutions to do this is a tall order; it will take enormous efforts and investments. We hope a next generation of professional researchers trained to co-produce knowledge by understanding and building appreciation that diverse knowledge cultures exist, and by demonstrating the building of bridges through everyday practice, can overcome the competitive vision of education in favour of a culture of collaboration and cooperation.

References

Canadian Commission for UNESCO. (2021). *Indigenous perspectives on higher education.* https://en.ccunesco.ca/-/media/Files/Unesco/Resources/2022/05/IndigneousPerspectivesHigherEducation.pdf

International Commission on the Futures of Education. (2021). *Reimagining our futures together: A new social contract for education.* UNESCO. https://unesdoc.unesco.org/ark:/48223/pf0000379707.locale=en

UNESCO. (2021). *UNESCO recommendation on open science.* UNESCO. https://unesdoc.unesco.org/ark:/48223/pf0000379949

UNESCO. (2022). *Global independent expert group on the universities and the 2030 agenda.* UNESCO.

Index

Printed in the United States
by Baker & Taylor Publisher Services